DEMOCRACY

D0022468

Key Concepts in Critical Theory
Series Editor
Roger S. Gottlieb

Published

JUSTICE
Edited by Milton Fisk

DEMOCRACY
Edited by Philip Green

ALIENATION AND SOCIAL CRITICISM
Edited by Richard Schmitt and Thomas E. Moody

Forthcoming

GENDER
Edited by Carol Gould

RACISM
Edited by Leonard Harris

DECONSTRUCTION AND SOCIAL THEORY
Edited by Bill Martin

ECOLOGY
Edited by Carolyn Merchant

EXPLOITATION
Edited by Kai Nielsen and Robert Ware

IMPERIALISM AND GLOBAL CAPITALISM
Edited by Robert Ross

Key Concepts in Critical Theory

DEMOCRACY

EDITED BY

Philip Green

HUMANITIES PRESS

NEW JERSEY

First published in 1993 by Humanities Press International, Inc.,
165 First Avenue, Atlantic Highlands, New Jersey 07716

This collection © 1993 by Humanities Press

Third Printing, 1994

Library of Congress Cataloging-in-Publication Data

Democracy / edited by Philip Green.
p. cm. — (Key concepts in critical theory)
Includes bibliographical references and index.
ISBN 0-391-03779-X
1. Democracy. I. Green, Philip, 1932– . II. Series.
JC423.D43977 1993
321.8—dc20 92-19823
CIP

A catalog record for this book is available from the British Library.

All rights reserved. No part of this publication may be reproduced or transmitted, in any form or by any means, without written permission from the publisher.

Printed in the United States of America

CONTENTS

Series Editor's Preface ix

Acknowledgments xi

PART I: INTRODUCTION

INTRODUCTION Philip Green
"Democracy" as a Contested Idea 2

SELECTION 1 Raymond Williams
from *Keywords* 19

PART II: THE CLASSICAL THEORY

SELECTION 2 Jean-Jacques Rousseau
from *The Social Contract* 24

SELECTION 3 John Stuart Mill
from *Considerations on Representative Government* 32

SELECTION 4 Alexis de Tocqueville
from *Democracy in America* 38

PART III: REPRESENTATIVE GOVERNMENT

SELECTION 5 James Madison
from *The Federalist #10* 44

SELECTION 6 John Stuart Mill
from *Considerations on Representative Government* 50

SELECTION 7 Robert A. Dahl
from *Democracy and Its Critics* 57

PART IV: THE THEORY OF DEMOCRATIC ELITISM

SELECTION 8 Robert Michels
from *Political Parties* 68

SELECTION 9 Max Weber
from *From Max Weber: Essays in Sociology* 74

SELECTION 10 Joseph A. Schumpeter
from *Capitalism, Socialism and Democracy* 83

SELECTION 11 Bernard Berelson, Paul Lazarsfeld, and William McPhee
from *Voting* 93

SELECTION 12 Michel J. Crozier, Samuel P. Huntington, and Joji Watanuki
from *The Crisis of Democracy* 99

SELECTION 13 Robert A. Dahl
from *Who Governs?* 104

PART V: THE CRITIQUE OF DEMOCRATIC ELITISM

SELECTION 14 John Dewey
from *The Public and Its Problems* 120

SELECTION 15 Peter Bachrach
from *The Theory of Democratic Elitism* 126

SELECTION 16 Kenneth Prewitt and Alan Stone
from *The Ruling Elites* 131

PART VI: THE PROBLEM OF INEQUALITY

SELECTION 17 Milton Friedman
from *Capitalism and Freedom* 146

SELECTION 18 C. B. Macpherson
from *Democratic Theory* 153

SELECTION 19 Michael Parenti
from *Inventing Reality* 158

SELECTION 20 Philip Green
from *Retrieving Democracy* 164

SELECTION 21 Samuel Bowles and Herbert Gintis
from *Democracy & Capitalism* 168

SELECTION 22 Stephen L. Elkin
from *The Democratic State* 175

SELECTION 23 Michael Parenti
from *Power and the Powerless* 185

SELECTION 24 Anne Phillips
from *Engendering Democracy* 192

PART VII: RADICAL DEMOCRACY REVISITED

Direct Action and Democracy

SELECTION 25 Rosa Luxemburg
from *The Russian Revolution* 204

SELECTION 26 Hannah Arendt
from *On Revolution* 209

SELECTION 27 April Carter
from *Direct Action and Liberal Democracy* 231

SELECTION 28 Michael Walzer
from *Dissent* 244

Participation and Representation

SELECTION 29 Carol C. Gould
from *Praxis International* 246

SELECTION 30 Philip Green
from *Retrieving Democracy* 257

SELECTION 31 Benjamin Barber
from *Strong Democracy* 269

PART VIII: DEMOCRATIC RIGHTS

Introduction to Part VIII 274

SELECTION 32 Jean-Jacques Rousseau
from *The Social Contract* 277

SELECTION 33 John Stuart Mill
from *On Liberty* 282

SELECTION 34 Christian Bay
from *The Structure of Freedom* 292

SELECTION 35 George Kateb
from *Political Science Quarterly* 297

SELECTION 36 Iris Marion Young
from *Justice and the Politics of Difference* 309

Bibliography 317

Index 319

SERIES EDITOR'S PREFACE

THE VISION OF A rational, just, and fulfilling social life, present in Western thought from the time of the Judaic prophets and Plato's *Republic*, has since the French Revolution been embodied in systematic *critical theories* whose adherents seek a fundamental political, economic, and cultural transformation of society.

These critical theories—varieties of Marxism, socialism, anarchism, feminism, gay/lesbian liberation, ecological perspectives, discourses by antiracist, anti-imperialist, and national liberation movements, and utopian/critical strains of religious communities—have a common bond that separates them from liberal and conservative thought. They are joined by the goal of sweeping social change; the rejection of existing patterns of authority, power, and privilege; and a desire to include within the realms of recognition and respect the previously marginalized and oppressed.

Yet each tradition of critical theory also has its distinct features: specific concerns, programs, and locations within a geometry of difference and critique. Because of their intellectual specificity and the conflicts among the different social groups they represent, these theories have often been at odds with one another, differing over basic questions concerning the ultimate cause and best response to injustice, the dynamics of social change, the optimum structure of a liberated society, the identity of the social agent who will direct the revolutionary change, and in whose interests the revolutionary change will be made.

In struggling against what is to some extent a common enemy, in overlapping and (at times) allying in the pursuit of radical social change, critical theories to a great extent share a common conceptual vocabulary. It is the purpose of this series to explore that vocabulary, revealing what is common and what is distinct, in the broad spectrum of radical perspectives.

For instance, although both Marxists and feminists may use the word "exploitation," it is not clear that they really are describing the same phenomenon. In the Marxist paradigm the concept identifies the surplus labor appropriated by the capitalist as a result of the wage-labor relation. Feminists have used the same term to refer as well to the unequal amounts of housework, emotional nurturance, and child raising performed by women in the nuclear family. We see some similarity in the notion of group inequality (capitalists/workers, husbands/wives) and of unequal exchange. But we also see critical differences: a previously "public" concept extended to the private realm; one first centered in the economy of goods now moved into the life of emotional relations. Or, for another example, when deep ecologists speak of "alienation" they may be exposing the contradictory and destructive relations of humans *to* nature. For socialists and anarchists, by contrast, "alienation" basically refers only to relations among human beings. Here we find a profound contrast between what is and is not included in the basic arena of politically significant relationships.

What can we learn from exploring the various ways different radical perspectives utilize the same terminology?

Most important, we see that these key concepts have histories and that the theories of which they are a part and the social movements whose spirit they embody take shape through a process of political struggle as well as of intellectual reflection. As a corollary, we can note that the creative tension and dissonance among the different uses of these concepts stem not only from the endless play of textual interpretation (the different understandings of classic texts, attempts to refute counterexamples or remove inconsistencies, rereadings of history, reactions to new theories), but also from the continual movement of social groups. Oppression, domination, resistance, passion, and hope are crystallized here. The feminist expansion of the concept of exploitation could only grow out of the women's movement. The rejection of a purely anthropocentric (human-centered, solely humanistic) interpretation of alienation is a fruit of people's resistance to civilization's lethal treatment of the biosphere.

Finally, in my own view at least, surveys of the differing applications of these key concepts of critical theory provide compelling reasons to see how complementary, rather than exclusive, the many radical perspectives are. Shaped by history and embodying the spirit of the radical movements that created them, these varying applications each have in them some of the truth we need in order to face the darkness of the current social world and the ominous threats to the earth.

ROGER S. GOTTLIEB

ACKNOWLEDGMENTS

ACKNOWLEDGMENT IS MADE TO the following for permission to quote from copyrighted material: for material from Raymond Williams, *Keywords*, William Collins Ltd.; for Robert A. Dahl, *Democracy and Its Critics*, Yale University Press, © 1989; for material from *From Max Weber: Essays in Sociology*, edited and translated by H. H. Gerth and C. Wright Mills, © 1946 by Oxford University Press, Inc., renewed 1973 by Hans H. Gerth, reprinted by permission of the publisher.

Excerpt from *The Ruling Elites* by Kenneth Prewitt and Alan Stone, © 1973 by Kenneth Prewitt and Alan Stone; reprinted by permission of HarperCollins Publishers.

Excerpt from *Capitalism, Socialism and Democracy* by Joseph A. Schumpeter, © 1942, 1947 by Joseph A. Schumpeter; reprinted by permission of HarperCollins Publishers.

Excerpt from *Voting*, Bernard Berelson et al., by permission of The University of Chicago Press.

For material from Robert A. Dahl, *Who Governs?*, Yale University Press, © 1961.

Excerpt from Milton Friedman, *Capitalism and Freedom*, The University of Chicago Press, © 1962.

Material reprinted from *Democratic Theory: Essays in Retrieval* by C. B. Macpherson (1973) by permission of Oxford University Press, © Oxford University Press, 1973.

From Michael Parenti, *Inventing Reality*, © 1986 by Michael Parenti; reprinted with special permission from St. Martin's Press, Inc., New York.

Excerpt from Philip Green, *Retrieving Democracy*, © Philip Green, 1985, Roman & Littlefield Publishers, Inc., by permission of the publisher.

Excerpt from *Democracy & Capitalism* by Samuel Bowles and Herbert Gintis, © 1988 by Basic Books, Inc., a division of HarperCollins Publishers.

Excerpt from *The Democratic State*, edited by Roger Benjamin and Stephen L. Elkin by permission of University Press of Kansas, © 1985 by University Press of Kansas.

Material from *Direct Action and Liberal Democracy* by April Carter, by permission of Routledge.

The article from *Dissent*, Spring 1990 by Michael Walzer, "A Credo for This Moment," is reprinted by permission of Michael Walzer.

Excerpt from *Power and the Powerless* by Michael Parenti, reprinted with permission of St. Martin's Press, Inc., © 1978.

Excerpt from *Engendering Democracy* by Anne Phillips by permission of Blackwell Publishers. Also from The Pennsylvania State University Press, 1991, pp. 156–168, © 1991 by The Pennsylvania State University; reproduced by permission of the publisher.

Material from *On Revolution* by Hannah Arendt, © 1963 by Hannah Arendt; used by permission of Viking Penguin, a division of Penguin Books USA, Inc.

Material reprinted from *The Structure of Freedom* by Christian Bay with the permission of the publisher, Stanford University Press, © 1958 by the Board of Trustees of the Leland Stanford Junior University.

Excerpt from "Socialism and Democracy" in *Praxis International*, I, 1, April 1981 by Carol Gould by permission of Basil Blackwell Ltd.

Excerpt from *Strong Democracy* by Benjamin Barber, University of California Press, © 1984 by University of California Press.

"The Majority Principle: Calhoun and His Antecedents" by George Kateb reprinted with permission from *Political Science Quarterly*, Vol. 84, No. 4, December 1969.

Excerpt from *Justice and the Politics of Difference* by Iris M. Young, © 1990 by Princeton University Press, reprinted by permission of Princeton University Press.

PART I

Introduction

INTRODUCTION

"*Democracy*" *as a Contested Idea*

PHILIP GREEN

DEMOCRACY IN THE LATE twentieth century is not only a contested concept but also a remarkably ambiguous one. Outside the few remaining outposts of strongman rule in Africa, Latin America, and Asia, virtually everyone with a claim to leadership seeks to legitimate that claim in democracy's name. It is probably impossible to eliminate ambiguity and even contradiction in these multifold usages, for they may well be built into the very concept; the moment we say something as (we think) innocuous as "democracy means rule by the people," we have already plunged into a definitional as well as practical morass. Thus conservatives in the United States oppose affirmative action programs in the name of democracy—that is, of majority rule. Liberals support the very same programs in the name of democracy—that is, of equal rights for minorities. The definition of democracy has in fact become a political project, ultimately to be decided if not on the battlefield at least in the voting booth.

Still, if we cannot settle on a definitive version of democracy, we can at least explore and critique its most salient alternative meanings. In particular, the great democratic revolution of Eastern Europe clearly demands some reassessment of democratic theory, for during its course there resurfaced a democratic practice—direct action by the mass of the people—that in the post–World War II era had virtually vanished from theoretical consideration. If only to know the possible range of democratic practices we may engage in, a theoretical investigation is essential.

As Raymond Williams notes (Selection 1), until fairly recently in historical time, *democracy* was an unpopular term, especially with political elites. That is because it was historically taken to mean direct rule by the people meeting in assembly—or, as its opponents thought of it, in a mob. This usage, which goes back to the Athenian city-state, is now known as the classical democratic ideal. It received a famous justification from Aristotle in the course of his discussion of citizenship in various polities. Even while he defined democracy as one of the "perverted" forms of constitution, Aristotle concluded "that the citizen of our definition [one holding the indeterminate office of judge in a court and member of an assembly] is particularly and especially the citizen of a democracy." (Aristotle, 1962, pp. 94–95). The virtue of democratic citizenship in this classical sense, both for the development of individual character and for the vitality of political life, is spelled out by John Stuart Mill and Alexis de Tocqueville (Selections 3 and 4); the most compelling description of a democratic state is found in Jean-Jacques Rousseau's *The Social Contract* (Selection 2). Rousseau's language, it must be noted, has occasioned much confusion, since at one point he remarks that "Were there a people of gods, their government would be democratic. . . . [such] a government is not for men." In context, though, it is clear that in categorizing the forms of "government" (democracy, aristocracy, and monarchy), Rousseau is actually discussing what we call "administration," that is, the execution of the laws. As for the making of the laws, or what we call legislation, there is only one legitimate procedure, according to Rousseau: laws must be formulated by the entire body of the people, meeting in general assembly. We may call the principle so inscribed that of popular self-government, or popular sovereignty, or self-determination; it is, in essence, the classical model of direct democracy.

Rousseau's homage to direct democracy is a notable example of the irony of history, for it came to us precisely at the moment when, in retrospect, the conditions for its realization seemed to vanish from the historical stage. Rousseau's is essentially a vision for small, premodern city-states, or even towns, which were about to lose any vestigial independence they might have retained to the sway of the modern imperial nation-state. Modernization, as Marx said of the bourgeoisie, "has put an end to all feudal, patriarchal, idyllic relations," and, apparently, to all ideals of communal unity as well. The significance of this denouement for the classical ideal has not been spelled out in detail until recently, but it was already perceived by Mill in the mid–nineteenth century. The chapter of *Considerations on Representative Government* from which Selection 3 is taken is titled "The Ideally Best Polity"; but at the very end of that chapter Mill adds this concluding sentence: "But since all cannot, in a community exceeding a single small town, participate personally in any but some very minor portions of the public business, it follows that the ideal type of a perfect government must be representative."

What does this conclusion mean for our understanding of democracy? What has happened is that democracy (this is most clear-cut in Dahl; see Selection 7) came to function both as a normative although impossible ideal and as the description of a concrete, yet quite different, contemporary reality. The ideal is constituted by a literal description of direct popular government as in the Athenian assembly or the New England town meeting; the reality, by a more "realistic" or "practical" or "possible" form of government, variously described as a republic (Madison, Selection 5), a "representative government" (Mill, Selection 6), or a "polyarchy" (Dahl, Selection 7). The honorific use of the classical term, with its implicit flattery of the presumptively sovereign "people," is applied to a state of affairs that both is and is not "democracy"—real, existing democracy. To be sure, democracy in the classical sense, and representative government in the contemporary sense, have in common that they are both legitimized in some degree by a philosophy of majority rule; but beyond that point, considerable divergence develops.

This conflation of divergent terms is a mid–nineteenth century innovation. As we see in the tenth *Federalist*, it would never have occurred, for example, to Madison. For him "democracy" was still not an honorific term, and he would hardly have thought to speak, as does Dahl, of the "idea of democracy" and the "institutions of polyarchy" (or a republic) in the same breath. This description of a democracy that is yet not quite a democracy begins with de Tocqueville (who in this as in other respects greatly influenced Mill) and achieves its most telling expression in *Considerations on Representative Government*. On first reading Mill's *Considerations* one may be struck, even wounded, by the rapidity of his descent from Chapter 3 ("there can be no kind of doubt that the passive type of character is favored by government of one or a few, and the active self-helping type by that of the Many") to his conclusion two chapters later in favor of

> . . . disjoining the office of control and criticism from the actual conduct of affairs, and devolving the former on the representatives of the Many, while securing for the latter, under strict responsibility to the nation, the acquired knowledge and practised intelligence of a specially trained and experienced Few.

The full significance of this passage is most visible in Mill's substitution of the abstract noun, "nation," for the expected climactic word, "people"—a substitution that more than anything else reveals the extent to which Mill retreated from his original panegyric to the benefits of popular "participation" in governance.

As a Victorian Englishman Mill himself still had enough ambivalence about democracy and its supposed excesses (majority tyranny, egalitarian leveling) not to be too heavily invested in saving the word. In his *Autobiography*, while calling himself a "Socialist," he spoke of going "far beyond Democracy" (p. 148). A century later, that language could no longer be used by any major political theorist. Democracy, after all, was what "the West" had fought two world wars to "save." Yet Mill's insight could not be gainsaid; how then could the legitimizing and flattering word be applied to a system that manifestly was not, in the traditional sense, democratic? It became a major task of post–World War II American political theory to rescue the term *democracy* from itself, so to speak, and somehow attach it to the much different institutions of representative government. That was particularly the self-imposed task of practitioners of the contemporary amalgam of social science and formal analysis that has come to be known as "empirical democratic theory."

Empirical democratic theory takes as its starting point the sociological treatises of Robert Michels on mass political parties (Selection 8) and Max Weber on bureaucracy (Selection 9). Building on their analyses, and reacting against the classical understanding of democracy as literally popular self-government, empirical democratic theorists have argued that direct democracy is logistically impossible beyond the scale of the small town or commune. But this revisionist argument now goes even further. Representative government itself, insofar as representatives might be thought of as directly responsible to the people, is now called into question. Neither lawmaking nor even accountability for lawmaking can really devolve on the people as a whole. As Joseph Schumpeter argued in the most famous statement of this kind, the people are capable of nothing but choosing leaders (see Selection 10). Other empirical democratic theorists add that in any event most people neither are competent to participate in governance nor actually desire to do so (see Selection 11). In practice, therefore, government "by the people" actually consists of government by elites. These elites, although not necessarily drawn from the people in any representative way, more or less represent the plurality of views and interests among them, and are even, allegedly, more faithfully attached to the democratic "rules of the game" than are their constituents. They are assisted also by experts who supply elected representatives with the knowledge and technical capabilities that most citizens lack. Thus political elites and experts govern; but they do not dominate, in that in the last analysis elections are controlling. This argument, made notorious by Peter Bachrach as "The Theory of Democratic Elitism" (Selection 15), has been given its most well-known and influential codification by the American political theorist Robert Dahl (see Selection 13).

Empirical democratic theory overall is best understood in light of the dual role that the notion of "democracy" plays in it. Democracy is on the one hand an ideal of which polyarchy, representative government, etc., are the existing approximations. Looking at it from this perspective, we are led inexorably to the question of whether the Rousseauistic mode of justification of the ideal is also appropriate for justifying the institutions and principles of real polities. Dahl especially has long argued against this conflation in practical terms: e.g., outside the very small town there is neither time nor space for every citizen to participate directly in political decision making or agenda setting. In this so-called practical usage, the element of equal participation in political decision making, fundamental to the classical or Rousseauistic notion, slips away, or is reduced solely to the act of voting—for the individual essentially an act of system affirmation rather than significant participation in the political realm. (One well-known political scientist is said, perhaps apocryphally, to have remarked that he never voted because there was a greater chance he'd be killed in an auto accident on the way to the polls than that his vote would alter the outcome of the election.) This is what many political theorists nowadays call "the democratic process." As Schumpeter put it in a moment of cynical candor, "Voters confine themselves to accepting [a candidate's] bid in preference to others or refusing to accept it. . . . Party and machine politicians are simply the response to the fact that the electoral mass is incapable of action other than a stampede." More politely, the contemporary social scientist Seymour Martin Lipset rephrased Schumpeter to define "democracy in a complex society" as

> . . . a political system which supplies regular constitutional opportunities for changing the governing officials, and a social mechanism which permits the largest possible part of the population to influence major decisions *by choosing among candidates for political office*. (Lipset, 1960, p. 45; emphasis added)

To this view Dahl more than anyone else has also added the hopeful notion that inequalities, although they do exist, are "dispersed" rather than "cumulative." Elites do not pyramid their power but compete with and check each other, on behalf of the various minorities of which any large polity really consists.

However, even with Dahl's emendation, in this slippage from "democracy" as a form of rule to "democracy" as a process much gets lost—one might say the essence of the term itself. By this I mean not the "impossible dream" of direct rule, but, at least, directly and meaningfully *accountable* rule. For example, Dahl begins his muted encomium to polyarchy with a reference to Aristotle, but even his ideal "criteria for a democratic process" are already a long way from what the Greeks called "democracy," since they have nothing to do with direct popular rule or popular participation of any kind. These criteria include, at a minimum, the opportunity for something called "effective participation," which is defined as the adequate and equal opportunity for "expressing preferences," including "adequate and equal opportunities for placing questions on the agenda" and voting equality.* This is the democratic process "narrowly" construed; later Dahl adds to this narrow sense two broader criteria: first, what might be called equal opportunity for enlightenment, and second, "final control of the agenda by the demos."

Aside from some degree of voting equality, none of this is remotely within the realm of possibility in polyarchies as presently constituted, and Dahl is aware of this. As he puts it,

> Inevitably, whenever democratic ideas are applied to the real world, actual democracy falls significantly short of ideal standards. For example, the criteria

---

*Dahl's earliest versions of "the democratic process" or "polyarchy" make no reference to any such requirement, but instead require that individuals be able to insert their "preferred alternative(s) among those scheduled for voting" (Dahl, 1956, p. 84). Dahl's explanation of this criterion has to do with avoiding the dangers of plebiscitary government and military dictatorship. Although he now uses the more expansive term "agenda-setting," it is not clear from his discussion whether he intends to make the notion do more than that limited amount of work. Bachrach and Baratz (1962), in a well-known critique of Dahl, pointed out that the agenda-setting process even in an independent, liberal polyarchy precludes real popular participation, but Dahl has not acknowledged their work or commented on the potential distinction.

> for the democratic process set out earlier have never been fully met and probably cannot be. What level of approximation are we to regard as in some sense satisfactory—sufficiently satisfactory, let us say, so that we may reasonably call some actual system a "democracy." . . . I shall argue . . . that an important threshold of democracy has been attained by a significant number of modern countries, as evidenced by a specific set of political institutions which, taken together, distinguishes the political system of these countries from all "democracies" and republics prior to the eighteenth century and from all "nondemocracies" in the contemporary world. Although these countries are ordinarily said to be "democracies," I will refer to their systems—distinguishable as I have said by virtue of their political institutions—as *polyarchies*. (See Selection 7)

The institutions of polyarchy (in a nutshell, competitive elections and civil liberties), he says later, should then be thought of as the necessary but not sufficient precondition to "the highest feasible attainment of the democratic process." However, nothing Dahl says thereafter leads the reader to think that such attainment is very feasible.

As an appreciation of political possibility, this continuum from polyarchy as a minimal necessary precondition for the democratic process, through various limited, attainable levels of the democratic process, to the ideal and unattainable democratic process, and finally to the myth of classical democracy is obviously sensible. But if we look closely at the lengthy passage quoted above, we see that Dahl equivocates with "democracy" just as Mill did with "self-government." Has the United States, for example, reached a "threshold," which some people "ordinarily" (and presumably imprecisely?) call "democracy"? Or, contrarily, can "we" (presumably sophisticated theorists with an ear for precision) call this "actual system" a "democracy," not just a mere "threshold"? The instant passage may be ambiguous, but the balance of Dahl's argument is tendentious in the same manner as is Chapter 5 of *Considerations on Representative Government*. In a dialogue elsewhere in *Democracy and Its Critics*, for example, "Critic" argues, "you know as well as I that political processes in all democratic countries are a long way from measuring up fully to the criteria of the democratic process. You seem to be talking about democracy in an ideal world, not democracy as we know it in the world we know." And "Advocate" (Dahl?) replies, "I can't deny that politics in democratic countries isn't by any means perfectly democratic" (p. 174). So the word now manages to occupy two places at once on the continuum, depending on whether "countries" or "politics" is being described. Here, clearly, "democracy" has become a kind of flattering verbal gloss applied to every invocation of what began as the distinct conception, polyarchy, and especially to every mention of the actual nations in which most of Dahl's readers live. When all of the real content has been leached out of such concepts as "enlightened understanding," "effective participation," and "control of the agenda," by their reduction to mere procedural requirements, the breach between democracy and polyarchy is almost complete. Seen in this light polyarchy indeed looks like a necessary precondition for democracy but is not in any particular respect (except that of voting equality) the thing itself.

In fact, the evidence of *Who Governs?* itself (which is a study of political decision making in New Haven, Connecticut, in the 1950s) casts a curious light on "democratic elitism." According to Dahl, the "Economic Notables" of New Haven were able "neither to agree on nor to put through a program of urban redevelopment, even under a Republican mayor anxious to retain their support" (p. 79). Only a liberal Democratic mayor, drawing on outside professionals and experts for program design, and on a "strange" coalition of voters that included even "the working-class and lower-middle-class ethnic groups, particularly Negroes and Italians, and their spokesmen," was able to negotiate the treacherous path to redevelopment (p. 129).

But this is exactly what the critics of polyarchy have always meant by "democratic elitism" (see Selection 15). If there were no adventurous political leaders coming to power precisely because "economic notables" can't agree on a common program—as Marx himself insisted they couldn't—then Bachrach and others would refer to our system as "elitism" pure and simple. The real process of polyarchies undergoing political change is usually as follows. There is a general perception of malaise, or decay, or crisis. If it is in the realm of economic structures, then most people will have no concrete ideas about it beyond the perception itself; only "economic notables," professional experts, and sometimes political leaders will be able to think about it as the object of concrete programs. Because capitalism is competitive, the economic notables will often not be able to agree among themselves as to the best specific program and will need to convert their influence into the power and authority of an elected official, if they can find one, who will cut through their own inertia. That official then creates a program by drawing on the assistance of experts, and a constituency by selling the program to elements of the public. From Louis Napoleon to Ronald Reagan that is how the process has worked in crisis. That the leader in question may be neither a Bonaparte nor a conservative Republican but a "liberal Democrat," capable of selling programs to a "working class" that still (in the 1950s) trusted Democrats and was susceptible to his kind of appeal, tells us much about how polyarchy actually works, or used to work, but almost nothing about "equal opportunity" or "control of the agenda," even among "competing elites." Furthermore, although the players have changed thirty years later, New Haven is still a city riven by deep material inequalities that have the same class (although a different racial) structure as before, regardless of how competitive its elites may have been.

More recently, to take another example, Mayor Koch of New York City managed to turn much of the borough of Manhattan entirely over to the interests of real estate developers, and he did so, with great and continued electoral success, in the name of the "people" who were being driven out of it by escalating housing costs (see, e.g., Newfield, 1988). This is the familiar story of public policy everywhere, that the power of entrenched economic elites has not been rooted out. In the end, not all minorities are equal or anything like equal. For most individuals as such, the gains they can achieve in political equality through civic participation or pressure group activity are negligible. Tigers and domestic cats both "influence" where dogs choose to take their constitutionals, but not equally.

Most liberal democrats, Dahl included, are well aware of this problem. Thus Dahl calls these requirements of the democratic process "necessary but not sufficient" for democracy and later explores possible additions to them, such as economic democracy, that is, the extension of the democratic process to the realm of production (see Selection 29). However, some advocates of representative government, as we have noted, reject the participatory element in democracy altogether. For Madison, for example, representative government was not a best possible substitute for classical democracy but was even itself in some respects a necessary evil; it could be justified only in tandem with the construction of mechanisms for hamstringing popular participation, as the majority was otherwise likely to make inroads against the rights of private property. The latter-day antipopulist Samuel Huntington (see Selection 12) goes beyond Madison in this respect. His concern is that too much democracy can lead to "democratic overload," and he complains that excluded groups make too many demands on government. Since most of those "demands" are ultimately funneled through the representative process, it is obviously representative government itself, or the democratic process, that Huntington would like to rein in.

For liberal democrats, however, representative government is justifiable chiefly because it realizes, or ideally may realize, those aspects of popular democracy that are practically attainable. For liberals, direct participation in "the general will" à la Rousseau may not be possible, but truly equal representation and true accountability of elites and experts are both possible and desirable. For this reason the invocation of "economic democracy" (what used to be called "socialism") has seemed to be a logical "next step" for liberal democratic theorists from Mill through John Dewey to Dahl; Mill, as we have seen, called himself a "Socialist" in his autobiography, and Dahl sometimes calls himself a "democratic socialist" today.

These theorists recognize—Dahl even asserts—that the requirements of the democratic process are purely formal. Merely stating them, or even attempting to implement them through a written constitution, does not of itself produce a general level of "enlightened understanding," or "effective participation," or "control of the agenda." And historically, the greatest obstacle to widespread citizen equality has been the existence of social and economic inequalities that render access to democratic institutions—the vote, the press, communication with representatives, the right to organize—either difficult or meaningless.

Not only socialists but liberals as well take this point. To be sure, one can assert, with Milton Friedman (Selection 17), that the so-called free market gives all people an equal chance to participate in the economic action of their choice. One man may choose to be a ditch digger, another may choose to own a newspaper; neither is coerced into doing what he would rather not do or restrained from doing what he would prefer to do. As C. B. Macpherson points out, however (see Selection 18), this idea that the "free market" eliminates coercion is absurd. The wealthy person who can own a newspaper and the poor person who can do nothing but engage in the struggle to survive are not in an equivalent position by any reasonable stretch of the imagination or of language; to call them equally "free" is to torture words out of their possible meaning.

Although liberal democrats have always recognized this difficulty, the liberal tradition has a past that is at the same time in conflict with itself. On one hand, struggles to extend the formal rights that make up the democratic process are a proud part of that tradition. On the other hand, the capitalist revolution was equally an outcome, or a concomitant, or even the causal condition, of the rise of liberalism. But the development, in a capitalist regime, of massive and (contrary to Friedman) structured inequalities in wealth, income, and property holdings ensures that some people will have much more realistic access to rulers (or even sometimes control over them) than the mass of voters. Selections 21 through 23 explore some of the ways in which unequal holdings of wealth and property necessarily reproduce themselves as unequal political power. The point of these selections is not necessarily to argue that institutions of democracy beyond representative government, conveying more than merely formal political rights to the mass of people, can never flower on capitalist soil. That would be a deeply pessimistic view, since capitalist soil is indeed the soil upon which we stand. Rather, what these authors suggest is that meaningful political change can only take place under certain conditions. Chiefly, some of the basic ground rules of capitalism—untrammeled accumulation, unalloyed private property right in the means of production, and a largely unregulated marketplace for labor—would at the same time have to be abolished, or at least modified to an extent that has yet to be defined.

In addition, democratic theorists have begun to stress an aspect of political domination and inequality rarely discussed in earlier considerations of democracy: private property, especially monopolistic private property, in the means of communication. It has been suggested recently that in the new age of advanced telecommunications a completely and equally wired society will be a truly democratic society. However, what advanced telecommunications makes possible is a far cry from what, given current patterns of ownership and control, it makes likely. In the immediate prospect, the revolution in telecommunications technology has rather been extraordinarily centralizing and demobilizing.

At the moment, the "promise" of mass television is to deliver mediated but *apparently unmediated* images of social and political reality that, for most people, virtually monopolize the cultural field. In the United States, the destructive effects on political campaigning, and thus on what is called the democratic process, are so obvious as to need no highlighting at this point. (See, for example, the series in the *New York Times* from March 17 through March 20, 1990.) However, although other contemporary democracies are beginning to imitate the American system, the condition of political campaigning in America is actually a special case and is controllable if Americans had the will. Abolish paid political broadcasting, and the problem of money and image making would in that respect disappear. But in any event, the peculiarly American problem of uncontrollable costs in political campaigning is only the tip of the iceberg. It is often forgotten that Walter Lippmann anatomized the helplessness of citizens in the presence of mass image making, long before television was even invented (Lippmann, 1925). Candidates at least do oppose each other; political campaigns still allow for the minimal citizen role envisaged by Schumpeter. Thus it would be excessive to say that citizens are making irrational voting choices, whatever that might mean; rational-choice theorists would feel vindicated by the fact that a business cycle-sensitive model is still the best predictive tool for national elections. However, the quantum change that mass market television imposes has to do not with voting behavior per se but with the entire field of information and education, and thus with Dahl's central rule about the equal citizen opportunity to be informed "between elections."

If we look again at Dahl's assessment of citizen politics in *Who Governs?* (Selection 13), the central distinction he makes there is between "homo civicus," who mobilizes himself politically only when his interests are visibly threatened, and "homo politicus," the political *man* who is always mobilized because politics is his profession. At one time it might have seemed that to fear for the citizens' capacity to know their own interests was to convict oneself of simple snobbery, or disdain for one's fellow citizens; this was the gist of John Dewey's scathing critique of rule by "experts" (Selection 14). Television in its contemporary form, however, raises quite a different issue: the colonization of the space within which consciousness can express itself, as the hunger of image makers for public spaces (today, even classrooms in public schools) that they can seize and privatize is insatiable (see Selections 19 and 20, and Schiller, 1989). Nor is it the case that we are all suffering from some mass epidemic of false consciousness in succumbing to the appeal of the media. Rather, for those whose input on major issues of the day is typical for a polyarchy—that is, next to nothing—television *is* the real political world, or as real a world as we will ever get close to. What one critic has called the "right to listen and watch" is the only real First Amendment right possessed by those who are not themselves wealthy or employed by the wealthy (Horwitz, 1989, p. 282). And the more attention we give to listening and watching, the less we have to give anywhere else. On the contrary, "elsewhere" must imitate television to procure our attention. Political campaigners do not use television to sell themselves to us; television uses them as one more product to sell itself to us: and they only succeed insofar as they become one more of its products. Incidentally, officeholders are chosen, and representative government seems to be preserved, but as politics becomes incidental to entertainment, the formal rules of the democratic process seem to be attaining a condition of stupefying irrelevance.

Beyond inequalities of ownership and control, whether of means of production or means of communication, there are other structural problems in "the theory of democratic elitism," or empirical democratic theory. For example, most democratic theorists properly make majority rule the centerpiece of the democratic process; the usual answer to complaints about the way it works in practice is that any less-than-majoritarian method of decision making will be worse. However, this approach neglects the history of what we might call "really existing majority rule." The philosopher Robert Nozick, for example, has explained one observable tendency of majority rule in societies dominated by a large middle class: "[A] voting coalition from the bottom won't form," he points out, "because it will be less expensive to the top group to buy off the swing middle group than to let it form"; thus "a society whose policies result from democratic elections will not find it easy to avoid having its redistributive programs most benefit the middle class" (Nozick, 1974, p. 275). British commentators on Thatcherism have called the politics of this kind of redistribution the "two-thirds/one-third strategy": the political isolation (in some contemporary polities, the United States not least) of the worst off in society.

Traditionally, both critics and supporters of majority rule, from Madison to Marx, assumed that absolute majoritarianism inevitably meant domination of the well-to-do by the working class, or debtors, or the poor, or however the "bottom part" of society might be defined. But that is no longer the case. Generalized need has been replaced by marginalized need, and electorates as a whole, through their representatives, now seem to respond sluggishly or not at all to the needs of the marginalized. ("Marginalized" in this context should not be taken to imply "few in number." In the United States, for example, we may be speaking of 30 or 40 million citizens or more.) Americans (and we are not the only ones, although among advanced industrial societies our record is perhaps the worst), for example, seem quite able to "tolerate" unnecessarily high rates of violent street crime, narcotics addiction, urban decay, and social morbidity, so long as that is the cost of maintaining racial privilege and the ghettoization of poverty.

In some societies, then, centralized majoritarianism may very well favor the needs of the well-to-do against those of the marginalized. Obviously this must be a difficulty for any version of democracy; but it is especially a problem for a theory that, like the revisionist theory, emphasizes process rather than substance, formal rules rather than desired outcomes. Greater "participation," clearly, is not by itself the solution to this difficulty. But, for example, to argue in favor of mechanisms to ensure effective representation for the disadvantaged, as does Iris Marion Young (Selection 36), is necessarily to go beyond the limits of what we currently mean by "representative government."

Much recent democratic theory tends also to be oblivious to the problem that gender poses for political analysis. There is an extensive literature that demonstrates the fundamentally (or bodily) engendered inscription both of traditional political theory and of the political institutions of representative government. (See, for example, Okin, 1979 and 1989; Pateman, 1983 and 1988; Eisenstein, 1988; MacKinnon, 1989; Bledsoe and Herring, 1990.) In the world of electoral competition political office is defined as a prize to be pursued by aggressive competitors. Implicitly, the prerequisite character traits of competitors for office are defined as forcefulness, adventurism, and the drive to dominance: all traits traditionally assigned to the realm of masculinity. Obviously there are women who possess those traits. But how are the traits that our culture assigns to the realm of the feminine—cooperativeness, caring, nurturing—to be expressed politically? In most contemporary societies the public sphere censors, constrains, and sometimes dominates the private ("female") sphere—but provides no space in which the needs of the latter can be represented. A political theory that fails even to recognize this problem is radically incomplete, as is a representative government, or polyarchy, that incarnates masculinity as rulership (see Selection 24). One of the most striking (and disturbing) features of the revolutions of 1989 was how women, so visibly active when the revolution was in the streets, quickly disappeared as soon as the revolutionary community came to be displaced by the nascent institutions and (male) rulers of "the democratic process."

Finally, on a broader scale we have to ask whether the combination of contemporary polyarchy, formal majority rule, and modern technology is not inherently plebiscitary, centralizing, and ultimately stifling of citizen autonomy. Thirty years ago, in a neglected essay, the political scientist Hans Morgenthau argued that modern technology has

> . . . given the government a decisive potential advantage over the people in the over-all distribution of power, [and] has also actually strengthened the hand of the government in its day-by-day operations. . . . The preferences of the people and their representatives, in so far as they can be articulated at all, have in these matters hardly any relevance for the substance of the policies of

> the executive branch. They may, however, influence greatly the manner in which these policies are presented to the public and the amount of information the executive branch is willing to make public to begin with. (Morgenthau, 1960, pp. 272–73)

The 1980s have indeed seen an unparalleled assault on open government in both the United States and Britain and an extensive recentralization of power in both societies (see Curry, 1988). Are we witnessing the future of polyarchy, or merely an Anglo-Saxon peculiarity? In any event, once again to limit our attention to "the democratic process" may blind us to the real prospect before us: that what we variously call "democracy," or "representative government," or "polyarchy" is really little more than elective monarchy in democratic guise.

It is against this background that we should understand the revival of classical democratic theory. The ground of the democratic process is safely secured against its traditional enemies: conservatives who distrust the masses and vanguardists who would make minority revolutions in the name of the majority. Aside from a few peculiar segments of the intelligentsia and ruling groups desperate to hang on to their power, no one any longer takes antidemocratic arguments seriously; no arguments for the virtue of polyarchy as opposed to oligarchy or tyranny are necessary. It is now clear that given the slightest weakening of resolve by their rulers, people anywhere will struggle for freedom and political equality.

Thus there is no need, as Dahl does in *Who Governs?* and as empirical democratic theory has habitually done, to look for cultural "conditions" or "elite" beliefs that conduce to democracy. Democracy, understood as the demand for equal voice and equal justice, is always on the agenda in any civil society. Furthermore, no matter what the survey research of empirical democratic theory purports to tell us about the allegedly greater dedication of elites than masses to "the democratic creed," it is the popular masses, not elites, who set the democratic agenda (see Selection 16). However, we have not seen the popular face of democracy because we have all been looking for it in the wrong place: in constitutions, in legislatures, in elective monarchs masquerading as presidents or prime ministers, and worst of all, in the abstract "attitudes" that respondents to survey research have toward these institutions of polyarchy.

We would do better, at least initially, to understand this hidden face of democracy as a series of moments: moments of popular insurgency and direct action, of unmediated politics. The history of democracy, then, is only in part a history of the Greek city-state and the later transition to modern nationhood. Both the city-state and the modern nation may have been, and may be, considerably more hospitable to the democratic moment than, say, ancient empires or feudal duchies; but they are democracy's framework, not the thing itself. Instead, we would do better to conceive of the real history of democracy as the history of popular struggle, in which the people learn, as Rosa Luxemburg put it, how to govern themselves (see Selection 26).

In the absence of any such understanding, ironically, our notion of "the democratic process" does not include the very process that, as in Eastern Europe, creates democracy—or even polyarchy. In Hannah Arendt's words, "in [the American] republic, as it presently turned out, there was no space reserved, no room left for the exercise of precisely those qualities which had been instrumental in building it" (see Selection 26). That is, although the *creative* democratic process occurs and reoccurs, it does so in opposition to, and often against the threat of suppression by, the entrenched institutions of polyarchy, of the formal democratic process. The great moments of the creative democratic process are not parliamentary sittings or elections but strikes, demonstrations, marches, occupations, even funerals (see Selection 27).

To take one well-known example: Until the fatal moment in 1911 when she threw herself in front of the King's horse at Epsom, Emily Wilding Davidson was a little-known militant on the violent fringe of suffragism; her martyrdom, although it would be forever, was in no way yet a moment of democracy. The next day, however, the leadership of the Women's Social and Political Union issued a call to women to march in her funeral procession wearing the colors of the WSPU; hundreds of thousands answered the call from all over Britain. The Home Secretary "banned" the procession and carefully instructed the constabulary not to enforce the ban. The deliberate symbolism of Davidson's death had raised the issue of women's suffrage to the highest possible political level. And the response of the mass of British women as well as that of the authorities made perfectly clear, even if the perception still existed below the level of consciousness for most people, that Britain could have a legitimate monarchy or males-only suffrage—but it could not have both. Thereafter only the Great War (and splits within the suffragist movement itself) could delay the day of reckoning (see Mackenzie, 1975).

Britain, of course, did not become fully democratic after the extension of the franchise (in fact, the price of that achievement was the retention of a property qualification for all voters); it did not even become a republic. It had only extended the democratic process in this one particular area; it remained a "polyarchy." But on the day of Davidson's funeral democracy existed in the streets of London; just as it existed in the streets of Barcelona in 1914, or in the streets of Toledo, San Francisco, and Minneapolis during the general strikes of 1934, or in the auto plants of Flint, Michigan in 1936–37, or on the highway into Selma in 1963, or in the public squares of Leipzig and Prague and East Berlin in 1989. No "competitive party process" or "competition for leadership" would have achieved women's suffrage in Britain, or the Civil Rights Act of 1964, or the National Labor Relations Act of 1935, or the upsurge in union organization after its passage. Our traditional theory, from this standpoint, has had it reversed: mass action is the heart of democracy; electoral and parliamentary politics, although indeed its "necessary condition," are too often the hardening of its arteries. Without democratic life in that, its most meaningful sense, the "democratic process" would be a lifeless shell (see Selection 28).

Direct action, admittedly, has always had a bad reputation with liberal democrats, for two obvious reasons in particular that require discussion. In the first place, the attraction of the formal democratic process is that, no matter how subject it may be (at a particular time and place) to accusations that it is a mere facade, no one ever hurts anyone else by engaging in it. Voting may be only symbolic, but at least it's done without weapons. The same can hardly be said in every case of direct action: one man's civil rights march is another man's violent riot. We can offer what look like formal principles, such as: demands for equal justice are democratic demands, whereas demands for the seizure of power or the coercion of others are not; but that is hardly compelling. Is the blockading of an abortion clinic a demand for equal justice for fetuses, or an assault on the privacy of women?

This is a serious objection, but it is hardly unique to a radical definition of democracy. Very few important disputes in political philosophy can be settled by an appeal to unambiguous principles. Does "equal opportunity" require only formal equality before the law, or does it require equalizing the condition of the runners before the "race" starts (and perhaps after every lap)? To the owners of General Motors, or the operators of buses and lunch counters in the South, the sit-down strikes and freedom rides may have looked like Mussolini's March on Rome; but any political theorist can tell the difference and should be able to explain it. There may have been mass movements that attempted to seize tyrannical power in the name of "democracy," but it is hard to think of many. The democratic aspect of the French Revolution died at the hands of self-anointed leaders, not the sans-culottes and bourgeois activists who initially made it.

Direct action also raises the question of representation: "Who elected *you*?" Elected representatives, it may be said, have at least been elected, as their title affirms; but who gave suffragists the right to block traffic in London? Here, though, the implied opposition is spurious. There may be rules for conducting an election, but there are no rules for being represented. People are represented if they think they are, and the notion that mass protests don't "represent" anyone but the protestors is patently false. A recent governor of my own state was an old friend of mine, and I always voted for him, but, except on a handful of issues, I did not feel represented by him in the slightest; contrarily, people whom I have never voted for in my life represent me faithfully and importantly in a variety of ways that have nothing to do with the electoral process. African-Americans were never represented by the legislative process until "outside agitators" represented them in the civil rights movement. Senator Wagner perhaps represented

American workers in some sense, but only very ambiguously and cautiously, and as part of a careful negotiating process with those who oppressed them. Union leaders such as John L. Lewis, Walter Reuther, Harry Bridges, not to mention the men who sat down at Fisher Body Number 1 in Flint and the women who formed a *cordon sanitaire* to protect them, were committed representatives of the American working class. The fundamental democratic right to organize and strike (a right that hardly ever appears as such in the lexicon of liberal theorists) would never have been won even temporarily without their acts of representation. Millions of British women gave the WSPU the "right" to tie up London's traffic, and they did not have to hold any election to do that.

To argue that only formal elections eventuate in representation is simply to argue by definition or to assume what has to be painstakingly proved. In this way the "democratic elitist" view tends to make elections into virtually absolute trumps—the only legitimate method for ascertaining the will of the only definable cast of characters known as "the people." But then the "necessary condition" in fact becomes the enemy of all attempts to eliminate injustices that are intrinsic to it; the good becomes the enemy of the better.

The more serious problem is not theoretical but practical. Democratic direct action is not in the same apparently utopian category (with respect to modern industrial states) as direct democracy, but its historical moments hardly seem to add up to a coherent set of permanent institutions. That is not to say, however, that it can never have any more substantial outcome than the local town meeting (which does not so much solve the problem of participation as remove it to another forum). At the moment we can only be speculative, but I think we can tell whether a society is becoming more democratic or is simply tightening the bonds of polyarchy. The kind of liberal reform that Jeremy Bentham and Mill and now Dahl have stood for can take us only so far, even when it comprehends a commitment to some version of worker control of industry.

Beyond that, we should be searching for a politics in which participation is understood as a right and as an essential element in the search for the conditions of self-determination that democracy is all about (see Selection 29). Of course it is not self-evident exactly what we might mean by this. Hannah Arendt, for example (Selection 26), insisted that an extended public participatory space could only be for what she assumed to be the special few who are truly dedicated to the expansion of the sphere of liberty; and she also believed that the public space of liberty would necessarily be contaminated by the intrusions of bread-and-butter politics, that is, by the demands of materially deprived people. However, we need not accept this elitist conclusion, at least not in the form Arendt gives it. On the contrary, if we turn her argument around we can see a different logic, which I have already suggested and which has appealed to democrats following in Arendt's footsteps: further realization of the democratic project must be preceded or accompanied by serious inroads against the kinds of material inequalities we in the United States sadly take for granted.

What might a more truly democratic politics look like? At a minimum, it would be a politics that is hospitable to informal conflict resolution in place of formal rules of order (see Mansbridge, 1980); rewards dialogue and discussion rather than one-way "communication"; deepens and broadens processes of representation, so that more people from early childhood on are involved in the direct action of representing and being represented; and as much as possible devolves rule-making powers, not of exclusion but of self-governance, to communities defined by and defining themselves through a project of joint action (see Selections 30 and 31; and Cockburn, 1977). The civic culture of this kind of democracy would not confuse an abstract pluralism with equal right (see the Introduction to Part VIII of this book, and Selection 36) and would not value formally democratic procedures to the exclusion of demands for equal right, but would rather encourage the direct expression of those demands. Seen in this light the United States, where the vital and long-standing tradition of grassroots political activism now has no link to either the media or the government, looks like a nation where polyarchy is indeed stable and enduring—but where democracy is (perhaps only momentarily) moribund.

The visible despair of the activists who toppled the German Democratic Republic, as they watched their democratic (and representative) revolution ousted from the streets of Berlin and the corridors of its public buildings, to become enmeshed in the monopolistic party politics of the Federal Republic, can be a lesson for all theorists of democracy. The real moment of challenge for democratic theory and practice begins when the momentary revolutions or rebellions of the enduring democratic struggle dissolve, as they always have heretofore, into the political party oligarchies and executive domination described so well by Michels and Morgenthau. Not "How can polyarchy be stabilized?" but "How can the democratic moment be prolonged beyond the moment?"; not "Who governs?" but "Who acts?" are the questions that democratic theory should now be addressing.

SELECTION 1
FROM
*Keywords**

RAYMOND WILLIAMS

DEMOCRACY IS A VERY old word but its meanings have always been complex. It came into English in the sixteenth century, from . . . a translation of *demokratia*, Greek, from the root words *demos*—people, and *kratos*—rule. . . . It is at once evident from Greek uses that everything depends on the senses given to *people* and to *rule*. Ascribed and doubtful early examples range from obeying "no master but the law" (?Solon) to "of the people, by the people, for the people" (?Cleon). More certain examples compare "the insolence of a despot" with "the insolence of the unbridled commonality" (cit. Herodotus) or define a government as democracy "because its administration is in the hands, not of the few, but of the many"; also, all that is opposed to despotic power, has the name of democracy" (cit. Thucydides). Aristotle (*Politics*, IV, 4) wrote: "a democracy is a state where the freemen and the poor, being in the majority, are invested with the power of the state." Yet much depends here on what is meant by "invested with power": whether it is ultimate sovereignty or, at the other extreme, practical and unshared rule. Plato made Socrates say (in *Republic*, VIII, 10) that "democracy comes into being after the poor have conquered their opponents, slaughtering some and banishing some, while to the remainder they give an equal share of freedom and power."

This range of uses, near the roots of the term, makes any simple derivation impossible. It can, however, be said at once that several of these uses—and especially those which indicate a form of popular class rule—are at some distance from any orthodox modern "Western" definition of *democracy*. Indeed the emergence of that orthodox definition, which has its own uncertainties, is what needs to be traced. "Democracy" is now often traced back to medieval precedents and given a Greek authority. But the fact is that, with only occasional exceptions, *democracy*, in the records that we have, was until the nineteenth century a strongly unfavorable term, and it is only since the late nineteenth and early twentieth centuries that a majority of political parties and tendencies have

*"Democracy," in *Keywords* (London: Fontana/Croom Helm, 1976): pp. 82–87.

united in declaring their belief in it. This is the most striking historical fact.

Aquinas defined *democracy* as popular power, where the ordinary people, by force of numbers, governed—oppressed—the rich; the whole people acting like a tyrant. This strong class sense remained the predominant meaning until the late eighteenth and early nineteenth centuries and was still active in mid-nineteenth century argument. . . . To this definition of the *people* as the *multitude* there was added a common sense of the consequent type of *rule*: a *democracy* was a state in which all had the right to rule and did actually rule; it was even contrasted (e.g., by Spinoza) with a state in which there was rule by representatives, including elected representatives. It was in this sense that the first political constitution to use the term *democracy*—that of Rhode Island in 1641—understood it:

> . . . popular government; that is to say it is in the power of the body of freemen orderly assembled, or major part of them, to make or constitute just Lawes, by which they will be regulated, and to depute from among themselves such ministers as shall see them faithfully executed between man and man.

This final clause needs to be emphasized, since a new meaning of democracy was eventually arrived at by an alteration of the concept here embodied. In the case of Rhode Island, the people or a major part of them made laws in orderly assembly; the ministers "faithfully executed" them. This is not the same as the *representative democracy* defined by Hamilton in 1777. He was referring to the earlier sense of *democracy* when he observed that

> when the deliberative or judicial powers are vested wholly or partly in the collective body of the people, you must expect error, confusion and instability. But a representative democracy, where the right of election is well secured and regulated, and the exercise of the legislative, executive and judicial authorities is vested in select persons . . . etc.

It is from this modified American use that a dominant modern sense developed. Bentham formulated a general sense of democracy as rule by the majority of the people, and then distinguished between "direct democracy" and "representative democracy," recommending the latter because it provided continuity and could be extended to large societies. These important practical reasons have since been both assumed and dropped, so that in the mid-twentieth century an assertion of *democracy* in the Rhode Island sense, or in Bentham's *direct* sense, could be described as "antidemocratic," since the first principle of *democracy* is taken to be rule by elected representatives. The practical arguments are of course serious, and in many circumstances decisive, but one of the two most significant changes in the meaning of *democracy* is this exclusive association with one of its derived forms, and the attempted exclusion of one of its original forms; at one period, its only form.

The second major change has to do with interpretation of *the people*. There is some significant history in the various attempts to limit "the people" to certain qualified groups: freemen, owners of property, the wise, white men, men, and so on. Where *democracy* is defined by a process of election, such limited constitutions can be claimed to be fully *democratic*: the mode of choosing representatives is taken as more important than the proportion of "the people" who have any part in this. The development of democracy is traced through institutions using this mode rather than through the relations between all the people and a form of government. This interpretation is orthodox in most accounts of the development of English democracy. Indeed *democracy* is said to have been "extended" stage by stage, where what is meant is clearly the right to vote for representatives rather than the old (and until the early nineteenth century normal English) sense of *popular power*. The distinction became critical in the period of the French Revolution. Burke was expressing an orthodox view when he wrote that "a perfect democracy" was "the most shameless thing in the world" (*Reflections on the Revolution in France*, 1790), for *democracy* was taken to be "uncontrolled" popular power under which, among other things, minorities (including especially the minority which held substantial property) would be suppressed or oppressed. *Democracy* was still a revolutionary or at least a radical term to the mid-nineteenth century, and the specialized development of *representative democracy* was at least in part a conscious reaction to this, over and above the practical reasons of extent and continuity.

It is from this point in the argument that two modern meanings of *democracy* can be seen to diverge. In the socialist tradition, *democracy* continued to mean *popular power*: a state in which the interests of the majority of the people were paramount and in which these interests were practically exercised and controlled by the majority. In the liberal tradition, *democracy* meant open election of representatives and certain conditions (*democratic rights*, such as free speech) which maintained the openness of election and political argument. These two conceptions, in their extreme forms, now confront each other as enemies. If the predominant criterion is popular power in the popular interest, other criteria are often taken as secondary (as in the *People's Democracies*) and their emphasis is specialized to "capitalist democracy" or "bourgeois democracy." If the predominant criteria are elections and free speech, other criteria are seen as secondary or are rejected; an attempt to exercise popular power in the popular interest, for example by a General Strike, is described as *antidemocratic*, since *democracy* has already been assured by other means; to claim economic equality as the essence of democracy is seen as leading to "chaos" or to *totalitarian democracy* or *government by trade unions*. These positions, with their many minor variants, divide the modern meanings of *democracy* between them, but this is not usually seen as a historical variation of the term; each position, normally, is described as "the only true meaning," and the alternative use is seen as propaganda or hypocrisy.

Democratic (from the early nineteenth century) is the normal adjective for one or other of these kinds of belief or institution. But two further senses should be noted. There is an observable use of *democratic* to describe the conditions of open argument, without necessary reference to elections or to power. Indeed, in one characteristic use freedom of speech and assembly are *the* "democratic rights," sufficient in themselves, without reference to the institution or character of political power. This is a limiting sense derived from the liberal emphasis, which in its full form has to include election and popular sovereignty (though not popular rule). There is also a derived sense from the early class reference to the "multitude": to be *democratic*, to have *democratic* manners or feelings, is to be unconscious of class distinctions, or consciously to disregard or overcome them in everyday behavior: acting *as if* all people were equal, and deserved equal respect, whether this is really so or not. Thus a man might be on "plain and natural" terms with everyone he met, and might further believe in free speech and free assembly, yet, following only these senses, could for example oppose universal suffrage, let alone government directed solely to the interests of the majority. The senses have in part been extended, in part moved away, from what was formerly and is probably still the primary sense of the character of political power.

No questions are more difficult than those of *democracy*, in any of its central senses. Analysis of variation will not resolve them, though it may sometimes clarify them. To the positive opposed senses of the socialist and liberal traditions we have to add, in a century which unlike any other finds nearly all political movements claiming to stand for *democracy* or *real democracy*, innumerable conscious distortions: reduction of the concepts of *election*, *representation* and *mandate* to deliberate formalities or merely manipulated forms; reduction of the concept of *popular power*, or government in the *popular interest*, to nominal slogans covering the rule of a bureaucracy or an oligarchy. It would sometimes be easier to believe in democracy, or to stand for it, if the nineteenth-century change had not happened and it were still an unfavorable or factional term. But that history has occurred, and the range of contemporary senses is its confused and still active record.

PART II

The Classical Theory

SELECTION 2
FROM
*The Social Contract**

JEAN-JACQUES ROUSSEAU

BOOK I, CHAPTER VI

[A]S THE FORCE AND liberty of each man are the chief instruments of his self-preservation, how can he pledge them without harming his own interests, and neglecting the care he owes to himself? This difficulty, in its bearing on my present subject, may be stated in the following terms:

"The problem is to find a form of association which will defend and protect with the whole common force the person and goods of each associate, and in which each, while uniting himself with all, may still obey himself alone, and remain as free as before." This is the fundamental problem of which the *Social Contract* provides the solution.

The clauses of this contract are so determined by the nature of the act that the slightest modification would make them vain and ineffective; so that, although they have perhaps never been formally set forth, they are everywhere the same and everywhere tacitly admitted and recognized, until, on the violation of the social compact, each regains his original rights and resumes his natural liberty, while losing the conventional liberty in favor of which he renounced it.

These clauses, properly understood, may be reduced to one—the total alienation of each associate, together with all his rights, to the whole community; for, in the first place, as each gives himself absolutely, the conditions are the same for all; and, this being so, no one has any interest in making them burdensome to others.

Moreover, the alienation being without reserve, the union is as perfect as it can be, and no associate has anything more to demand: for, if the individuals retained certain rights, as there would be no common superior to decide between them and the public, each, being on one point his own judge, would ask to be so on all; the state of nature would thus continue, and the association would necessarily become inoperative or tyrannical.

**The Social Contract* and *Discourses*, G. D. H. Cole (Trans.) (New York: E. P. Dutton [Everyman's Library], 1950). From *The Social Contract*, Book I, Ch. 6; Book III, Chs. 12–18. The author's original capitalization and punctuation have been maintained here for historical accuracy.

Finally, each man, in giving himself to all, gives himself to nobody; and as there is no associate over which he does not acquire the same right as he yields others over himself, he gains an equivalent for everything he loses, and an increase of force for the preservation of what he has.

If then we discard from the social compact what is not of its essence, we shall find that it reduces itself to the following terms:

> Each of us puts his person and all his power in common under the supreme direction of the general will, and, in our corporate capacity, we receive each member as an indivisible part of the whole.

At once, in place of the individual personality of each contracting party, this act of association creates a moral and collective body, composed of as many members as the assembly contains voters, and receiving from this act its unity, its common identity, its life, and its will. This public person, so formed by the union of all other persons, formerly took the name of *city*, . . . and now takes that of *Republic* or *body politic*; it is called by its members *State* when passive, *Sovereign* when active, and *Power* when compared with others like itself. Those who are associated in it take collectively the name *people*, and severally are called *citizens*, as sharing in the sovereign power, and *subjects*, as being under the laws of the State. But these terms are often confused and taken one for another: it is enough to know how to distinguish them when they are being used with precision.

Book III, Chapter XII
How the Sovereign Authority Maintains Itself

The Sovereign having no force other than legislative power, acts only by means of the laws; and the laws being solely the authentic acts of the general will, the Sovereign cannot act save when the people is assembled. The people in assembly, I shall be told, is a mere chimera. It is so today, but two thousand years ago it was not so. Has man's nature changed?

The bounds of possibility, in moral matters, are less narrow than we imagine: it is our weaknesses, our vices, and our prejudices that confine them. Base souls have no belief in great men; vile slaves smile in mockery at the name of liberty.

Let us judge of what can be done by what has been done. I shall say nothing of the Republics of ancient Greece; but the Roman Republic was, to my mind, a great State, and the town of Rome a great town. The last census showed that there were in Rome four hundred thousand citizens capable of bearing arms, and the last computation of the population of the Empire showed over four million citizens, excluding subjects, foreigners, women, children, and slaves.

What difficulties might not be supposed to stand in the way of the frequent assemblage of the vast population of this capital and its neighborhood. Yet few weeks passed without the Roman people being in assembly, and even being so several times. It exercised not only the rights of Sovereignty, but also a part of those of government. It dealt with certain matters, and judged certain cases, and this whole people was found in the public meeting-place hardly less often as magistrates than as citizens.

If we went back to the earliest history of nations, we should find that most ancient governments, even those of monarchical form, such as the Macedonian and the Frankish, had similar councils. In any case, the one incontestable fact I have given is an answer to all difficulties; it is good logic to reason from the actual to the possible.

CHAPTER XIII
THE SAME (CONTINUED)

It is not enough for the assembled people to have once fixed the constitution of the State by giving its sanction to a body of law; it is not enough for it to have set up a perpetual government, or provided once for all for the election of magistrates. Besides the extraordinary assemblies unforeseen circumstances may demand, there must be fixed periodical assemblies which cannot be abrogated or prorogued so that on the proper day the people is legitimately called together by law, without need of any formal summoning.

But, apart from these assemblies authorized by their date alone, every assembly of the people not summoned by the magistrates appointed for that purpose, and in accordance with the prescribed forms, should be regarded as unlawful, and all its acts as null and void, because the command to assemble should itself proceed from the law.

The greater or less frequency with which lawful assemblies should occur depends on so many considerations that no exact rules about them can be given. It can only be said generally that the stronger the government the more often should the Sovereign show itself.

This, I shall be told, may do for a single town; but what is to be done when the State includes several? Is the sovereign authority to be divided? Or is it to be concentrated in a single town to which all the rest are made subject?

Neither the one nor the other, I reply. First, the sovereign authority is one and simple, and cannot be divided without being destroyed. In the second place, one town cannot, any more than one nation, legitimately be made subject to another, because the essence of the body politic lies in the reconciliation of obedience and liberty, and the words subject and Sovereign are identical correlatives the idea of which meets in the single word "citizen."

I answer further that the union of several towns in a single city is always bad, and that, if we wish to make such a union, we should not expect to avoid its natural disadvantages. It is useless to bring up abuses that belong to great States against one who desires to see only small ones; but how can small States be given the strength to resist great ones, as formerly the Greek towns resisted the Great King, and more recently Holland and Switzerland have resisted the House of Austria?

Nevertheless, if the State cannot be reduced to the right limits, there remains still one resource; this is, to allow no capital, to make the seat of government move from town to town, and to assembly by turn in each the Provincial Estates of the country.

People the territory evenly, extend everywhere the same rights, bear to every place in it abundance and life: by these means will the State become at once as strong and as well governed as possible. Remember that the walls of towns are built of the ruins of the houses of the countryside. For every palace I see raised in the capital, my mind's eye sees a whole country made desolate.

CHAPTER XIV
THE SAME (CONTINUED)

The moment the people legitimately assembled as a sovereign body, the jurisdiction of the government wholly lapses, the executive power is suspended, and the person of the meanest citizen is as sacred and inviolable as that of the first magistrate; for in the presence of one person represented, representatives no longer exist. Most of the tumults that arose in the comitia at Rome were due to ignorance or neglect of this rule. The consuls were in them merely the presidents of the people; the tribunes were mere speakers; . . . the senate was nothing at all.

These intervals of suspension, during which the prince recognizes or ought to recognize an actual superior, have always been viewed by him with alarm; and these assemblies of the people, which are the aegis of the body politic and the curb on the government, have at all times been the horror of rulers: who therefore never spare pains, objections, difficulties, and promises, to stop the citizens from having them. When the citizens are greedy, cowardly, and pusillanimous, and love ease more than liberty, they do not long hold out against the redoubled efforts of the government; and thus, as the resisting force incessantly grows, the sovereign authority ends by disappearing, and most cities fall and perish before their time.

But between the sovereign authority and arbitrary government there sometimes intervenes a mean power of which something must be said.

CHAPTER XV
DEPUTIES OR REPRESENTATIVES

As soon as public service ceases to be the chief business of the citizens and they would rather serve with their money than with their persons, the State is not far from its fall. When it is necessary to march out to war, they pay troops and stay at home: when it is necessary to meet in council, they name deputies and stay at home. By reason of idleness and money, they end by having soldiers to enslave their country and representatives to sell it.

It is through the hustle of commerce and the arts, through the greedy self-interest of profit, and through softness and love of amenities that personal services are replaced by money payments. Men surrender a part of their profits in order to have time to increase them at leisure. Make gifts of money, and you will not be long without chains. The word "finance" is a slavish word, unknown in the city-state. In a country that is truly free, the citizens do everything with their own arms and nothing by means of money; so far from paying to be exempted from their duties, they would even pay for the privilege of fulfilling them themselves. I am far from taking the common view: I hold enforced labor to be less opposed to liberty than taxes.

The better the constitution of a state is, the more do public affairs encroach on private in the minds of the citizens. Private affairs are even of much less importance, because the aggregate of the common happiness furnishes a greater proportion of that of each individual, so that there is less for him to seek in particular cares. In a well-ordered city every man flies to the assemblies: under a bad government no one cares to stir a step to get to them, because no one is interested in what happens there, because it is foreseen that the general will will not prevail, and lastly because domestic cares are all-absorbing. Good laws lead to the making of better ones; bad ones bring about worse. As soon as any man says of the affairs of the State *What does it matter to me?* the State may be given up for lost.

The lukewarmness of patriotism, the activity of private interests, the vastness of States, conquest, and the abuse of government suggested the method of having deputies or representatives of the people in the national assemblies. These are what, in some countries, men have presumed to call the Third Estate. Thus the individual interest of two orders is put first and second; the public interest occupies only the third place.

Sovereignty, for the same reason as makes it inalienable, cannot be represented; it lies essentially in the general will, and will does not admit of representation: it is either the same, or other; there is no intermediate possibility. The deputies of the people, therefore, are not and cannot be its representatives: they are merely its stewards, and can carry through no definitive acts. Every law the people has not ratified in person is null and void—is, in fact, not a law. The people of England regards itself as free: but it is grossly mistaken: it is free only during the election of members of parliament. As soon as they are elected, slavery overtakes it, and it is nothing. The use it makes of the short moments of liberty it enjoys shows indeed that it deserves to lose them.

The idea of representation is modern; it comes to us from feudal government, from that iniquitous and absurd system which degrades humanity and dishonors the name of man. In ancient republics and even in monarchies, the people never had representatives; the word itself was unknown. It is very singular that in Rome, where the tribunes were so sacrosanct, it was never even imagined that they could usurp the functions of the people, and that in the midst of so great a multitude they never attempted to pass on their own authority a single *plebiscitum*. . . .

In Greece, all that the people had to do, it did for itself; it was constantly assembled in the public square. The Greeks lived in a mild climate; they had no natural greed; slaves did their work for them; their great concern was with liberty. Lacking the same advantages, how can you preserve the same rights? Your severer climates add to your needs; . . . for half the year your public squares are uninhabitable; the flatness of your languages unfits them for being heard in the open air; you sacrifice more for your profit than for liberty, and fear slavery less than poverty.

What then? Is liberty maintained only by the help of slavery? It may be so. Extremes meet. Everything that is not in the course of nature has its disadvantages, civil society most of all. There are some unhappy circumstances in which we can only keep our liberty at others' expense, and where the citizen can be perfectly free only when the slave is most a slave. Such was the case with Sparta. As for you, modern peoples, you have no slaves, but you are slaves yourselves; you pay for their liberty with your own. It is in vain that you boast of this preference; I find in it more cowardice than humanity.

I do not mean by all this that it is necessary to have slaves, or that the right of slavery is legitimate: I am merely giving the reasons why modern peoples, believing themselves to be free, have representatives, while ancient peoples had none. In any case, the moment a people allows itself to be represented, it is no longer free: it no longer exists.

All things considered, I do not see that it is possible henceforth for the Sovereign to preserve among us the exercise of its rights, unless the city is very small. But if it is very small, it will be conquered? No, I will show later on how the external strength of a great people . . . may be combined with the convenient polity and good order of a small State.

Chapter XVI
That the Institution of Government Is Not a Contract

The legislative power once well established, the next thing is to establish similarly the executive power; for this latter, which operates only by particular acts, not being of the essence of the former, is naturally separate from it. Were it possible for the Sovereign, as such, to possess the executive power, right and fact would be so confounded that no one could tell what was law and what was not;

and the body politic, thus disfigured, would soon fall a prey to the violence it was instituted to prevent.

As the citizens, by the social contract, are all equal, all can prescribe what all should do, but no one has a right to demand that another shall do what he does not do himself. It is strictly this right, which is indispensable for giving the body politic life and movement, that the Sovereign, in instituting the government, confers upon the prince.

It has been held that this act of establishment was a contract between the people and rulers it sets over itself—a contract in which conditions were laid down between the two parties binding the one to command and the other to obey. It will be admitted, I am sure, that this is an odd kind of contract to enter into. But let us see if this view can be upheld.

First, the supreme authority can no more be modified than it can be alienated; to limit it is to destroy it. It is absurd and contradictory for the Sovereign to set a superior over itself; to bind itself to obey a master would be to return to absolute liberty.

Moreover, it is clear that this contract between the people and such and such persons would be a particular act; and from this it follows that it can be neither a law nor an act of Sovereignty, and that consequently it would be illegitimate.

It is plain too that the contracting parties in relation to each other would be under the law of nature alone and wholly without guarantees of their mutual undertakings, a position wholly at variance with the civil state. He who has force at his command being always in a position to control execution, it would come to the same thing if the name "contract" were given to the act of one man who said to another: "I give you all my goods, on condition that you give me back as much of them as you please."

There is only one contract in the State, and that is the act of association, which in itself excludes the existence of a second. It is impossible to conceive of any public contract that would not be a violation of the first.

Chapter XVII
The Institution of Government

Under what general idea then should the act by which government is instituted be conceived as falling? I will begin by stating that the act is complex, as being composed of two others—the establishment of the law and its execution.

By the former, the Sovereign decrees that there shall be a governing body established in this or that form; this act is clearly a law.

By the latter, the people nominates the rulers who are to be entrusted with the government that has been established. This nomination, being a particular act, is clearly not a second law, but merely a consequence of the first and a function of government.

The difficulty is to understand how there can be a governmental act before government exists, and how the people, which is only Sovereign or subject, can, under certain circumstances, become a prince or magistrate.

It is at this point that there is revealed one of the astonishing properties of the body politic, by means of which it reconciles apparently contradictory operations; for this is accomplished by a sudden conversion of Sovereignty into democracy, so that, without sensible change, and merely by virtue of a new relation of all to all, the citizens become magistrates and pass from general to particular acts, from legislation to the execution of the law. . . .

It is, indeed, the perculiar advantage of democratic government that it can be established in actuality by a simple act of the general will. Subsequently, this provisional government remains in power, if this form is adopted, or else establishes in the name of the Sovereign the government that is prescribed by law; and thus the whole proceeding is regular. It is impossible to set up government in any other manner legitimately and in accordance with the principles so far laid down.

Chapter XVIII
How to Check the Usurpations of Government

What we have just said confirms Chapter XVI, and makes it clear that the institution of government is not a contract, but a law; that the depositaries of the executive power are not the people's masters, but its officers; that it can set them up and pull them down when it likes; that for them there is no question of contract, but of obedience; and that in taking charge of the functions the State imposes on them they are doing no more than fulfilling their duty as citizens, without having the remotest right to argue about the conditions. . . .

The opening of these assemblies, whose sole object is the maintenance of the social treaty, should always take the form of putting two propositions that may not be suppressed, which should be voted on separately.

The first is: "Does it please the Sovereign to preserve the present form of Government?"

The second is: "Does it please the people to leave its administration in the hands of those who are actually in charge of it?"

I am here assuming what I think I have shown; that there is in the State no fundamental law that cannot be revoked, not excluding the social compact itself; for if all the citizens assembled of one accord to break the compact, it is impossible to doubt that it would be very legitimately broken. Grotius even thinks that each man can renounce his membership of his own State, and recover his natural liberty and his goods on leaving the country. . . . It would be indeed absurd if all the citizens in assembly could not do what each can do by himself.

SELECTION 3
FROM
*Considerations on Representative Government**

JOHN STUART MILL

THERE IS NO DIFFICULTY in showing that the ideally best form of government is that in which the sovereignty, or supreme controlling power in the last resort, is vested in the entire aggregate of the community; every citizen not only having a voice in the exercise of that ultimate sovereignty, but being, at least occasionally, called on to take an actual part in the government, by the personal discharge of some public function, local or general.

To test this proposition, it has to be examined in reference to the two branches into which, as pointed out in the last chapter, the inquiry into the goodness of a government conveniently divides itself, namely, how far it promotes the good management of the affairs of society by means of the existing faculties, moral, intellectual, and active, of its various members, and what is its effect in improving or deteriorating those faculties.

The ideally best form of government, it is scarcely necessary to say, does not mean one which is practicable or eligible in all states of civilization, but the one which, in the circumstances in which it is practicable and eligible, is attended with the greatest amount of beneficial consequences, immediate and prospective. A completely popular government is the only polity which can make out any claim to this character. It is preeminent in both the departments between which the excellence of a political constitution is divided. It is both more favorable to present good government, and promotes a better and higher form of national character, than any other polity whatsoever.

Its superiority in reference to present well-being rests upon two principles, of as universal truth and applicability as any general propositions which can be laid down respecting human affairs. The first is, that the rights and interests of every or any person are only secure from being disregarded when the person interested is himself able, and habitually disposed, to stand up for them. The second is,

* (New York: E. P. Dutton [Everyman's Library], 1951): Chs. 3 and 5.

that the general prosperity attains a greater height, and is more widely diffused, in proportion to the amount and variety of the personal energies enlisted in promoting it.

Putting these two propositions into a shape more special to their present application; human beings are only secure from evil at the hands of others in proportion as they have the power of being, and are self-*protecting*; and they only achieve a high degree of success in their struggle with Nature in proportion as they are self-*dependent*, relying on what they themselves can do, either separately or in concert, rather than on what others do for them.

The former proposition—that each is the only safe guardian of his own rights and interests—is one of those elementary maxims of prudence, which every person, capable of conducting his own affairs, implicitly acts upon, wherever he himself is interested. Many, indeed, have a great dislike to it as a political doctrine, and are fond of holding it up to obloquy, as a doctrine of universal selfishness. To which we may answer, that whenever it ceases to be true that mankind, as a rule, prefer themselves to others, and those nearest to them to those more remote, from that moment communism is not only practicable, but the only defensible form of society; and will, when that time arrives, be assuredly carried into effect. For my own part, not believing in universal selfishness, I have no difficulty in admitting that communism would even now be practicable among the elite of mankind, and may become so among the rest. But as this opinion is anything but popular with those defenders of existing institutions who find fault with the doctrine of the general predominance of self-interest, I am inclined to think they do in reality believe that most men consider themselves before other people. It is not, however, necessary to affirm even thus much in order to support the claim of all to participate in the sovereign power. We need not suppose that when power resides in an exclusive class, that class will knowingly and deliberately sacrifice the other classes to themselves: it suffices that, in the absence of its natural defenders, the interest of the excluded is always in danger of being overlooked; and, when looked at, is seen with very different eyes from those of the persons whom it directly concerns. In this country, for example, what are called the working classes may be considered as excluded from all direct participation in the government. I do not believe that the classes who do participate in it have in general any intention of sacrificing the working classes to themselves. They once had that intention; witness the persevering attempts so long made to keep down wages by law. But in the present day their ordinary disposition is the very opposite: they willingly make considerable sacrifices, especially for their pecuniary interest, for the benefit of the working classes, and err rather by too lavish and indiscriminating beneficence; nor do I believe that any rulers in history have been actuated by a more sincere desire to do their duty towards the poorer portion of their countrymen. Yet does Parliament, or almost any of the members composing it, ever for an instant look at any question with the eyes of a working man? When a subject arises in which the laborers as such have an interest, is it regarded from any point of view but that of the employers of labor? I do not say that the working men's view of these questions is in general nearer to the truth than the other: but it is sometimes quite as near; and in any case it ought to be respectfully listended to, instead of being, as it is, not merely turned away from, but ignored. On the question of strikes, for instance, it is doubtful if there is so much as one among the leading members of either House who is not firmly convinced that the reason of the matter is unqualifiedly on the side of the masters, and that the men's view of it is simply absurd. Those who have studied the question know well how far this is from being the case; and in how different, and how definitely less superficial a manner the point would have to be argued, if the classes who strike were able to make themselves heard in Parliament. . . .

It is an adherent condition of human affairs that no intention, however sincere, of protecting the interests of others can make it safe or salutary to tie up their own hands. Still more obviously true is it, that by their own hands only can any positive and durable improvement of their circumstances in life be worked out. . . .

It must be acknowledged that the benefits of freedom, so far as they have hitherto been enjoyed, were obtained by the extension of its privileges to a part only of the community; and that a government in which they are extended impartially to all is a desideratum still unrealized. But though every approach to this has an independent value, and in many cases more than an approach could not, in the existing state of general improvement, be made, the participation of all in these benefits is the ideally perfect conception of free government. In proportion as any, no matter who, are excluded from it, the interests of the excluded are left without the guarantee accorded to the rest, and they themselves have less scope and encouragement than they might otherwise have to that exertion of their energies for the good of themselves and of the community, to which the general prosperity is always proportioned.

Thus stands the case as regards present well-being; the good management of the affairs of the existing generation. If we now pass to the influence of the form of government upon character, we shall find the superiority of popular government over every other to be, if possible, still more decided and indisputable.

This question really depends upon a still more fundamental one, viz., which of two common types of character, for the general good of humanity, it is most desirable should predominate—the active, or the passive type; that which struggles against evils, or that which endures them; that which bends to circumstances, or that which endeavors to make circumstances bend to itself. . . .

Now there can be no kind of doubt that the passive type of character is favored of one or a few, and the active self-helping type by that of the Many. Irresponsible rulers need the quiescence of the ruled more than they need any activity but that which they can compel. Submissiveness to the prescriptions of men as necessities of nature is the lesson inculcated by all governments upon those who are wholly without participation in them. The will of superiors, and the law as the will of superiors, must be passively yielded to. But no men are mere instruments or materials in the hands of their rulers who have will or spirit or a spring of internal activity in the rest of their proceedings: and any manifestation of these qualities, instead of receiving encouragement from despots, has to get itself forgiven by them. Even when irresponsible rulers are not sufficiently conscious of danger from the mental activity of their subjects to be desirous of repressing it, the position itself is a repression. Endeavor is even more effectually restrained by the certainty of its impotence than by any positive discouragement. Between subjection to the will of others and the virtues of self-help and self-government, there is a natural incompatibility. This is more or less complete, according as the bondage is strained or relaxed. Rulers differ very much in the length to which they carry the control of the free agency of their subjects, or the supersession of it by managing their business for them. But the difference is in degree, not in principle; and the best despots often go the greatest lengths in chaining up the free agency of their subjects. A bad despot, when his own personal indulgences have been provided for, may sometimes be willing to let the people alone; but a good despot insists on doing them good, by making them do their own business in a better way than they themselves know of. The regulations which restricted to fixed processes all the leading branches of French manufactures were the work of the great Colbert.

Very different is the state of the human faculties where a human being feels himself under no other external restraint than the necessities of nature, or mandates of society which he has his share in imposing, and which it is open to him, if he thinks them wrong, publicly to dissent from, and exert himself actively to get altered. No doubt, under a government partially popular, this freedom may be exercised even by those who are not partakers in the full privileges of citizenship. But it is a great additional stimulus to anyone's self-help and self-reliance when he starts from even ground, and has not to feel that his success depends on the impression he can make upon the sentiments and dispositions of a body of whom he is not one. It is a great discouragement to an individual, and a still greater one to a class, to be left out of the constitution; to be reduced to plead from outside the door to the arbiters of their destiny, not taken into consultation within. The maximum of the invigorating effect of freedom upon the character is only obtained when the person acted on either is, or is looking forward to becoming, a citizen as fully privileged as any other. What is still more important than even this matter of feeling is the practical discipline which the character obtains from the occasional demand made upon the citizens to exercise, for a time and in their turn, some social function. It is not sufficiently considered how little there is in most men's ordinary life to give any largeness either to their conceptions or to their sentiments. Their work is a routine; not a labor of love, but of self-interest in the most elementary form, the satisfaction of daily wants; neither the thing done, nor the process of doing it, introduces the mind to thoughts or feelings extending beyond individuals; if instructive books are within their reach, there is no stimulus to read them; and in most cases the individual has no access to any person of cultivation much superior to his own. Giving him something to do for the public, supplies, in a measure, all these deficiencies. If circumstances allow the amount of public duty assigned him to be considerable, it makes him an educated man. Notwithstanding the defects of the social system and moral ideas of antiquity, the practice of the dicastery and the ecclesia raised the intellectual standard of an average Athenian citizen far beyond anything of which there is yet an example in any other mass of men, ancient or modern. The proofs of this are apparent in every page of our great historian of Greece; . . . but we need scarcely look further than to the high quality of the addresses which their great orators deemed best calculated to act with effect on their understanding and will. A benefit of the same kind, though far less in degree, is produced on Englishmen of the lower-middle class by their liability to be placed on juries and to serve parish offices; which, though it does not occur to so many, nor is so continuous, nor introduces them to so great a variety of elevated considerations, as to admit of comparison with the public education which every citizen of Athens obtains from her democratic institutions, must make them nevertheless very different beings, in range of ideas and development of faculties, from those who have done nothing in their lives but drive a quill, or sell goods over a counter. Still more salutary is the moral part of the instruction afforded by the participation of the private citizen, if even rarely, in public functions. He is called upon, while so engaged, to weigh interests not his own; to be guided, in case of conflicting claims, by another rule than his private partialities; to apply, at every turn, principles and maxims which have for their reason of existence the common good: and he usually finds associated with him in the same work minds more familiarized than his own with these ideas and operations, whose study it will be to supply reasons to his understanding, and stimulation to his feeling for the general interest. He is made to feel himself one of the public, and whatever is for their benefit to be for his benefit. Where his school of public spirit does not exist, scarcely any sense is entertained that private persons, in no eminent social situation, owe any duties to society, except to obey the laws and submit to the government. There is no unselfish sentiment of identification with the public. . . . Every thought or feeling, either of interest or of duty, is absorbed in the individual and in the family. The man never thinks of any collective interest, of any objects to be pursued jointly with others, but only in competition with them, and in some measure at their expense. A neighbor, not being an ally or an associate, since he is never engaged in any common undertaking for joint benefit, is therefore only a rival. Thus even private morality suffers, while public is actually extinct. Were this the universal and only possible state of things, the utmost aspirations of the lawgiver or the moralist could only stretch to make the bulk of the community a flock of sheep innocently nibbling the grass side by side.

From these accumulated considerations it is evident that the only government which can fully satisfy all the exigencies of the social state is one in which the whole people participate; that any participation, even in the smallest public function, is useful; that the participation should everywhere be as great as the general degree of improvement of the community will allow; and that nothing less can be ultimately desirable than the admission of all to a share in the sovereign power of the state. . . .

SELECTION 4
FROM
*Democracy in America**

ALEXIS DE TOCQUEVILLE

IT IS NOT ONLY the fortunes of men that are equal in America; even their acquirements partake in some degree of the same uniformity. I do not believe that there is a country in the world where, in proportion to the population, there are so few ignorant and at the same time so few learned individuals. Primary instruction is within the reach of everybody; superior instruction is scarcely to be obtained by any. This is not surprising; it is, in fact, the necessary consequence of what I have advanced above. Almost all the Americans are in easy circumstances and can therefore obtain the first elements of human knowledge.

In America there are but few wealthy persons; nearly all Americans have to take a profession. Now, every profession requires an apprenticeship. The Americans can devote to general education only the early years of life. At fifteen they enter upon their calling, and thus their education generally ends at the age when ours begins. If it is continued beyond that point, it aims only towards a particular specialized and profitable purpose; one studies science as one takes up a business; and one takes up only those applications whose immediate practicality is recognized.

In America most of the rich men were formerly poor; most of those who now enjoy leisure were absorbed in business during their youth; the consequence of this is that when they might have had a taste for study, they had no time for it, and when the time is at their disposal, they have no longer the inclination.

There is no class, then, in America, in which the taste for intellectual pleasures is transmitted with hereditary fortune and leisure and by which the labors of the intellect are held in honor. Accordingly, there is an equal want of the desire and the power of application to these objects.

A middling standard is fixed in America for human knowledge. All approach as near to it as they can; some as they rise, others as they descend. Of course, a multitude of persons are to be found who entertain the same number of ideas on

*(New York: A. A. Knopf [Vintage Books Edition], 1945): Volume 1, Chs. 3 and 4.

religion, history, science, political economy, legislation, and government. The gifts of intellect proceed directly from God, and man cannot prevent their unequal distribution. But it is at least a consequence of what I have just said that although the capacities of men are different, as the Creator intended they should be, the means that Americans find for putting them to use are equal.

In America the aristocratic element has always been feeble from its birth; and if at the present day it is not actually destroyed, it is at any rate so completely disabled that we can scarcely assign to it any degree of influence on the course of affairs.

The democratic principle, on the contrary, has gained so much strength by time, by events, and by legislation, as to have become not only predominant, but all-powerful. No family or corporate authority can be perceived; very often one cannot even discover in it any very lasting individual influence.

America, then, exhibits in her social state an extraordinary phenomenon. Men are there seen on a greater equality in point of fortune and intellect, or, in other words, more equal in their strength, than in any other country of the world, or in any age of which history has preserved the remembrance.

. . . The political consequences of such a social condition as this are easily deducible.

It is impossible to believe that equality will not eventually find its way into the political world, as it does everywhere else. To conceive of men remaining forever unequal upon a single point, yet equal on all others, is impossible; they must come in the end to be equal upon all.

Now, I know of only two methods of establishing equality in the political world; rights might be given to every citizen, or none at all to anyone. For nations which are arrived at the same stage of social existence as the Anglo-Americans, it is, therefore, very difficult to discover a medium between the sovereignty of all and the absolute power of one man: and it would be vain to deny that the social condition which I have been describing is just as liable to one of these consequences as to the other.

There is, in fact, a manly and lawful passion for equality that incites men to wish all to be powerful and honored. This passion tends to elevate the humble to the rank of the great; but there exists also in the human heart a depraved taste for equality, which impels the weak to attempt to lower the powerful to their own level and reduces men to prefer equality in slavery to inequality with freedom. Not that those nations whose social condition is democratic naturally despise liberty; on the contrary, they have an instinctive love of it. But liberty is not the chief and constant object of their desires; equality is their idol: they make rapid and sudden efforts to obtain liberty and, if they miss their aim, resign themselves to their disappointment; but nothing can satisfy them without equality, and they would rather perish than lose it.

On the other hand, in a state where the citizens are all practically equal, it becomes difficult for them to preserve their independence against the aggressions of power. No one among them being strong enough to engage in the struggle alone with advantage, nothing but a general combination can protect their liberty. Now, such a union is not always possible.

From the same social position, then, nations may derive one or the other of two great political results; these results are extremely different from each other, but they both proceed from the same cause.

The Anglo-Americans are the first nation who, having been exposed to this formidable alternative, have been happy enough to escape the dominion of absolute power. They have been allowed by their circumstances, their origin, their intelligence, and especially by their morals to establish and maintain the sovereignty of the people.

. . . Whenever the political laws of the United States are to be discussed, it is with the doctrine of the sovereignty of the people that we must begin.

The principle of the sovereignty of the people, which is always to be found, more or less, at the bottom of almost all human institutions, generally remains there concealed from view. It is obeyed without being recognized, or if for a moment it is brought to light, it is hastily cast back into the gloom of the sanctuary.

"The will of the nation" is one of those phrases that have been most largely abused by the wily and the despotic of every age. Some have seen the expression of it in the purchased suffrages of a few of the satellites of power; others, in the votes of a timid or an interested minority; and some have even discovered it in the silence of a people, on the supposition that the fact of submission established the right to command.

In America the principle of the sovereignty of the people is neither barren nor concealed, as it is with some other nations; it is recognized by the customs and proclaimed by the laws; it spreads freely; and arrives without impediment at its most remote consequences. If there is a country in the world where the doctrine of the sovereignty of the people can be fairly appreciated, where it can be studied in its application to the affairs of society, and where its dangers and its advantages may be judged, that country is assuredly America.

I have already observed that, from their origin, the sovereignty of the people was the fundamental principle of most of the British colonies in America. It was far, however, from then exercising as much influence on the government of society as it now does. Two obstacles, the one external, the other internal, checked its invasive progress.

It could not ostensibly disclose itself in the laws of colonies which were still forced to obey the mother country; it was therefore obliged to rule secretly in the provincial assemblies, and especially in the townships.

American society at that time was not yet prepared to adopt it with all its consequences. Intelligence in New England and wealth in the country to the south of the Hudson . . . long exercised a sort of aristocratic influence, which tended to keep the exercise of social power in the hands of a few. Not all the public functionaries were chosen by popular vote, nor were all the citizen voters. The electoral franchise was everywhere somewhat restricted and made dependent on a certain qualification, which was very low in the North and more considerable in the South.

The American Revolution broke out, and the doctrine of the sovereignty of the people came out of the townships and took possession of the state. Every class was enlisted in its cause; battles were fought and victories obtained for it; it became the law of laws.

A change almost as rapid was effected in the interior of society, where the law of inheritance completed the abolition of local influences.

As soon as this effect of the laws and of the Revolution became apparent to every eye, victory was irrevocably pronounced in favor of the democratic cause. All power was, in fact, in its hands, and resistance was no longer possible. The higher orders submitted without a murmur and without a struggle to an evil that was thenceforth inevitable. The ordinary fate of falling powers awaited them: each of their members followed his own interest; and as it was impossible to wring the power from the hands of a people whom they did not detest sufficiently to brave, their only aim was to secure its goodwill at any price. The most democratic laws were consequently voted by the very men whose interests they impaired: and thus, although the higher classes did not excite the passions of the people against their order, they themselves accelerated the triumph of the new state of things; so that, by a singular change, the democratic impulse was found to be most irresistible in the very states where the aristocracy had the firmest hold. The state of Maryland, which had been founded by men of rank, was the first to proclaim universal suffrage . . . and to introduce the most democratic forms into the whole of its government.

When a nation begins to modify the elective qualification, it may easily be foreseen that, sooner or later, that qualification will be entirely abolished. There is no more invariable rule in the history of society: the further electoral rights are extended, the greater is the need of extending them; for after each concession the strength of the democracy increases, and its demands increase with its strength. The ambition of those who are below the appointed rate is irritated in exact proportion to the great number of those who are above it. The exception at last becomes the rule, concession follows concession, and no stop can be made short of universal suffrage.

At the present day the principle of the sovereignty of the people has acquired in the United States all the practical development that the imagination can conceive. It is unencumbered by those fictions that are thrown over it in other countries, and it appears in every possible form, according to the exigency of the occasion. Sometimes the laws are made by the people in a body, as at Athens;

and sometimes its representatives, chosen by universal suffrage, transact business in its name and under its immediate supervision.

In some countries a power exists which, though it is in a degree foreign to the social body, directs it, and forces it to pursue a certain track. In others the ruling force is divided, being partly within and partly without the ranks of the people. But nothing of the kind is to be seen in the United States; there society governs itself for itself. All power centers in its bosom, and scarcely an individual is to be met with who would venture to conceive or, still less, to express the idea of seeking it elsewhere. The nation participates in the making of its laws by the choice of its legislators, and in the execution of them by the choice of the agents of the executive government; it may almost be said to govern itself, so feeble and so restricted is the share left to the administration, so little do the authorities forget their popular origin and the power from which they emanate. The people reign in the American political world as the Deity does in the universe. They are the cause and the aim of all things; everything comes from them, and everything is absorbed in them.

PART III

Representative Government

SELECTION 5
FROM
*The Federalist #10**

JAMES MADISON

TO THE PEOPLE OF the State of New York:

Among the numerous advantages promised by a well-constructed Union, none deserves to be more accurately developed than its tendency to break and control the violence of faction. The friend of popular governments never finds himself so much alarmed for their character and fate, as when he contemplates their propensity to this dangerous vice. He will not fail, therefore, to set a due value on any plan which, without violating the principles to which he is attached, provides a proper cure for it. The instability, injustice, and confusion introduced into the public councils, have, in truth, been the mortal diseases under which popular governments have everywhere perished; as they continue to be the favorite and fruitful topics from which the adversaries to liberty derive their most specious declamations. The valuable improvements made by the American constitutions on the popular models, both ancient and modern, cannot certainly be too much admired; but it would be an unwarrantable partiality, to contend that they have as effectually obviated the danger on this side, as was wished and expected. Complaints are everywhere heard from our most considerate and virtuous citizens, equally the friends of public and private faith, and of public and personal liberty, that our governments are too unstable, that the public good is disregarded in the conflicts of rival parties, and that measures are too often decided, not according to the rules of justice and the rights of the minor party, but by the superior force of an interested and overbearing majority. However anxiously we may wish that these complaints had no foundation, the evidence of known facts will not permit us to deny that they are in some degree true. It will be found, indeed, on a candid review of our situation, that some of the distresses under which we labor have been erroneously charged on the operation of our governments; but it will be found, at the same time, that other causes will not alone account for many of our heaviest misfortunes; and, particularly, for that prevailing and increasing distrust of

*(New York: Random House [The Modern Library], n. d.)

public engagements, one end of the continent to the other. These must be chiefly, if not wholly, effects of the unsteadiness and injustice with which a factious spirit has tainted our public administrations.

By a faction, I understand a number of citizens, whether amounting to a majority or minority of the whole, who are united and actuated by some common impulse of passion, or of interest, adverse to the rights of other citizens, or to the permanent and aggregate interests of the community.

There are two methods of curing the mischiefs of faction: the one, by removing its causes; the other, by controlling its effects.

There are again two methods of removing the causes of faction: the one, by destroying the liberty which is essential to its existence; the other, by giving to every citizen the same opinions, the same passions, and the same interests.

It could never be more truly said than of the first remedy, that it was worse than the disease. Liberty is to faction what air is to fire, an aliment without which it instantly expires. But it could not be less folly to abolish liberty, which is essential to political life, because it nourishes faction, than it would be to wish the annihilation of air, which is essential to animal life, because it imparts to fire its destructive agency.

The second expedient is as impracticable as the first would be unwise. As long as the reason of man continues fallible, and he is at liberty to exercise it, different opinions will be formed. As long as the connection subsists between his reason and his self-love, his opinions and his passions will have a reciprocal influence on each other; and the former will be objects to which the latter will attach themselves. The diversity in the faculties of men, from which the rights of property originate, is not less an insuperable obstacle to a uniformity of interests. The protection of these faculties is the first object of government. From the protection of different and unequal faculties of acquiring property, the possession of different degrees and kinds of property immediately results; and from the influence of these on the sentiments and views of the respective proprietors, ensues a division of the society into different interests and parties.

The latent causes of faction are thus sown in the nature of man; and we see them everywhere brought into different degrees of activity, according to the different circumstances of civil society. A zeal for different opinions concerning religion, concerning government, and many other points, as well of speculation as of practice; and attachment to different leaders ambitiously contending for preeminence and power; or to persons of other descriptions whose fortunes have been interesting to the human passions, have, in turn, divided mankind into parties, inflamed them with mutual animosity, and rendered them much more disposed to vex and oppress each other than to cooperate for their common good. So strong is this propensity of mankind to fall into mutual animosities, that where no substantial occasion presents itself, the most frivolous and fanciful distinctions have been sufficient to kindle their unfriendly passions and excite their most violent conflicts. But the most common and durable source of factions has been the various and unequal distribution of property. Those who hold and those who are without property have ever formed distinct interests in society. Those who are creditors, and those who are debtors, fall under a like discrimination. A landed interest, a manufacturing interest, a mercantile interest, a moneyed interest, with many lesser interests, grow up of necessity in civilized nations, and divide them into different classes, actuated by different sentiments and views. The regulation of these various and interfering interests forms the principal task of modern legislation, and involves the spirit of party and faction in the necessary and ordinary operations of the government.

No man is allowed to be a judge in his own cause, because his interest would certainly bias his judgment, and, not improbably, corrupt his integrity. With equal, nay with greater reason, a body of men are unfit to be both judges and parties at the same time; yet what are many of the most important acts of legislation, but so many judicial determinations, not indeed concerning the rights of single persons, but concerning the rights of large bodies of citizens? And what are the different classes of legislators but advocates and parties to the causes which they determine? Is a law proposed concerning private debts? It is a question to which the creditors are parties on one side and the debtors on the other. Justice ought to hold the balance between them. Yet the parties are, and must be, themselves the judges; and the most numerous party, or, in other words, the most powerful faction must be expected to prevail. Shall domestic manufactures be encouraged, and in what degree, by restrictions on foreign manufactures? [These] are questions which would be differently decided by the landed and the manufacturing classes, and probably by neither with a sole regard to justice and the public good. The apportionment of taxes on the various descriptions of property is an act which seems to require the most exact impartiality; yet there is, perhaps, no legislative act in which greater opportunity and temptation are given to a predominant party to trample on the rules of justice. Every shilling with which they overburden the inferior number, is a shilling saved to their own pockets.

It is in vain to say that enlightened statesmen will be able to adjust these clashing interests, and render them all subservient to the public good. Enlightened statesmen will not always be at the helm. Nor, in many cases, can such an adjustment be made at all without taking into view indirect and remote considerations, which will rarely prevail over the immediate interest which one party may find in disregarding the rights of another or the good of the whole.

The inference to which we are brought is, that the *causes* of faction cannot be removed, and that relief is only to be sought in the means of controlling its *effects*.

If a faction consists of less than a majority, relief is supplied by the republican principle, which enables the majority to defeat its sinister views by regular vote.

It may clog the administration, it may convulse the society; but it will be unable to execute and mask its violence under the forms of the Constitution. When a majority is included in a faction, the form of popular government, on the other hand, enables it to sacrifice to its ruling passion or interest both the public good and the rights of other citizens. To secure the public good and private rights against the danger of such a faction, and at the same time to preserve the spirit and the form of popular government, is then the great object to which our inquiries are directed. Let me add that it is the great desideratum by which this form of government can be rescued from the opprobrium under which it has so long labored, and be recommended to the esteem and adoption of mankind.

By what means is this object attainable? Evidently by one of two only. Either the existence of the same passion or interest in a majority at the same time must be prevented, or the majority, having such coexistent passion or interest, must be rendered, by their number and local situation, unable to concert and carry into effect schemes of oppression. If the impulse and the opportunity be suffered to coincide, we well know that neither moral nor religious motives can be relied on as an adequate control. They are not found to be such on the injustice and violence of individuals, and lose their efficacy in proportion to the number combined together, that is, in proportion as their efficacy becomes needful.

From this view of the subject it may be concluded that a pure democracy, by which I mean a society consisting of a small number of citizens, who assemble and administer the government in person, can admit of no cure for the mischiefs of faction. A common passion or interest will, in almost every case, be felt by a majority of the whole; a communication and concert result from the form of government itself; and there is nothing to check the inducements to sacrifice the weaker party or an obnoxious individual. Hence it is that such democracies have ever been spectacles of turbulence and contention; have ever been found incompatible with personal security or the rights of property; and have in general been as short in their lives as they have been violent in their deaths. Theoretic politicians, who have patronized this species of government, have erroneously supposed that by reducing mankind to a perfect equality in their political rights, they would, at the same time, be perfectly equalized and assimilated in their possessions, their opinions, and their passions.

A republic, by which I mean a government in which the scheme of representation takes place, opens a different prospect, and promises the cure for which we are seeking. Let us examine the points in which it varies from pure democracy, and we shall comprehend both the nature of the cure and the efficacy which it must derive from the Union.

The two great points of difference between a democracy and a republic are: first, the delegation of the government, in the latter, to a small number of citizens elected by the rest; secondly, the greater number of citizens, and greater sphere of country, over which the latter may be extended.

The effect of the first difference is, on the one hand, to refine and enlarge the public views, by passing them through the medium of a chosen body of citizens, whose wisdom may best discern the true interest of their country, and whose patriotism and love of justice will be least likely to sacrifice it to temporary or partial considerations. Under such a regulation, it may well happen that the public voice, pronounced by the representatives of the people, will be more consonant to the public good than if pronounced by the people themselves, convened for the purpose. On the other hand, the effect may be inverted. Men of factious tempers, of local prejudices, or of sinister designs, may, by intrigue, by corruption, or by other means, first obtain the suffrages, and then betray the interests, of the people. The question resulting is, whether small or extensive republics are more favorable to the election of proper guardians of the public weal; and it is clearly decided in favor of the latter by two obvious considerations:

In the first place, it is to be remarked that, however small the republic may be, the representatives must be raised to a certain number, in order to guard against the cabals of a few; and that, however large it may be, they must be limited to a certain number, in order to guard against the confusion of a multitude. Hence, the number of representatives in the two cases not being in proportion to that of the two constituents, and being proportionally greater in the small republic, it follows that, if the proportion of fit characters be not less in the large than in the small republic, the former will present a greater option, and consequently a greater probability of a fit choice.

In the next place, as each representative will be chosen by a greater number of citizens in the large than in the small republic, it will be more difficult for unworthy candidates to practise with success the vicious arts by which elections are too often carried; and the suffrages of the people being more free, will be more likely to center in men who possess the most attractive merit and the most diffusive and established characters.

It must be confessed that in this, as in most other cases, there is a mean, on both sides of which inconveniences will be found to lie. By enlarging too much the number of electors, you render the representative too little acquainted with all their local circumstances and lesser interests; as by reducing it too much, you render him unduly attached to these, and too little fit to comprehend and pursue great and national objects. The federal Constitution forms a happy combination in this respect; the great and aggregate interests being referred to the national, the local and particular to the State legislatures.

The other point of difference is, the greater number of citizens and extent of territory which may be brought within the compass of republican than of democratic government; and it is this circumstance principally which renders factious combinations less to be dreaded in the former than in the latter. The smaller the society, the fewer probably will be the distinct parties and interests composing it; the fewer the distinct parties and interests, the more frequently will a majority be found of the same party; and the smaller the number of individuals composing a majority, and the smaller the compass within which they are placed, the more easily will they concert and execute their plans of oppression. Extend the sphere, and you take in a greater variety of parties and interests; you make it less probable that a majority of the whole will have a common motive to invade the rights of other citizens; or if such a common motive exists, it will be more difficult for all who feel it to discover their own strength, and to act in unison with each other. . . .

The influence of factious leaders may kindle a flame within their particular States, but will be unable to spread a general conflagration through the other States. A religious sect may degenerate into a political faction in a part of the Confederacy; but the variety of sects dispersed over the entire face of it must secure the national councils against any danger from that source. A rage for paper money, for an abolition of debts, for an equal division of property, or for any other improper or wicked project, will be less apt to pervade the whole body of the Union than a particular member of it; in the same proportion as such a malady is more likely to taint a particular county or district, than an entire State.

In the extent and proper structure of the Union, therefore, we behold a republican remedy for the diseases most incident to republican government. And according to the degree of pleasure and pride we feel in being republicans, ought to be our zeal in cherishing the spirit and supporting the character of Federalists.

PUBLIUS

SELECTION 6
FROM
Considerations on Representative Government[*]

JOHN STUART MILL

IN TREATING OF REPRESENTATIVE government, it is above all necessary to keep in view the distinction between its idea or essence, and the particular forms in which the idea has been clothed by accidental historical developments, or by the notions current at some particular period.

The meaning of representative government is, that the whole people, or some numerous portion of them, exercise through deputies periodically elected by themselves the ultimate controlling power, which, in every constitution, must reside somewhere. This ultimate power they must possess in all its completeness. They must be masters, whenever they please, of all the operations of government. There is no need that the constitutional law should itself give them this mastery. It does not in the British Constitution. But what it does give practically amounts to this. The power of final control is as essentially single, in a mixed and balanced government, as in a pure monarchy or democracy. This is the portion of truth in the opinion of the ancients, revived by greater authorities in our own time, that a balanced constitution is impossible. There is almost always a balance, but the scales never hang exactly even. Which of them preponderates is not always apparent on the face of the political institutions. In the British Constitution, each of the three coordinate members of the sovereignty is invested with powers which, if fully exercised, would enable it to stop all the machinery of government. Nominally, therefore, each is invested with equal power of thwarting and obstructing the others: and if, by exerting that power, any of the three could hope to better its position, the ordinary course of human affairs forbids us to doubt that the power would be exercised. There can be no question that the full powers of each would be employed defensively if it found itself assailed by one or both of the others. What then prevents the same powers from being exerted aggressively? The unwritten maxims of the Constitution—in

---

[*] (New York: E. P. Dutton [Everyman's Library], 1951): from Ch. 5.

other words, the positive political morality of the country: and this positive political morality is what we must look to, if we would know in whom the really supreme power in the Constitution resides.

. . . But while it is essential to representative government that the practical supremacy in the state should reside in the representatives of the people, it is an open question what actual functions, what precise part in the machinery of government, shall be directly and personally discharged by the representative body. Great varieties in this respect are compatible with the essence of representative government, provided the functions are such as secure to the representative body the control of everything in the last resort.

There is a radical distinction between controlling the business of government and actually doing it. The same person or body may be able to control everything, but cannot possibly do everything; and in many cases its control over everything will be more perfect the less it personally attempts to do. The commander of an army could not direct its movements effectually if he himself fought in the ranks, or led an assault. It is the same with bodies of men. Some things cannot be done except by bodies; other things cannot be well done by them. It is one question, therefore, what a popular assembly should control, another what it should itself do. It should, as we have already seen, control all the operations of government. But in order to determine through what channel this general control may most expediently be exercised, and what portion of the business of government the representative assembly should hold in its own hands, it is necessary to consider what kinds of business a numerous body is competent to perform properly. That alone which it can do well it ought to take personally upon itself. With regard to the rest, its proper province is not to do it, but to take means for having it well done by others.

For example, the duty which is considered as belonging more peculiarly than any other to an assembly representative of the people, is that of voting the taxes. Nevertheless, in no country does the representative body undertake, by itself or its delegated officers, to prepare the estimates. . . .

The principles which are involved and recognized in this constitutional doctrine, if followed as far as they will go, are a guide to the limitation and definition of the general functions of representative assemblies. In the first place, it is admitted in all countries in which the representative system is practically understood, that numerous representative bodies ought not to administer. The maxim is grounded not only on the most essential principles of good government, but on those of the successful conduct of business of any description. No body of men, unless organized and under command, is fit for action, in the proper sense. Even a select board, composed of few members, and these specially conversant with the business to be done, is always an inferior instrument to some one individual who could be found among them, and would be improved in character if that one person were made the chief, and all the others reduced to subordinates. What can be done better by a body than by an individual is deliberation. When it is necessary or important to secure hearing and consideration to many conflicting opinions, a deliberative body is indispensable. Those bodies, therefore, are frequently useful, even for administrative business, but in general only as advisers; such business being, as a rule, better conducted under the responsibility of one. Even a joint-stock company has always in practice, if not in theory, a managing director; its good or bad management depends essentially on some one person's qualifications, and the remaining directors, when of any use, are so by their suggestions to him, or by the power they possess of watching him, and restraining or removing him in case of misconduct. That they are ostensibly equal sharers with him in the management is no advantage, but a considerable set-off against any good which they are capable of doing: it weakens greatly the sense in his own mind, and in those of other people, of that individual responsibility in which he should stand forth personally and undividedly.

But a popular assembly is still less fitted to administer, or to dictate in detail to those who have the charge of administration. Even when honestly meant, the interference is almost always injurious. Every branch of public administration is a skilled business, which has its own peculiar principles and traditional rules, many of them not even known, in any effectual way, except to those who have at some time had a hand in carrying on the business, and none of them likely to be duly appreciated by persons not practically acquainted with the department. I do not mean that the transaction of public business has esoteric mysteries, only to be understood by the initiated. Its principles are all intelligible to any person of good sense, who has in his mind a true picture of the circumstances and conditions to be dealt with: but to have this he must know those circumstances and conditions; and the knowledge does not come by intuition. There are many rules of the greatest importance in every branch of public business (as there are in every private occupation), of which a person fresh to the subject neither knows the reason or even suspects the existence, because they are intended to meet dangers or provide against inconveniences which never entered into his thoughts. I have known public men, ministers, of more than ordinary natural capacity, who on their first introduction to a department of business new to them, have excited the mirth of their inferiors by the air with which they announced as a truth hitherto set at nought, and brought to light by themselves, something which was probably the first thought of everybody who ever looked at the subject, given up as soon as he had got on to a second. It is true that a great statesman is he who knows when to depart from traditions, as well as when to adhere to them. But it is a great mistake to suppose that he will do this better for being ignorant of the traditions. No one who does not thoroughly know the modes of action which common experience has sanctioned is capable of judging of the circumstances which require a departure from those ordinary modes of action. The interests dependent on the acts done by a public department, the consequences liable to follow from any particular mode of conducting it, require for weighing and estimating them a kind of knowledge, and of specially exercised judgment, almost as rarely found in those not bred to it, as the capacity to reform the law in those who have not professionally studied it. All these difficulties are sure to be ignored by a representative assembly which attempts to decide on special acts of administration. At its best, it is inexperience sitting in judgment on experience, ignorance on knowledge: ignorance which never suspecting the existence of what it does not know, is equally careless and supercilious, making light of, if not resenting, all pretensions to have a judgment better worth attending to than its own. Thus it is when no interested motives intervene: but when they do, the result is jobbery more unblushing and audacious than the worst corruption which can well take place in a public office under a government of publicity. . . .

The proper duty of a representative assembly in regard to matters of administration is not to decide them by its own vote, but to take care that the persons who have to decide them shall be the proper persons. Even this they cannot advantageously do by nominating the individuals. There is no act which more imperatively requires to be performed under a strong sense of individual responsibility than the nomination to employments. The experience of every person conversant with public affairs bears out the assertion, that there is scarcely any act respecting which the conscience of an average man is less sensitive; scarcely any case in which less consideration is paid to qualifications, partly because men do not know, and partly because they do not care for, the difference in qualifications between one person and another. When a minister makes what is meant to be an honest appointment, that is when he does not actually job it for his personal connections or his party, an ignorant person might suppose that he would try to give it to the person best qualified. No such thing. An ordinary minister thinks himself a miracle of virtue if he gives it to a person of merit, or who has a claim on the public on any account, though the claim or the merit may be of the most opposite description to that required. . . . The qualifications which fit special individuals for special duties can only be recognized by those who know the individuals, or who make it their business to examine and judge of persons from what they have done, or from the evidence of those who are in a position to judge. When these conscientious obligations are so little regarded by great public officers who can be made responsible for their appointments, how must it be with assemblies who cannot? Even now, the worst appointments are those which are made for the sake of gaining support or disarming opposition in the representative body: what might we expect if they were made by the body itself? Numerous bodies never regard special qualifications at all. Unless a man is fit for the gallows, he is thought to be about as fit as other people for almost anything for which he can offer himself as a candidate. When appointments made by a public body are not decided, as they almost always are, by party connection or private jobbing, a man is appointed either because he has a reputation, often quite undeserved, for *general* ability, or frequently for no better reason than that he is personally popular.

. . . Any government fit for a high state of civilization would have as one of its fundamental elements a small body, not exceeding in number the members of a Cabinet, who should act as a Commission of Legislation, having for its appointed office to make the laws. If the laws of this country were, as surely they will soon be, revised and put into a connected form, the Commission of Codification by which this is effected should remain as a permanent institution, to watch over the work, protect it from deterioration, and make further improvements as often as required. No one would wish that this body should of itself have any power of *enacting* laws: the Commission would only embody the element of intelligence in their construction; Parliament would represent that of will. No measure would become a law until expressly sanctioned by Parliament: and Parliament, or either House, would have the power not only of rejecting but of sending back a Bill to the Commission for reconsideration or improvement. Either House might also exercise its initiative, by referring any subject to the Commission, with directions to prepare a law. The Commission, of course, would have no power of refusing its instrumentality to any legislation which the country desired. Instructions, concurred in by both Houses, to draw up a Bill which should effect a particular purpose, would be imperative on the Commissioners, unless they preferred to resign their office. Once framed, however, Parliament should have no power to alter the measure, but solely to pass or reject it; or, if partially disapproved of, remit it to the Commission for reconsideration. . . .

. . . By such arrangements as these, legislation would assume its proper place as a work of skilled labor and special study and experience; while the most important liberty of the nation, that of being governed only by laws assented to by its elected representatives, would be fully preserved, and made more valuable by being detached from the serious, but by no means unavoidable, drawbacks which now accompany it in the form of ignorant and ill-considered legislation.

Instead of the function of governing, for which it is radically unfit, the proper office of a representative assembly is to watch and control the government: to throw the light of publicity on its acts: to compel a full exposition and justification of all of them which any one considers questionable; to censure them if found condemnable, and, if the men who compose the government abuse their trust, or fulfill it in a manner which conflicts with the deliberate sense of the nation, to expel them from office, and either expressly or virtually appoint their successors. This is surely ample power, and security enough for the liberty of the nation. In addition to this, the Parliament has an office, not inferior even to this in importance; to be at once the nation's Committee of Grievances, and its

Congress of Opinions; an arena in which not only the general opinion of the nation, but that of every section of it, and as far as possible of every eminent individual whom it contains, can produce itself in full light and challenge discussion; where every person in the country may count upon finding somebody who speaks his mind, as well or better than he could speak it himself—not to friends and partisans exclusively, but in the face of opponents, to be tested by adverse controversy; where those whose opinion is overruled, feel satisfied that it is heard, and set aside not by a mere act of will, but for what are thought superior reasons, and commend themselves as such to the representatives of the majority of the nation; where every party or opinion in the country can muster its strength, and be cured of any illusion concerning the number or power of its adherents; where the opinion which prevails in the nation makes itself manifest as prevailing, and marshals its hosts in the presence of the government, which is thus enabled and compelled to give way to it on the mere manifestation, without the actual employment, of its strength; where statesmen can assure themselves, far more certainly than by any other signs, what elements of opinion and power are growing, and what declining, and are enabled to shape their measures with some regard not solely to present exigencies, but to tendencies in progress. Representative assemblies are often taunted by their enemies with being places of mere talk and *bavardage*. There has seldom been more misplaced derision. I know not how a representative assembly can more usefully employ itself than in talk, when the subject of talk is the great public interests of the country, and every sentence of it represents the opinion either of some important body of persons in the nation, or of an individual in whom some such body have reposed their confidence. A place where every interest and shade of opinion in the country can have its cause even passionately pleaded, in the face of the government and of all other interests and opinions, can compel them to listen, and either comply, or state clearly why they do not, is in itself, if it answered no other purpose, one of the most important political institutions that can exist anywhere, and one of the foremost benefits of free government. Such "talking" would never be looked upon with disparagement if it were not allowed to stop "doing"; which it never would, if assemblies knew and acknowledged that talking and discussion are their proper business, while *doing*, as the result of discussion, is the task not of a miscellaneous body, but of individuals specially trained to it; that the fit office of an assembly is to see that those individuals are honestly and intelligently chosen, and so interfere no further with them, except by unlimited latitude of suggestion and criticism, and by applying or withholding the final seal of national assent. It is for want of this judicious reserve that popular assemblies attempt to do what they cannot do well—to govern and legislate—and provide no machinery but their own for much of it, when of course every hour spent in talk is an hour withdrawn from actual business. But the very fact which most unfits such bodies for a Council of Legislation qualifies them the more for their other office—namely, that they are not a selection of the greatest political minds in the country, from whose opinions little could with certainty be inferred concerning those of the nation, but are, when properly constituted, a fair sample of every grade of intellect among the people which is at all entitled to a voice in public affairs. Their part is to indicate wants, to be an organ for popular demands, and a place of adverse discussion for all opinions relating to public matters, both great and small; and, along with this, to check by criticism, and eventually by withdrawing their support, those high public officers who really conduct the public business, or who appoint those by whom it is conducted. Nothing but the restriction of the function of representative bodies within these rational limits will enable the benefits of popular control to be enjoyed in conjunction with the no less important requisites (growing ever more important as human affairs increase in scale and in complexity) of skilled legislation and administration. There are no means of combining these benefits except by separating the functions which guarantee the one from those which essentially require the other; by disjoining the office of control and criticism from the actual conduct of affairs, and devolving the former on the representatives of the Many, while securing for the latter, under strict responsibility to the nation, the acquired knowledge and practiced intelligence of a specially trained and experienced Few.

SELECTION 7
FROM
*Democracy and Its Critics**

ROBERT A. DAHL

CRITERIA FOR A DEMOCRATIC PROCESS

SUPPOSE, THEN, THAT SOME persons wish to constitute a political order. Suppose further that the assumptions justifying a *democratic* political order are valid with respect to this group. Because these assumptions are valid, we conclude that they ought to adopt a democratic order and therefore that the process by which the demos is to arrive at its decisions ought to meet certain criteria. When I say that the process ought to meet certain criteria, I mean that if one believes in the assumptions, then one must reasonably affirm the desirability of the criteria; conversely, to reject the criteria is in effect to reject one or more of the assumptions. . . .

The five criteria are standards—ideal standards, if you like—against which procedures proposed ought to be evaluated in any association to which the assumptions apply. Any process that met them perfectly would be a perfect democratic process, and the government of the association would be a perfect democratic government. I take for granted that a perfect democratic process and a perfect democratic government might never exist in actuality. They represent ideas of human possibilities against which actualities may be compared. Even if the criteria can never be perfectly satisfied, they are useful in appraising real world possibilities, as I shall show. Naturally they do not eliminate all elements of judgment in evaluation. For example, the criteria do not specify any particular procedures, such as majority rule, for specific procedures cannot be directly extracted from the criteria. And judgments will have to take into account the specific historical conditions under which a democratic association is to be developed. However, no one should be surprised that democratic theory, like all other normative theories, cannot furnish completely unambiguous answers for every concrete situation in which a choice has to be made between alternative proposals.

---

*(New Haven, CT: Yale University Press, 1989): pp. 108–14, 220–23.

What criteria, then, will be uniquely consistent with our assumptions and thereby provide us with the distinguishing features of a democratic process?

EFFECTIVE PARTICIPATION

Throughout the process of making binding decisions, citizens ought to have an adequate opportunity, and an equal opportunity, for expressing their preferences as to the final outcome. They must have adequate and equal opportunities for placing questions on the agenda and for expressing reasons for endorsing one outcome rather than another.

To deny any citizen adequate opportunities for effective participation means that because their preferences are unknown or incorrectly perceived, they cannot be taken into account. But not to take their preferences as to the final outcome equally into account is to reject the principle of equal consideration of interests.

VOTING EQUALITY AT THE DECISIVE STAGE

At the decisive stage of collective decisions, each citizen must be ensured an equal opportunity to express a choice that will be counted as equal in weight to the choice expressed by any other citizen. In determining outcomes at the decisive stage, these choices, and only these choices, must be taken into account.

Because the choices are, of course, what we ordinarily mean by voting, this may be said to require voting equality at the decisive stage.

Obviously something like this requirement has been a mainstay of democratic theory and practice from classical Greece onward. But on what rational ground? Its justification rests, I think, on the practical judgment that voting equality at the decisive stage is necessary in order to provide adequate protection for the intrinsic equality of citizens and the Presumption of Personal Autonomy. Without it, citizens would face the prospect of an infinite regress of potential inequalities in their influence over decisions, with no final court of appeal in which, as political equals, they could decide whether their interests, as they interpreted them, were given equal consideration. Just as inequalities in other resources could give advantages to some persons in securing special consideration for their interests, and handicap others, so too, without a requirement of equal voting at the decisive stage, inequalities in votes could work cumulatively to violate the Principle of Equal Consideration of Interests.

Notice, however, what the criterion of voting equality at the decisive stage does not specify. To begin with, it does not require voting equality at preceding stages. A demos might reasonably decide that the interests of some persons could best be given equal consideration by weighing their votes more heavily at earlier stages. On the same grounds the demos might delegate some decisions to citizen bodies in which votes were unequally weighted. Arrangements like these might be exceptional, as they have been historically in democratic countries, but they would not necessarily violate the criterion. The criterion would be violated, however, if the demos were no longer free to alter such arrangements whenever they failed to achieve their purposes or threatened to cause the demos to lose its final control over collective decisions.

Moreover, the criterion does not specify a particular method of voting or elections. To require that citizens have equal opportunities to express their choices could be satisfied if the votes or voters were selected randomly, that is, by lot. Nor does equal voting mean that each citizen should necessarily be entitled to an equal vote in districts of equal numbers of voters or residents; a system of proportional representation might serve as well or better. How citizens may best express their choices, and what specific rules and procedures should be adopted, are questions that require additional practical judgments. But procedures that meet the criterion better ought to be chosen over those that meet it worse. That the better procedure should be preferred to the worse holds even if all the procedures proposed are in some respects defective, as might often be the case.

Finally, the criterion does not explicitly require an association to adopt the principle of majority rule for its decisions. It requires only that majority rule and alternatives to it be evaluated according to this and other criteria, including the principles and assumptions that justify this criterion, such as the principle of equal consideration of interests, and that the solution that best meets the criteria should be adopted. Whether majority rule is the best solution is thus left open. . . . The problem posed by majority rule and the alternatives to it is one of extreme difficulty for which no completely satisfactory solutions have yet been found. Judging what decision rule best meets the criterion of voting equality, whether generally or in a specific context, is a question on which persons who are committed to voting equality continue to disagree.

I think it is consistent with historic usage to say that any association whose government satisfies the criteria of effective participation and voting equality governs itself, to that limited extent, by means of a democratic process. In order to leave room for some important distinctions to come, I want to say that such an association is governed by a *democratic process in a narrow sense*. Though the process is narrower in scope than a fully democratic process, the two criteria enable us to evaluate a large number of possible procedures. To be sure, they cannot be decisive in cases where a procedure is better according to one criterion and worse by the other. Moreover, any evaluation would ordinarily require additional judgments about the facts of the particular situation or about general tendencies and regularities of human behavior and action. Nonetheless, the criteria are far from vacuous. Although I will not introduce a rigorous argument here, it would be hard to deny that procedures providing for decisions by a randomly selected sample of citizens would satisfy the criteria better than a procedure by which one citizen makes binding decisions for all the rest; or that a voting scheme allocating one vote to each citizen at the decisive stage would be better than a scheme in which some citizens had ten votes and others none. I do not mean to imply, however, that judgments about alternatives like these would follow as unassailable conclusions from a perfectly rigorous argument.

ENLIGHTENED UNDERSTANDING

As I have already suggested, judgments about the existence, composition, and boundaries of a demos are highly contestable. Thus one might simply challenge such judgments outright by asserting that some citizens are more qualified than the rest to make the decisions required. This objection of course raises the challenge to democracy posed by guardianship, which we have already considered at length. What I wish to consider now, however, is a second objection that might run like this:

> I agree—the objector might say—that the citizens are equally well qualified, taken all around. I agree also that none among them, or among the other members, or among nonmembers are so definitely better qualified as to warrant their making the decisions instead of the demos. Yet for all that, I think the citizens are not as well qualified as they might be. They make mistakes about the means to the ends they want; they also choose ends they would reject if they were more enlightened. I agree then that they ought to govern themselves by procedures that are satisfactory according to the criteria of a democratic process, narrowly defined. Yet a number of different procedures will satisfy the criteria equally well; among these, however, some are more likely to lead to a more enlightened demos—and thus to better decisions—than others. Surely these are better procedures and ought to be chosen over the others.

One might object, I suppose, that enlightenment has nothing to do with democracy. But I think this would be a foolish and historically false assertion. It is foolish because democracy has usually been conceived as a system in which "rule by the people" makes it more likely that the "people" will get what it wants, or what it believes is best, than alternative systems like guardianship in which an elite determines what is best. But to know what it wants, or what is best, the people might be enlightened, at least to some degree. And because advocates of democracy have invariably recognized this and placed great stress on the means to an informed and enlightened demos, such as education and public discussion, the objection is also historically false.

I propose therefore to amplify the meaning of the democratic process by adding a third criterion. Unfortunately, I do not know how to formulate the criterion except in words that are rich in meaning and correspondingly ambiguous. Let me, however, offer this formulation for the criterion of enlightened understanding:

Each citizen ought to have adequate and equal opportunities for discovering and validating (within the time permitted by the need for a decision) the choice on the matter to be decided that would best serve the citizen's interests.

This criterion implies, then, that alternative procedures for making decisions ought to be evaluated according to the opportunities they furnish citizens for acquiring an understanding of means and ends, of one's interests and the expected consequences of policies for interests, not only for oneself but for all other relevant persons as well. Insofar as a citizen's good or interests requires attention to a public good or general interest, then citizens ought to have the opportunity to acquire an understanding of these matters. Ambiguous as the criterion may be, it provides guidance for determining the shape that institutions should take. Thus the criterion makes it hard to justify procedures that would cut off or suppress information which, were it available, might well cause citizens to arrive at a different decision; or that would give some citizens much easier access than others to information of crucial importance; or that would present citizens with an agenda of decisions that had to be decided without discussion, though time was available; and so on. To be sure, these may look like easy cases, but a great many political systems—perhaps most—operate according to the worse not the better procedures.

CONTROL OF THE AGENDA

If an association were to satisfy all three criteria, it could properly be regarded as a full procedural democracy with respect to its agenda and in relation to its demos. The criteria are to be understood as aspects of the best possible political system, from a democratic point of view; while no actual system could be expected to satisfy the criteria perfectly, systems could be judged more democratic or less, and to that extent better or worse, according to how nearly they meet the criteria.

Yet to say that a system is governed by a fully democratic process "with respect to an agenda" and "in relation to a demos" suggests the possibility that the three criteria are incomplete. The two qualifying clauses imply the possibility of restrictions—of democratic decision-making processes limited to a narrow agenda, or responsive to a highly exclusive demos, or both. To judge whether a demos is appropriately inclusive and exercises control over an appropriate agenda requires additional standards.

In order to see more clearly why a fourth criterion is needed, let us suppose that Philip of Macedon, having defeated the Athenians at Chaeronea, deprives the Athenian assembly of the authority to make any decisions on matters of foreign and military policy. The citizens continue to assemble some forty times a year and decide on many matters, but on some of the most important questions they must remain silent. With respect to "local" matters, the Athenian polis is no less democratic than before, but with respect to foreign and military affairs the Athenians are now governed hierarchically by Philip or his minions. Would we want to say that Athens was now fully democratic or was as democratic as it had been before?

Although outside control makes the point more dramatically, control over the agenda may also be taken from citizens by some of its own members. Let us imagine an independent country where the three criteria we have discussed are relatively well met, and in addition there are no limitations on the matters that citizens may decide. Their agenda of collective decisions is completely open. Suppose that an antidemocratic movement somehow seizes power. In a move to placate the democratic sentiments of their fellow countrymen the new rulers leave the old constitution symbolically in place. However, they modify it in one respect. Hereafter, the people may use their old democratic political institutions for only a few matters—purely local questions, let us say, such as traffic control, street maintenance, and residential zoning. The rulers keep all the rest strictly under their own control. Even if the new system were to meet the first three criteria perfectly and thus was "fully democratic with respect to its agenda," it would be a travesty of democracy. For citizens could not democratically decide matters they felt to be important other than those the rulers had allowed to remain on the pitifully shrunken agenda of the neutered democracy. The control of nondemocratic rulers over the agenda could be much less blatant and more subtle. In some countries, for example, military leaders are under the nominal control of elected civilians who know, however, that they will be removed from office, and worse, unless they tailor their decisions to meet the wishes of the military.

These considerations suggest a fourth criterion, final control of the agenda by the demos.

The demos must have the exclusive opportunity to decide how matters are to be placed on the agenda of matters that are to be decided by means of the democratic process.

The criterion of final control is perhaps what is also meant when we say that in a democracy the people must have the final say, or must be sovereign. A system that satisfies this criterion as well as the other three could be regarded as having a fully democratic process in relation to its demos.

According to this criterion, a political system would employ a fully democratic process even if the demos decided that it would not make every decision on every matter but instead chose to have some decisions on some matters made, say, in a hierarchical fashion by judges or administrators. As long as the demos could effectively retrieve any matter for decision by itself, the criterion would be met. In this respect, then, the criterion for a democratic process presented here allows more latitude for delegation of decision making than would be permissible by Rousseau's eccentric definition of democracy in *The Social Contract*. Because he defined democracy so as to make delegation impermissible, Rousseau concluded that "if there were a people of Gods, it would govern itself democratically. Such a perfect government is not suited to men" (Rousseau, Roger D. Masters, ed., Judith R. Masters, trans., St. Martin's, 1978, Bk. 3, Ch. 4, p. 85).

Thus the criterion of final control does not presuppose a judgment that the demos is qualified to decide every question requiring a binding decision. It does presuppose a judgment that the demos is qualified to decide (1) which matters do or do not require binding decisions, (2) of those that do, which matters the demos is qualified to decide for itself, and (3) the terms on which the demos delegates authority. To accept the criterion as appropriate is therefore to imply that the demos is the best judge of its own competence and limits. Consequently, to say that certain matters ought to be placed beyond the final reach of the demos—in the sense that the demos ought to be prohibited from dealing with them at all—is to say that on these matters the demos is not qualified to judge its own competence and limits.

By delegation I mean a revocable grant of authority, subject to recovery by the demos. Empirically, of course, the boundaries between delegation and alienation are not always sharp, and what begins as delegation might end as alienation. Moreover, the empirical problem of judging whether the final agenda is covertly controlled by certain leaders outside the democratic process—like the military, in the example given earlier—is necessarily complicated by the covert nature of the control. But, however difficult it may be to draw the line in practice, the theoretical distinction between delegation and alienation is nonetheless crucial. In a system employing a fully democratic process, decisions about delegation would be made according to democratic procedures. But alienation of control over the final agenda (or its appropriation by leaders outside the democratic process) would clearly violate the criterion of final control and would be inconsistent with the judgment that the full condition of equal qualification exists among citizens. . . .

The criterion of final control completes the requirements for *a fully democratic process in relation to a demos*. If all the members are judged equally qualified, in the full sense, and if the other conditions set out earlier are held to exist among them, then the procedures according to which these persons, the citizens, make binding decisions ought to be evaluated according to the four criteria. . . .*

POLYARCHY

Polyarchy is a political order distinguished at the most general level by two broad characteristics: Citizenship is extended to a relatively high proportion of adults, and the rights of citizenship include the opportunity to oppose and vote out the

*[Dahl adds later that "The demos should include all adults subject to the binding collective decisions of the association. This proposition constitutes the fifth and final criterion for a full democratic process."—ED.]

highest officials in the government. The first characteristic distinguishes polyarchy from more exclusive systems of rule in which, though opposition is permitted, governments and their legal oppositions are restricted to a small group, as was the case in Britain, Belgium, Italy, and other countries before mass suffrage. The second characteristic distinguishes polyarchy from regimes in which, though most adults are citizens, citizenship does not include the right to oppose and vote out the government, as in modern authoritarian regimes.

THE INSTITUTIONS OF POLYARCHY

More specifically, and giving greatest content to these two general features, polyarchy is a political order distinguished by the presence of seven institutions, all of which must exist for a government to be classified as a polyarchy.

1. *Elected officials*. Control over government decisions about policy is constitutionally vested in elected officials.
2. *Free and fair elections*. Elected officials are chosen in frequent and fairly conducted elections in which coercion is comparatively uncommon.
3. *Inclusive suffrage*. Practically all adults have the right to vote in the election of officials.
4. *Right to run for office*. Practically all adults have the right to run for elective offices in the government, though age limits may be higher for holding office than for the suffrage.
5. *Freedom of expression*. Citizens have a right to express themselves without the danger of severe punishment on political matters broadly defined, including criticism of officials, the government, the regime, the socioeconomic order, and the prevailing ideology.
6. *Alternative information*. Citizens have a right to seek out alternative sources of information. Moreover, alternative sources of information exist and are protected by laws.
7. *Associational autonomy*. To achieve their various rights, including those listed above, citizens also have a right to form relatively independent associations or organizations, including independent political parties and interest groups.

It is important to understand that these statements characterize actual and not merely nominal rights, institutions, and processes. In fact, the countries of the world may be assigned approximate rankings according to the extent to which each of the institutions is present in a realistic sense. Consequently the institutions can serve as criteria for deciding which countries are governed by polyarchy today or were in earlier times. These rankings and classifications can then be used, as we shall see later, to investigate the conditions that favor or harm the chances for polyarchy.

POLYARCHY AND DEMOCRACY

However, it is obvious that we are not concerned with polyarchy merely because it is a type of political order distinctive to the modern world. It interests us here primarily because of its bearing on democracy. How then *is* polyarchy related to democracy?

Briefly, the institutions of polyarchy are necessary to democracy on a large scale, particularly the scale of the modern national state. To put the matter in a slightly different way, all the institutions of polyarchy are necessary to the highest feasible attainment of the democratic process in the government of a country. To say that all seven institutions are necessary is not to say that they are sufficient. . . .

The relation between polyarchy and the requirements of the democratic process are set out in Table 1.

TABLE 1
POLYARCHY AND THE DEMOCRATIC PROCESS

The following institutions . . .	*are necessary to satisfy the following criteria*
1. Elected officials	I. Voting equality
3. Free and fair elections	
1. Elected officials	II. Effective participation
3. Inclusive suffrage	
4. Right to run for office	
5. Freedom of expression	
6. Alternative information	
7. Associational autonomy	
5. Freedom of expression	III. Enlightened understanding
6. Alternative information	
7. Associational autonomy	
1. Elected officials	IV. Control of the agenda
2. Free and fair elections	
3. Inclusive suffrage	
4. Right to run for office	
5. Freedom of expression	
6. Alternative information	
7. Associational autonomy	
3. Inclusive suffrage	V. Inclusion
4. Right to run for office	
5. Freedom of expression	
6. Alternative information	
7. Associational autonomy	

Appraising Polyarchy

Typical of democrats who live in countries governed by authoritarian regimes is a fervent hope that their country will one day reach the threshold of polyarchy. Typical of democrats who live in countries long governed by polyarchy is a belief that polyarchy is insufficiently democratic and should be made more so. Yet, while democrats describe many different visions of what the next stage of democratization should be, so far no country has transcended polyarchy to a "higher" stage of democracy.

While intellectuals in democratic countries where polyarchy has existed without interruption for several generations or more often grow jaded with its institutions and contemptuous of their shortcomings, it is not hard to understand why democrats deprived of these institutions find them highly desirable, warts and all. For polyarchy provides a broad array of human rights and liberties that no actually existing real world alternative to it can match. Integral to polyarchy itself is a generous zone of freedom and control that cannot be deeply or persistently invaded without destroying polyarchy itself. And because people in democratic countries, as we have seen, have a liking for other rights, liberties, and empowerments, that essential zone is enlarged even more. Although the institutions of polyarchy do not guarantee the ease and vigor of citizen participation that could exist, in principle, in a small city-state, nor ensure that governments are closely controlled by the citizens or that policies invariably correspond with the desires of a majority of citizens, they make it unlikely in the extreme that a government will long pursue policies that deeply offend a majority of citizens. What is more, those institutions even make it rather uncommon for a government to enforce policies to which a substantial number of citizens object and try to overturn by vigorously using the rights and opportunities available to them. If citizen control over collective decisions is more anemic than the robust control they would exercise if the dream of participatory democracy were ever realized, the capacity of citizens to exercise a veto over the reelection and policies of elected officials is a powerful and frequently exercised means for preventing officials from imposing policies objectionable to many citizens.

Compared then with its alternatives, historical and actual, polyarchy is one of the most extraordinary of all human artifacts. Yet it unquestionably falls well short of achieving the democratic process.

PART IV

The Theory of Democratic Elitism

SELECTION 8
FROM *Political Parties**

ROBERT MICHELS

LEADERSHIP IS A NECESSARY phenomenon in every form of social life. Consequently it is not the task of science to inquire whether this phenomenon is good or evil, or predominantly one or the other. But there is great scientific value in the demonstration that every system of leadership is incompatible with the most essential postulates of democracy. We are now aware that the law of the historic necessity of oligarchy is primarily based upon a series of facts of experience. Like all other scientific laws, sociological laws are derived from empirical observation. In order, however, to deprive our axiom of its purely descriptive character, and to confer upon it that status of analytical explanation which can alone transform a formula into a law, it does not suffice to contemplate from a unitary outlook those phenomena which may be empirically established; we must also study the determining causes of these phenomena. Such has been our task.

Now, if we leave out of consideration the tendency of the leaders to organize themselves and to consolidate their interests, and if we leave also out of consideration the gratitude of the led toward the leaders, and the general immobility and passivity of the masses, we are led to conclude that the principal cause of oligarchy in the democratic parties is to be found in the technical indispensability of leadership.

The process which has begun in consequence of the differentiation of functions in the party is completed by a complex of qualities which the leaders acquire through their detachment from the mass. At the outset, leaders arise SPONTANEOUSLY; their functions are ACCESSORY AND GRATUITOUS. Soon, however, they become PROFESSIONAL leaders, and in this second stage of development they are STABLE and IRREMOVABLE.

It follows that the explanation of the oligarchical phenomenon which thus results is partly PSYCHOLOGICAL; oligarchy derives, that is to say, from the

***Political Parties: A Sociological Study of the Oligarchical Tendencies of Modern Democracies* (New York: Collier Books, 1962): Part 6, pp. 364–71.

psychical transformations which the leading personalities in the parties undergo in the course of their lives. But also, and still more, oligarchy depends upon what we may term the PSYCHOLOGY OF ORGANIZATION ITSELF, that is to say, upon the tactical and technical necessities which result from the consolidation of every disciplined political aggregate. Reduced to its most concise expression, the fundamental sociological law of political parties (the term "political" being here used in its most comprehensive significance) may be formulated in the following terms: "It is organization which gives birth to the dominion of the elected over the electors, of the mandataries over the mandators, of the delegates over the delegators. Who says organization, says oligarchy."

Every party organization represents an oligarchical power grounded upon a democratic basis. We find everywhere electors and elected. Also we find everywhere that the power of the elected leaders over the electing masses is almost unlimited. The oligarchical structure of the building suffocates the basic democratic principle. That which IS oppresses THAT WHICH OUGHT TO BE. For the masses, this essential difference between the reality and the ideal remains a mystery. Socialists often cherish a sincere belief that a new elite of politicians will keep faith better than did the old. The notion of the representation of popular interests, a notion to which the great majority of democrats . . . cleave with so much tenacity and confidence, is an illusion engendered by a false illumination, is an effect of mirage. . . . The modern proletariat, enduringly influenced by glib-tongued persons intellectually superior to the mass, ends by believing that by flocking to the polls and entrusting its social and economic cause to a delegate, its direct participation in power will be assured.

The formation of oligarchies within the various forms of democracy is the outcome of organic necessity, and consequently affects every organization, be it socialist or even anarchist. . . . The supremacy of the leaders in the democratic and revolutionary parties has to be taken into account in every historic situation present and to come, even though only a few and exceptional minds will be fully conscious of its existence. The mass will never rule except *in abstracto*. Consequently the question we have to discuss is not whether ideal democracy is realizable, but rather to what point and in what degree democracy is desirable, possible, and realizable at a given moment. In the problem as thus stated we recognize the fundamental problem of politics as a science. Whoever fails to perceive this must . . . either be so blind and fanatical as not to see that the democratic current daily makes undeniable advance, or else must be so inexperienced and devoid of critical faculty as to be unable to understand that all order and all civilization must exhibit aristocratic features. The great error of socialists, an error committed in consequence of their lack of adequate psychological knowledge, is to be found in their combination of pessimism regarding the present, with rosy optimism and immeasurable confidence regarding the future. A realistic view of the mental condition of the masses shows beyond question that even if we admit the possibility of moral improvement in mankind, the human materials with whose use politicians and philosophers cannot dispense in their plans of social reconstruction are not of a character to justify excessive optimism. Within the limits of time for which human provision is possible, optimism will remain the exclusive privilege of utopian thinkers.

The socialist parties, like the trade unions, are living forms of social life. As such they react with the utmost energy against any attempt to analyze their structure or their nature, as if it were a method of vivisection. When science attains to results which conflict with their apriorist ideology, they revolt with all their power. Yet their defense is extremely feeble. Those among the representatives of such organizations whose scientific earnestness and personal good faith make it impossible for them to deny outright the existence of oligarchical tendencies in every form of democracy, endeavor to explain these tendencies as the outcome of a kind of atavism in the mentality of the masses, characteristic of the youth of the movement. The masses, they assure us, are still infected by the oligarchic virus simply because they have been oppressed during long centuries of slavery, and have never yet enjoyed an autonomous existence. The socialist regime, however, will soon restore them to health, and will furnish them with all the capacity necessary for self-government. Nothing could be more antiscientific than the supposition that as soon as socialists have gained possession of governmental power it will suffice for the masses to exercise a little control over their leaders to secure that the interests of these leaders shall coincide perfectly with the interests of the led. . . .

The objective immaturity of the mass is not a mere transitory phenomenon which will disappear with the progress of democratization *au lendemain du socialisme* ["on the morning of socialism"—ED.]. On the contrary, it derives from the very nature of the mass as mass, for this, even when organized, suffers from an incurable incompetence for the solution of the diverse problems which present themselves for solution—because the mass per se is amorphous, and therefore needs division of labor, specialization, and guidance. . . . Man as individual is by nature predestined to be guided, and to be guided all the more in proportion as the functions of life undergo division and subdivision. To an enormously greater degree is guidance necessary for the social group.

From this chain of reasoning and from these scientific convictions it would be erroneous to conclude that we should renounce all endeavors to ascertain the limits which may be imposed upon the powers exercised over the individual by oligarchies (state, dominant class, party, etc.). It would be an error to abandon the desperate enterprise of endeavoring to discover a social order which will render possible the complete realization of the idea of popular sovereignty. In the present work, as the writer said at the outset, it has not been his aim to indicate new paths. But it seemed necessary to lay considerable stress upon the pessimistic aspect of democracy which is forced on us by historical study. We had to inquire whether, and within what limits, democracy must remain purely ideal, possessing no other value than that of a moral criterion which renders it possible to appreciate the varying degrees of that oligarchy which is immanent in every social regime. In other words, we have had to inquire if, and in what degree, democracy is an ideal which we can never hope to realize in practice. A further aim of this work was the demolition of some of the facile and superficial democratic illusions which trouble science and lead the masses astray. Finally, the author desired to throw light upon certain sociological tendencies which oppose the reign of democracy, and to a still greater extent oppose the reign of socialism.

The writer does not wish to deny that every revolutionary working-class movement, and every movement sincerely inspired by the democratic spirit, may have a certain value as contributing to the enfeeblement of oligarchic tendencies. The peasant in the fable, when on his deathbed, tells his sons that a treasure is buried in the field. After the old man's death the sons dig everywhere in order to discover the treasure. They do not find it. But their indefatigable labor improves the soil and secures for them a comparative well-being. The treasure in the fable may well symbolize democracy. Democracy is a treasure which no one will ever discover by deliberate search. But in continuing our search, in laboring indefatigably to discover the indiscoverable, we shall perform a work which will have fertile results in the democratic sense. We have seen, indeed, that within the bosom of the democratic working-class party are born the very tendencies to counteract which that party came into existence. Thanks to the diversity and to the unequal worth of the elements of the party, these tendencies often give rise to manifestations which border on tyranny. . . . Historical evolution mocks all the prophylactic measures that have been adopted for the prevention of oligarchy. If laws are passed to control the dominion of the leaders, it is the laws which gradually weaken, and not the leaders. Sometimes, however, the democratic principle carries with it, if not a cure, at least a palliative, for the disease of oligarchy. . . . It is, in fact, a general characteristic of democracy, and hence also of the labor movement, to stimulate and to strengthen in the individual the intellectual aptitudes for criticism and control. We have seen how the progressive bureaucratization of the democratic organism tends to neutralize the beneficial effects of such criticism and such control. Nonetheless it is true that the labor movement, in virtue of the theoretical postulates it proclaims, is apt to bring into existence (in opposition to the will of the leaders) a certain number of free spirits who, moved by principle, by instinct, or by both, desire to revise the base upon which authority is established. Urged on by conviction or by temperament, they are never weary of asking an eternal "Why?" about every human institution. Now this predisposition toward free inquiry, in which we cannot fail to recognize one of the most precious factors of civilization, will gradually increase in proportion as the economic status of the masses undergoes improvement and becomes more stable, and in proportion as they are admitted more effectively to the advantages of civilization. A wider education involves an increasing capacity for exercising control. Can we not observe every day that among the well-to-do the authority of the leaders over the led, extensive though it be, is never so unrestricted as in the case of the leaders of the poor? Taken in the mass, the poor are powerless and disarmed vis-à-vis their leaders. Their intellectual and cultural inferiority makes it impossible for them to see whither the leader is going, or to estimate in advance the significance of his actions. It is, consequently, the great task of social education to raise the intellectual level of the masses, so that they may be enabled, within the limits of what is possible, to counteract the oligarchical tendencies of the working-class movement.

In view of the perennial incompetence of the masses, we have to recognize the existence of two regulative principles:

1. The *ideological* tendency of democracy toward criticism and control;
2. The *effective* countertendency of democracy toward the creation of parties ever more complex and ever more differentiated—parties, that is to say, which are increasingly based upon the competence of the few.

To the idealist, the analysis of the forms of contemporary democracy cannot fail to be a source of bitter deceptions and profound discouragement. Those alone, perhaps, are in a position to pass a fair judgment upon democracy who, without lapsing into dilettantist sentimentalism, recognize that all scientific and human ideals have relative values. If we wish to estimate the value of democracy, we must do so in comparison with its converse, pure aristocracy. The defects inherent in democracy are obvious. It is nonetheless true that as a form of social life we must choose democracy as the least of evils. The ideal government would doubtless be that of an aristocracy of persons at once morally good and technically efficient. But where shall we discover such an aristocracy? We may find it sometimes, though very rarely, as the outcome of deliberate selection; but we shall never find it where the hereditary principle remains in operation. Thus monarchy in its pristine purity must be considered as imperfection incarnate, as the most incurable of ills; from the moral point of view it is inferior even to the most revolting of demagogic dictatorships, for the corrupt organism of the latter at least contains a healthy principle upon whose working we may continue to base hopes of social [recovery]. It may be said, therefore, that the more humanity comes to recognize the advantages which democracy, however imperfect, presents over aristocracy, even at its best, the less likely is it that a recognition of the defects of democracy will provoke a return to aristocracy. Apart from certain formal differences and from the qualities which can be acquired only by good education and inheritance (qualities in which aristocracy will always have the advantage over democracy—qualities which democracy either neglects altogether, or, in attempting to imitate them, falsifies to the point of caricature), the defects of democracy will be found to inhere in its inability to get rid of its aristocratic scoriae. On the other hand, nothing but a serene and frank examination of the oligarchical dangers of democracy will enable us to minimize these dangers, even though they can never be entirely avoided.

The democratic currents of history resemble successive waves. They break ever on the same shoal. They are ever renewed. This enduring spectacle is simultaneously encouraging and depressing. When democracies have gained a certain stage of development, they undergo a gradual transformation, adopting the aristocratic spirit, and in many cases also the aristocratic forms, against which at the outset they struggled so fiercely. Now new accusers arise to denounce the traitors; after an era of glorious combats and of inglorious power, they end by fusing with the old dominant class; whereupon once more they are in their turn attacked by fresh opponents who appeal to the name of democracy. It is probable that this cruel game will continue without end.

SELECTION 9
FROM
*From Max Weber: Essays in Sociology**

MAX WEBER

THE DECISIVE REASON FOR the advance of bureaucratic organization has always been its purely technical superiority over any other form of organization. The fully developed bureaucratic mechanism compares with other organizations exactly as does the machine with the nonmechanical modes of production.

Precision, speed, unambiguity, knowledge of the files, continuity, discretion, unity, strict subordination, reduction of friction and of material and personal costs—these are raised to the optimum point in the strictly bureaucratic administration, and especially in its monocratic form. As compared with all collegiate, honorific, and avocational forms of administration, trained bureaucracy is superior on all these points. And as far as complicated tasks are concerned, paid bureaucratic work is not only more precise but, in the last analysis, it is often cheaper than even formally unremunerated honorific service.

Honorific arrangements make administrative work an avocation and, for this reason alone, honorific service normally functions more slowly, being less bound to schemata and being more formless. Hence it is less precise and less unified than bureaucratic work because it is less dependent upon superiors and because the establishment and exploitation of the apparatus of subordinate officials and filing services are almost unavoidably less economical. Honorific service is less continuous than bureaucratic and frequently quite expensive. This is especially the case if one thinks not only of the money costs to the public treasury—costs which bureaucratic administration, in comparison with administration by notables, usually substantially increases—but also of the frequent economic losses of the governed caused by delays and lack of precision. The possibility of

*"Bureaucracy," in *From Max Weber: Essays in Sociology*, H. H. Gerth and C. Wright Mills (Eds. and Trans.) (New York: Oxford University Press, 1946; Galaxy Book Edition, 1958): Part 2, Ch. 8, pp. 214–42.

administration by notables normally and permanently exists only where official management can be satisfactorily discharged as an avocation. With the qualitative increase of tasks the administration has to face, administration by notables reaches its limits. . . . Work organized by collegiate bodies causes friction and delay and requires compromises between colliding interests and views. The administration, therefore, runs less precisely and is more independent of superiors; hence, it is less unified and slower. . . .

Today, it is primarily the capitalist market economy which demands that the official business of the administration be discharged precisely, unambiguously, continuously, and with as much speed as possible. Normally, the very large, modern capitalist enterprises are themselves unequaled models of strict bureaucratic organization. Business management throughout rests on increasing precision, steadiness, and, above all, the speed of operations. This, in turn, is determined by the peculiar nature of the modern means of communication, including, among other things, the news service of the press. The extraordinary increase in the speed by which public announcements, as well as economic and political facts, are transmitted exerts a steady and sharp pressure in the direction of speeding up the tempo of administrative reaction toward various situations. The optimum of such reaction time is normally attained only by a strictly bureaucratic organization. . . .

Bureaucratization offers above all the optimum possibility for carrying through the principle of specializing administrative functions according to purely objective considerations. Individual performances are allocated to functionaries who have specialized training and who by constant practice learn more and more. The "objective" discharge of business primarily means a discharge of business according to *calculable rules* and "without regard for persons."

"Without regard for persons" is also the watchword of the "market" and, in general, of all pursuits of naked economic interests. A consistent execution of bureaucratic domination means the leveling of status "honor." Hence, if the principle of the free market is not at the same time restricted, it means the universal domination of the "class situation." That this consequence of bureaucratic domination has not set in everywhere, parallel to the extent of bureaucratization, is due to the differences among possible principles by which polities may meet their demands.

The second element mentioned, "calculable rules," also is of paramount importance for modern bureaucracy. The peculiarity of modern culture, and specifically of its technical and economic basis, demands this very "calculability" of results. . . . Its specific nature, which is welcomed by capitalism, develops the more perfectly the more the bureaucracy is "dehumanized," the more completely it succeeds in eliminating from official business love, hatred, and all purely personal, irrational, and emotional elements which escape calculation. This is the specific nature of bureaucracy and it is appraised as its special virtue.

The more complicated and specialized modern culture becomes, the more its external supporting apparatus demands the personally detached and strictly "objective" *expert*, in lieu of the master of older social structures, who was moved by personal sympathy and favor, by grace and gratitude. Bureaucracy offers the attitudes demanded by the external apparatus of modern culture in the most favorable combination. As a rule, only bureaucracy has established the foundation for the administration of a rational law conceptually systematized on the basis of such enactments as the latter Roman imperial period first created with a high degree of technical perfection. During the Middle Ages, this law was received along with the bureaucratization of legal administration, that is to say, with the displacement of the old trial procedure which was bound to tradition or to irrational presuppositions, by the rationally trained and specialized expert. . . .

For the field of administrative activity proper, that is, for all state activities that fall outside the field of law creation and court procedure, one is accustomed to claiming the freedom and paramountcy of individual circumstances. General norms are held to play primarily a negative role as barriers to the official's positive and "creative" activity, which should never be regulated. The bearing of this thesis may be disregarded here. Yet the point that this "freely" creative administration (and possibly judicature) does not constitute a realm of *free*, arbitrary action, of mercy, and of *personally* motivated favor and valuation, as we shall find to be the case among prebureaucratic forms, is a very decisive point. The rule and the rational estimation of "objective" purposes, as well as devotion to them, always exist as a norm of conduct. In the field of executive administration, especially where the "creative" arbitrariness of the official is most strongly built up, the specifically modern and strictly "objective" idea of "reasons of state" is upheld as the supreme and ultimate guiding star of the official's behavior.

Of course, and above all, the sure instincts of the bureaucracy for the conditions of maintaining its power in its own state (and through it, in opposition to other states) are inseparably fused with the canonization of the abstract and "objective" idea of "reasons of state." In the last analysis, the power interests of the bureaucracy only give a concretely exploitable content to this by no means unambiguous ideal; and, in dubious cases, power interests tip the balance. We cannot discuss this further here. The only decisive point for us is that in principle a system of rationally debatable "reasons" stands behind every act of bureaucratic administration, that is, either subsumption under norms or a weighing of ends and means.

The position of all "democratic" currents, in the sense of currents that would minimize "authority," is necessarily ambiguous. "Equality before the law" and the demand for legal guarantees against arbitrariness demand a formal and rational "objectivity" of administration, as opposed to the personally free discretion flowing from the "grace" of the old patrimonial domination. If, however, an "ethos"—not to speak of instincts—takes hold of the masses on some individual question, it postulates *substantive* justice oriented toward some concrete instance and person; and such an "ethos" will unavoidably collide with the formalism and the rule-bound and cool "matter-of-factness" of bureaucratic administration. For this reason, the ethos must emotionally reject what reason demands.

The propertyless masses especially are not served by a formal "equality before the law" and a "calculable" adjudication and administration, as demanded by "bourgeois" interests. Naturally, in their eyes justice and administration should serve to compensate for their economic and social life-opportunities in the face of the propertied classes. Justice and administration can fulfill this function only if they assume an informal character to a far-reaching extent. It must be informal because it is substantively "ethical" ("Kadi-justice"). Every sort of "popular justice"—which usually does not ask for reasons and norms—as well as every sort of intensive influence on the administration by so-called public opinion, crosses the rational course of justice and administration just as strongly, and under certain conditions far more so, as the "star chamber" proceedings of an "absolute" ruler has been able to do. In this connection, that is, under the conditions of mass democracy, public opinion is communal conduct born of irrational "sentiments." Normally it is staged or directed by party leaders and the press. . . .

Bureaucratic organization has usually come into power on the basis of a leveling of economic and social differences. This leveling has been at least relative, and has concerned the significance of social and economic differences for the assumption of administrative functions.

Bureaucracy inevitably accompanies modern *mass democracy* in contrast to the democratic self-government of small homogeneous units. This results from the characteristic principle of bureaucracy: the abstract regularity of the execution of authority, which is a result of the demand for "equality before the law" in the personal and functional sense—hence, of the horror of "privilege," and the principled rejection of doing business "from case to case." Such regularity also follows from the social preconditions of the origin of bureaucracies. The non-bureaucratic administration of any large social structure rests in some way upon the fact that existing social, material, or honorific preferences and ranks are connected with administrative functions and duties. This usually means that a direct or indirect economic exploitation or a "social" exploitation of position, which every sort of administrative activity gives to its bearers, is equivalent to the assumption of administrative functions.

Bureaucratization and democratization within the administration of the state therefore signify and increase the cash expenditures of the public treasury. And this is the case in spite of the fact that bureaucratic administration is usually more "economical" in character than other forms of administration. . . . Mass democracy makes a clean sweep of the feudal, patrimonial, and—at least in intent—the plutocratic privileges in administration. Unavoidably it puts paid professional labor in place of the historically inherited avocational administration by notables. . . .

The progress of bureaucratization in the state administration itself is a parallel phenomenon of democracy, as is quite obvious in France, North America, and now in England. Of course one must always remember that the term "democratization" can be misleading. The demos itself, in the sense of an inarticulate mass, never "governs" larger associations; rather, it is governed, and its existence only changes the way in which the executive leaders are selected and the measure of influence which the demos, or better, which social circles from its midst are able to exert upon the content and the direction of administrative activities by supplementing what is called "public opinion." "Democratization," in the sense here intended, does not necessarily mean an increasingly active share of the governed in the authority of the social structure. This may be a result of democratization, but it is not necessarily the case.

We must expressly recall at this point that the political concept of democracy, deduced from the "equal rights" of the governed, includes these postulates: (1) prevention of the development of a closed status group of officials in the interest of a universal accessibility of office, and (2) minimization of the authority of officialdom in the interest of expanding the sphere of influence of "public opinion" as far as practicable. Hence, wherever possible, political democracy strives to shorten the term of office by election and recall and by not binding the candidate to a special expertness. Thereby democracy inevitably comes into conflict with the bureaucratic tendencies which, by its fight against notable rule, democracy has produced. The generally loose term "democratization" cannot be used here, insofar as it is understood to mean the minimization of the civil servants' ruling power in favor of the greatest possible "direct" rule of the demos, which in practice means the respective party leaders of the demos. The most decisive thing here—indeed it is rather exclusively so—is the *leveling of the governed* in opposition to the ruling and bureaucratically articulated group, which in its turn may occupy a quite autocratic position, both in fact and in form. . . .

Once it is fully established, bureaucracy is among those social structures which are the hardest to destroy. Bureaucracy is *the* means of carrying "community action" over into rationally ordered "societal action." Therefore, as an instrument for "societalizing" relations of power, bureaucracy has been and is a power instrument of the first order—for the one who controls the bureaucratic apparatus.

Under otherwise equal conditions, a "societal action," which is methodically ordered and led, is superior to every resistance of "mass" or even of "communal action." And where the bureaucratization of administration has been completely carried through, a form of power relation is established that is practically unshatterable.

The individual bureaucrat cannot squirm out of the apparatus in which he is harnessed. In contrast to the honorific or avocational "notable," the professional bureaucrat is chained to his activity by his entire material and ideal existence. In the great majority of cases, he is only a single cog in an ever-moving mechanism which prescribes to him an essentially fixed route of march. The official is entrusted with specialized tasks and normally the mechanism cannot be put into motion or arrested by him, but only from the very top. The individual bureaucrat is thus forged to the community of all the functionaries who are integrated into the mechanism. They have a common interest in seeing that the mechanism continues its functions and that the societally exercised authority carries on.

The ruled, for their part, cannot dispense with or replace the bureaucratic apparatus of authority once it exists. For this bureaucracy rests upon expert training, a functional specialization of work, and an attitude set for habitual and virtuoso-like mastery of single yet methodically integrated functions. If the official stops working, or if his work is forcefully interrupted, chaos results, and it is difficult to improvise replacements from among the governed who are fit to master such chaos. This holds for public administration as well as for private economic management. More and more the material fate of the masses depends upon the steady and correct functioning of the increasingly bureaucratic organizations of private capitalism. The idea of eliminating these organizations becomes more and more utopian.

The discipline of officialdom refers to the attitude-set of the official for precise obedience within his *habitual* activity, in public as well as in private organizations. This discipline increasingly becomes the basis of all order, however great the practical importance of administration on the basis of the filed documents may be. The naive idea of Bakuninism of destroying the basis of "acquired rights" and "domination" by destroying public documents overlooks the settled orientation of *man* for keeping to the habitual rules and regulations that continue to exist independently of the documents. Every reorganization of beaten or dissolved troops, as well as the restoration of administrative orders destroyed by revolt, panic, or other catastrophes, is realized by appealing to the trained orientation of obedient compliance to such orders. Such compliance has been conditioned into the officials, on the one hand, and, on the other hand, into the governed. If such an appeal is successful it brings, as it were, the disturbed mechanism into gear again.

The objective indispensability of the once-existing apparatus, with its peculiar, "impersonal" character, means that the mechanism — in contrast to feudal orders based upon personal piety — is easily made to work for anybody who knows how to gain control over it. A rationally ordered system of officials continues to function smoothly after the enemy has occupied the area; he merely needs to change the top officials. This body of officials continues to operate because it is to the vital interest of everyone concerned, including above all the enemy. . . .

It is clear that the bureaucratic organization of a social structure, and especially of a political one, can and regularly does have far-reaching economic consequences. But what sort of consequences? Of course in any individual case it depends upon the distribution of economic and social power, and especially upon the sphere that is occupied by the emerging bureaucratic mechanism. The consequences of bureaucracy depend therefore upon the direction which the powers using the apparatus give to it. And very frequently a crypto-plutocratic distribution of power has been the result. . . .

. . . The mere fact of bureaucratic organization does not unambiguously tell us about the concrete direction of its economic effects, which are always in some manner present. At least it does not tell us as much as can be told about its relatively leveling effect socially. In this respect, one has to remember that bureaucracy as such is a precision instrument which can put itself at the disposal of quite varied interests in domination purely political as well as purely economic ones, or any other sort. Therefore the measure of its parallelism with democratization must not be exaggerated, however typical it may be. . . . The express reservation of offices for certain status groups is very frequent, and actual reservations are even more frequent. The democratization of society in its totality, and in the *modern* sense of the term, whether actual or perhaps merely formal, is an especially favorable basis of bureaucratization, but by no means the only possible one. After all, bureaucracy strives merely to level those powers that stand in its way and in those areas that, in the individual case, it seeks to occupy. We must remember this fact—which we have encountered several times and which we shall have to discuss repeatedly: that "democracy" as such is opposed to the "rule" of bureaucracy, in spite and perhaps because of its unavoidable yet unintended promotion of bureaucratization. Under certain conditions, democracy creates obvious ruptures and blockages to bureaucratic organization. Hence, in every individual historical case, one must observe in what special direction bureaucratization has developed. . . .

We cannot here analyze the far-reaching and general cultural effects that the advance of the rational bureaucratic structure of domination, as such, develops quite independently of the areas in which it takes hold. Naturally, bureaucracy promotes a "rationalist" way of life, but the concept of rationalism allows for widely differing contents. Quite generally, one can only say that the bureaucratization of all domination very strongly furthers the development of "rational matter-of-factness" and the personality type of the professional expert. This has far-reaching ramifications, but only one important element of the process can be briefly indicated here: its effect upon the nature of training and education.

Educational institutions on the European continent, especially the institutions of higher learning—the universities, as well as technical academies, business colleges, gymnasiums, and other middle schools—are dominated and influenced by the need for the kind of "education" that produces a system of special examinations and the trained expertness that is increasingly indispensable for modern bureaucracy.

"Democracy" also takes an ambivalent stand in the face of specialized examinations, as it does in the face of all the phenomena of bureaucracy—although democracy itself promotes these developments. Special examinations, on the one hand, mean or appear to mean a "selection" of those who qualify from all social strata rather than a rule by notables. On the other hand, democracy fears that a merit system and educational certificates will result in a privileged "caste." Hence, democracy fights against the special-examination system. . . .

The modern development of full bureaucratization brings the system of rational, specialized, and expert examinations irresistibly to the fore. The civil-service reform gradually imports expert training and specialized examinations into the United States. In all other countries this system also advances, stemming from its main breeding place, Germany. The increasing bureaucratization of administration enhances the importance of the specialized examination in England. In China, the attempt to replace the semipatrimonial and ancient bureaucracy by a modern bureaucracy brought the expert examination; it took the place of a former and quite differently structured system of examinations. The bureaucratization of capitalism, with its demand for expertly trained technicians, clerks, et cetera, carries such examinations all over the world. Above all, the development is greatly furthered by the social prestige of the educational certificates acquired through such specialized examinations. This is all the more the case as the educational patent is turned to economic advantage. Today, the certificate of education becomes what the test for ancestors has been in the past, at least where the nobility has remained powerful: a prerequisite for equality of birth, a qualification for a canonship, and for state office.

The development of the diploma from universities and business and engineering colleges, and the universal clamor for the creation of educational certificates in all fields make for the formation of a privileged stratum in bureaus and in offices. Such certificates support their holders' claims for intermarriages with notable families (in business offices people naturally hope for preferment with regard to the chief's daughter), claims to be admitted into the circles that adhere to "codes of honor," claims for a "respectable" remuneration rather than remuneration for work done, claims for assured advancement and old-age insurance, and, above all, claims to monopolize socially and economically advantageous positions. When we hear from all sides the demand for an introduction of regular curricula and special examinations, the reason behind it is, of course, not a suddenly awakened "thirst for education" but the desire for restricting the supply for these positions and their monopolization by the owners of educational certificates. Today, the "examination" is the universal means of this monopolization, and therefore examinations irresistibly advance. As the education prerequisite to the acquisition of the educational certificate requires considerable expense and a period of waiting for full remuneration, this striving means a setback for talent (charisma) in favor of property. For the "intellectual" costs of educational certificates are always low, and with the increasing volume of such certificates, their intellectual costs do not increase, but rather decrease. . . .

. . . [B]ureaucracy seeks to secure the official position, the orderly advancement, and the provision for old age. In this, the bureaucracy is supported by the "democratic" sentiment of the governed, which demands that domination be minimized. Those who hold this attitude believe themselves able to discern a weakening of the master's prerogatives in every weakening of the arbitrary disposition of the master over the officials. To this extent, bureaucracy, both in business offices and in public service, is a carrier of specific "status" development, as have been the quite differently structured officeholders of the past. We have already pointed out that these status characteristics are usually also exploited, and that by their nature they contribute to the technical usefulness of the bureaucracy in fulfilling its specific tasks.

"Democracy" reacts precisely against the unavoidable "status" character of bureaucracy. Democracy seeks to put the election of officials for short terms in the place of appointed officials; it seeks to substitute the removal of officials by election for a regulated procedure of discipline. Thus, democracy seeks to replace the arbitrary disposition of the hierarchically superordinate "master" by the equally arbitrary disposition of the governed and the party chiefs dominating them.

SELECTION 10

FROM *Capitalism, Socialism and Democracy*[*]

JOSEPH A. SCHUMPETER

THERE IS FOR EVERYONE, within a much wider horizon, a narrower field—widely differing in extent as between different groups and individuals and bounded by a broad zone rather than a sharp line—which is distinguished by a sense of reality or familiarity or responsibility. And this field harbors relatively definite individual volitions. These may often strike us as unintelligent, narrow, egotistical; and it may not be obvious to everyone why, when it comes to political decisions, we should worship at their shrine, still less why we should feel bound to count each of them for one and none of them for more than one. If, however, we do choose to worship we shall at least not find the shrine empty. . . .

Now this comparative definiteness of volition and rationality of behavior does not suddenly vanish as we move away from those concerns of daily life in the home and in business which educate and discipline us. In the realm of public affairs there are sectors that are more within the reach of the citizen's mind than others. This is true, first, of local affairs. Even there we find a reduced power of discerning facts, a reduced preparedness to act upon them, a reduced sense of responsibility. We all know the man—and a very good specimen he frequently is—who says that the local administration is not his business and callously shrugs his shoulders at practices which he would rather die than suffer in his own office. High-minded citizens in a hortatory mood who preach the responsibility of the individual voter or taxpayer invariably discover the fact that this voter does not feel responsible for what the local politicians do. Still, especially in communities not too big for personal contacts, local patriotism may be a very important factor in "making democracy work." Also, the problems of a town are in many respects akin to the problems of a manufacturing concern. The man

[*] (New York: Harper & Row, 1950; 3rd Edition): Chs. 21 and 23, pp. 259–64, 269–74, 282–83.

who understands the latter also understands, to some extent, the former. The manufacturer, grocer, or workman need not step out of his world to have a rationally defensible view (that may of course be right or wrong) on street cleaning or town halls.

Second, there are many national issues that concern individuals and groups so directly and unmistakably as to evoke volitions that are genuine and definite enough. The most important instance is afforded by issues involving immediate and personal pecuniary profit to individual voters and groups of voters, such as direct payments, protective duties, silver policies, and so on. Experience that goes back to antiquity shows that by and large voters react promptly and rationally to any such chance. But the classical doctrine of democracy evidently stands to gain little from displays of rationality of this kind. Voters thereby prove themselves bad and indeed corrupt judges of such issues, . . . and often they even prove themselves bad judges of their own long-run interests, for it is only the short-run promise that tells politically and only short-run rationality that asserts itself effectively.

However, when we move still farther away from the private concerns of the family and the business office into those regions of national and international affairs that lack a direct and unmistakable link with those private concerns, individual volition, command of facts, and method of inference soon cease to fulfill the requirements of the classical doctrine. What strikes me most of all and seems to me to be the core of the trouble is the fact that the sense of reality . . . is so completely lost. Normally, the great political questions take their place in the psychic economy of the typical citizen with those leisure-hour interests that have not attained the rank of hobbies, and with the subjects of irresponsible conversation. These things seem so far off; they are not at all like a business proposition; dangers may not materialize at all and if they should they may not prove so very serious; one feels oneself to be moving in a fictitious world.

This reduced sense of reality accounts not only for a reduced sense of responsibility but also for the absence of effective volition. One has one's phrases, of course, and one's wishes and daydreams and grumbles; especially, one has one's likes and dislikes. But ordinarily they do not amount to what we call a will—the psychic counterpart of purposeful responsible action. In fact, for the private citizen musing over national affairs there is no scope for such a will and no task at which it could develop. He is a member of an unworkable committee, the committee of the whole nation, and this is why he expends less disciplined effort on mastering a political problem than he expends on a game of bridge. . . .

The reduced sense of responsibility and the absence of effective volition in turn explain the ordinary citizen's ignorance and lack of judgment in matters of domestic and foreign policy which are if anything more shocking in the case of educated people and of people who are successfully active in nonpolitical walks of life than it is with uneducated people in humble stations. Information is plentiful and readily available. But this does not seem to make any difference. Nor should we wonder at it. We need only compare a lawyer's attitude to his brief and the same lawyer's attitude to the statements of political fact presented in his newspaper in order to see what is the matter. In the one case the lawyer has qualified for appreciating the relevance of his facts by years of purposeful labor done under the definite stimulus of interest in his professional competence; and under a stimulus that is no less powerful he then bends his acquirements, his intellect, his will to the contents of the brief. In the other case, he has not taken the trouble to qualify; he does not care to absorb the information or to apply to it the canons of criticism he knows so well how to handle; and he is impatient of long or complicated argument. All of this goes to show that without the initiative that comes from immediate responsibility, ignorance will persist in the face of masses of information however complete and correct. It persists even in the face of the meritorious efforts that are being made to go beyond presenting information and to teach the use of it by means of lectures, classes, discussion groups. Results are not zero. But they are small. People cannot be carried up the ladder.

Thus the typical citizen drops down to a lower level of mental performance as soon as he enters the political field. He argues and analyzes in a way which he would readily recognize as infantile within the sphere of his real interests. He becomes a primitive again. His thinking becomes associative and effective. . . . And this entails two further consequences of ominous significance.

First, even if there were no political groups trying to influence him, the typical citizen would in political matters tend to yield to extrarational or irrational prejudice and impulse. The weakness of the rational processes he applies to politics and the absence of effective logical control over the results he arrives at would in themselves suffice to account for that. Moreover, simply because he is not "all there," he will relax his usual moral standards as well and occasionally give in to dark urges which the conditions of private life help him to repress. But as to the wisdom or rationality of his inferences and conclusions, it may be just as bad if he gives in to a burst of generous indignation. This will make it still more difficult for him to see things in their correct proportions or even to see more than one aspect of one thing at a time. Hence, if for once he does emerge from his usual vagueness and does display the definite will postulated by the classical doctrine of democracy, he is as likely as not to become still more unintelligent and irresponsible than he usually is. At certain junctures, this may prove fatal to his nation. . . .

Second, however, the weaker the logical element in the processes of the public mind and the more complete the absence of rational criticism and of the rationalizing influence of personal experience and responsibility, the greater are the opportunities for groups with an ax to grind. These groups may consist of professional politicians or of exponents of an economic interest or of idealists of one kind or another or of people simply interested in staging and managing political shows. The sociology of such groups is immaterial to the argument in hand. The only point that matters here is that, Human Nature in Politics being what it is, they are able to fashion and, within very wide limits, even to create the will of the people. What we are confronted with in the analysis of political processes is largely not a genuine but a manufactured will. And often this artifact is all that in reality corresponds to the *volonté générale* ["general will"; the term is Rousseau's—see Selection 2—though Schumpeter incorrectly attributed it to Bentham—ED.] of the classical doctrine. So far as this is so, the will of the people is the product and not the motive power of the political process.

The ways in which issues and the popular will on any issue are being manufactured is exactly analogous to the ways of commercial advertising. We find the same attempts to contact the subconscious. We find the same technique of creating favorable and unfavorable associations which are the more effective the less rational they are. We find the same evasions and reticences and the same trick of producing opinion by reiterated assertion that is successful precisely to the extent to which it avoids rational argument and the danger of awakening the critical faculties of the people. And so on. Only, all these arts have infinitely more scope in the sphere of public affairs than they have in the sphere of private and professional life. The picture of the prettiest girl that ever lived will in the long run prove powerless to maintain the sales of a bad cigarette. There is no equally effective safeguard in the case of political decisions. Many decisions of fateful importance are of a nature that makes it impossible for the public to experiment with them at its leisure and at moderate cost. Even if that is possible, however, judgment is as a rule not so easy to arrive at as it is in the case of the cigarette, because effects are less easy to interpret.

But such arts also vitiate, to an extent quite unknown in the field of commercial advertising, those forms of political advertising that profess to address themselves to reason. To the observer, the antirational or, at all events, the extrarational appeal and the defenselessness of the victim stand out more and not less clearly when cloaked in facts and arguments. We have seen above why it is so difficult to impart to the public unbiased information about political problems and logically correct inferences from it and why it is that information and arguments in political matters will "register" only if they link up with the citizen's preconceived ideas. As a rule, however, these ideas are not definite enough to determine particular conclusions. Since they can themselves be manufactured, effective political argument almost inevitably implies the attempt to twist existing volitional premises into a particular shape and not merely the attempt to implement them or to help the citizen to make up his mind.

Thus information and arguments that are really driven home are likely to be the servants of political intent. Since the first thing man will do for his ideal or interest is to lie, we shall expect, and as a matter of fact we find, that effective information is almost always adulterated or selective . . . and that effective reasoning in politics consists mainly in trying to exalt certain propositions into axioms and to put others out of court; it thus reduces to the psycho-technics mentioned before. The reader who thinks me unduly pessimistic need only ask himself whether he has never heard—or said himself—that this or that awkward fact must not be told publicly, or that a certain line of reasoning, though valid, is undesirable. If men who according to any current standard are perfectly honorable or even high-minded reconcile themselves to the implications of this, do they not thereby show what they think about the merits or even the existence of the will of the people?

There are of course limits to all this. . . . And there is truth in Jefferson's dictum that in the end the people are wiser than any single individual can be, or in Lincoln's about the impossibility of "fooling all the people all the time." But both dicta stress the long-run aspect in a highly significant way. It is no doubt possible to argue that given time the collective psyche will evolve opinions that not infrequently strike us as highly reasonable and even shrewd. History however consists of a succession of short-run situations that may alter the course of events for good. If all the people can in the short run be "fooled" step by step into something they do not really want, and if this is not an exceptional case which we could afford to neglect, then no amount of retrospective common sense will alter the fact that in reality they neither raise nor decide issues but that the issues that shape their fate are normally raised and decided for them. More than anyone else the lover of democracy has every reason to accept this fact and to clear his creed from the aspersion that it rests upon make-believe. . . .

. . . I think that most students of politics have by now come to accept the criticisms leveled at the classical doctrine of democracy in the preceding chapter. I also think that most of them agree, or will agree before long, in accepting another theory which is much truer to life and at the same time salvages much of what sponsors of the democratic method really mean by this term. Like the classical theory, it may be put into the nutshell of a definition.

It will be remembered that our chief troubles about the classical theory centered in the proposition that "the people" hold a definite and rational opinion about every individual question and that they give effect to this opinion—in a democracy—by choosing "representatives" who will see to it that that opinion is carried out. Thus the selection of the representatives is made secondary to the primary purpose of the democratic arrangement, which is to vest the power of deciding political issues in the electorate. Suppose we reverse the roles of these two elements and make the deciding of issues by the electorate secondary to the election of the men who are to do the deciding. To put it differently, we now take the view that the role of the people is to produce a government, or else an intermediate body which in turn will produce a national executive . . . or government. And we define the democratic method as that institutional arrangement for arriving at political decisions in which individuals acquire the power to decide by means of a competitive struggle for the people's vote.

Defense and explanation of this idea will speedily show that, as to both plausibility of assumptions and tenability of propositions, it greatly improves the theory of the democratic process.

First of all, we are provided with a reasonably efficient criterion by which to distinguish democratic governments from others. We have seen that the classical theory meets with difficulties on that score because both the will and the good of the people may be, and in many historical instances have been, served just as well or better by governments that cannot be described as democratic according to any accepted usage of the term. Now we are in a somewhat better position partly because we are resolved to stress a *modus procedendi* the presence or absence of which it is in most cases easy to verify. . . .

For instance, a parliamentary monarchy like the English one fulfills the requirements of the democratic method because the monarch is practically constrained to appoint to cabinet office the same people as parliament would elect. A "constitutional" monarchy does not qualify to be called democratic because electorates and parliaments, while having all the other rights that electorates and parliaments have in parliamentary monarchies, lack the power to impose their choice as to the governing committee: the cabinet ministers are in this case servants of the monarch, in substance as well as in name, and can in principle be dismissed as well as appointed by him. Such an arrangement may satisfy the people. The electorate may reaffirm this fact by voting against any proposal for change. The monarch may be so popular as to be able to defeat any competition for the supreme office. But since no machinery is provided for making this competition effective the case does not come within our definition.

Second, the theory embodied in this definition leaves all the room we may wish to have for a proper recognition of the vital fact of leadership. The classical theory did not do this but, as we have seen, attributed to the electorate an altogether unrealistic degree of initiative which practically amounted to ignoring leadership. But collectives act almost exclusively by accepting leadership—this is the dominant mechanism of practically any collective action which is more than a reflex. Propositions about the working and the results of the democratic method that take account of this are bound to be infinitely more realistic than propositions which do not. They will not stop at the execution of a *volonté générale* but will go some way toward showing how it emerges or how it is substituted or faked. What we have termed "manufactured will" is no longer outside the theory, an aberration for the absence of which we piously pray; it enters on the ground floor as it should.

Third, however, so far as there are genuine group-wise volitions at all—for instance the will of the unemployed to receive unemployment benefits or the will of other groups to help—our theory does not neglect them. On the contrary we are now able to insert them in exactly the role they actually play. Such volitions do not as a rule assert themselves directly. Even if strong and definite they remain latent, often for decades, until they are called to life by some political leader who turns them into political factors. This he does, or else his agents do it for him, by organizing these volitions, by working them up, and by including eventually appropriate items in his competitive offering. The interaction between sectional interests and public opinion and the way in which they produce the pattern we call the political situation appear from this angle in a new and much clearer light.

Fourth, our theory is of course no more definite than is the concept of competition for leadership. This concept presents similar difficulties as the concept of competition in the economic sphere, with which it may be usefully compared. In economic life competition is never completely lacking, but hardly ever is it perfect. . . . Similarly, in political life there is always some competition, though perhaps only a potential one, for the allegiance of the people. To simplify matters we have restricted the kind of competition for leadership which is to define democracy, to free competition for a free vote. The justification for this is that democracy seems to imply a recognized method by which to conduct the competitive struggle, and that the electoral method is practically the only one available for communities of any size. But though this excludes many ways of securing leadership which should be excluded, . . . such as competition by military insurrection, it does not exclude the cases that are strikingly analogous to the economic phenomena we label "unfair" or "fraudulent" competition or restraint of competition. And we cannot exclude them because if we did we should be left with a completely unrealistic ideal. . . . Between this ideal case which does not exist and the cases in which all competition with the established leader is prevented by force, there is a continuous range of variation within which the democratic method of government shades off into the autocratic one by imperceptible steps. But if we wish to understand and not to philosophize, this is as it should be. The value of our criterion is not seriously impaired thereby.

Fifth, our theory seems to clarify the relation that subsists between democracy and individual freedom. If by the latter we mean the existence of a sphere of individual self-government the boundaries of which are historically variable—*no* society tolerates absolute freedom even of conscience and of speech, *no* society reduces that sphere to zero—the question clearly becomes a matter of degree. We have seen that the democratic method does not necessarily guarantee a greater amount of individual freedom than another political method would permit in similar circumstances. It may well be the other way round. But there is still a relation between the two. If, on principle at least, everyone is free to compete for political leadership . . . by presenting himself to the electorate, this will in most cases though not in all mean a considerable amount of freedom of discussion *for all.* In particular it will normally mean a considerable amount of freedom of the press. This relation between democracy and freedom is not absolutely stringent and can be tampered with. But, from the standpoint of the intellectual, it is nevertheless very important. At the same time, it is all there is to that relation.

Sixth, it should be observed that in making it the primary function of the electorate to produce a government (directly or through an intermediate body) I intended to include in this phrase also the function of evicting it. The one means simply the acceptance of a leader or a group of leaders, the other means simply the withdrawal of this acceptance. This takes care of an element the reader may have missed. He may have thought that the electorate controls as well as installs. But since electorates normally do not control their political leaders in any way except by refusing to reelect them or the parliamentary majorities that support them, it seems well to reduce our ideas about this control in the way indicated by our definition. Occasionally, spontaneous revulsions occur which upset a government or an individual minister directly or else enforce a certain course of action. But they are not only exceptional; they are, as we shall see, contrary to the spirit of the democratic method.

Seventh, our theory sheds much-needed light on an old controversy. Whoever accepts the classical doctrine of democracy and in consequence believes that the democratic method is to guarantee that issues be decided and policies framed according to the will of the people must be struck by the fact that, even if that will were undeniably real and definite, decision by simple majorities would in many cases distort it rather than give effect to it. Evidently the will of the majority is the will of the majority and not the will of "the people." The latter is a mosaic that the former completely fails to "represent." To equate both by definition is not to solve the problem. Attempts at real solutions have however been made by the authors of the various plans for proportional representation.

These plans have met with adverse criticism on practical grounds. It is in fact obvious not only that proportional representation will offer opportunities for all sorts of idiosyncrasies to assert themselves but also that it may prevent democracy from producing efficient governments and thus prove a danger in times of stress. . . . But before concluding that democracy becomes unworkable if its principle is carried out consistently, it is just as well to ask ourselves whether this principle really implies proportional representation. As a matter of fact it does not. If acceptance of leadership is the true function of the electorate's vote, the case for proportional representation collapses because its premises are no longer binding. The principle of democracy then merely means that the reins of government should be handed to those who command more support than do any of the competing individuals or teams. And this in turn seems to assure the standing of the majority system within the logic of the democratic method, although we might still condemn it on grounds that lie outside of that logic. . . .

. . . We may sum up as follows. In observing human societies we do not as a rule find it difficult to specify, at least in a rough commonsense manner, the various ends that the societies under study struggle to attain. These ends may be said to provide the rationale or meaning of corresponding individual activities. But it does not follow that the social meaning of a type of activity will necessarily provide the motive power, hence the explanation of the latter. If it does not, a theory that contents itself with an analysis of the social end or need to be served cannot be accepted as an adequate account of the activities that serve it. For instance, the reason why there is such a thing as economic activity is of course that people want to eat, to clothe themselves, and so on. To provide the means to satisfy those wants is the social end or meaning of production. Nevertheless we all agree that this proposition would make a most unrealistic starting point for a theory of economic activity in commercial society and that we shall do much better if we start from propositions about profits. Similarly, the social meaning or function of parliamentary activity is no doubt to turn out legislation and, in part, administrative measures. But in order to understand how democratic politics serve this social end, we must start from the competitive struggle for power and office and realize that the social function is fulfilled, as it were, incidentally—in the same sense as production is incidental to the making of profits.

. . . Finally, as to the role of the electorate, only one additional point need be mentioned. We have seen that the wishes of the members of a parliament are not the ultimate data of the process that produces government. A similar statement must be made concerning the electorate. Its choice—ideologically glorified into the Call from the People—does not flow from its initiative but is being shaped, and the shaping of it is an essential part of the democratic process. Voters do not decide issues. But neither do they pick their members of parliament from the eligible population with a perfectly open mind. In all normal cases the initiative lies with the candidate who makes a bid for the office of member of parliament and such local leadership as that may imply. Voters confine themselves to accepting this bid in preference to others or refusing to accept it. Even most of those exceptional cases in which a man is *genuinely* drafted by the electors come into the same category for either of two reasons: naturally a man need not bid for leadership if he has acquired leadership already; or it may happen that a local leader who can control or influence the vote but is unable or unwilling to compete for election himself designates another man who then may seem to have been sought out by the voters acting on their own initiative.

But even as much of electoral initiative as acceptance of one of the competing candidates would in itself imply is further restricted by the existence of parties. A party is not, as classical doctrine (or Edmund Burke) would have us believe, a group of men who intend to promote public welfare "upon some principle on which they are all agreed." This rationalization is so dangerous because it is so tempting. For all parties will of course, at any given time, provide themselves with a stock of principles or planks and these principles or planks may be as characteristic of the party that adopts them and as important for its success as the brands of goods a department store sells are characteristic of it and important for its success. But the department store cannot be defined in terms of its brands and a party cannot be defined in terms of its principles. A party is a group whose members propose to act in concert in the competitive struggle for political power. If that were not so it would be impossible for different parties to adopt exactly or almost exactly the same program. Yet this happens as everyone knows. Party and machine politicians are simply the response to the fact that the electoral mass is incapable of action other than a stampede, and they constitute an attempt to regulate political competition exactly similar to the corresponding practices of a trade association. The psycho-technics of party management and party advertising, slogans and marching tunes, are not accessories. They are of the essence of politics. So is the political boss.

SELECTION 11
FROM
*Voting**

BERNARD BERELSON, PAUL LAZARSFELD, AND WILLIAM MCPHEE

INDIVIDUAL VOTERS TODAY SEEM unable to satisfy the requirements for a democratic system of government outlined by political theorists. But the *system of democracy* does meet certain requirements for a going political organization. The individual members may not meet all the standards, but the whole nevertheless survives and grows. This suggests that where the classic theory is defective is in its concentration on the *individual citizen*. What are undervalued are certain collective properties that reside in the electorate as a whole and in the political and social system in which it functions.

The political philosophy we have inherited, then, has given more consideration to the virtues of the typical citizen of the democracy than to the working of the *system* as a whole. Moreover, when it dealt with the system, it mainly considered the single constitutive institutions of the system, not those general features necessary if the institutions are to work as required. For example, the rule of law, representative government, periodic elections, the party system, and the several freedoms of discussion, press, association, and assembly have all been examined by political philosophers seeking to clarify and to justify the idea of political democracy. But liberal democracy is more than a political system in which individual voters and political institutions operate. For political democracy to survive, other features are required: the intensity of conflict must be limited, the rate of change must be restrained, stability in the social and economic structure must be maintained, a pluralistic social organization must exist, and a basic consensus must bind together the contending parties.

Such features of the system of political democracy belong neither to the constitutive institutions nor to the individual voter. It might be said that they form the atmosphere or the environment in which both operate. In any case, such features have not been carefully considered by political philosophers, and it

*(Chicago: University of Chicago Press, 1954): pp. 306–7, 311–23.

is on these broader properties of the democratic political system that more reflection and study by political theory is called for. In the most tentative fashion let us explore the values of the political system, as they involve the electorate, in the light of the foregoing considerations.

Underlying the paradox is an assumption that the population is homogeneous socially and should be homogeneous politically: that everybody is about the same in relevant social characteristics; that, if something is a political virtue (like interest in the election), then everyone should have it; that there is such a thing as *the* typical citizen on whom uniform requirements can be imposed. The tendency of classic democratic literature to work with an image of *the* voter was never justified. For, as we will attempt to illustrate here, some of the most important requirements that democratic values impose on a system require a voting population that is not homogeneous but heterogeneous in its political qualities.

The need for heterogeneity arises from the contradictory functions we expect our voting system to serve. We expect the political system to adjust itself and our affairs to changing conditions; yet we demand too that it display a high degree of stability. We expect the contending interests and parties to pursue their ends vigorously and the voters to care; yet, after the election is over, we expect reconciliation. We expect the voting outcome to serve what is best for the community; yet we do not want disinterested voting unattached to the purposes and interests of different segments of that community. We want voters to express their own free and self-determined choices; yet, for the good of the community, we would like voters to avail themselves of the best information and guidance available from the groups and leaders around them. We expect a high degree of rationality to prevail in the decision; but were all irrationality and mythology absent, and all ends pursued by the most coldly rational selection of political means, it is doubtful if the system would hold together.

In short, our electoral system calls for apparently incompatible properties—which, although they cannot all reside in each individual voter, can (and do) reside in a heterogeneous electorate. What seems to be required of the electorate as a whole is a *distribution* of qualities along important dimensions. We need some people who are active in a certain respect, others in the middle, and still others passive. The contradictory things we want from the total require that the parts be different. This can be illustrated by taking up a number of important dimensions by which an electorate might be characterized.

How could a mass democracy work if all the people were deeply involved in politics? Lack of interest by some people is not without its benefits, too. True, the highly interested voters vote more, and know more about the campaign, and read and listen more, and participate more; however, they are also less open to persuasion and less likely to change. Extreme interest goes with extreme partisanship and might culminate in rigid fanaticism that could destroy democratic processes if generalized throughout the community. Low affect toward the election—not caring much—underlies the resolution of many political problems; votes can be resolved into a two-party split instead of fragmented into many parties (the splinter parties of the left, for example, splinter because their advocates are *too* interested in politics). Low interest provides maneuvering room for political shifts necessary for a complex society in a period of rapid change. Compromise might be based upon sophisticated awareness of costs and returns—perhaps impossible to demand of a mass society—but it is more often induced by indifference. Some people are and should be highly interested in politics, but not everyone is or needs to be. Only the doctrinaire would deprecate the moderate indifference that facilitates compromise.

Hence, an important balance between action motivated by strong sentiments and action with little passion behind it is obtained by heterogeneity within the electorate. Balance of this sort is, in practice, met by a distribution of voters rather than by a homogeneous collection of "ideal" citizens.

A similar dimension along which an electorate might be characterized is stability-flexibility. The need for change and adaptation is clear, and the need for stability ought equally to be (especially from observation of current democratic practice in, say, certain Latin American countries).

How is political stability achieved? There are a number of social sources of political stability: the training of the younger generation before it is old enough to care much about the matter, the natural selection that surrounds the individual voter with families and friends who reinforce his own inclinations, the tendency to adjust in favor of the majority of the group, the self-perpetuating tendency of political traditions among ethnic and class and regional strata where like-minded people find themselves socially together. Political stability is based upon social stability. Family traditions, personal associations, status-related organizational memberships, ethnic affiliations, socioeconomic strata—such ties for the individual do not change rapidly or sharply, and since his vote is so importantly a product of them, neither does it. In effect, a large part of the study of voting deals not with why votes change but rather with why they do not.

In addition, the varying conditions facing the country, the varying political appeals made to the electorate, and the varying dispositions of the voters activated by these stimuli—these, combined with the long-lasting nature of the political loyalties they instill, produce an important cohesion within the system. . . .

What of flexibility? Curiously, the voters least admirable when measured against individual requirements contribute most when measured against the aggregate requirement for flexibility. For those who change political preferences most readily are those who are least interested, who are subject to conflicting social pressures, who have inconsistent beliefs and erratic voting histories.

Without them—if the decision were left only to the deeply concerned, well-integrated, consistently-principled, ideal citizens—the political system might easily prove too rigid to adapt to changing domestic and international conditions.

In fact, it may be that the very people who are most sensitive to changing social conditions are those most susceptible to political change. For, in either case, the people exposed to membership in overlapping strata, those whose former life-patterns are being broken up, those who are moving about socially or physically, those who are forming new families and new friendships—it is they who are open to adjustments of attitudes and tastes. They may be the least partisan and the least interested voters, but they perform a valuable function for the entire system. Here again is an instance in which an individual "inadequacy" provides a positive service for the society: the campaign can be a reaffirming force for the settled majority and a creative force for the unsettled minority. There is stability on both sides and flexibility in the middle. . . .

Lord Bryce pointed out the difficulties in a theory of democracy that assumes that each citizen must himself be capable of voting intelligently.

Orthodox democratic theory assumes that every citizen has, or ought to have, thought out for himself certain opinions, i.e., ought to have a definite view, defensible by argument, of what the country needs, of what principles ought to be applied in governing it, of the man to whose hands the government ought to be entrusted. There are persons who talk, though certainly very few who act, as if they believed this theory, which may be compared to the theory of some ultra-Protestants that every good Christian has or ought to have . . . worked out for himself from the Bible a system of theology.

In the first place, however, the information available to the individual voter is not limited to that directly possessed by him. True, the individual casts his own personal ballot. But, as we have tried to indicate, . . . that is perhaps the most individualized action he takes in an election. His vote is formed in the midst of his fellows in a sort of group decision—if, indeed, it may be called a decision at all—and the total information and knowledge possessed in the group's present and past generations can be made available for the group's choice. Here is where opinion-leading relationships, for example, play an active role.

Second, and probably more important, the individual voter may not have a great deal of detailed information, but he usually has picked up the crucial *general* information as part of his social learning itself. He may not know the parties' positions on the tariff, or who is for reciprocal trade treaties, or what are the differences on Asiatic policy, or how the parties split on civil rights, or how many security risks were exposed by whom. But he cannot live in an American community without knowing broadly where the parties stand. He has learned that the Republicans are more conservative and the Democrats more liberal—and he can locate his own sentiments and cast his vote accordingly. After all, he must vote for one or the other party, and, if he knows the big thing about the parties, he does not need to know all the little things. The basic role a party plays as an institution in American life is more important to his voting than a particular stand on a particular issue.

It would be unthinkable to try to maintain our present economic style of life without a complex system of delegating to others what we are not competent to do ourselves, without accepting and giving training to each other about what each is expected to do, without accepting our dependence on others in many spheres and taking responsibility for their dependence on us in some spheres. And, like it or not, to maintain our present political style of life, we may have to accept much the same interdependence with others in collective behavior. We have learned slowly in economic life that it is useful not to have everyone a butcher or a baker, any more than it is useful to have no one skilled in such activities. The same kind of division of labor—as repugnant as it may be in some respects to our individualistic tradition—is serving us well today in mass politics. There is an implicit division of political labor within the electorate.

In short, when we turn from requirements for "average" citizens to requirements for the survival of the total democratic system, we find it unnecessary for the individual voter to be an "average citizen" cast in the classic or any other single mold. With our increasingly complex and differentiated citizenry has grown up an equally complex political system, and it is perhaps not simply a fortunate accident that they have grown and prospered together.

But it is a dangerous act of mental complacency to assume that conditions found surviving together are, therefore, positively "functional" for each other. The apathetic segment of America probably has helped to hold the system together and cushioned the shock of disagreement, adjustment, and change. But that is not to say that we can stand apathy without limit. Similarly, there must be some limit to the degree of stability or nonadaptation that a political society can maintain and still survive in a changing world. And surely the quality and amount of conformity that is necessary and desirable can be exceeded, as it has been in times of war and in the present Communist scare, to the damage of the society itself and of the other societies with which it must survive in the world.

How can our analysis be reconciled with the classical theory of liberal political democracy? Is the theory "wrong"? Must it be discarded in favor of empirical political sociology? Must its ethical or normative content be dismissed as incompatible with the nature of modern man or of mass society? That is not our view. Rather, it seems to us that modern political theory of democracy stands in need of revision and not replacement by empirical sociology. The classical political philosophers were right in the direction of their assessment of the virtues of the citizen. But they demanded those virtues in too extreme or doctrinal a form. The voter does have some principles, he does have information and rationality, he does have interest—but he does not have them in the extreme, elaborate, comprehensive, or detailed form in which they were uniformly recommended by political philosophers. Like Justice Hand, the typical citizen has other interests in life, and it is good, even for the political system, that he pursue them. The classical requirements are more appropriate for the opinion leaders in the society, but even they do not meet them directly. Happily for the system, voters distribute themselves along a continuum.

And it turns out that this distribution itself, with its internal checks and balances, can perform the functions and incorporate the same values ascribed by some theorists to each individual in the system as well as to the constitutive political institutions!

SELECTION 12
FROM
*The Crisis of Democracy**

MICHEL J. CROZIER, SAMUEL P. HUNTINGTON, AND JOJI WATANUKI

AMERICAN SOCIETY IS CHARACTERIZED by a broad consensus on democratic, liberal, egalitarian values. For much of the time, the commitment to these values is neither passionate nor intense. During periods of rapid social change, however, these democratic and egalitarian values of the American creed are reaffirmed. The intensity of belief during such creedal passion periods leads to the challenging of established authority and to major efforts to change governmental structure to accord more fully with those values. In this respect, the democratic surge of the 1960s shares many characteristics with the comparable egalitarian and reform movements of the Jacksonian and Progressive eras. Those "surges" like the contemporary one also occurred during periods of realignment between party and governmental institutions, on the one hand, and social forces, on the other. . . . The slogans, goals, values, and targets of all three movements are strikingly similar. To the extent this analysis is valid, the causes of the democratic surge in the United States would be specific to the United States and limited in duration but potentially recurring at some point in the future.

Predictively, the implication of this analysis is that in due course the democratic surge and its resulting dual distemper in government will moderate. Prescriptively, the implication is that these developments ought to take place in order to avoid the deleterious consequences of the surge and to restore balance between vitality and governability in the democratic system.

Al Smith once remarked that "the only cure for the evils of democracy is more democracy." Our analysis suggests that applying that cure at the present time could well be adding fuel to the flames. Instead, some of the problems of governance in the United States today stem from an excess of democracy—an

**The Crisis of Democracy: Report on the Governability of Democracies to the Trilateral Commission* (New York: New York University Press, 1975): Chs. 3 and 5, pp. 112–15, 161–64.

"excess of democracy" in much the same sense in which David Donald used the term to refer to the consequences of the Jacksonian revolution which helped to precipitate the Civil War. Needed, instead, is a greater degree of moderation in democracy.

In practice, this moderation has two major areas of application. First, democracy is only one way of constituting authority, and it is not necessarily a universally applicable one. In many situations the claims of expertise, seniority, experience, and special talents may override the claims of democracy as a way of constituting authority. During the surge of the 1960s, however, the democratic principle was extended to many institutions where it can, in the long run, only frustrate the purposes of those institutions. A university where teaching appointments are subject to approval by students may be a more democratic university but it is not likely to be a better university. In similar fashion, armies in which the commands of officers have been subject to veto by the collective wisdom of their subordinates have almost invariably come to disaster on the battlefield. The arenas where democratic procedures are appropriate are, in short, limited.

Second, the effective operation of a democratic political system usually requires some measure of apathy and noninvolvement on the part of some individuals and groups. In the past, every democratic society has had a marginal population, of greater or lesser size, which has not actively participated in politics. In itself, this marginality on the part of some groups is inherently undemocratic, but it has also been one of the factors which has enabled democracy to function effectively. Marginal social groups, as in the case of the blacks, are now becoming full participants in the political system. Yet the danger of overloading the political system with demands which extend its functions and undermine its authority still remains. Less marginality on the part of some groups thus needs to be replaced by more self-restraint on the part of all groups.

The Greek philosophers argued that the best practical state would combine several different principles of government in its constitution. The Constitution of 1787 was drafted with this insight very much in mind. Over the years, however, the American political system has emerged as a distinctive case of extraordinarily democratic institutions joined to an exclusively democratic value system. Democracy is more of a threat to itself in the United States than it is in either Europe or Japan where there still exist residual inheritances of traditional and aristocratic values. The absence of such values in the United States produces a lack of balance in society which, in turn, leads to the swing back and forth between creedal passion and creedal passivity. Political authority is never strong in the United States, and it is peculiarly weak during a creedal passion period of intense commitment to democratic and egalitarian ideals. In the United States, the strength of democracy poses a problem for the governability of democracy in a way which is not the case elsewhere.

The vulnerability of democratic government in the United States thus comes not primarily from external threats, though such threats are real, nor from internal subversion from the left or the right, although both possibilities could exist, but rather from the internal dynamics of democracy itself in a highly educated, mobilized, and participant society. "Democracy never lasts long," John Adams observed. "It soon wastes, exhausts, and murders itself. There never was a democracy yet that did not commit suicide." That suicide is more likely to be the product of overindulgence than of any other cause. A value which is normally good in itself is not necessarily optimized when it is maximized. We have come to recognize that there are potentially desirable limits to the indefinite extension of political democracy. Democracy will have a longer life if it has a more balanced existence.

Quite apart from the substantive policy issues confronting democratic government, many specific problems have arisen which seem to be an intrinsic part of the functioning of democracy itself. The successful operation of democratic government has given rise to tendencies which impede that functioning.

1. The pursuit of the democratic virtues of equality and individualism has led to the delegitimation of authority generally and the loss of trust in leadership.
2. The democratic expansion of political participation and involvement has created an "overload" on government and the imbalanced expansion of governmental activities, exacerbating inflationary tendencies in the economy.
3. The political competition essential to democracy has intensified, leading to a disaggregation of interests and the decline and fragmentation of political parties.
4. The responsiveness of democratic government to the electorate and to societal pressures encourages nationalistic parochialism in the way in which democratic societies conduct their foreign relations.

1. The Delegitimation of Authority

In most of the Trilateral countries [Japan, United States, Western Europe—Ed.] in the past decade [1960s—Ed.] there has been a decline in the confidence and trust which the people have in government, in their leaders, and, less clearly but most importantly, in each other. Authority has been challenged not only in government, but in trade unions, business enterprises, schools and universities, professional associations, churches, and civic groups. In the past, those institutions which have played the major role in the indoctrination of the young in their rights and obligations as members of society have been the family, the church, the school, and the army. The effectiveness of all these institutions as a means of socialization has declined severely. The stress has been increasingly on individuals and their rights, interests, and needs, and not on the community and its rights, interests, and needs. These attitudes have been particularly prevalent in the young, but they have also appeared in other age groups, especially among those who have achieved professional, white-collar, and middle-class status. The success of the existing structures of authority in incorporating large elements of the population into the middle class, paradoxically, strengthens precisely those groups which are disposed to challenge the existing structures of authority.

The democratic spirit is egalitarian, individualistic, populist, and impatient with the distinctions of class and rank. The spread of that spirit weakens the traditional threats to democracy posed by such groups as the aristocracy, the church, and the military. At the same time, a pervasive spirit of democracy may pose an intrinsic threat and undermine all forms of association, weakening the social bonds which hold together family, enterprise, and community. Every social organization requires, in some measure, inequalities in authority and distinctions in function. To the extent that the spread of the democratic temper corrodes all of these, exercising a leveling and a homogenizing influence, it destroys the bases of trust and cooperation among citizens and creates obstacles to collaboration for any common purpose.

Leadership is in disrepute in democratic societies. Without confidence in its leadership, no group functions effectively. When the fabric of leadership weakens among other groups in society, it is also weakened at the top political levels of government. The governability of a society at the national level depends upon the extent to which it is effectively governed at the subnational, regional, local, functional, and industrial levels. In the modern state, for instance, powerful trade union "bosses" are often viewed as a threat to the power of the state. In actuality, however, responsible union leaders with effective authority over their members are less of a challenge to the authority of the national political leaders than they are a prerequisite to the exercise of authority by those leaders. If the unions are disorganized, if the membership is rebellious, if extreme demands and wildcat strikes are the order of the day, the formulation and implementation of a national wage policy become impossible. The weakening of authority throughout society thus contributes to the weakening of the authority of government.

2. The Overloading of Government

Recent years in the Trilateral countries have seen the expansion of the demands on government from individuals and groups. The expansion takes the form of: (1) the involvement of an increasing proportion of the population in political activity; (2) the development of new groups and of new consciousness on the part of old groups, including youth, regional groups, and ethnic minorities; (3) the diversification of the political means and tactics which groups use to secure their ends; (4) an increasing expectation on the part of groups that government has the responsibility to meet their needs; and (5) an escalation in what they conceive those needs to be.

The result is an "overload" on government and the expansion of the role of government in the economy and society. During the 1960s governmental expenditures, as a proportion of GNP, increased significantly in all the principal Trilateral countries, except for Japan. This expansion of governmental activity was attributed not so much to the strength of government as to its weakness and the inability and unwillingness of central political leaders to reject the demands made upon them by numerically and functionally important groups in their society. The impetus to respond to the demands which groups made on government is deeply rooted in both the attitudinal and structural features of a democratic society. The democratic idea that government should be responsive to the people creates the expectation that government should meet the needs and correct the evils affecting particular groups in society. Confronted with the structural imperative of competitive elections every few years, political leaders can hardly do anything else.

Inflation is obviously not a problem which is peculiar to democratic societies, and it may well be the result of causes quite extrinsic to the democratic process. It may, however, be exacerbated by a democratic politics and it is, without doubt, extremely difficult for democratic systems to deal with effectively. The natural tendency of the political demands permitted and encouraged by the dynamics of a democratic system helps governments to deal with the problems of economic recession, particularly unemployment, and it hampers them in dealing effectively with inflation. In the face of the claims of business groups, labor unions, and the beneficiaries of governmental largesse, it becomes difficult if not impossible for democratic governments to curtail spending, increase taxes, and control prices and wages. In this sense, inflation is the economic disease of democracies.

SELECTION 13
FROM
*Who Governs?**

ROBERT A. DAHL

IN THE UNITED STATES as a whole, an industrial society followed an agrarian society. In New Haven, an industrial society followed a hierarchical urban society dominated by a patrician oligarchy. In the agrarian society, political resources were dispersed in an approximation to equality such as the civilized world had never before seen. In the old oligarchy of New Haven, political resources were concentrated in the familiar pattern of hierarchical societies. Against the background of an agrarian society, the institutions and processes of industrial society produced a concentration of political resources. Against the background of oligarchy in New Haven, the institutions and processes of industrial society produced a dispersion of political resources.

But this dispersion did not recapture the equalitarian distribution of political resources that existed in agrarian America. Industrial society dispersed, it did not eradicate, political inequality.

In the political system of the patrician oligarchy, political resources were marked by a cumulative inequality: when one individual was much better off than another in one resource, such as wealth, he was usually better off in almost every other resource—social standing, legitimacy, control over religious and educational institutions, knowledge, office. In the political system of today, inequalities in political resources remain, but they tend to be *noncumulative*. The political system of New Haven, then, is one of *dispersed inequalities*.

The patrician-Congregationalist-Federalist elite that ruled New Haven prior to 1840 was a tiny group that combined the highest social standing, education, and wealth with key positions in religion, the economy, and public life. The entrepreneurs drove a wedge into this unified elite; social standing and education remained with the patricians, but wealth and key positions in corporate and public life went to the new men of industry. With the rise of the ex-plebes there occurred a further fragmentation of political resources. Rising out of the newly created urban proletariat, of immigrant backgrounds and modest social standing,

---

*(New Haven, CT: Yale University Press, 1961): Chs. 7, 19, and 28, pp. 85–86, 223–28, 315–25.

the ex-plebes had one political resource of extraordinary importance in a competitive political system: they were popular with the voters. Popularity gave them office, and office gave them other political resources, such as legality and city jobs. Office, legality, and jobs gave the ex-plebes influence over government decisions.

Within a century a political system dominated by one cohesive set of leaders had given way to a system dominated by many different sets of leaders, each having access to a different combination of political resources. It was, in short, a pluralist system. If the pluralist system was very far from being an oligarchy, it was also a long way from achieving the goal of political equality advocated by the philosophers of democracy and incorporated into the creed of democracy and equality practically every American professes to uphold.

An elite no longer rules New Haven. But in the strict democratic sense, the disappearance of elite rule has not led to the emergence of rule by the people. Who, then, rules in a pluralist democracy?

On the Species *Homo Politicus*

We have now discovered and exposed the anatomy of political influence in New Haven. We have described the long-run changes from oligarchy to pluralism; we have analyzed the distribution and patterns of influence; we have traced the short-run changes from spheres of influence to an executive-centered order. We know now *how* the system works. Can we explain *why*?

Let us start with man himself: with his opportunities and resources for gaining influence and the way he exploits—or more often neglects to exploit—his political potentialities.

Homo Civicus

Civic man is, at heart, simply man; man is the child grown up; the child is the human species after millions of years of evolution. In spite of ideas and ideals, the human organism still relentlessly insists on its primordial quest for gratifications and release from pain. The child and the youth learn various forms of gratifying experience; they learn of love, and food, of play, work, and rest, of the pursuit of curiosity, the perception of order and pattern, sex, friendship, self-esteem, social esteem. Throughout man's life, experiences like these channel his efforts, his energies, his attention. They represent his hungers, his needs, his wants.

The child, the budding civic man, learns all too soon that he cannot indulge himself without stint. Constraints are imposed on his liberty to gratify himself, both by nature herself in the form of physiological, mechanical, and psychological limitations and also by other individuals—his family, to begin with, then playmates, teachers, and later a host of others. The child struggles, resists, and is caught, more or less firmly, in a net woven by himself and his society.

He learns how to delay his gratifying experiences; because of the various barriers imposed on him, the routes he now chooses to his goals are frequently complex and time-consuming, sometimes boring, occasionally painful, at times dangerous.

He discovers that just as others constrain him in his efforts to achieve his primary goals, he too has resources that he can use to influence others to gain his own ends. At first these resources are closely attached to his own person and consist of simple, direct actions and reactions like affection, friendliness, anger, hostility, crying, destructiveness. But the world, as he gradually learns, contains many resources that can be used more indirectly. In our own culture, for example, he soon finds that money has a magical power to induce the compliance of many different people for many different purposes.

Thus *homo civicus* begins to develop strategies, ways of using his resources to achieve his goals. Even in choosing strategies, he discovers, he does not enjoy complete freedom. Some strategies are banned, some are permissible, others are encouraged, many are all but unavoidable. Schooling and a job are presented to him as compulsory strategies; it is made clear that any attempt to depart from these paths will be visited not only by a great loss in his capacity to attain his goals but possibly even by outright punishment. Schooling is considered instrumental in gaining knowledge, and knowledge is a resource of widespread applicability; a job is instrumental in acquiring income and social standing, resources that are important for a variety of ends.

Young *homo civicus* learns that his choices are constrained by laws enforced by the police, by courts, and by many other officials. He learns of clusters of institutions and men called governments, toward some of which he develops sentiments of loyalty or cynicism. He may accept the constraints on his choices flowing from the actions of these governments, or he may try to evade them, but in either case he gradually learns that the range of permissible strategies in dealing with governments is a good deal wider and includes many subtler alternatives than he had first assumed. Among his resources for influencing officials, *homo civicus* discovers the ballot. Although the prevailing public doctrine of American society places a high value on this resource, and *homo civicus* may himself give lip service to that doctrine, in fact he may doubt its value and rarely if ever employ it, or he may vote merely out of habit and sense of duty. Or he may see the ballot as a useful device for influencing politicians.

Homo civicus has other resources, too, For example, he can forego a movie or two in order to make a contribution to a political campaign; he can forego an evening of television in order to distribute propaganda for a candidate. But the chances are very great that political activity will always seem rather remote from the main focus of his life. Typically, as a source of direct gratification, political activity will appear to *homo civicus* as less attractive than a host of other activities; and, as a strategy to achieve his gratifications indirectly, political action will seem considerably less efficient than working at his job, earning more money, taking out insurance, joining a club, planning a vacation, moving to another neighborhood or city, or coping with an uncertain future in manifold other ways.

Sometimes, however, the actions or inactions of governments may threaten the primary goals of *homo civicus* (as in the cases of Miss Grava and her neighbors when they were threatened by the metal houses, or the New Haven school teachers threatened by declining salaries and poor schools). Then *homo civicus* may set out deliberately to use the resources at his disposal in order to influence the actions of governments. But when the danger passes, *homo civicus* may usually be counted on to revert to his normal preoccupation with nonpolitical strategies for attaining his primary goals.

Homo civicus is not, by nature, a political animal.

Homo Politicus

Despite several thousand years of richly insightful speculation, not much can be said with confidence about the factors that shape *homo politicus* out of the apolitical clay of *homo civicus*. Presumably, in the course of development some individuals find that political action is a powerful source of gratifications, both direct and indirect. If and when the primary goals that animate *homo civicus* become durably attached to political action, a new member of the genus *homo politicus* is born. Political man, unlike civic man, deliberately allocates a very sizable share of his resources to the process of gaining and maintaining control over the policies of government. Control over policies usually requires control over officials. And where, as in the United States, key officials are elected by voters, political man usually allocates an important share of his resources to the process of gaining and maintaining influence over voters. Because the acquiescence of *homo civicus* is always a necessary condition for rulership, and to gain his consent is often economical, in all political systems *homo politicus* deliberately employs some resources to influence the choices of *homo civicus*. Political man invariably seeks to influence civic man directly, but even in democratic systems civic man only occasionally seeks to influence political man directly.

Like civic man, political man develops strategies that govern the ways in which he uses the resources at his disposal. Like civic man, political man chooses his strategies from a narrowly limited set. In some political systems, the limits imposed on *homo politicus* are broad; in others the limits are relatively narrow. In pluralistic, democratic political systems with wide political consensus the range of acceptable strategies is narrowed by beliefs and habits rooted in traditions of legality, constitutionality, and legitimacy that are constantly reinforced by a great variety of social processes for generating agreement on and adherence to political norms. Whoever departs from these acceptable strategies incurs a high risk of defeat, for the resources that will be mounted against the political deviant are almost certain to be vastly greater than the resources the political deviant can himself muster. Even *homo civicus* (under the prodding of rival political leaders) can be counted on to rise briefly out of his preoccupation with apolitical goals and employ some of his resources to smite down the political man who begins to deviate noticeably in his choice of strategies from the norms prescribed in the political culture.

Resources

The resources available to political man for influencing others are limited, though not permanently fixed. For our purposes in this book, a resource is anything that can be used to sway the specific choices or the strategies of another individual. Or, to use different language, whatever may be used as an inducement is a resource.

How one classifies resources is to some extent arbitrary. It would be possible to list resources in great detail, distinguishing one from the other with the utmost subtlety or to deal in very broad categories. One could search for a comprehensive and logically exhaustive classification or simply list resources according to the dictates of common sense. One could employ elaborate psychological categories derived from theories of modern psychology, or one could use more commonplace terms to classify resources. To the extent that we can explain the patterns of influence in New Haven, it will do, I think, to use categories dictated by common sense; to do more at this stage of our knowledge would be pseudoscientific window dressing.

Some resources can be used more or less directly as inducements. Or, put another way, the kinds of effective and cognitive experiences mentioned a moment ago as peculiarly fundamental and universal depend rather directly on some kinds of resources and more indirectly on others.

A list of resources in the American political system might include an individual's own time; access to money, credit, and wealth; control over jobs; control over information; esteem or social standing; the possession of charisma, popularity, legitimacy, legality; and the rights pertaining to public office. The list might also include solidarity: the capacity of a member of one segment of society to evoke support from others who identify him as like themselves because of similarities in occupation, social standing, religion, ethnic origin, or racial stock. The list would include the right to vote, intelligence, education, and perhaps even one's energy level.

One could easily think of refinements and additions to this list; it is not intended as an exhaustive list so much as an illustration of the richness and variety of political resources. All too often, attempts to explain the distribution and patterns of influence in political systems begin with an a priori assumption that everything can be explained by reference to only one kind of resource. On the contrary, the various manifestations of influence in New Haven . . . can be explained, as we shall see, only by taking into account a number of different political resources.

Although the kinds and amounts of resources available to political man are always limited and at any given moment fixed, they are not, as was pointed out a moment ago, permanently fixed as to either kind or amount. Political man can use his resources to gain influence, and he can then use his influence to gain more resources. Political resources can be pyramided in much the same way that a man who starts out in business sometimes pyramids a small investment into a large corporate empire. To the political entrepreneur who has skill and drive, the political system offers unusual opportunities for pyramiding a small amount of initial resources into a sizable political holding. . . .

. . . [W]e saw how the monopoly over public life enjoyed by the Congregational patrician families of New Haven was destroyed, how the entrepreneurs without inherited social position and education acquired the prerogatives of office, and how these men were in their turn displaced by ex-plebes who lacked the most salient resources of influence possessed by their predecessors: hereditary social status, wealth, business prominence, professional attainments, and frequently even formal education beyond high school. . . .

This change in New Haven is fully consistent with three of the key hypotheses in this study. First, a number of old American cities, of which New Haven is one, have passed through a roughly similar transformation from a system in which resources of influence were highly concentrated to a system in which they are highly dispersed. Second, the present dispersion is a consequence of certain fundamental aspects of the social, economic, and political structures of New Haven. Third, the present dispersion does not represent equality of resources but fragmentation. The revolution in New Haven might be said to constitute a change from a system of *cumulative inequalities* in political resources to a system of noncumulative or *dispersed inequalities* in political resources.

This system of dispersed inequalities is, I believe, marked by the following six characteristics.

1. Many different kinds of resources for influencing officials are available to different citizens.

2. With few exceptions, these resources are unequally distributed.

3. Individuals best off in their access to one kind of resource are often badly off with respect to many other resources.

4. No one influence resource dominates all the others in all or even in most key decisions.

5. With some exceptions, an influence resource is effective in some issue areas or in some specific decisions but not in all.

6. Virtually no one, and certainly no group of more than a few individuals, is entirely lacking in some influence resources.

If, as we have just hypothesized, New Haven is a system of dispersed inequalities possessing the six characteristics of such a system, how does this help us to account for the patterns of influence described in earlier chapters [of *Who Governs?*—ED.]?

One way to answer the question is to look at the ways in which resources are distributed in New Haven. It would be tedious to examine in detail *all* the kinds of resources existing in the community. Keeping in mind the great variety of political resources listed a moment ago, we can proceed to consider a list of resources short enough to be manageable and yet long enough to permit us to test some alternative explanations for the distribution, patterns, and changes of influence in New Haven. This shortened list of political resources will consist of social standing, . . . access to cash, credit, and wealth . . . access to certain resources at the disposal of elected leaders, such as the legal powers of public office, popularity, and jobs . . . and control over information. . . .

Consensus as a Process

Most of us, I suppose, are ready to recognize long-run changes in the beliefs expressed by the more articulate segments of the political stratum and the intelligentsia, and we can infer from various kinds of evidence—all of it, alas, highly debatable—that changes of some sort take place over long periods of time in the attitudes about democracy held in the general population. We tend to assume, however, that except for these long-run shifts, beliefs about democracy are more or less static. I want to propose an alternative explanation, namely that democratic beliefs, like other political beliefs, are influenced by a recurring *process* of interchange among political professionals, the political stratum, and the great bulk of the population. The process generates enough agreement on rules and norms so as to permit the system to operate, but agreement tends to be incomplete, and typically it decays. So the process is frequently repeated. "Consensus," then, is not at all a static and unchanging attribute of citizens. It is a variable element in a complex and more or less continuous process.

This process seems to me to have the following characteristics:

1. Over long periods of time the great bulk of the citizens possess a fairly stable set of democratic beliefs at a high level of abstraction. Let me call these beliefs the democratic creed. . . . We can, I think, confidently conclude that most Americans believe in democracy as the best form of government, in the desirability of rights and procedures insuring a goodly measure of majority rule and minority freedom, and in a wide but not necessarily comprehensive electo-

rate. At a somewhat lower level of agreement, probably the great majority of citizens also believe in the essential legitimacy of certain specific American political institutions: the presidency, Congress, the Supreme Court, the states, the local governments, etc.

2. Most citizens assume that the American political system is consistent with the democratic creed. Indeed, the common view seems to be that our system is not only democratic but is perhaps the most perfect expression of democracy that exists anywhere; if deficiencies exist, either they can, and ultimately will, be remedied, or else they reflect the usual gap between ideal and reality that men of common sense take for granted. Moreover, because leading officials with key roles in the legitimate political institutions automatically acquire authority for their views on the proper functioning of the political institutions, as long as these various officials seem to agree, the ordinary citizen is inclined to assume that existing ways of carrying on the public business do not violate, at least in an important way, the democratic creed to which he is committed.

3. Widespread adherence to the democratic creed is produced and maintained by a variety of powerful social processes. Of these, probably formal schooling is the most important. The more formal education an American has, the more democratic formulas he knows, expresses, and presumably believes. But almost the entire adult population has been subjected to *some* degree of indoctrination through the schools. Beliefs acquired in school are reinforced in adult life through normal exposure to the democratic creed, particularly as the creed is articulated by leading political figures and transmitted through the mass media.

These social processes have an enormous impact on the citizen, partly because they begin early in life and partly because the very unanimity with which the creed is espoused makes rejection of it almost impossible. To reject the creed is infinitely more than a simple matter of disagreement. To reject the creed is to reject one's society and one's chances of full acceptance of it—in short, to be an outcast. (As a mental experiment, try to imagine the psychic and social burdens an American child in an American school would incur if he steadfastly denied to himself and others that democracy is the best form of government.)

To reject the democratic creed is in effect to refuse to be an American. As a nation we have taken great pains to insure that few citizens will ever want to do anything so rash, so preposterous—in fact, so wholly un-American. . . . vast social energies have been poured into the process of "Americanization," teaching citizens what is expected in the way of words, beliefs, and behavior if they are to earn acceptance as Americans, for it was obvious to the political stratum that unless the immigrants and their children quickly accepted American political norms, the flood of aliens, particularly from countries with few traditions of self-government, would disrupt the political system. In a characteristic response, the Board of Education of the city of New Haven created a supervisor for Americanization (a post, incidentally, that still exists). . . .

In one form or another the process of Americanization has absorbed enormous social energies all over the United States. As a factor in shaping American behavior and attitudes, the process of Americanization must surely have been as important as the frontier, or industrialization, or urbanization. That regional, ethnic, racial, religious, or economic differences might disrupt the American political system has been a recurring fear among the political stratum of the United States from the very beginning of the republic. Doubtless this anxiety was painfully stimulated by the Civil War. It was aroused again by the influx of immigrants. Throughout the country, then, the political stratum has seen to it that new citizens, young and old, have been properly trained in "American" principles and beliefs. Everywhere, too, the pupils have been highly motivated to talk, look, and believe as Americans should. The result was as astonishing an act of voluntary political and cultural assimilation and speedy elimination of regional, ethnic, and cultural dissimilarities as history can provide. The extent to which Americans agree today on the key propositions about democracy is a measure of the almost unbelievable success of this deliberate attempt to create a seemingly uncoerced nationwide consensus.

4. Despite wide agreement on a general democratic creed, however, citizens frequently disagree on specific applications. Many citizens oppose what some political philosophers would regard as necessary implications of the creed. Many citizens also disagree with the way the creed is actually applied—or perhaps it would be more accurate to say, with the existing rules of the game, the prevailing political norms. Again and again, for example, surveys indicate that a large number of Americans, sometimes even a majority, do not approve of the extension of important rights, liberties, and privileges to individuals and groups that do in fact enjoy them.

A citizen is able to adhere to these seemingly inconsistent beliefs for a great variety of reasons. For one thing, he himself need not see any inconsistency in his beliefs. The creed is so vague (and incomplete) that strict deductions are difficult or impossible even for sophisticated logicians. Moreover, propositions stated in universal terms are rarely assumed by men of common sense to imply universality in practice; to the frequent dismay of logicians, a common tendency of mankind—and not least of Americans—is to qualify universals in application while leaving them intact in rhetoric. Then, too, the capacity for (or interest in) working out a set of consistent political attitudes is rather limited. As the authors of *The American Voter* have shown, most voters seem to operate at a low level of ideological sophistication; even among intelligent (though not necessarily highly educated) citizens, conceptions of politics are often of a simplicity that the political philosopher might find it hard to comprehend. . . . In addition, most citizens operate with a very small fund of political information; often they lack the elementary information required even to be aware of inconsistencies between their views and what is actually happening in the political system, particularly if the subject is (as most questions of rights and procedures are) arcane and complex. Again, questions that bother theorists are often not interesting or salient to most voters; their attention and energies are diverted elsewhere, usually to activities that lie entirely outside the political arena. As long as a citizen believes that democracy is the best political system, that the United States is a democracy, and that the people in office can be trusted, by and large, to apply the abstract creed to specific cases, issues of democratic theory and practice hotly discussed by political philosophers, or even by publicists and columnists, are likely never to penetrate through the manifold barriers to abstract political thinking that are erected by the essentially apolitical culture in which he lives. Finally, even if the issues do manage to get through, many citizens feel themselves incompetent to decide them; this, after all, is what Supreme Court judges, presidents, and members of Congress are supposed to do. Worse yet, many citizens feel that no one in public office will care much about their opinions anyway.

5. Members of the political stratum (who live in a much more politicized culture) are more familiar with the "democratic" norms, more consistent, more ideological, more detailed and explicit in their political attitudes, and more completely in agreement on the norms. They are more in agreement not only on what norms are implied by the abstract democratic creed but also in supporting the norms currently operating. This relatively higher degree of support for the prevailing norms in the existing political system is generated and maintained by a variety of processes. Because members of the political stratum have on the average considerably more formal education than the population as a whole, they have been more thoroughly exposed to the creed and its implications. Because they are more involved in, concerned with, and articulate about politics, they invest more time and effort in elaborating a consistent ideology. Because they participate more extensively in politics, they more frequently express and defend their views, encounter criticism, and face the charge of inconsistency. They know more about politics, read more, experience more, see more.

Within the political stratum, the professionals tend to agree even more on what the norms should be, what they are, and the desirability of maintaining them substantially as they are. Agreement among the professionals is generated by all the factors that account for it among the rest of the political stratum and even among the apolitical strata. Mastery over the existing norms of the political system represents the particular stockpile of skills peculiar to the professional's vocation. Norms also tend to legitimate his power and position in the political system, furnish an agreed-on method of getting on with the immediate tasks at hand, carry the authority of tradition, and help to reduce the baffling uncertainty that surrounds the professional's every choice. Finally, the professional is likely to support the existing norms because his own endorsement of existing norms was initially a criterion in his own recruitment and advancement; complex processes of political selection and rejection tend to exclude the deviant who challenges the prevailing norms of the existing political system. Most of the professionals might properly be called democratic "legitimists."

6. The professionals, of course, have access to extensive political resources which they employ at a high rate with superior efficiency. Consequently, a challenge to the existing norms is bound to be costly to the challenger, for legitimist professionals can quickly shift their skills and resources into the urgent task of doing in the dissenter. As long as the professionals remain substantially legitimist in outlook, therefore, the critic is likely to make little headway. Indeed, the chances are that anyone who advocates extensive changes in the prevailing democratic norms is likely to be treated by the professionals, and even by a fair share of the political stratum, as an outsider, possibly even as a crackpot whose views need not be seriously debated. No worse fate can befall the dissenter, for unless he can gain the attention of the political stratum, it is difficult for him to gain space in the mass media; if he cannot win space in the mass media, it is difficult for him to win a large following; if he cannot win a large following, it is difficult for him to gain the attention of the political stratum.

7. Sometimes, of course, disagreements over the prevailing norms occur within the political stratum and among the professionals themselves. But these disagreements need not, and perhaps ordinarily do not, produce much effort to involve the general public in the dispute. The disagreements are not, to be sure, secret; the electorate is not *legally* barred from finding out about the conflict and becoming involved. It does not need to be. Given the low salience of politics in the life of the average citizen, most conflicts over the prevailing norms might attract more attention if they were held behind locked doors. Unless a professional is willing to invest very great resources in whipping up public interest, he is not likely to get much effective support. In any case, public involvement may seem undesirable to the legitimist, for alterations in the prevailing norms are often subtle matters, better obtained by negotiation than by the crudities and oversimplifications of public debate.

8. Among the rules and procedures supported strongly by the legitimists in the political stratum, and particularly by the professionals, are some that prescribe ways of settling disagreements as to rules and procedures. These involve appeals to authorities who give decisions widely accepted as binding, authoritative, and legitimate—though not necessarily as "good" or "correct." Typically these include appeals to courts or quasi-judicial institutions that ostensibly arrive at their decisions by appeals to norms, codes, formulas, and beliefs that appear to transcend partisan and policy differences in the political stratum.

9. Ordinarily, then, it is not difficult for a stable system of rights and privileges to exist that, at least in important details, does not have widespread

public support and occasionally even lacks majority approval. As long as the matter is not a salient public issue—and whether it is or not depends partly on how the political stratum handles it—the question is substantially determined within the political stratum itself. When disagreements arise, these are adjudicated by officials who share the beliefs of the political stratum rather than those of the populace; and even when these officials adopt positions that do not command the undivided support of the political stratum, members of the political stratum, and particularly the professionals, tend to accept a decision as binding until and unless it can be changed through the accepted procedures. This is the essence of their code of democratic legitimism.

10. Occasionally, however, a sizable segment of the political stratum develops doubts that it can ever achieve the changes it seeks through accepted procedures that are, in a sense, internal to the political stratum and the professionals. One or more of these dissenters may push his way into the professional group, or the dissenters may be numerous and vocal enough to acquire a spokesman or two among the professionals. The strategy of the dissenters may now begin to shift. Instead of adjudicating the matter according to the accepted procedures, the dissenters attempt to arouse public support for their proposals, hoping that when a sufficient number of voters are won over to their cause, other professionals—legitimist or not—will have to come around.

The professionals, as I have said, live in a world of uncertainty. They search for omens and portents. If the auguries indicate that the appeal to the populace has failed, then the legitimists may confidently close ranks against the dissenter. But if the auguries are uncertain or unfavorable, then the legitimists, too, are forced to make a counterappeal to the populace.

If the dissenters succeed in forcing the issue out beyond the political stratum, and dissenters and legitimists begin making appeals to the populace, then the nature of the debate begins to change. Technical questions, subtle distinctions, fine matters of degree are shed. The appeal is now shaped to the simple democratic creed which nearly every citizen believes in. Because the creed does not constitute a tightly logical system, it is possible for the legitimists to demonstrate that existing norms are necessary consequences of the creed, and for the dissenters to show that existing norms run counter to the creed. Because the creed is deeply laden with tradition and sentiment, emotion rises and reasoned discussion declines.

11. Ordinary citizens who normally remain outside these debates now find their attention—and their votes—solicited by both sides. They become aware that the very officials who ordinarily decide these matters, to whom the citizen himself turns for his cues as to what is legitimate and consistent with the creed, are locked in deadly, heated battle. These citizens must now find ways of applying the creed to the issue. One way is to withdraw even more deeply into the political shadows; a citizen can simply refuse to choose. Many do. In March

1937, at the height of the debate over President Roosevelt's proposal to enlarge the Supreme Court, 50 percent of the people interviewed in a Gallup poll had listened to neither of the president's two recent radio speeches defending his plan. A month later, one out of seven persons who were asked whether Congress should pass the president's bill expressed no opinion. . . . In New Haven, after several years of public discussion and debate over charter reform, when a sample of registered voters was asked in 1959 whether they personally would do anything if a revision of the charter was proposed that would make the mayor stronger, over 40 percent of those who disapproved of such an idea said they would do nothing to oppose it, and nearly three-quarters of those who approved said they would do nothing to support it. (These seemed to be tolerably honest responses; in the preceding election, after wide discussion among the political stratum and hot debate among the professionals over a new charter, less than half the voters who went to the polls even bothered to vote on the charter.) Thus when dissenters and legitimists appeal to the populace to settle questions they ordinarily decide among themselves, they cannot be at all sure that they will actually produce much of a response no matter how much they try to stir up the public.

However, citizens who *do* make up their minds must find some ways for arriving at a choice. For many citizens the decision is eased by their existing loyalties to parties or political leaders. In April 1937, 68 percent of the Democrats in a Gallup poll said that Congress should pass Roosevelt's court plan; 93 percent of the Republicans said Congress should not. Those who had no strong party identifications were, as one might expect, split—42 percent in favor and 58 percent against. . . .

If the parties give no clear guidance, citizens may look to particular leaders or institutions. They may turn to spokesmen in their churches, for example, or trade unions, or regions. They often turn, of course, to attitudes prevalent in their own circle of intimates, friends, associates, acquaintances. If their search yields no consistent cues, they may give up. In the struggle over charter reform in New Haven in 1958, when Democratic leaders were split from the top down, judging from a sample of registered voters interviewed shortly after the election the proportion of people who went to the polls and voted in the general election but did not vote either for or against the charter was higher among Democrats than among either Republicans or independents.

12. An appeal to the populace may terminate in several ways. The appeal may simply fail to create a stir. Interest in political matters wanes rather quickly; since complex issues of democratic norms nearly always lack a direct relation to the ongoing life of an individual, they have even less capacity for holding attention than many other issues. However passionately the dissenters feel about their case, life does move on, old questions become tiresome, and the newspapers begin to shove the conflict to the inside pages. Perhaps the legitimists,

buoyed by their reading of the electorate, defeat the dissenters in a clear-cut trial of strength and, having done so, close ranks and go on to the next business. Perhaps the dissenters win, or a compromise is worked out; if so the dissenters, like as not, turn into the next generation of legitimists.

THE ROLE OF DEMOCRATIC BELIEFS

The specific beliefs of the average citizen thus have a rather limited though important function. Ordinarily, conflicts over democratic norms are resolved among the professionals, with perhaps some involvement by parts of the political stratum but little or no involvement by most citizens. Thus the fact that a large number of citizens do not believe in the political norms actually applied, particularly extending political liberties to unpopular individuals and groups, has slight effect on the outcome.

The beliefs of the ordinary citizen become relevant only when professionals engage in an intensive appeal to the populace. Even then, the actual outcome of the appeal does not necessarily reflect majority attitudes at all accurately. These are not always known; they are guessed at in a variety of inaccurate ways, and they have to be filtered through the tighter mesh of the political stratum and the professionals before they can become public policy.

Nonetheless, wide consensus on the democratic creed does have two important kinds of consequences. On the one hand, this very consensus makes occasional appeal all but inevitable, for the creed itself gives legitimacy to an appeal to the populace. On the other hand, widespread adherence to the creed limits the character and the course of an appeal. It insures that no appeal is likely to succeed unless it is framed in terms consistent with the creed—which is perhaps not so small a constraint. Some solutions pretty evidently are *not* consistent. Because an appeal must take place in the face of criticism from legitimists and extensive appraisal by members of the political stratum, blatant inconsistencies are likely to be exposed. Moreover, because the appeal is legitimized by the creed, it provides an orderly way to conduct a dispute that exceeds the capacities of the professionals to resolve among themselves.

No one, I imagine, has ever supposed that the existence of the creed entails no risks. People can be deceived by appeals intended to destroy democracy in the name of democracy. Dissenters who believe in the democratic creed may unwittingly advocate or legitimists may insist on preserving rules of the game destined to have unforeseen and unintended consequences disastrous to the stability and perhaps the survival of the democracy.

Nonetheless, we can be reasonably sure of this: even if universal belief in a democratic creed does not guarantee the stability of a democratic system, a substantial decline in the popular consensus would greatly increase the chance of serious instability. How the professionals act, what they advocate, what they are likely to believe, are all constrained by the wide adherence to the creed that exists throughout the community. If a substantial segment of the electorate begins to doubt the creed, professionals will quickly come forth to fan that doubt. The nature and course of an appeal to the populace will change. What today is a question of applying the fundamental norms of democracy will become tomorrow an inquiry into the validity of these norms. If a substantial number of citizens begin to deny not merely to *some* minorities but to minorities *as such* the rights and powers prescribed in the creed, an appeal to the populace is likely to end sooner or later in a call to arms.

Thus consensus on political beliefs and practices has much in common with other aspects of a democratic system. Here, too, leaders lead—and often are led. Citizens are very far indeed from exerting equal influence over the content, application, and development of the political consensus. Yet widely held beliefs by Americans in a creed of democracy and political equality serve as a critical limit on the ways in which leaders can shape the consensus.

Neither the prevailing consensus, the creed, nor even the political system itself are immutable products of democratic ideas, beliefs, and institutions inherited from the past. For better or worse, they are always open, in some measure, to alteration through those complex processes of symbiosis and change that constitute the relations of leaders and citizens in a pluralistic democracy.

PART V

The Critique of Democratic Elitism

SELECTION 14
FROM
*The Public and Its Problems**

JOHN DEWEY

WHEN WE SAY THAT thinking and beliefs should be experimental, not absolutistic, we have then in mind a certain logic of method, not, primarily, the carrying on of experimentation like that of laboratories. Such a logic involves the following factors: First, that those concepts, general principles, theories, and dialectical developments which are indispensable to any systematic knowledge be shaped and tested as tools of inquiry. Secondly, that policies and proposals for social action be treated as working hypotheses, not as programs to be rigidly adhered to and executed. They will be experimental in the sense that they will be entertained subject to constant and well-equipped observation of the consequences they entail when acted upon and subject to ready and flexible revision in the light of observed consequences. The social sciences, if these two stipulations are fulfilled, will then be an apparatus for conducting investigation, and for recording and interpreting (organizing) its results. The apparatus will no longer be taken to be itself knowledge, but will be seen to be intellectual means of making discoveries of phenomena having social import and understanding their meaning. Differences of opinion in the sense of differences of judgment as to the course which it is best to follow, the policy which it is best to try out, will still exist. But opinion in the sense of beliefs formed and held in the absence of evidence will be reduced in quantity and importance. No longer will views generated in view of special situations be frozen into absolute standards and masquerade as eternal truths.

This phase of the discussion may be concluded by consideration of the relation of experts to a democratic public. A negative phase of the earlier argument for political democracy has largely lost its force. For it was based upon hostility to dynastic and oligarchic aristocracies, and these have largely been reft of power. The oligarchy which now dominates is that of an economic class. It claims to rule, not in virtue of birth and hereditary status, but in virtue of ability in management and of the burden of social responsibilities which it carries, in

*(Denver, CO: Alan Swallow, n. d.): pp. 202–11, 216–19. Originally published in 1927.

virtue of the position which superior abilities have conferred upon it. At all events, it is a shifting, unstable oligarchy, rapidly changing its constituents, who are more or less at the mercy of accidents they cannot control and of technological inventions. Consequently, the shoe is now on the other foot. It is argued that the check upon the oppressive power of this particular oligarchy lies in an intellectual aristocracy, not in appeal to an ignorant, fickle mass whose interests are superficial and trivial, and whose judgments are saved from incredible levity only when weighted down by heavy prejudice.

It may be argued that the democratic movement was essentially transitional. It marked the passage from feudal institutions to industrialism, and was coincident with the transfer of power from landed proprietors, allied to churchly authorities, to captains of industry, under conditions which involved an emancipation of the masses from legal limitations which had previously hemmed them in. But, so it is contended in effect, it is absurd to convert this legal liberation into a dogma which alleges that release from old oppressions confers upon those emancipated the intellectual and moral qualities which fit them for sharing in regulation of affairs of state. The essential fallacy of the democratic creed, it is urged, is the notion that a historic movement which effected an important and desirable release from restrictions is either a source or a proof of capacity in those thus emancipated to rule, when in fact there is no factor common in the two things. The obvious alternative is rule by those intellectually qualified, by expert intellectuals.

This revival of the Platonic notion that philosophers should be kings is the more taking because the idea of experts is substituted for that of philosophers, since philosophy has become something of a joke, while the image of the specialist, the expert in operation, is rendered familiar and congenial by the rise of the physical sciences and by the conduct of industry. A cynic might indeed say that the notion is a pipe dream, a reverie entertained by the intellectual class in compensation for an impotence consequent upon the divorce of theory and practice, upon the remoteness of specialized science from the affairs of life: the gulf being bridged not by the intellectuals but by inventors and engineers hired by captains of industry. One approaches the truth more nearly when one says that the argument proves too much for its own cause. If the masses are as intellectually irredeemable as its premise implies, they at all events have both too many desires and too much power to permit rule by experts to obtain. The very ignorance, bias, frivolity, jealousy, instability, which are alleged to incapacitate them from share in political affairs, unfit them still more for passive submission to rule by intellectuals. Rule by an economic class may be disguised from the masses; rule by experts could not be covered up. It could be made to work only if the intellectuals became the willing tools of big economic interests. Otherwise they would have to ally themselves with the masses, and that implies, one more, a share in government by the latter.

A more serious objection is that expertness is most readily attained in specialized technical matters, matters of administration and execution which postulate that general policies are already satisfactorily framed. It is assumed that the policies of the experts are in the main both wise and benevolent, that is, framed to conserve the genuine interests of society. The final obstacle in the way of any aristocratic rule is that in the absence of an articulate voice on the part of the masses, the best do not and cannot remain the best, the wise cease to be wise. It is impossible for highbrows to secure a monopoly of such knowledge as must be used for the regulation of common affairs. In the degree in which they become a specialized class, they are shut off from knowledge of the needs which they are supposed to serve.

The strongest point to be made in behalf of even such rudimentary political forms as democracy has already attained, popular voting, majority rule and so on, is that to some extent they involve a consultation and discussion which uncover social needs and troubles. This fact is the great asset on the side of the political ledger. De Tocqueville wrote it down almost a century ago in his survey of the prospects of democracy in the United States. Accusing a democracy of a tendency to prefer mediocrity in its elected rules, and admitting its exposure to gusts of passion and its openness to folly, he pointed out in effect that popular government is educative as other modes of political regulation are not. It forces a recognition that there are common interests, even though the recognition of *what* they are is confused; and the need it enforces of discussion and publicity brings about some clarification of what they are. The man who wears the shoe knows best that it pinches and where it pinches, even if the expert shoemaker is the best judge of how the trouble is to be remedied. Popular government has at least created public spirit even if its success in informing that spirit has not been great.

A class of experts is inevitably so removed from common interests as to become a class with private interests and private knowledge, which in social matters is not knowledge at all. The ballot is, as often said, a substitute for bullets. But what is more significant is that counting of heads compels prior recourse to methods of discussion, consultation, and persuasion, while the essence of appeal to force is to cut short resort to such methods. Majority rule, just as majority rule, is as foolish as its critics charge it with being. But it never is *merely* majority rule. As a practical politician, Samuel J. Tilden, said a long time ago: "The means by which a majority comes to be a majority is the more important thing": antecedent debates, modification of views to meet the opinions of minorities, the relative satisfaction given the latter by the fact that it has had a chance and that next time it may be successful in becoming a majority. Think of the meaning of the "problem of minorities" in certain European states, and compare it with the status of minorities in countries having popular government. It is true that all valuable as well as new ideas begin with minorities, perhaps a minority of one. The important consideration is that opportunity be given that idea to spread and to become the possession of the multitude. No government by experts in which the masses do not have the chance to inform the experts as to their needs can be anything but an oligarchy managed in the interests of the few. And the enlightenment must proceed in ways which force the administrative specialists to take account of the needs. The world has suffered more from leaders and authorities than from the masses.

The essential need, in other words, is the improvement of the methods and conditions of debate, discussion, and persuasion. That is *the* problem of the public. We have asserted that this improvement depends essentially upon freeing and perfecting the processes of inquiry and of dissemination of their conclusions. Inquiry, indeed, is a work which devolves upon experts. But their expertness is not shown in framing and executing policies, but in discovering and making known the facts upon which the former depend. They are technical experts in the sense that scientific investigators and artists manifest *expertise*. It is not necessary that the many should have the knowledge and skill to carry on the needed investigations; what is required is that they have the ability to judge of the bearing of the knowledge supplied by others upon common concerns.

It is easy to exaggerate the amount of intelligence and ability demanded to render such judgments fitted for their purpose. In the first place, we are likely to form our estimate on the basis of present conditions. But indubitably one great trouble at present is that the data for good judgment are lacking; and no innate faculty of mind can make up for the absence of facts. Until secrecy, prejudice, bias, misrepresentation, and propaganda as well as sheer ignorance are replaced by inquiry and publicity, we have no way of telling how apt for judgment of social policies the existing intelligence of the masses may be. It would certainly go much further than at present. In the second place, *effective* intelligence is not an original, innate endowment. No matter what are the differences in native intelligence (allowing for the moment that intelligence can be native), the actuality of mind is dependent upon the education which social conditions effect. Just as the specialized mind and knowledge of the past is embodied in implements, utensils, devices, and technologies which those of a grade of intelligence which could not produce them can now intelligently use, so it will be when currents of public knowledge blow through social affairs.

The level of action fixed by *embodied* intelligence is always the important thing. In savage culture a superior man will be superior to his fellows, but his knowledge and judgment will lag in many matters far behind that of an inferiorly endowed person in an advanced civilization. Capacities are limited by the objects and tools at hand. They are still more dependent upon the prevailing habits of attention and interest which are set by tradition and institutional customs. Meanings run in the channels formed by instrumentalities of which, in the end, language, the vehicle of thought as well as of communication, is the most important. A mechanic can discourse of ohms and amperes as Sir Isaac Newton could not in his day. Many a man who has tinkered with radios can judge of things which Faraday did not dream of. It is aside from the point to say that if Newton and Faraday were here now, the amateur and mechanic would be infants beside them. The retort only brings out the point: the difference made by different objects to think of and by different meanings in circulation. A more intelligent state of social affairs, one more informed with knowledge, more directed by intelligence, would not improve original endowments one whit, but it would raise the level upon which the intelligence of all operates. The height of this level is much more important for judgment of public concerns than are differences in intelligence quotients. As Santayana has said:

> Could a better system prevail in our lives a better order would establish itself in our thinking. It has not been for want of keen senses, or personal genius, or a constant order in the outer world, that mankind has fallen back repeatedly into barbarism and superstition. It has been for want of good character, good example, and good government.

The notion that intelligence is a personal endowment or personal attainment is the great conceit of the intellectual class, as that of the commercial class is that wealth is something which they personally have wrought and possess.

Whatever the future may have in store, one thing is certain. Unless local communal life can be restored, the public cannot adequately resolve its most urgent problem: to find and identify itself. But if it be reestablished, it will manifest a fullness, variety, and freedom of possession and enjoyment of meanings and goods unknown in the contiguous associations of the past. For it will be alive and flexible as well as stable, responsive to the complex and worldwide scene in which it is enmeshed. While local, it will not be isolated. Its larger relationships will provide an exhaustible and flowing fund of meanings upon which to draw, with assurance that its drafts will be honored. Territorial states and political boundaries will persist; but they will not be barriers which impoverish experience by cutting man off from his fellows; they will not be hard and fast divisions whereby external separation is converted into inner jealousy, fear, suspicion, and hostility. Competition will continue, but it will be less rivalry for acquisition of material goods and more an emulation of local groups to enrich direct experience with appreciatively enjoyed intellectual and artistic wealth. If the technological age can provide mankind with a firm and general basis of material security, it will be absorbed in a humane age. It will take its place as an instrumentality of shared and communicated experience. But without passage through a machine age, mankind's hold upon what is needful as the precondition of a free, flexible, and many-colored life is so precarious and inequitable that competitive scramble for acquisition and frenzied use of the results of acquisition for purposes of excitation and display will be perpetuated.

We have said that consideration of this particular condition of the generation of democratic communities and an articulate democratic public carries us beyond the question of intellectual method into that of practical procedure. But the two questions are not disconnected. The problem of securing diffused and seminal intelligence can be solved only in the degree in which local communal life becomes a reality. Signs and symbols, language, are the means of communication by which a fraternally shared experience is ushered in and sustained. But the wingèd words of conversation in immediate intercourse have a vital import lacking in the fixed and frozen words of written speech. Systematic and continuous inquiry into all the conditions which affect association and their dissemination in print is a precondition of the creation of a true public. But it and its results are but tools after all. Their final actuality is accomplished in face-to-face relationships by means of direct give-and-take. Logic in its fulfillment recurs to the primitive sense of the word: dialogue. Ideas which are not communicated, shared, and reborn in expression are but soliloquy, and soliloquy is but broken and imperfect thought. It, like the acquisition of material wealth, marks a diversion of the wealth created by associated endeavor and exchange to private ends. It is more genteel, and it is called more noble. But there is no difference in kind.

In a word, that expansion and reinforcement of personal understanding and judgment by the cumulative and transmitted intellectual wealth of the community which may render nugatory the indictment of democracy drawn on the basis of the ignorance, bias and levity of the masses, can be fulfilled only in the relations of personal intercourse in the local community. The connections of the ear with vital and outgoing thought and emotion are immensely closer and more varied than those of the eye. Vision is a spectator; hearing is a participator. Publication is partial and the public which results is partially informed and formed until the meanings it purveys pass from mouth to mouth. There is no limit to the liberal expansion and confirmation of limited personal intellectual endowment which may proceed from the flow of social intelligence when that circulates by word of mouth from one to another in the communications of the local community. That and that only gives reality to public opinion. We lie, as Emerson said, in the lap of an immense intelligence. But that intelligence is dormant and its communications are broken, inarticulate, and faint until it possesses the local community as its medium.

SELECTION 15

FROM
The Theory of Democratic Elitism[*]

PETER BACHRACH

WHILE IT IS TRUE that there are many theories of democracy, . . . it is also true that there is a general theory of democracy which is supported by most leading theorists and which reflects the main currents of thought in social science today. It is a theory largely explanatory rather than normative in approach; directed toward clarifying ongoing democratic systems rather than suggesting how they ought to operate. Yet it is a theory which reflects, on the one hand, a receptiveness toward the existing structure of power and elite decision making in large industrial societies, and on the other, an impatience with old myths and sentiments associated with phrases such as "will of the people," "grass-roots democracy," and "the dignity of the common man."

This general theory purports to be above ideology but is in reality deeply rooted in an ideology, an ideology which is grounded upon a profound distrust of the majority of ordinary men and women, and a reliance upon the established elites to maintain the values of civility and the "rules of the game" of democracy. It is an ideology which is closely attached to and protective of the liberal principles embodied in the rule of law and in the rights of the individual to freedom of conscience, expression, and privacy. While embracing liberalism it rejects, in effect, the major tenet of classical democratic theory—belief and confidence in the people. The suspicion that liberalism and classical theory are fundamentally incompatible is manifested in the key explanatory concepts of democratic elitism.

Democracy conceived solely as a political method is one of these concepts. Since democracy is not seen as embodying an overriding objective, such as enhancing the self-esteem and development of the individual, the democratic-elite theorist frees himself from the charge that democratic means have failed to

---

[*] *The Theory of Democratic Elitism: A Critique* (Boston, MA: Little Brown, 1967): pp. 93–98, 100–102.

achieve democratic ends. He holds only that democracy must be self-perpetuating as method, and thus able to secure the open society through time. In focusing upon openness qua openness—avoiding the question of openness for whom—he is in a position to show that the system is in good health, while acknowledging at the same time that a large number of people are probably alienated from the social and political life around them.

While the concept of democracy as political method is not inherently elitist, it does serve as a formidable defense of the elite-mass structure of ongoing democratic systems. The charge, for example, that the common man is not given sufficient opportunity to participate in meaningful decision making and is therefore deprived of an essential means to develop his faculties and broaden his outlook is, under this concept, irrelevant. For conceived as political method, the standard for judging democracy is not the degree of centralization or devolution in the decision-making process but rather the degree to which the system conforms to the basic principles of the democratic method: political equality (universal suffrage), freedom of discussion, majority rule, free periodic elections, and the like. When these principles are adhered to, the system is characterized by the accountability of political elites to nonelites. And in being held accountable, the former, owing to the phenomenon of anticipated reactions, normally rules in the interests of the latter. Thus, although democracy as a political method is defined in terms of procedural principles, it invariably is defended today on the basis of its service to the interests of the people.

This defense of democracy construes the interests of the people narrowly and the democratic elite theorist has little difficulty in accepting it. He posits that the value of the democratic system for ordinary individuals should be measured by the degree to which the "outputs" of the system, in the form of security, services, and material support, benefit them. On the basis of this reasoning, the less the individual has to participate in politics on the "input" and demand side of the system in order to gain his interests on the output side, the better off he is. With rare exception elites are available to represent his interest in the decision-making process, relegating to him the comparatively painless task of paying nominal dues and occasionally attending a meeting and casting a ballot. By assuming a one-dimensional view of political interest, the democratic elitist is led to the conclusion that there is a natural division of labor within a democratic system between elite rule and nonelite interest.

By conceiving of man's political interest solely in terms of that which accrues to him from government, the democratic elitist implicitly rejects the contention of classical theorists that interests also include the opportunity for development which accrues from participation in meaningful political decisions. This two-dimensional view of political interests—interests as end results and interest in the process of participation—is rejected by the democratic elitists on the ground that it has little relevance to the reality of political life in large-scale industrial societies, and that it is based on the concept of equality of power in decision making which is completely at odds with existing practices in modern democracies, where key political decisions must of necessity be made by a small minority. The main thrust of the elitist argument is incontestable. However, although participation in key political decisions on the national level must remain extremely limited, is there any sound reason, within the context of democratic theory, why participation in political decisions by the constituencies of "private" bureaucratic institutions of power could not be widely extended on those issues which primarily affect their lives within these institutions?

The answer to the question turns on what constitutes "political." If private organizations, at least the more powerful among them, were considered political—on the ground that they are organs which regularly share in authoritatively allocating values for society—then there would be a compelling case, in terms of the democratic principle of equality of power, to expand participation in decision making within these organizations. . . . This could be achieved by radically altering their hierarchical structures to facilitate the devolution of the decision-making process. However, if one holds, as the democratic elite theorist does, to a narrow and institutional concept of "political" (when referring to political elites and political equality), this line of reasoning is effectively excluded from democratic theory. If "political" is confined to governmental decision making and that which relates to it, the clearly nongovernmental institutions, irrespective of the power which they may wield and the impact of their decisions on society, are not political. And in being not political, they are exempt, as far as the reach of democratic theory goes, from democratization.

The importance to the theory of democratic elitism of interpreting narrowly the integral and key concept "political" cannot be overemphasized. First, on the basis of this interpretation, the argument for expanding democracy to encompass a portion of the economic sector can be discarded out of hand as irrelevant. Democracy is a *political* method, neither intended nor designed to operate beyond the political realm. Second, this narrow concept supports the legitimacy of the elite decision-making process within the corporations and other large private institutions. It is common knowledge that corporate elites, who regularly make decisions directly affecting social values, are accountable largely, if not solely, to themselves. But this is not considered to be an irresponsible exercise of political power since corporate managers act as private citizens on nonpolitical matters. Finally, and most important, by accepting a rigid and narrow concept of "political," the elite theorist removes from consideration (within the context of democratic theory) the question of the feasibility of increasing participation in decision making by enlarging the political scope to include the more powerful private institutions. The existing elite-nonelite relationship is consequently made immune to attack by democratic theorists loyal to the classical tradition.

If the area of politics is conceived narrowly for purposes of democratic theory, then it is understandable that the principle of equality of power, long identified as an ideal of democracy, must give way to the more realistic principle of equality of opportunity to obtain a position of power. For the former principle is only meaningful as an ideal to strive for in a society in which there is hope of obtaining a more equalitarian base for decision making. The latter principle is suited to a political system in which power is highly stratified.

In sum, the explanatory side of democratic elite theory, in the form of its conceptualization of "method," "interest," "political," and "equality," unmistakably leads to a twofold conclusion: (1) ongoing democratic systems, characterized by elite rule and mass passivity, handsomely meet the requirements of democratic theory; and (2) any suggestion that a departure from the system in the direction of obtaining a more equalitarian relationship between elites and nonelites is, on objective grounds, unrealistic.

These conclusions are in harmony with and support the normative judgment, as reflected in the writing of democratic elitists, that the illiberal propensity of the masses is the overriding threat to the free society, which, if it does survive, will do so because of the wisdom and courage of established elites. The theory of democratic elitism is not a theory of the status quo. For on the one hand it is completely in tune with the rapid change toward greater concentration of power in the hands of managerial elites, and on the other, it manifests an uneasiness that, in the absence of the creation of an elite consensus, the system is doomed.

Classical theory, as I emphasized at the outset of this essay, is based on the supposition that man's dignity, and indeed his growth and development as a functioning and responsive individual in a free society, is dependent upon an opportunity to participate actively in decisions that significantly affect him. . . .

. . . Stripped of normative ends, political theory, including democratic theory, cannot perform the crucial function of providing direction to man's actions. To argue that we must be content to struggle modestly forward by combating social evil as it arises is to assume that a series of incremental moves to combat various evils will add up over time to a step forward. That need not be and often is not the case. In any event, the fundamental issue is not whether democracy should or should not have an overriding objective; it is rather whether its objective should be implicitly dedicated to the viability of a democratic elitist system or explicitly to the self-development of the individual.

In opting for the latter objective, I believe that a theory of democracy should be based upon the following assumptions and principles: the majority of individuals stand to gain in self-esteem and growth toward a fuller affirmation of their personalities by participating more actively in meaningful community decisions;* people generally, therefore, have a twofold interest in politics—interest in end results and interest in the process of participation; benefits from the latter interest are closely related to the degree to which the principle of equality of power is realized; and progress toward the realization of this principle is initially dependent upon the acceptance by social scientists of a realistic concept of what constitutes the political sector of society.

The elite-mass structure of present-day society is very much a reality. But it is an unalterable structure only if political decision making is viewed narrowly, as governmental decision making. I have argued that such a view is untenable, that the evidence will simply not support a *twofold* definition of "political." To define "political" broadly for general purposes and then, when concerned with the meaning of political elites or political equality, to retreat to a nineteenth-century notion of the concept is to remove an important area of politics from political research. If the political scientist is to be realistic, he must recognize that large areas within existing so-called private centers of power are political and therefore potentially open to a wide and democratic sharing in decision making.

---

*. . . Under what concrete conditions will man's capacities be developed and under what conditions will development be frustrated? How will democratic theory provide the developmental conditions? Definitive answers to these questions must await empirical research. Tentatively, however, I would suggest that beneficial results from participation can best be assured if two conditions are present: (1) that the participants are roughly equal in the power they are capable of exerting in the decision-making process; (2) that diverse interests are represented within the participating group. The first condition would tend to prevent manipulation and the second would tend to prevent the pressures of conformity from being overbearing on those sharing in the decision-making process. Democratic theory must therefore include among its principles equality of power and pluralism.

SELECTION 16
FROM
*The Ruling Elites**

KENNETH PREWITT AND ALAN STONE

PLATO'S *REPUBLIC*, THEN, IS protected from tendencies toward irresponsible rulers or decay in the ruling class *by the values of the ruling class itself*. It is to the inward convictions of the elite that we turn for an explanation of how to stabilize the just society. That is, the safeguard against unjust rule was to have just rulers. And the way in which to get these rulers is to educate and nurture them in the values of the republic.

In somewhat disguised forms, the Platonic ideal lingers on in contemporary thought. Certainly there are strains of Platonism in various interpretations of the viability and stability of representative democracy in America. These interpretations proceed in four steps.

1. The mass public in the United States has an uncomfortably low regard for democratic rights and procedures. Although the public agrees to an abstract democratic creed, when the issue of specific application faces it, the public has low levels of tolerance for free speech, deviant political opinions, judicial processes, and the like. More than a quarter of the general electorate feels that the majority has a right to outlaw minorities if it wants to; and, again, a quarter of the populace reports that we cannot afford to depend on the slow and unreliable methods of courts in dealing with dangerous enemies like the Communists. Approximately half the population would deny the vote to those who cannot do so intelligently; and again half the populace would prevent publication of a book that contains "wrong" political views, while nearly three-fifths reject the idea that freedom implies the right to teach "foreign ideas" in our schools. . . . These and similar survey findings have caused some question about the mass public as a repository of the values of democracy.

2. The same surveys, however, show the political leadership to have a consistently firmer grasp of and commitment to the democratic creed. Writing of political influentials, one commentator notes that this commitment to democracy is "evidenced in their stronger approval of democratic ideas, their greater

*(New York: Harper & Row, 1973): Ch. 8, pp. 189–204, 213–21.

tolerance and regard for proper procedures and citizen rights; their superior understanding and acceptance of the 'rules of the game,' and their more affirmative attitudes toward the political system in general." This author continues,

> Compared with the electorate, whose ordinary members are submerged in an ideological babble of poorly informed and discordant opinions, the members of the political minority inhabit a world in which political ideas are vastly more salient, intellectual consistency is more frequently demanded, attitudes are related to principles, actions are connected to beliefs, "correct" opinions are rewarded and "incorrect" opinions are punished. . . . The net effect of these influences is to heighten their sensitivity to political ideas and to unite them more firmly behind the values of the American tradition. . . .

3. The manner in which the elite come to hold to the democratic values bears more than a little resemblance to Plato's hopes in *The Republic*. The political influentials constitute, in effect,

> a subculture with its own peculiar set of norms of behavior, motives, and approved standards. Processes of indoctrination internalize such norms among those who are born to or climb to positions of power and leadership; they serve as standards of action, which are reinforced by a social discipline among the political activists.

. . . Another student of American democracy reasons in a similar vein about the effects of political recruitment: The political professional

> is likely to support the existing norms because his own endorsement of existing norms was initially a criterion in his own recruitment and advancement; complex processes of political selection and rejection tend to exclude the deviant who challenges the prevailing norms of the existing political system. Most of the professionals might properly be called democratic "legitimists." . . .

An emphasis on recruitment, training, and education also accounts for the failure among the public to appreciate and defend the principles of democracy:

> Democratic beliefs and habits are obviously not "natural" but must be learned; and they are learned more slowly by men and women whose lives are circumscribed by apathy, ignorance, provincialism and social or physical distance from the centers of intellectual activity. In the absence of knowledge and experience—as we can readily observe from the fidgety course of growth in newly emerging nations—the presuppositions and complex obligations of democracy, the rights it grants and the self-restraints it imposes, cannot be quickly comprehended. Even in a highly developed nation like the United States, millions of people continue to possess only the most rudimentary understanding of democratic ideology. . . .

4. The inference drawn from these three observations is reminiscent of the Platonic concept. Democratic viability and social stability are saved by the elite, not by mass participation. Indeed, it is to the benefit of society that

> those who are most confused about democratic ideas are also likely to be politically apathetic and without significant influence. Their role in the nation's decision process is so small that their "misguided" opinions or nonopinions have little practical consequence for stability.

. . . Their passive rule is countered by the active defense of democracy by the elite.

> The longer one frets with the puzzle of how democratic regimes manage to function, the more plausible it appears that a substantial part of the explanation is to be found in the motives that actuate the leadership echelon; the values that it holds, in the rules of the political game to which it adheres, in the expectations which it entertains about its own status in society, and perhaps in some of the objective circumstances, both material and institutional, in which it functions. . . .

The skill with which the elite maintain the democratic tradition rests somewhat on the extensive political resources they command; "consequently, a challenge to the existing norms is bound to be costly to the challenger, for legitimist professionals can quickly shift their skills and resources into the urgent task of doing in the dissenter." . . . Given the resources of the elites, it is fortunate that their values bid them to serve the public welfare rather than their own parochial interests. The modal norms of the ruling classes of a democratic order have been described in the following terms:

> Fundamental is a regard for public opinion, a belief that in some way or another it should prevail. . . . The basic doctrine goes further to include a sense of trusteeship for the people generally and an adherence to the basic doctrine that collective efforts should be dedicated to the promotion of mass gains rather than of narrow class advantage. . . .

The thesis paraphrased and summarized in the previous four points reduces to the simple proposition that representative democracy depends on the values of the elite more than the actions of the nonelite. It recalls Plato's insistence that the cause of justice is served by the "inward conviction" of the guardian and not by the moods and manners of those on whose behalf justice prevails.

. . . Can we rely on the "inward convictions" of the elite to protect the democratic tradition? There are two reasons for expressing doubt.

First, and most important, the record of the elite is not promising. Compliance with democratic rules demands great self-restraint, especially for the elite. It requires that they forebear from using their immense resources of patronage and media control to stifle groups seen as repugnant. Further, it requires also that they consider public preferences even when they, the elite, "know best" what the society needs. It requires that they refrain, as individuals, from furthering private interests through their access to contracts, contacts, and the public treasury. And it requires that they resist the tendency to isolate themselves from the broader public and resist the temptation to select their own successors on narrow grounds. On all counts, and others which could be listed, the elite fail to achieve the standards Plato expected of the Guardians, and fail as well to measure up even to the requirements established by those contemporary theorists who would force American democracy into the mold of Platonic elitism. Consider a few dramatic, although not atypical, cases.

Senator Joseph McCarthy of Wisconsin, in the name of uprooting un-American activities, disregarded democratic traditions for nearly half a decade. He was contemptuous and destructive of exactly those "rules of the game" which the elite are supposed to preserve. And he had enormous influence on American politics, an influence weakened but not yet expurgated two decades later. Richard Rovere provides a useful summary to help us recall the early 1950s:

> He held two presidents captive—or as nearly captive as any Presidents of the United States have ever been held; in their conduct of the nation's affairs, Harry S. Truman and Dwight D. Eisenhower, from early 1950 through late 1954, could never act without weighing the effect of their plans upon McCarthy and the forces he led, and in consequence there were times when, because of this man, they could not act at all. He had enormous impact on American foreign policy at a time when that policy bore heavily on the course of world history, and American diplomacy might bear a different aspect today if McCarthy had never lived. In the Senate, his headquarters and his hiding place, he assumed the functions of the Committee of the Whole; he lived in thoroughgoing contempt of the Congress of which he was a member, of the rules it had made for itself, and—whenever they ran counter to his purposes—of the laws enacted for the general welfare. . . .

That one United States Senator should show flagrant disdain for reasoned discourse, for free speech, for due process, and for the principle of innocent until proven guilty does not, of course, prove anything about the broader elite. But if this broader elite either passively permitted or actively supported transparent violations of procedural democracy, then there is reason to doubt the commitment of the Guardians. And the evidence gives ample support to the notion that McCarthy was sustained by exactly those persons thought to be the repository of the democratic creed. Political elites

> helped dramatize his issues and fight his fights. Conservative Republican activists provided money and enthusiasm for the Senator's cause. In Wisconsin, for example, McCarthy did not mobilize the mass of voters. But he did mobilize the local elites of the Republican Party. . . . He had succeeded in

harnessing respectable elites and respectable institutions to which the populace paid deference. . . .

The elite in government were slow to judge their own, reasoning, as did Senator McClellan of Arkansas, "I do not want to do unto one of my colleagues what I would not want him to do unto me under the same circumstances.". . .

It is not necessary to go back forty years to find evidence that the commitment of the political elite to democracy is more tarnished in practice than in theory. We need not impugn the motives of the small clique who took American society deeper and deeper into the Vietnam War; perhaps they were men of good intentions sincerely attempting to serve their country. But there can be little doubt that the public was deceived and Congress deliberately misled, and that this was accomplished on a massive scale, with little more than quiet grumbling from all but a handful of senators and congressmen. If the Kennedys and McNamaras and Rostows and Johnsons can conceive, plan, and initiate a "secret war," how are we to remain confident that the principles of representative democracy rest secure in the inward convictions of the elite? How the elite responded to political, often aggressive dissent on the war gives concern as well. We need not here take sides one way or the other with Attorney General Mitchell's political views to raise questions about his commitment to due process when some 800 antiwar demonstrators were arrested, with his approval, although no charge was pressed against them. The attempt to transform political dissent into treason, which is an old trick, of course, cannot but raise doubts about the wisdom of relying on the good faith of the elite to sustain the First Amendment freedoms.

But if there are doubts about the government elite, there are even more reasons for pessimism about the economic elite. There certainly are many corporate executives who have a sense of responsibility and who care about the society they so substantially influence, but it is doubtful whether these personal values adequately establish anything remotely approaching the responsiveness and accountability promised in the democratic creed. Instances of public fraud are uncovered every day, and it is safe to say that there are many that have not been uncovered. Even the hallowed commitment to "free enterprise" is undermined by price-fixing and related arrangements. . . .

Certainly it is comforting to be told that the military elite, being professionals, know their place in relation to civilian control. But the comfort evaporates when the role of the Joint Chiefs of Staff is carefully examined, because the Joint Chiefs of Staff have great latitude and near autonomy in matters of intelligence, of military strategy, and of expenditures and weapon development. Whatever their professional norms, the admirals and generals protect their spheres of influence with a tenacity that questions their concern with civilian control. Moreover, the realm of military justice gives evidence that the "democratic principles" are defined very differently within than without the military. Officers and soldiers alike who have attempted to exercise their rights as citizens have learned, to their dismay, that the Bill of Rights does not extend to even their off-duty activities.

If we are less than sanguine about "inward convictions" as the guarantor of democracy, it is largely because of the record itself. The survey data testifying to the special political culture of the elite are important, but they do not tell the entire story. The commitment of the elite seems to crumble when pressures mount, as they did in the McCarthy era and as they did again in the late 1960s. That is, it is exactly in those times of crisis when the democratic procedures are most vulnerable that the presumed defenders weaken.

We should briefly record a second flaw in the contemporary versions of Plato's dream state. The thesis has a curious if little noticed logical property. The standards by which the elite measure themselves are often self-generated. To have political power is to have at least some control over the institutions, such as media and schools that shape and give operational meaning to the values of society. And, in this regard, the elite hold themselves accountable to standards that they themselves fix. Note, for instance, that the four points listed above emphasize procedural issues to the almost total neglect of substantive issues. Thus, the elite is honored if it stoutly defends universal suffrage, First Amendment freedoms, and due process of law. And we do not wish to make light of how important it is that the elite do, in fact, defend these principles. But it is possible for the elite to take their stand on procedural issues while pursuing policies (or nonpolicies) that lead to decay of cities, imperialistic adventurism, entrenchment of racist institutions, and a growing disparity in income and living conditions between those below and those above the poverty line. And if the elite themselves are assigning blame and credit, it is unlikely that they measure themselves in terms of social deterioration.

What, in brief, the theory of electoral accountability does is link the elitists' observation that the few rule the many with the democrats' observation that the few represent the many. This marriage comes about as follows: To be sure, a very few men direct and control the society, but this tiny elite is not indifferent to public needs and preference. Because the public is an electorate, the few, being either elected officials or dependent for their powers and privileges on elected officials, stand in fear of the wrath of the electorate. The accountability of the few to the many is insured because men are ambitious to gain and control the apparatus of the State, and such ambitions can be realized only by paying due attention to the electorate. Because the electorate, through periodic elections, grants or withholds the privilege of government, men who enjoy governing pursue policies they believe will satisfy the voters.

This anticipation of voter responses is what links elite rule and political representation; the electorate, in these formulations, does indeed control their governors. Schumpeter writes that "electorates normally do not control their political leaders in any way except by refusing to re-elect them or the parliamentary majorities which support them," . . . a point elaborated by Lipset when he writes that representative democracy is practically synonymous with the permanent insecurity of the governors: "Thus every incumbent of a position of high status within a truly democratic system must of necessity anticipate the loss of his position by the operation of the normal political process." . . .

It is easy to see why this line of argument is popular. . . . The ancient task of preventing tyranny by an elite is solved by the simple institutional device of periodic elections. Not too much is expected, therefore, of the public, which is a good thing, because, in general, the average citizen is ignorant about political matters and largely indifferent to them. Most citizens will rouse themselves to vote every two or four years, but more than this should not be expected. Thus the thesis of "electoral accountability" is realistic; it makes no assumptions about the masses that are not confirmed by social surveys. It is realistic in a second sense as well. The fact that everywhere societies are "divided into two classes—a class that rules and a class that is ruled" need not be denied, but instead can be incorporated into a political theory that makes a virtue of this fact. Electoral accountability insures that political representation constrains elite rule, and thus saves democracy from the enemy within: the tendency of power to accumulate in the hands of a small group.

In short, the theory of electoral accountability replaces a commitment to participatory democracy (considered unworkable and unrealistic) with a faith in elite competition. The first requirement of representative democracy is an intra-elite struggle to control political office, and this struggle is periodically decided by the mass electorate. In choosing who shall govern them, the public is also choosing how it shall be governed.

There is an important point to be made about this conception. . . . The "theory of electoral accountability" is much more than an academic notion. Rather, this idea and the package of assumptions it incorporates is integral to the operating political beliefs of many American citizens. "Electoral accountability" is a core term in what Mosca has called the "political formula," and what others have called the "symbolic universe of politics." For Mosca, the power of any political class rests on the political formula (set of moral principles) used to justify their rule. The formula in the United States is that "the powers of all lawmakers, magistrates and governmental officials in the United States emanate directly or indirectly from the vote of the voters, which is held to be the expression of the sovereign will of the whole American people." . . . This belief is held by the overwhelming majority of Americans. Studies of very young children show that voting is often chosen as a symbol of the government, and, indeed, that democracy is conceptualized in terms of voting privileges. One set of data about political beliefs of grade school children is summarized as follows:

> To young children, voting and elections are important democratic activities. The conflict which is present in every campaign is minimized. Throughout the age span there typically is a positive attitude toward candidates: they are viewed as concerned more with the public welfare than with selfish gains. Elections are perceived as crucial to the goals of the democratic process even though they may result in removal of incumbents for whom the child feels personal attachment. . . . The high value placed upon the election process may also encourage the acceptance of a newly elected President. Though the campaign winner may not be his personal favorite, a child's trust in the election process assures him that any person chosen by election will be capable and trustworthy.

This report continues by emphasizing how children believe that the defeated candidate "should help the winner to do a good job" and that citizens themselves should "go along with the man who was elected even if you didn't vote for him." . . .

That such beliefs are well established even among ten-year-olds is perhaps not surprising. Elections are part of every American child's school experience. Even in the earliest grades there are elections to choose the captain of the safety patrol; there are elections to choose the head cheerleader; there are votes about what to do on a school outing. The child considers these elections to be important and attaches great value to the significance of his vote. As an adult, he may realize that such powers were fictitious and that the teachers and other authorities controlled all the important decisions. Thus, with maturity, his confidence in elections is weakened, but he still retains his basic belief that representative democracy is insured by the competition of leaders for the electoral support of the public.

The thesis of electoral accountability has several weaknesses. First, the reader should recall one of our central conceptions—that critical political decisions in America are made by important members of the economic elite, especially the managers and directors of our largest corporations. When this is granted, it is readily seen that some of the important sectors of the governing elite are relatively untouched by the central institution purportedly designed to promote responsiveness.

There are, to be sure, "elections" in other than political sectors: Stockholders vote for corporation directors, trade union members vote for union officials, and even consumers can be said to vote by investing their capital. But these forms of elections do not begin to establish the type of accountability and responsiveness necessary for representative democracy to be workable. The reasons for this are well known: Most stockholder or union elections involve nothing other than the choice to support incumbent leaders and their policies or to vote "no" by abstention; two slates of candidates or two programs of actions are seldom if ever presented. Attempts to wage "proxy fights" have usually proven very unsuccessful because of the great advantages accruing to extant directors due to their control of the organization. Moreover, not all citizens get to vote for the Board of Directors of General Motors; this privilege is given only to the stockholders (in proportion to the stock they control). However, it is not just the stockholders who are affected by the actions of General Motors. The same is true of union elections; the protectionist and racist policies of the building and construction unions are possible because the blacks who cannot gain admittance to these unions are also unable to participate in their elections. Thus, elections within a particular sector, even if presenting alternatives and offering competing slates, are necessarily limited elections.

But there is another substantial flaw to the theory of electoral accountability. Implicit in the model is the notion that the relationship between elites and voters is akin to that of the traditional New England town meeting: Elites articulate the reasons for their held positions in a rational manner before the informed electorate, which then exercises its collective judgment in choosing between the candidates on the basis of reason.

Even a cursory comparison between this picture and the way in which American election campaigns are conducted will reveal a yawning chasm indeed. Those seeking office are more often than not content to campaign on the basis of slogans, such as "law and order" or "support your local policy," designed to elicit emotional responses from the electorate, rather than to form the basis for a rational debate. Moreover, candidates will often conceal their true positions on issues from the electorate; consider only President Johnson's 1964 presidential campaign statements that he would not expand America's role in the Vietnam War when he had every intention of doing so at the time. Again, campaigns are also replete with false issues, as, in 1960, when candidate John Kennedy raised the specter of a "missile gap" between the American and Russian arsenals, a gap which was in fact nonexistent. Finally, we only briefly note the recently developed manipulatory public relations techniques designed to present candidates with different personality characteristics than they actually possess.

On the other side of the ledger, as we shall discuss shortly, the voter is ill informed. Thus, the election system is far removed from the rational model of an informed electorate choosing among candidates who present rationally held positions. It is often not a system whereby candidates are held accountable for their actions, but rather one in which there is frequently no accountability for *political* actions. Rather, accountability is a perverted conception involving elites' abilities to manipulate electorates through fear, deception, and distorted personality characteristics.

Pressure Organizations and the Petitioning Process

Americans, it has been said, are a nation of "joiners." They flock to the innumerable voluntary associations and organizations which dot the social landscape. And the extensive and complex group life which results is not without consequences, mostly benign, for representative democracy. At least, this is what one line of reasoning proposes. How do voluntary associations and pressure organizations contribute to checking the elite and forcing them to be responsive? An answer to this question comes out of a rich literature on American politics; we can provide only a brief overview as preface to expressing our own doubts about how well the "group process" establishes representative democracy.

The beginning point is to recognize the importance of group activity to political life, an importance which cannot be denied. As summarized by one observer,

> Group interests are the animating forces in the political process. The exercise of the power of governance consists in the promotion of group objectives regarded as legitimate, in the reconciliation and mediation of conflicting group ambitions, and in the restraint of group tendencies judged to be socially destructive. . . .

This active role by groups benefits representative democracy in several respects. Organizations are linkages between the elite and the nonelite. Whereas the individual voter or petitioner may be scarcely noticed by elites, the citizen whose strength is augmented by collective pressure of a large and well-financed organization has less difficulty being heard. "Voluntary associations are the prime means by which the function of mediating between the individual and the state is performed. Through them the individual is able to relate himself effectively and meaningfully to the political system," is the conclusion of two political scientists. . . .

This linkage role is particularly important to augment the electoral process. Elections occur infrequently, and when the excitement and flurry of the contest is past, the elite once again retreat into the company of peers and close advisors. But the lobbying activity of pressure groups reminds them of the wishes and demands of the public. And this reminder comes at an opportune time, for it is in the period between elections when laws are passed (or not), when public monies are spent, and when commitments on behalf of the entire society are made. The group process establishes a dual system of representation. Not only does the citizen have elected leaders to represent him, but he has group leaders and spokesmen to carry his wishes into the elite circles. In being "represented twice," the citizen has a double check on the elite. Group spokesmen press demands on the elite and report back the results to the group members.

But an active group life does more than take up the slack in the representational process. It facilitates social consensus and political moderation. This viewpoint is well summarized in the following passage:

> The United States is a large and diverse nation with many different kinds of people holding many different values. The pursuit of these diverse values

> often occurs through the medium of interest groups which contend against one another for the influence and power to gain their values. The competition among so many groups moderates the claims and counterclaims by forcing compromise and bargaining. It disciplines the groups thereby and they adjust and adapt to one another. If any sector of society is aggrieved, it may organize and seek redress through the bargaining among groups. Freedom for each group is thus maximized, goals are moderated, and social consensus is promoted. . . .

Thus, an active group life moderates the conflicts and tensions that might otherwise be unmanageable in a society committed to the democratic principle that every viewpoint should receive a hearing.

Finally, it has been argued, organizations check tendencies that can be destructive to the political order within which representative democracy thrives. Associational activity mediates between the elite and the nonelite in a way that protects each from the excesses of the other. The excesses of the elite would be aloofness, isolation, arbitrariness, and, ultimately, tyranny. The excesses of the nonelite would be ill-informed and ill-formulated political viewpoints, shifting moods and unreasonable demands, sporadic and poorly considered political activities, and, ultimately, social anomie and alienation. Tyrannical elites and anomic masses are unlikely if the "space" between them is filled by an active group life. Organizations monitor and check the tendencies of elites and they organize and stabilize the viewpoints and activities of the public.

We thus see that the antidemocratic possibilities when society is directed by an elite are modified, even prevented, in three different ways by an active group life. First, pressure organizations are a channel by which citizens express themselves to the elite and thus these organizations provide a necessary complement to elections. Second, because of the variety of organizations, very diverse political viewpoints have the type of outlet that moderates social conflict and tension. Third, two of the severest dangers to a democracy—elite tyranny and mass anomie—are effectively checked by a layer of associational activity mediating between elites and nonelites, and reducing the antidemocratic excesses of both.

These, then, are some of the major propositions that have connected group politics with an understanding of representative democracy. While there is an element of truth in them, there are also some grave difficulties. Indeed, there are aspects of group politics that *reduce* the responsiveness of elites, and these aspects must be considered if our understanding of elites and political representation is to be complete. Let us then consider the evidence on organizations and their political role.

Thus, insofar as an active group life connects citizen and elite, it does so more effectively for the middle and upper-middle classes than it does for the lower strata. The strong association between social status and organizational membership in the United States is particularly revealing when measured against data from other nations. The class bias in organizational membership is much higher in the United States than, for example, in Britain, Germany, or Italy. In each of these latter nations, lower-class citizens have greater opportunities to express themselves politically through the group process than they do in the United States. This discrepancy partly reflects the fact that in Britain, Germany, and Italy there have been deliberate efforts to mobilize and politically involve the lower classes by radical or working-class political parties.

America has simply never developed a lower-class organizational infrastructure. And thus an undue emphasis on group politics has a clear socioeconomic bias. It provides an additional resource and channel of access to those who already benefit from the social system, and it denies a linkage to those already penalized by lack of resources.

The correspondence in the United States between organizational membership and higher social status plus the tendency for those in organizations to participate more actively in politics than do nonmembers suggests that the group process very imperfectly connects the mass of citizens with the elite. The following table demonstrates the low levels of participation by those who are doubly penalized: first, by being without social and economic resources and second, by being without an organizational home. . . .

Only one out of every ten citizens penalized by low status and isolated from the interest-group system is likely to be politically active. In contrast, three of every four citizens who hold high status positions and who are involved in organizations are also politically active. It is evident, therefore, that, as we have already observed, the group process very imperfectly connects the mass of citizens with the elite. Intense minorities, especially those based in the middle and upper-middle classes, are advantaged by group politics. The majority is not so effectively served. As one critic [E. E. Schattschneider—Ed.] summarized the evidence,

> The vice in the groupist theory is that it conceals the most significant aspect of the system. The flaw in the pluralist heaven is that the heavenly chorus

TABLE 1
ORGANIZATIONAL INVOLVEMENT

	High		*Medium*		*Low*	
	High social status	Low social status	High status	Low status	High status	Low status
Proportion who are politically active	75%	67%	41%	27%	32%	10%

> sings with a strong upper-class accent. Probably about 90 percent of the people cannot get into the pressure system. . . .

The class bias in membership and activity gives a conservative hue to the pressure system, but it is not the only factor contributing to this conservatism. Equally, if not more, important is the simple fact that well-established, entrenched organizations are more powerful than organizations in the process of being born. The established, organized interests have budgets, professional lobbying staffs, contacts in Washington and state capitals, and a long, often distinguished, record of public involvement. The upstart organization lacks all of these assets. But it is often the upstart organizations which represent dissatisfaction with the status quo and which enter politics to reform institutions and to change policies. They are met and more often than not beaten back by the conservative interests which have shaped the status quo and understandably intend to protect it. Thus, the NAACP has been more conservative and accommodating than the more recently formed Southern Christian Leadership Conference, which, in turn, has taken a more cautious stance than the newest entries into the black politics arena. Moreover, the newer organizations are disregarded by the parties bent on preserving the extant group system with which they have a long-standing accommodation.

The pressure-group system has a class and a conservative bias, both of which weaken its effectiveness in bringing about political representation and elite accountability. It would be in error to conclude that representation and accountability are not in some respects furthered by group politics, but it would be even more erroneous to conclude that just because a society has an active group life it has perfected and protected a representative democracy.

The thesis that an organizational layer between elite and nonelite insures representative politics is flawed in another manner as well. The thesis depends on active competition between different groups, but a plurality of groups does not necessarily imply group competition. As we noted in a previous chapter, powerful interest groups are capable of capturing entire sectors of public policy. The policy-making elites might be representative of a particular constituency, but it is often a constituency that is narrow and parochial in its demands. Agricultural policy provides a clear example. The powerful interest organizations that represent the farmer, especially the large, commercial farmer, have literally captured the public agencies that are supposed to regulate the agricultural section.

In one extended criticism of pluralism and group politics, the author contends that the all-important distinction between private power and public authority has nearly been eliminated in American society: "This has been accomplished not by public expropriation of private domain—as would be true of the nationalization that Americans fear—but by private expropriation of public authority."

. . . Powerful private interests rule their own fiefdoms with the blessing of public authority and with the largess[e] of the public treasury.

To the extent that capture rather than competition describes group politics, political representation again suffers. Broad interests are sacrificed to narrow ones, and elites are cushioned from public reprisal by the protective envelope of friendly and powerful, if parochial, groups.

Summary

Three separate arguments about political representation and elite accountability have been reviewed: (1) Elites are held in check by internalized values, which include a healthy respect for democratic norms and a commitment to serve the public interest. (2) Elites are held in check by a competitive election system, which penalizes and rewards according to how faithfully the public interest has been represented. And (3) elites are held in check by a vigorous interest-group system which provides a vast network through which the nonelite shape and constrain public policy in accord with majority preferences. Our review has revealed that each argument is flawed in major and minor ways, although each argument has some merit.

We conclude on a pessimistic note. Not only are elites well entrenched in American society, which is what we expect of any large-scale industrial nation, but they are more immune from popular control than the rhetoric of democracy implies.

PART VI

The Problem of Inequality

SELECTION 17
FROM
*Capitalism and Freedom**

MILTON FRIEDMAN

HOW CAN WE BENEFIT from the promise of government while avoiding the threat to freedom? Two broad principles embodied in our Constitution give an answer that has preserved our freedom so far, though they have been violated repeatedly in practice while proclaimed as precept.

First, the scope of government must be limited. Its major function must be to protect our freedom both from the enemies outside our gates and from our fellow citizens: to preserve law and order, to enforce private contracts, to foster competitive markets. Beyond this major function, government may enable us at times to accomplish jointly what we would find it more difficult or expensive to accomplish severally. However, any such use of government is fraught with danger. We should not and cannot avoid using government in this way. But there should be a clear and large balance of advantages before we do. By relying primarily on voluntary cooperation and private enterprise, in both economic and other activities, we can insure that the private sector is a check on the powers of the governmental sector and an effective protection of freedom of speech, of religion, and of thought.

The second broad principle is that government power must be dispersed. If government is to exercise power, better in the country than in the state, better in the state than in Washington. If I do not like what my local community does, be it in sewage disposal, or zoning, or schools, I can move to another local community, and though few may take this step, the mere possibility acts as a check. If I do not like what my state does, I can move to another. If I do not like what Washington imposes, I have few alternatives in this world of jealous nations.

The very difficulty of avoiding the enactments of the federal government is of course the great attraction of centralization to many of its proponents. It will enable them more effectively, they believe, to legislate programs that—as they see it—are in the interest of the public, whether it be the transfer of income

* (Chicago: University of Chicago Press, 1962): pp. 2–4, 12–19.

from the rich to the poor or from private to governmental purposes. They are in a sense right. But this coin has two sides. The power to do good is also the power to do harm; those who control the power today may not tomorrow; and, more important, what one man regards as good, another may regard as harm. The great tragedy of the drive to centralization, as of the drive to extend the scope of government in general, is that it is mostly led by men of good will who will be the first to rue its consequences.

The preservation of freedom is the protective reason for limiting and decentralizing governmental power. But there is also a constructive reason. The great advances of civilization, whether in architecture or painting, in science or literature, in industry or agriculture, have never come from centralized government. Columbus did not set out to seek a new route to China in response to a majority directive of a parliament, though he was partly financed by an absolute monarch. Newton and Leibnitz; Einstein and Bohr; Shakespeare, Milton, and Pasternak; Whitney, McCormick, Edison, and Ford; Jane Addams, Florence Nightingale, and Albert Schweitzer; no one of these opened new frontiers in human knowledge and understanding, in literature, in technical possibilities, or in the relief of human misery in response to governmental directives. Their achievements were the product of individual genius, of strongly held minority views, of a social climate permitting variety and diversity.

Government can never duplicate the variety and diversity of individual action. At any moment in time, by imposing uniform standards in housing, or nutrition, or clothing, government could undoubtedly improve the level of living of many individuals; by imposing uniform standards in schooling, road construction, or sanitation, central government could undoubtedly improve the level of performance in many local areas and perhaps even on the average of all communities. But in the process, government would replace progress by stagnation, it would substitute uniform mediocrity for the variety essential for that experimentation which can bring tomorrow's laggards above today's mean.

The basic problem of social organization is how to coordinate the economic activities of large numbers of people. Even in relatively backward societies, extensive division of labor and specialization of function is required to make effective use of available resources. In advanced societies, the scale on which coordination is needed, to take full advantage of the opportunities offered by modern science and technology, is enormously greater. Literally millions of people are involved in providing one another with their daily bread, let alone with their yearly automobiles. The challenge to the believer in liberty is to reconcile this widespread interdependence with individual freedom.

Fundamentally, there are only two ways of coordinating the economic activities of millions. One is central direction involving the use of coercion—the technique of the army and of the modern totalitarian state. The other is voluntary cooperation of individuals—the technique of the marketplace.

The possibility of coordination through voluntary cooperation rests on the elementary—yet frequently denied—proposition that both parties to an economic transaction benefit from it, *provided the transaction is bilaterally voluntary and informed.*

Exchange can therefore bring about coordination without coercion. A working model of a society organized through voluntary exchange is a *free private enterprise exchange economy*—what we have been calling competitive capitalism.

In its simplest form, such a society consists of a number of independent households—a collection of Robinson Crusoes, as it were. Each household uses the resources it controls to produce goods and services that it exchanges for goods and services produced by other households, on terms mutually acceptable to the two parties to the bargain. It is thereby enabled to satisfy its wants indirectly by producing goods and services for others, rather than directly by producing goods for its own immediate use. The incentive for adopting this indirect route is, of course, the increased product made possible by division of labor and specialization of function. Since the household always has the alternative of producing directly for itself, it need not enter into any exchange unless it benefits from it. Hence, no exchange will take place unless both parties do benefit from it. Cooperation is thereby achieved without coercion.

Specialization of function and division of labor would not go far if the ultimate productive unit were the household. In a modern society, we have gone much farther. We have introduced enterprises which are intermediaries between individuals in their capacities as suppliers of service and as purchasers of goods. And similarly, specialization of function and division of labor could not go very far if we had to continue to rely on the barter of product for product. In consequence, money has been introduced as a means of facilitating exchange, and of enabling the acts of purchase and of sale to be separated into two parts.

Despite the important role of enterprises and of money in our actual economy, and despite the numerous and complex problems they raise, the central characteristic of the market technique of achieving coordination is fully displayed in the simple exchange economy that contains neither enterprises nor money. As in that simple model, so in the complex enterprise and money-exchange economy, cooperation is strictly individual and voluntary *provided*: (1) that enterprises are private, so that the ultimate contracting parties are individuals, and (2) that individuals are effectively free to enter or not to enter into any particular exchange, so that every transaction is strictly voluntary.

It is far easier to state these provisos in general terms than to spell them out in detail, or to specify precisely the institutional arrangements most conducive to their maintenance. Indeed, much of technical economic literature is concerned with precisely these questions. The basic requisite is the maintenance of law and order to prevent physical coercion of one individual by another and to enforce contracts voluntarily entered into, thus giving substance to "private." Aside from this, perhaps the most difficult problems arise from monopoly—which inhibits effective freedom by denying individuals alternatives to the particular exchange—and from "neighborhood effects"—effects on third parties for which it is not feasible to charge or recompense them. . . .

So long as effective freedom of exchange is maintained, the central feature of the market organization of economic activity is that it prevents one person from interfering with another in respect of most of his activities. The consumer is protected from coercion by the seller because of the presence of other sellers with whom he can deal. The seller is protected from coercion by the consumer because of other consumers to whom he can sell. The employee is protected from coercion by the employer because of other employers for whom he can work, and so on. And the market does this impersonally and without centralized authority.

Indeed, a major source of objection to a free economy is precisely that it does this task so well. It gives people what they want instead of what a particular group thinks they ought to want. Underlying most arguments against the free market is a lack of belief in freedom itself.

The existence of a free market does not of course eliminate the need for government. On the contrary, government is essential both as a forum for determining the "rules of the game" and as an umpire to interpret and enforce the rules decided on. What the market does is to reduce greatly the range of issues that must be decided through political means, and thereby to minimize the extent to which government need participate directly in the game. The characteristic feature of action through political channels is that it tends to require or enforce substantial conformity. The great advantage of the market, on the other hand, is that it permits wide diversity. It is, in political terms, a system of proportional representation. Each man can vote, as it were, for the color of tie he wants and get it; he does not have to see what color the majority wants and then, if he is in the minority, submit.

It is this feature of the market that we refer to when we say that the market provides economic freedom. But this characteristic also has implications that go far beyond the narrowly economic. Political freedom means the absence of coercion of a man by his fellow men. The fundamental threat to freedom is power to coerce, be it in the hands of a monarch, a dictator, an oligarchy, or a momentary majority. The preservation of freedom requires the elimination of such concentration of power to the fullest possible extent and the dispersal and distribution of whatever power cannot be eliminated—a system of checks and balances. By removing the organization of economic activity from the control of political authority, the market eliminates this source of coercive power. It enables economic strength to be a check to political power rather than a reinforcement.

Economic power can be widely dispersed. There is no law of conservation which forces the growth of new centers of economic strength to be at the expense of existing centers. Political power, on the other hand, is more difficult to decentralize. There can be numerous small independent governments. But it is far more difficult to maintain numerous equipotent small centers of political power in a single large government than it is to have numerous centers of economic strength in a single large economy. There can be many millionaires in one large economy. But can there be more than one really outstanding leader, one person on whom the energies and enthusiasms of his countrymen are centered? If the central government gains power, it is likely to be at the expense of local governments. There seems to be something like a fixed total of political power to be distributed. Consequently, if economic power is joined to political power, concentration seems almost inevitable. On the other hand, if economic power is kept in separate hands from political power, it can serve as a check and a counter to political power.

The force of this abstract argument can perhaps best be demonstrated by example. Let us consider first, a hypothetical example that may help to bring out the principles involved, and then some actual examples from recent experience that illustrate the way in which the market works to preserve political freedom.

One feature of a free society is surely the freedom of individuals to advocate and propagandize openly for a radical change in the structure of the society—so long as the advocacy is restricted to persuasion and does not include force or other forms of coercion. It is a mark of the political freedom of a capitalist society that men can openly advocate and work for socialism. Equally, political freedom in a socialist society would require that men be free to advocate the introduction of capitalism. How could the freedom to advocate capitalism be preserved and protected in a socialist society?

In order for men to advocate anything, they must in the first place be able to earn a living. This already raises a problem in a socialist society, since all jobs are under the direct control of political authorities. It would take an act of self-denial whose difficulty is underlined by experience in the United States after World War II with the problem of "security" among federal employees, for a socialist government to permit its employees to advocate policies directly contrary to official doctrine.

But let us suppose this act of self-denial to be achieved. For advocacy of capitalism to mean anything, the proponents must be able to finance their cause—to hold public meetings, publish pamphlets, buy radio time, issue newspapers and magazines, and so on. How could they raise the funds? There might and probably would be men in the socialist society with large incomes, perhaps even large capital sums in the form of government bonds and the like, but these would of necessity be high public officials. It is possible to conceive of a minor socialist official retaining his job although openly advocating capitalism.

It strains credulity to imagine the socialist top brass financing such "subversive" activities.

The only recourse for funds would be to raise small amounts from a large number of minor officials. But this is no real answer. To tap these sources, many people would already have to be persuaded, and our whole problem is how to initiate and finance a campaign to do so. Radical movements in capitalist societies have never been financed this way. They have typically been supported by a few wealthy individuals who have become persuaded—by a Frederick Vanderbilt Field, or an Anita McCormick Blaine, or a Corliss Lamont, to mention a few names recently prominent, or by a Friedrich Engels, to go farther back. This is a role of inequality of wealth in preserving political freedom that is seldom noted—the role of the patron.

In a capitalist society, it is only necessary to convince a few wealthy people to get funds to launch any idea, however strange, and there are many such persons, many independent foci of support. And, indeed, it is not even necessary to persuade people or financial institutions with available funds of the soundness of the ideas to be propagated. It is only necessary to persuade them that the propagation can be financially successful; that the newspaper or magazine or book or other venture will be profitable. The competitive publisher, for example, cannot afford to publish only writing with which he personally agrees; his touchstone must be the likelihood that the market will be large enough to yield a satisfactory return on his investment.

In this way, the market breaks the vicious circle and makes it possible ultimately to finance such ventures by small amounts from many people without first persuading them. There are no such possibilities in the socialist society; there is only the all-powerful state.

Let us stretch our imagination and suppose that a socialist government is aware of this problem and is composed of people anxious to preserve freedom. Could it provide the funds? Perhaps, but it is difficult to see how. It could establish a bureau for subsidizing subversive propaganda. But how could it choose whom to support? If it gave to all who asked, it would shortly find itself out of funds, for socialism cannot repeal the elementary economic law that a sufficiently high price will call forth a large supply. Make the advocacy of radical causes sufficiently remunerative, and the supply of advocates will be unlimited.

Moreover, freedom to advocate unpopular causes does not require that such advocacy be without cost. On the contrary, no society could be stable if advocacy of radical change were costless, much less subsidized. It is entirely appropriate that men make sacrifices to advocate causes in which they deeply believe. Indeed, it is important to preserve freedom only for people who are willing to practice self-denial, for otherwise freedom degenerates into license and irresponsibility. What is essential is that the cost of advocating unpopular causes be tolerable and not prohibitive.

But we are not yet through. In a free market society, it is enough to have the funds. The suppliers of paper are as willing to sell it to the *Daily Worker* as to the *Wall Street Journal.* In a socialist society, it would not be enough to have the funds. The hypothetical supporter of capitalism would have to persuade a government factory making paper to sell to him, the government printing press to print his pamphlets, a government post office to distribute them among the people, a government agency to rent him a hall in which to talk, and so on.

Perhaps there is some way in which one could overcome these difficulties and preserve freedom in a socialist society. One cannot say it is utterly impossible. What is clear, however, is that there are very real difficulties in establishing institutions that will effectively preserve the possibility of dissent. So far as I know, none of the people who have been in favor of socialism and also in favor of freedom have really faced up to this issue, or made even a respectable start at developing the institutional arrangements that would permit freedom under socialism. By contrast, it is clear how a free market capitalist society fosters freedom.

SELECTION 18
FROM
Democratic Theory *

C. B. MACPHERSON

PROFESSOR FRIEDMAN'S DEMONSTRATION THAT the capitalist market economy can coordinate economic activities without coercion rests on an elementary conceptual error. His argument runs as follows. He shows first that in a simple market model, where each individual or household controls resources enabling it to produce goods and services either directly for itself or for exchange, there will be production for exchange because of the increased product made possible by specialization. But

> since the household always has the alternative of producing directly for itself, it need not enter into any exchange unless it benefits from it. Hence no exchange will take place unless both parties do benefit from it. Cooperation is thereby achieved without coercion. (*Capitalism and Freedom*, p. 13; hereafter CF)

So far, so good. It is indeed clear that in this simple exchange model, assuming rational maximizing behavior by all hands, every exchange will benefit both parties, and hence that no coercion is involved in the decision to produce for exchange or in any act of exchange.

Professor Friedman then moves on to our actual complex economy, or rather to his own curious model of it:

> As in [the] simple model, so in the complex enterprise and money-exchange economy, cooperation is strictly individual and voluntary *provided*: (1) that enterprises are private, so that the ultimate contracting parties are individuals and (2) that individuals are effectively free to enter or not to enter into any particular exchange, so that every transaction is strictly voluntary. (CF, p. 14)

One cannot take exception to proviso (1): it is clearly required in the model to produce a cooperation that is "strictly individual." One might, of course,

---

* *Democratic Theory: Essays in Retrieval* (London: Oxford University Press, 1973): pp. 143–49.

suggest that a model containing this stipulation is far from corresponding to our actual complex economy, since in the latter the ultimate contracting parties who have the most effect on the market are not individuals but corporations, and moreover, corporations which in one way or another manage to opt out of the fully competitive market. This criticism, however, would not be accepted by all economists as self-evident: some would say that the question who has most effect on the market is still an open question (or is a wrongly posed question). More investigation and analysis of this aspect of the economy would be valuable. But political scientists need not await its results before passing judgment on Friedman's position, nor should they be tempted to concentrate their attention on proviso (1). If they do so they are apt to miss the fault in proviso (2), which is more fundamental, and of a different kind. It is not a question of the correspondence of the model to the actual: it is a matter of the inadequacy of the proviso to produce the model.

Proviso (2) is "that individuals are effectively free to enter or not to enter into any particular exchange," and it is held that with this proviso "every transaction is strictly voluntary." A moment's thought will show that this is not so. The proviso that is required to make every transaction strictly voluntary is *not* freedom not to enter into any *particular* exchange, but freedom not to enter into any exchange *at all*. This, and only this, was the proviso that proved the simple model to be voluntary and noncoercive; and nothing less than this would prove the complex model to be voluntary and noncoercive. But Professor Friedman is clearly claiming that freedom not to enter into any *particular* exchange is enough: "The consumer is protected from coercion by the seller because of the presence of other sellers with whom he can deal. . . . The employee is protected from coercion by the employer because of other employers for whom he can work . . ." (*CF*, pp. 14–15).

One almost despairs of logic, and of the use of models. It is easy to see what Professor Friedman has done, but it is less easy to excuse it. He has moved from the simple economy of exchange between independent producers to the capitalist economy, without mentioning the most important thing that distinguishes them. He mentions money instead of barter, and "enterprises which are intermediaries between individuals in their capacities as suppliers of services and as purchasers of goods" (*CF*, pp. 13–14), as if money and merchants were what distinguished a capitalist economy from an economy of independent producers. What distinguishes the capitalist economy from the simple exchange economy is the separation of labor and capital, that is, the existence of a labor force without its own sufficient capital and therefore without a choice as to whether to put its labor in the market or not. Professor Friedman would agree that where there is no choice there is coercion. His attempted demonstration that capitalism coordinates without coercion therefore fails.

Since all his specific arguments against the welfare and regulatory state depend on his case that the market economy is not coercive, the reader may spare himself the pains (or, if an economist, the pleasure) of attending to the careful and persuasive reasoning by which he seeks to establish the minimum to which coercion could be reduced by reducing or discarding each of the main regulatory and welfare activities of the state. None of this takes into account the coercion involved in the separation of capital from labor, or the possible mitigation of this coercion by the regulatory and welfare state. Yet it is because this coercion can in principle be reduced by the regulatory and welfare state, and thereby the amount of effective individual liberty be increased, that liberals have been justified in pressing, in the name of liberty, for infringements on the pure operation of competitive capitalism. . . .

The argument that competitive capitalism is necessary to political freedom is itself conducted on two levels, neither of which shows a necessary relation.

1. The first, on which Friedman properly does not place very much weight, is a historical correlation. No society that has had a large measure of political freedom "has not also used something comparable to a free market to organize the bulk of economic activity" (*CF*, p. 9). Professor Friedman rightly emphasizes "how limited is the span of time and the part of the globe for which there has ever been anything like political freedom" (*CF*, p. 9); he believes that the exceptions to the general rule of "tyranny, servitude and misery" are so few that the relation between them and certain economic arrangements can easily be spotted. "The nineteenth century and early twentieth century in the Western world stand out as striking exceptions to the general trend of historical development. Political freedom in this instance clearly came along with the free market and the development of capitalist institutions" (*CF*, pp. 9–10). Thus, for Professor Friedman, "history suggests . . . that capitalism is a necessary condition for political freedom" (*CF*, p. 10).

The broad historical correlation is fairly clear, though in cutting off the period of substantial political freedom in the West at the "early twentieth century" Friedman seems to be slipping into thinking of economic freedom and begging the question of the relation of political freedom to economic freedom. But granting the correlation between the emergence of capitalism and the emergence of political freedom, what it may suggest to the student of history is the converse of what it suggests to Professor Friedman: i.e., it may suggest that political freedom was a necessary condition for the development of capitalism. Capitalist institutions could not be fully established until political freedom (ensured by a competitive party system with effective civil liberties) had been won by those who wanted capitalism to have a clear run: a liberal state (political freedom) was needed to permit and facilitate a capitalist market society.

If this is the direction in which the causal relation runs, what follows (assuming the same relation to continue to hold) is that freedom, or rather specific kinds and degrees of freedom, will be or not be maintained according as those who have a stake in the maintenance of capitalism think them useful or necessary. In fact, there has been a complication in this relation. The liberal state which had, by the mid-nineteenth century in England, established the political freedoms needed to facilitate capitalism, was not democratic: that is, it had not extended political freedom to the bulk of the people. When, later, it did so, it began to abridge market freedom. The more extensive the political freedom, the less extensive the economic freedom became. At any rate, the historical correlation scarcely suggests that capitalism is a necessary condition for political freedom.

2. Passing from historical correlation, which "by itself can never be convincing," Professor Friedman looks for "logical links between economic and political freedom" (*CF*, pp. 11–12). The link he finds is that "the kind of economic organization that provides economic freedom directly, namely, competitive capitalism, also promotes political freedom because it separates economic power from political power and in this way enables the one to offset the other" (*CF*, p. 9). The point is developed a few pages later. The greater the concentration of coercive power in the same hands, the greater the threat to political freedom (defined as "the absence of coercion of a man by his fellow men"). The market removes the organization of economic activity from the control of the political authority. It thus reduces the concentration of power and "enables economic strength to be a check to political power rather than a reinforcement" (*CF*, p. 15).

Granted the validity of these generalizations, they tell us only that the market *enables* economic power to offset rather than reinforce political power. They do not show any necessity or inherent probability that the market *leads to* the offsetting of political power by economic power. We may doubt that there is any such inherent probability. What can be shown is an inherent probability in the other direction, i.e., that the market leads to political power being used not to offset but to reinforce economic power. For the more completely the market takes over the organization of economic activity, that is, the more nearly the society approximates Friedman's ideal of a competitive capitalist market society, where the state establishes and enforces the individual right of appropriation and the rules of the market but does not interfere in the operation of the market, the more completely is political power being used to reinforce economic power.

Professor Friedman does not see this as any threat to political freedom because he does not see that the capitalist market necessarily gives coercive power to those who succeed in amassing capital. He knows that the coercion whose absence he equates with political freedom is not just the physical coercion of police and prisons, but extends to many forms of economic coercion, e.g., the power some men may have over others' terms of employment. He sees the coercion possible (he thinks probable) in a socialist society where the political authority can enforce certain terms of employment. He does not see the coercion in a capitalist society where the holders of capital can enforce certain terms of employment. He does not see this because of his error about freedom not to enter into any particular exchange being enough to prove the uncoercive nature of entering into exchange at all.

The placing of economic coercive power and political coercive power in the hands of different sets of people, as in the fully competitive capitalist economy, does not lead to the first checking the second but to the second reinforcing the first. It is only in the welfare-state variety of capitalism, which Friedman would like to have dismantled, that there is a certain amount of checking of economic power by political power.

The logical link between competitive capitalism and political freedom has not been established.

SELECTION 19
FROM
*Inventing Reality**

MICHAEL PARENTI

DO THE MEDIA MANAGE OUR MINDS?

ARE THE MEDIA INDEPENDENT of government influence? If not, what is the nature of that influence? Are the media dominated by particular class interests? If so, does this dominance carry over into news content? Does control of news content translate into propaganda? Does propaganda translate into indoctrination of the public mind? And does indoctrination translate into support for policies? These questions guide the present inquiry: let us run through them again, a little more slowly.

1. In the United States a free press is defined as one unhampered by repressive laws. As we shall find, government interference with the news is not the only or even the major problem. More often the danger is that the press goes along willingly with officialdom's view of things at home and abroad, frequently manifesting a disregard for accuracy equal to that of policymakers. To be sure, questions are sometimes raised and criticisms voiced, but most of these are confined to challenging the *efficacy* of a particular policy rather than its underlying interests, especially if the interests are powerful ones.

2. The newspeople who participate in the many forums on freedom of the press usually concentrate on threats to the press from without, leaving untouched the question of coercion from within, specifically from media owners. . . . Are the media free from censorial interference by their owners? Does ownership translate into actual control over information, or does responsibility for the news still rest in the hands of journalists and editors who are free to report what they want—limited only by professional canons of objectivity? As we shall see, the working press, including newspaper editors and television news producers and even the top media executives, are beholden to media owners and corporate advertisers. More specifically, the owners exercise control through the power to hire and fire, to promote and demote anyone they

*(New York: St. Martin's Press, 1986): pp. 19–24.

want and by regularly intervening directly into the news production process with verbal and written directives.

3. But does control over media content and personnel translate into ruling class propaganda? Even if we allow that owners ultimately determine what is or is not publicized, can it be assumed that the end product serves their interests and gives only their viewpoint? I will argue that, except for momentary departures, a capitalist ideological perspective regarding events at home and abroad rather consistently predominates. The system of control works, although not with absolute perfection, and is not devoid of items that might at times be discomforting to the rich and powerful.

4. A final concern: Does ruling class propaganda translate into indoctrination of the public? It might be argued that even if the news is cast in a capitalist ideological mold, the public does not swallow it and has ways of withstanding the propaganda. The news may be manipulated by the press lords, but are we manipulated by the news? It is this last question I want to deal with here at some length. For if the press exercises only an inconsequential influence over the public, then we are dealing with a tempest in a teapot and are being unduly alarmist about "mind management."

Early studies of the media's impact on voting choices found that people seem surprisingly immune from media manipulation. Campaign propaganda usually reinforced the public's preferences rather than altered them. People exposed themselves to media appeals in a selective way, giving more credence and attention to messages that bolstered their own views. Their opinions and information intake also were influenced by peers, social groups, and community, so the individual did not stand without a buffer against the impact of the media. The press, it was concluded, had only a "minimal effect." . . .

At first glance, these findings are reassuring: People seem fairly self-directed in their responses to the media and do not allow themselves to be mindlessly directed. Democracy is safe. But troublesome questions remain. If through "selective exposure" and "selective attention" we utilize the media mainly to reinforce our established predispositions, where do the predispositions themselves come from? We can point to various socializing agencies: family, school, peer groups, work place—and the media themselves. Certainly some of our internalized political predispositions come from the dominant political culture that the media have had a hand in shaping—and directly from earlier exposure to the media themselves.

Our ability to discriminate is limited in part by how we have been conditioned by previous media exposures. The selectivity we exercise is not an autonomous antidote to propaganda but may feed right into it, choosing one or another variation of the same establishment offering. Opinions that depart too far from the mainstream are likely to be rejected out of hand. In such situations, our "selectivity" is designed to *avoid* information and views that contradict the dominant propaganda, a propaganda we long ago implicitly embraced as representative of "the nature of things." Thus, an implanted set of conditioned responses are now mistakenly identified as our self-generated political perceptions, and the public's selective ingestion of the media's conventional fare is wrongly treated as evidence of the "minimal effect" of news organizations.

In addition, more recent empirical evidence suggests that, contrary to the earlier "minimal effects" theory, the news media are able to direct our attention to certain issues and shape our opinions about them. One study found that "participants exposed to a steady stream of news about defense or about pollution came to believe that defense or pollution were more consequential problems." . . . Other studies found the fluctuations in public concern for problems like civil rights, Vietnam, crime, and inflation over the last two decades reflected variations in the attention paid to them by the major media. . . .

Theorists who maintain that the media have only a minimal effect on campaigns ought to try convincing those political candidates who believe they survive and perish because of media exposure or the lack of it. And as we saw earlier, the inability to buy media time or attract press coverage consigns third-party candidates to the dim periphery of American politics. The power to ignore political viewpoints other than the standard two-party offerings is more than minimal, it is monumental. Media exposure frequently may be the single most crucial mobilizer of votes, even if certainly not the only one.

If much of our informational and opinion intake is filtered through our previously established mental predilections, these predilections are often not part of our conscious discernment but of our unexamined perceptual conditioning—which brings us back to an earlier point: *Rather than being rational guardians against propaganda, our predispositional sets, having been shaped by prolonged exposure to earlier outputs of that same propaganda, may be active accomplices.*

Furthermore, there are many things about which we may not have a predetermined opinion. Lacking any competing information, we often unwarily embrace what we read or hear. In those instances, the media are not merely reinforcing previously held opinions, they are implanting new ones, although these implants themselves seldom fall upon tabula rasa brains and usually do not conflict too drastically with established biases. For example, millions of Americans who have an unfavorable view of the Sandinista government in Nicaragua came by that opinion through exposure to press reports rather than from direct contact with the Nicaraguan revolution. Here then is an original implant; people are prepared to hate and fear a foreign government on the basis of what they read in the papers or hear on television and radio. But this negative view is persuasive to them also because it is congruous with a long-standing and largely uncriticized anticommunist, cold war propaganda that has shaped the climate of opinion for decades.

Thus the press can effectively direct our perceptions when we have no information to the contrary and when the message seems congruent with earlier notions about these events (which themselves may be in part media created). In this way the original implant is also a reinforcement of earlier perceptions. Seemingly distinct reports about diverse events have a hidden continuity and a cumulative impact that again support previous views. To see this process as one of "minimal effects" because it merely reinforces existing views and does not change them is to overlook the fact that it was never intended to change them and was indeed designed to reinforce the dominant orthodoxy.

As to whether the negative view of the Sandinistas translates into support for a United States government policy of aggression against Nicaragua is yet another question. For an entirely different set of reasons, such as fear of loss of American lives, fear of a larger war, opposition to the draft and to the higher taxes needed to pay for war, people may be reluctant to go along with United States intervention. Yet the negative image about Nicaragua propagated by government and press does leave policymakers with a lot of room to carry out aggressive measures short of direct intervention by United States troops. So even if the press does not elicit total public support for a particular policy, it is stil not without a substantial influence in creating a *climate of opinion* that allows the government to get away with a lot, and it prevents a competing opinion about Nicaragua from occupying the high ground in the political arena. Even if those who are antagonistic toward Nicaragua constitute but a minority of the public, members of Congress and other politicians find it difficult, if not impossible, to say a positive word about the Sandinista revolution given the *publicly visible opinion* created by media and government around that issue and given the way that opinion hooks into decades of anticommunist propaganda. . . .

If the press cannot mold our every opinion, it can frame the perceptual reality around which our opinions take shape. Here may lie the most important effect of the news media: they set the issue agenda for the rest of us, choosing what to emphasize and what to ignore or suppress, in effect organizing much of our political world for us. *The media may not always be able to tell us what to think, but they are strikingly successful in telling us what to think about.* . . .

Along with other social, cultural, and educational agencies, the media teach us tunnel vision, conditioning us to perceive the problems of society as isolated particulars, thereby stunting our critical vision. Larger causalities are reduced to immediately distinct events, while the linkages of wealth, power, and policy go unreported or are buried under a congestion of surface impressions and personalities. There is nothing too essential and revealing that cannot be ignored by the American press and nothing too trivial and superficial that cannot be accorded protracted play.

In sum, the media set the limits on public discourse and public understanding. They may not always mold opinion but they do not always have to. It is enough that they create opinion visibility, giving legitimacy to certain views and illegitimacy to others. The media do the same to substantive issues that they do to candidates, raising some from oblivion and conferring legitimacy upon them, while consigning others to limbo. This power to determine the issue agenda, the information flow, and the parameters of political debate so that it extends from ultra-right to no further than moderate center, is, if not total, still totally awesome.

BEYOND ORWELL'S *1984*

The news media operate with far more finesse than did the heartless, lacerating instruments of control portrayed in George Orwell's *1984*. . . . The picture Orwell draws of a Spartan barracks society with a centrally controlled electronic surveillance system barking exercise commands at a hapless, demoralized Winston Smith in his home, leaves no doubt in Winston's mind and ours that he is being oppressed. Something quite different goes on with our news media. For instance, for twenty-five years the United States portrayed the Shah of Iran just as the State Department and the big oil companies wanted: a benign ruler and modernizer of his nation, rather than as the autocrat and plunderer he was. Hailed as a staunch ally of the West, the Shah was photographed with presidents and senators and regularly interviewed on American television. Personality profiles and features were run on him and his family, making him a familiar and perfectly likable public personage—with not a word about the thousands of men, women, and children, the students, workers and peasants this personable fellow had tortured and murdered. Here was an Orwellian inversion of the truth if ever there was one, but most of us didn't know it.

When the Iranian students took over the United States embassy in 1979 and took American hostages, one of the demands was that the United States media publicize the Shah's atrocities. For a short time, the American public was treated to some of the truth, to testimony by persons who had suffered unspeakable oppression. We heard of parents and children tortured in front of each other, including one youngster displayed before the cameras, who had had his arms chopped off in the presence of his father. It left many people shocked, including members of Congress who, like the rest of us, had been taught by the media to think of the Shah as an upright person worthy of millions of dollars in United States aid and CIA assistance.

The sinister commandant who tortures Winston in Orwell's *1984* lets us know he is an oppressor. The vision of the future is of a boot pressing down on a human face, he tells his victim. The ideological control exercised in the United States today is far more insidious. Power is always more secure when cooptive, covert, and manipulative than when nakedly brutish. The support elicited through the control of minds is more durable than the support extracted at the point of a bayonet. The essentially undemocratic nature of the mainstream media, like the other business-dominated institutions of society, must be hidden behind a neutralistic, voluntaristic, pluralistic facade. "For manipulation to be most effective, evidence of its presence should be nonexistent. . . . It is essential, therefore, that people who are manipulated believe in the neutrality of their key social institutions," writes Herbert Schiller. . . .

If Big Brother comes to America, he will not be a fearsome, foreboding figure with a heart-chilling, omnipresent glare as in *1984*. He will come with a smile on his face, a quip on his lips, a wave to the crowd, and a press that (1) dutifully reports the suppressive measures he is taking to save the nation from internal chaos and foreign threat; and (2) gingerly questions whether he will be able to succeed.

SELECTION 20
FROM
*Retrieving Democracy**

PHILIP GREEN

FULL AND FREE PUBLIC discussion and debate is an absolute prerequisite to any process of democratic decision making. And in this realm technology not only makes a difference, it makes a decisive difference. If ideas are communicated on paper, then to be without access to a printing press may be to be effectively prohibited from expressing them. If ideas are communicated along coaxial cables, lack of access to a television studio will have the same effect. The democractic guarantee of the vote requires only the legitimation of political competition to realize itself; the democratic guarantee of participation and representation requires only the existence and legal protection of autonomous communities and groups; the democratic guarantee of equal protection requires a climate of tolerance and the protection of securely independent judicial institutions. But the democratic guarantee of free speech, free press, and full public discussion requires more than protection, legitimation, or tolerance. It requires actual access to the means of communication; without that it is empty. By positive liberty or empowerment here I mean to restate the democratic requirement suggested by the late A. J. Liebling's famous epigram, "What good is a free press if you don't have one?"

What might this requirement mean in practice? The first approximation of an answer to that question may seem drastic, or even drastically simple-minded, but it is unarguable nonetheless. Democratic equality requires the dismantling of the entire structure of monopolized mass communication—newspaper chains, nationwide network television, mass-market book publishers—that we have come to take for granted as the very heart of consumer civilization itself.

Whoever controls the image in a world dominated by the mass communication of images ultimately controls that world. . . . That is so because the very structure of mass media of communication is incompatible with the structure of democratic citizenship itself: of genuine representation, of nonalienated and mutual linkage, and of continuing rotation in role and responsibility between

* (Totowa, NJ: Rowman and Allanheld, 1985): Ch. 10, pp. 219–24.

those who represent and those who are represented. There is no way that the controllers of the mass image can ever be representative of any constituency or can ever engage in anything but alienating communication.

The mass-produced image abstracts from, negates, and distorts the actual images that particular human beings have of their world, and then returns the alienated image to them as though it were their own. Lacking the technical, or technological, facility to produce the competing images of our own understanding of the world, we are all reduced to being a consumer of someone else's worldview. If for a moment we think (with apologies) of the social decisions that make up collective life as commodities, then a citizen is someone who produces those commodities, at least his or her share of them. I do not have to make my own shoes or build my own home to be a full-fledged citizen; but the person who simply consumes the commodity of social life is a pseudocitizen.

Images are not just any commodity. In the absence of resistance, of the carefully thought-out production of counterimages, they are authoritative; they irradiate, so to speak, the field of potentially autonomous communication. I am implicated in no fundamental political or social contradiction when I accept that a Florsheim shoe is really a shoe, an ingot from Bethlehem Steel is really an ingot. But if I accept that Archie Bunker is really a human being or that *Time*'s depersonalized account of this week's events is the authoritative account, then I am necessarily surrendering my own experience of what is human to a concocted experience that is necessarily a lie and a sham. It is a lie and a sham because we cannot obtain a mass audience by communicating true particulars, except in the rarest of circumstances; and yet this lie and sham is also more vivid, more real, than my own devalued experience. At the very best, our own local knowledge of what social life is all about is always going to be competing with the grander, more global, more compellingly expressed knowledge of someone else: of a dominant class.

Moreover, to have representatives to the world of mass communications is useless. What will they represent, other than what they represent today—the presence of censorship, of resistance to particular kinds of stereotyping, etc.? All that can accomplish is a further cleansing of the mass image, usually making it even more abstracted from reality, and robbing us of the one dialectical element in our relationship with the mass image: our ability to be made angry by it. What our representatives can never do, either in this world or in a more democratic one, is substitute our particular truths for the mass untruth, for then we would no longer be dealing with a medium of mass communication.

As for the democratic pluralist solution, by itself it will not do either. Given the existence of a culturally authoritative mass communications medium, the thousand local flowers that bloom in its shadow will either be infiltrated by it (that is already happening to cable television in the United States) or imitate it, but less authoritatively, catering to minority tastes that it ignores. . . . Suppose that somehow we do genuinely open ourselves to the communication of our experience by the people of one region, locality, or neighborhood to another. That would still just be a democratic undercurrent, a democratic counterculture, in an antidemocratic milieu. That's a prescription for marginal reform in a pseudodemocracy and perhaps valuable for that purpose; but as to real democracy, a prescription for abandoning it.

All social formations decay, and an egalitarian formation may well decay even quicker than others. If there is one overriding meaning to life in a democracy, though, it has to be that participating in the shared production of products and of culture is what is easy and can be accomplished by any ordinary person; whereas to subvert public life on behalf of some elite's imperial vision requires the saboteur to be extraordinarily scheming and manipulative, and pathologically ambitious. Democratic pluralism can countenance almost any set of organizational arrangements, perhaps; but it cannot countenance any arrangement whereby communal democracy is the counterculture, and alienated mass pseudodemocracy is the normative culture.

How images, whether in one's home on a screen, in a collective gathering place, in print or on a newswire, should be best collocated and communicated, is a topic that would require an entirely separate discussion. At the minimum, however, we obviously have to talk about making sure that the technology of print and picture media are widely available to individuals or groups among the public, through the sharing of technical facilities and distribution networks; and through the maintenance of enough channels of public communication to ensure that no single private entrepreneur or public corporation could dominate discussion anywhere. This is another area, clearly, where several desirable principles must exist in an uneasy balance. The value of being able to generate knowledge or images of events of national or even global interest to disparate regions and localities exists side by side with the requirement that authority and power to control their distribution be decentralized. The requirement of cooperative social ownership of communications media, in order to ensure the equal access for and thus the empowerment of the voices of all citizens, exists side by side with the equally democratic necessities that there be free room for private competition with community institutions that will inevitably fail to satisfy all needs; and that there be constitutional protection for the expression of dissident views, and for minority access to the tools of communication that might be denied by a monolithic public voice.

The reference to private competition especially requires further explication, for that is a proposition that in this realm has traditionally been ignored or denigrated by socialists, egalitarians, and advocates of community control. It will not do to substitute community control of the means of communication for either the dominated mass market model or the centralized state control model and think that we have accomplished something. If all printing presses, television equipment, and so forth, were owned by local publics, who or what would guarantee access to those means of communication for dissidents, nonconformists, and the like? Judicial review alone is not a satisfactory answer, for that is the last line of defense of our rights. In an egalitarian society, any litigant who appears before the ultimate tribunal demanding equal access to some community newspaper will by then have undergone so much struggle, obloquy, and perhaps ostricization that triumph seems hardly worthwhile. Liebling's rhetorical question is as relevant for the advocates of community control, or of workplace democracy, as it is for advocates of the free market.

. . . The market for communication of ideas, moreover, is the one market that ought to be entirely and truly free. Neither corporate oligopolies nor state nor local monopolies in the means of communication are compatible with democratic equality. . . . A democratic system of communications must do more than make room for local control and individual right of access; it must encourage and protect a genuine pluralism in the sources of access. A democratic constitution, therefore, ought to provide special protection for and encouragement of the private as well as communal ownership of the means of communication in particular. This might be done via either tax incentives of programs of direct subsidy or in some other manner. However it is done, the principle of maintaining a privileged position for the publication and communication of ideas and images by independent persons or groups has to be part of the central philosophy of democratic political equality, and constitutionally protected.

SELECTION 21
FROM
*Democracy & Capitalism**

SAMUEL BOWLES AND HERBERT GINTIS

[I]T IS CLEARLY INCONSISTENT to consider a society to be democratic when the rights of popular determination and individual choice do not extend to the social relations through which preferences themselves are formed. This principle is of course recognized in liberal doctrine, but only in a dichotomized learning-choosing form. For example, compulsory education is held accountable through the democratic character of government, and such "private" institutions of preference formation as churches, the various communications media, and proprietary educational institutions are held accountable through the freedom of market choice and voluntary association.

Philosophical critiques of the liberal treatment of the economy have, reasonably enough, centered on questions of distributional justice and allocational efficiency. The learning-choosing partition, however, sheds additional light upon the shortcomings of the liberal justification of capitalism. Liberal discourse clearly presents the economy not only as a set of private institutions, but as a sphere of social life within which "choosing" rather than "learning" occurs. This notion is sanctified in liberal economic theory which, following the liberal economist Lionel Robbins, defines economics as "the science which studies human behavior as a relationship between given ends and scarce means which have alternative uses." This is the source of the commonsense notion of the economy as a site that produces *things* according to the *preferences* of its participants. . . .

But the economy produces people. The experience of individuals as economic actors is a major determinant of their personal capacities, attitudes, choices, interpersonal relations, and social philosophies. Individuals develop their needs, powers, capacities, consciousness, and personal attributes partly through the way they go about transforming and appropriating their natural environment. Moreover, individuals and groups regulate their own development in part to the extent that they succeed in controlling their own labor. Thus under ideal

*(New York: Basic Books, 1986): pp. 131–45.

circumstances, developmental practices form an essential and intentional element of production itself. Our critique of the capitalist economy in this respect is that it renders the developmental practices of workers in production relatively ineffective and sharply circumscribed while giving broad scope to educational practices of employers, and that the effects of these arrangements, both intended and unintended, are antithetical to the development of a democratic culture.

To the extent that the experiences of production constitute an important learning environment, then, the despotic character of the capitalist economy obstructs the ability of liberal democratic capitalism to foster generalized popular control over personal development. If, as we argue . . . the economy is a public sphere generally unaccountable to its participants, these participants will not possess the social power to control their own development either as workers or, insofar as development through work suffuses their personalities and capacities, as citizens and family members. The problem concerns not only the dubious status of a liberal capitalist society as democratic but the ability of such a society in the long run to support and reproduce even minimally the liberal democratic systems of state decision making. This broader claim requires a sustained investigation of the relationship between the capitalist economy and democratic culture.

By democratic culture we mean a broad diffusion of politically relevant information, skills, and attitudes of political effectiveness, as well as the availability of forms of discourse conducive to the effective functioning of democratic institutions. A frequent claim of the defenders of liberal democratic capitalism is that it promotes precisely such a democratic culture. These claims . . . cannot be summarily dismissed. The discourse of individual rights, the near-universal spread of literacy, the extension of social interaction to ever-wider circles of contact, the consequent destruction of many forms of patriarchy, parochialism, and political deference are all integral to democratic culture, and at least in some measure they are promoted by the extension of the capitalist economy.

But we find the claim that capitalism supports the generation and regeneration of democratic culture not altogether persuasive. Our arguments for a critical reconsideration of this claim concern the division of labor within the capitalist enterprise and the market.

Consider, first, the experience of production as it may affect the formation of people and communities. Our analysis of the organization of the labor process within the capitalist enterprise suggests that it may be a powerful influence on human development, one that is antithetical to the production of a democratic culture. . . .

. . . [U]nder conditions of capitalist production the division of labor within the enterprise quite generally exhibits four relevant characteristics. These are the minute fragmentation of tasks, the separation of the conception of tasks from their execution, the hierarchical control of the labor process, and the assignment of persons to positions on the basis of race, sex, age, and academic credentials. These four characteristics would appear to promote the *opposite* of a democratic culture, as they concentrate information, information processing, and decision-making skills at the narrow pinnacle of a pyramidal structure. At the same time, the structure of capitalist production promotes a sense of political ineffectiveness, and assigns to racial, sexual, and other differences a set of hierarchical meanings that are as inconsistent with tolerance and respect as they are hostile to the forms of solidarity and cooperation necessary for effective political action.

But can these antidemocratic effects be traced to the specifically capitalist structure of production? Each of the four characteristics might well be taken as a lamentable manifestation of the technically or genetically determined requirements of efficient production. These would then presumably appear in any system, and thus would present natural rather than social limits to democratic accountability.

If labor were like any other input in the textbook rendition of neoclassical economics, and its use were governed simply by costlessly enforced contractual relations, the liberal counterclaims would be compelling. But . . . the neoclassical representation of labor is incoherent: it cannot make sense of even the most rudimentary facts and enduring tendencies of the capitalist economy such as unemployment. It is precisely the noncontractual aspect of the relationship between boss and worker (the extraction of labor from the worker) that simultaneously explains the above-mentioned four characteristics of the labor process and forces a divergence between efficiency and profitability even under competitive conditions. The minute fragmentation of tasks and the separation of conception from execution make individual workers dispensable (and hence susceptible to threat of dismissal) by restricting the areas of production involving high levels of skill and expertise; fragmentation renders the worker's activities more susceptible to measurement and supervision. The hierarchical control of the labor process, whatever its technical properties, is required to enforce the delivery of labor services, and the assignment of persons to positions on the basis of race, sex, age, or academic credentials serves to legitimate the hierarchical division of labor and divide workers against each other. It is on this basis that we can claim that the hierarchical structure of the labor process is consistent with a competitive equilibrium of profit-maximizing noncolluding capitalists, but it is not reducible to the imperatives of technical efficiency in production. . . . We are thus permitted to say that these characteristics of the division of labor within the enterprise are not the result of technological requirements or genetic limitations and that they are (at least in part) the results of the specifically capitalist structure of production even in its idealized competitive form.

If the antidemocratic nature of the labor process has been all but ignored by advocates of the liberal democratic argument, the other major facet of the coordination of the division of labor in capitalist society—the private and decentralized coordination of the activities of the producers of diverse commodities through the medium of markets—has provided its foundation. It is true, to be sure, that since de Tocqueville few liberal theorists have made much of the relationship between markets and culture. Where the issue has been raised, as in Milton Friedman's classic defense of markets, it has been to assert that markets inhibit prejudice, censorship, and the arbitrary use of power. . . .

The strength of the argument lies in the anonymity and range of choise offered in markets, which explain, to return to Friedman's example, why the consumer of bread does not know whether it was produced by "a Negro, by a Christian or a Jew." The shortcoming of the argument consists in overlooking the relationship between markets, political participation, and the formation of a democratic culture.

Demonstrating this shortcoming is quite straightforward. A democratic culture is produced and reproduced through the activities that people undertake. Perhaps the most important of these activities is democratic politics itself. Under what conditions will people engage in learning democratic culture by doing democratic politics? Clearly, the answer is where such opportunities exist and where there are incentives to participate. The incentives to participate will be greater where something important is at stake, or to put it differently, where the opportunity cost of not participating is high.

Markets minimize the cost to the individual of not participating in democratic political practices, for markets promote exit over voice and hence provide an alternative to political participation as a means toward achieving desired ends. The extensive reliance upon markets thus undermines the conditions conducive to a high level of participation and a vibrant democratic culture. If most important social outcomes are generated by market processes, the stakes of democratically constituted decision processes are severely circumscribed. That markets might undermine democratic political participation through limiting the stakes and reducing the opportunity costs of not participating is perhaps not surprising. For it is precisely this reduction in the "need" for collective decision making that is so much applauded in liberal social theory.

Perhaps an example will make our point clear. Consider the disgruntled parent of an elementary-school student seeking to rectify the inadequacy of the curriculum at the neighborhood public school. Assuming that the parent's suggestions have been ignored, he or she may organize others to elect a new school board, or may threaten to do so. Or he or she may withdraw the child, curtail competing expenditures if possible, and send the child to a private school with the preferred curriculum. The opportunities open to the parent are voice or exit. Markets inhibit participation by ensuring that the option of exit is always present, thus undercutting the commitment to voice.

The example may appear limited, but it is not. The person who feels strongly about street crime or air pollution can either organize to improve the social and physical environment, or can "shop" for a community with a more desirable bundle of characteristics. The disgruntled individual with limited resources and less mobility can buy an air conditioner, or a gun.

In short, the issue of market versus nonmarket decision making, which is traditionally seen as an "economic" debate to be decided on grounds of allocational efficiency, must also be political and cultural. The issue cannot be resolved in favor of market or planning, we submit, for the same reason that a reasonable political philosophy does not choose between liberty and popular sovereignty.

The capitalist economy, then, produces people; and the people it produces are far from ideally equipped with democratic sentiments and capacities. The instrumental conception of action, which has diverted liberal attention from this problem in the evaluation of economic structure, is no more auspicious as a basis for a theory of specifically political action. . . .

Our objections to the instrumental conception of politics parallel our reservations concerning instrumentalism in economic theory. First, by abstracting from the formation of wills and the process of human development, this conception extols exit and denigrates voice, and hence reduces democratic government to representative government. By devaluing political participation (or rather, reducing participation to the act of registering one's preferences—voting), it counsels against politically empowering forms of community association which lie between the individual and the state itself.

The liberal approach thereby effectively identifies the democratization of a sphere of social life (such as the economy), either with its organization according to principles of unimpeded exit or with its assimilation into the liberal democratic state. As a result, the liberal mind has difficulty expanding the menu of democratic choices beyond the conservative reliance on the market and the social democratic disposition toward an enlarged state. The affirmation of the desirability of heterogeneous forms of social power, each governed by an interaction of exit and voice, is thus precluded by the instrumental conception of political action. . . .

. . . The instrumental conception of politics renders liberalism indifferent or hostile to the formation of those loyalties and social bonds upon which a vibrant democracy must depend. This is nowhere more clear than in its devaluation of decentralized autonomous communities.

Far from fostering . . . a democratic pluralism, liberal capitalism has produced a political wasteland stretching between the individual and the state. The problem, according to Hannah Arendt, is not the scale of social life, but its substance: "What makes mass society so difficult to bear is not the number of people involved, but the fact that the world between them has lost its power to gather them together . . . and to separate them." . . . But the era of the ballot box and the marketplace did not so much destroy the intervening communities as it did disempower and depoliticize them. As a result the state came to monopolize politics. . . .

The great liberal thinkers themselves did not pretend that choice based on instrumental action could form the universal model of social practice. Obligation, loyalty, love, shame, civic virtue, and a host of other sentiments and commitments were variously held to be essential influences upon social action. Even Bernard Mandeville, who shocked his eighteenth-century readers with *The Fable of the Bees*, did not envision that private greed would yield public virtue in all realms of society; instead he focused on the economy. . . . Early liberal economic thinkers—notably Smith and Bentham—showed a lively interest in both the learning and choosing aspects of economic life, pondering the kinds of human beings that the emerging capitalist system would produce and advocating institutions to guide and correct this process. The celebrated ability of markets to reconcile individual interests and collective rationality—or at least to substantially attenuate the contradiction between the two—was always viewed as conditional on a kind of morality and moral action. We cannot agree more with Denis O'Brien on this point:

> While the classical writers were the earliest fully to appreciate the allocative mechanism of the market, and the power, subtlety and efficiency of this mechanism, they were perfectly clear that it could operate only within a framework of restrictions. Such restrictions were partly legal and partly religious, moral and conventional; and they were designed to ensure the coincidence of self and community interest. . . .

The early liberals recognized that the perpetuation of these moral, religious, and conventional commitments could not be taken for granted. But later views, especially those inspired by the instrumental theory of action exemplified by neoclassical economics, came to embrace a much simpler conception: the exogenous individual. Custom, community, and commitment might still be the bedrock of social interaction, but liberal thinkers—rejecting Edmund Burke's activitism on behalf of tradition—increasingly saw these as the result of a more or less historical legacy rather than as the outcomes of ongoing projects of cultural reproduction. Accordingly, the problem of the reproduction of a culture consistent with the workings of the market, the ballot box, and the other institutions favored by liberalism dropped from theoretical debate.

To some extent the eclipse of cultural practices as a theoretical concern has flowed from the logic of liberal discourse itself. By couching its fundamental principles in terms of an individual and asocial conception of rights, liberal discourse makes it difficult to express solidarity and cooperation as goals of political practices. . . . The sole forms of social solidarity explicitly sanctioned in liberal discourse are nationality, based on common citizenship, and kinship, based on the family. It is perhaps for this reason that among the most effective forms of "the politics of becoming" in some advanced capitalist countries today are nationalism and antifeminist defense of the patriarchal family.

Paradoxically, the disappearance from *theoretical* discussion of the problem of cultural reproduction in the nineteenth century coincided with a growing awareness that heightened labor mobility, urbanization, economic dynamism, and other outcomes of the growth of capitalist economy itself had undermined many traditional bases of morality and social control. Just as the issue of cultural reproduction fell from theoretical view, it began to assume immense practical importance in the minds and work of the growing army of reformers and administrators who since the nineteenth century have attempted to construct state surrogates for the rapidly eroding family, neighborhood community, craft guild, church, community, and the like. The result was the erection of compulsory schools, asylums, and prisons on an unprecedented scale during an era that prided itself on tearing down other walls in the interest of economic freedom. These costs of enforcing the liberal capitalist order have continued to mount in the twentieth century.

A fundamental problem of liberal social theory, then, is that it takes as axiomatic the reproduction of those cultural, moral, and economic conditions which are necessary to make good the normative claims made on behalf of its favored institutions. In the absence of vital communities standing between the individual and the state, liberalism's cherished political principle, liberty, is experienced more as loneliness than as freedom. And the putative allocative efficiency of the market is challenged by the proliferation of enforcement costs arising from the exercise of instrumental self-interest in a conflict-ridden economy inhabited by strangers.

In its more modern variants liberalism is thus not only temperamentally ill-disposed but conceptually ill-equipped to address the problem of the forms of learning promoted by the spread of markets and elections as the dominant framework for choosing.

SELECTION 22
FROM
*The Democratic State**

STEPHEN L. ELKIN

IT MAY BE POSSIBLE to argue that some measure of popular control is, in fact, an essential feature of the capitalist system and, thus, that when the state works to reproduce the system, it is doing more than serving the interests of capital. Unless this line of argument is developed considerably beyond its present position, however, we simply have an elaborate way of noting that in liberal democracies, popular control and the promotion of business interests can operate simultaneously. . . . We are still left with the theoretical problem of how the two are joined together in practice. . . . It is to this and related tasks that the discussion now turns.

We may best start by reiterating the opening remarks concerning the liberal democratic division of labor. Liberal democracy is a type of regime where the distinction between "public" and "private" is central, signifying the distinction between authority and production and how each is to be organized. When we talk about the regime, we are then referring to the basic organizing principles of the society. The state itself is the constitutional-legal entity that sets out the authoritative policies of the society and wields much of the organized means of coercion. The extent of its legitimacy may range anywhere from mere acquiescence to active support.

A state that is operating in a liberal democratic regime requires "satisfactory" economic performance from the private holders and managers of productive assets, and it needs this for at least two reasons. . . . First, most of its important officials are directly subject to popular approval through elections or indirectly through appointment by those who have been elected. Sustained poor performance, and thus low or declining levels of material well-being, will mean electoral difficulties and possibly electoral rout. . . . Even many of those whose appointments do not depend on electoral returns are also concerned about

*"Pluralism in Its Place: State and Regime in Liberal Democracy," in *The Democratic State*, Roger Benjamin and Stephen L. Elkin (Eds.) (Lawrence, KS: University Press of Kansas, 1985): pp. 186–96.

consistently poor economic performance, since it may result in an undesired rearrangement of their responsibilities.

Second, state activities require revenues, the production of which is not in the hands of state officials. . . . Economic performance to produce revenue is required for a variety of reasons, ranging from officials paying for their perquisites to financing policies that are central to their careers and to their conception of larger national purposes. The performance of owners and managers of productive assets is of even more concern to the state to the degree that a substantial portion of national revenues originates through trading abroad. If the nation is highly integrated into the world economy, owners and managers in effect become public officials, helping to earn the nation's keep. So much is obvious. The implications are less so.

A first step toward seeing the implications is to summarize the preceding discussion as a basic premise of the liberal democratic state: officials of the state are beholden to the citizenry but cannot meet the citizens' concerns, serve their own careers, or manage the state without a satisfactory level of economic performance. Public officials cannot run the state without at least the tacit cooperation of owners and managers of productive assets. Of course, the extent of officials' concern will vary, not least because the citizens' interest in economic performance and their ability to forcefully express their views are subject to variation across space and time. Public officials *will*, however, be concerned about the level of economic performance.

None of this would be a problem if businessmen on their own would engage in the necessary activities. Economic performance would be high enough so as not to outrage citizens, and at least modest levels of state action would be possible. But whereas businessmen will clearly make some investments, take some risks, and employ some labor, even in difficult times, the great productive apparatus that is required to employ a growing population, to generate future investment capital, to provide public services, and otherwise to pay the public bill will not arise unaided. Commanding businessmen to perform will clearly not be sufficient, precisely to the degree they are guaranteed disposition over productive assets. As Lindblom puts it, owners and managers must be *induced* to perform, and public officials have long engaged in making such inducements (Lindblom, 1977, ch. 13). At the heart of the matter is likely to be the large scale of investment that is required and the high degree of uncertainty, which necessitate some fragile combination of the following: daring entrepreneurial vision—or at least "animal spirits"—and the promise that risks can be controlled, that rewards will be high, and that compensation for failure is possible. These last three are at the center of the state's inducements to perform. . . .

Public officials therefore really have two tasks (Block, 1977). On the negative side, they must try to avoid reducing the confidence of businessmen. Low confidence means low investment. Erratic management of the currency or talk about nationalization will distress businessmen and make them less inclined to take risks. On the positive side, actual inducements must be offered. These may run from tax incentives and state provision of research money and research findings, to facilitating the granting of various permits. The latter may involve punishing rapacious officials and replacing them with those who will perform in nonarbitrary ways. Not only are the alternatives manifold; they can be organized in a variety of ways. In some liberal democratic states, everything may be accomplished centrally, while in others—the United States being a conspicuous example—much will be done locally. . . . Thus, there are many ways to be concerned with economic performance, but once again, public officials *will* be concerned.

It is important to emphasize the differences between the view that is elaborated here and any theory built around the great power of owners and holders of productive assets. We might be tempted to conclude from the preceding discussion that the connection between market and state is much as the ruling-class thesis proposes, with perhaps a clearer understanding of just why property holders are so powerful. Public officials are more or less completely dependent on owners and managers for economic performance and thus are subject to manipulation: businessmen are powerful because they are needed, or so it would be argued. If there were no more than this to the regime argument, it would indeed be in danger of collapsing into an assertion about the power of actors. The essential feature of the liberal democratic regime, however, is not that owners and managers can exert power but is the very shape of the regime itself, particularly the division between market and popularly controlled state. Public officials do not have to be told to worry about economic performance or to facilitate it: they understand that for them to do their job as public officials, to stay in office, and to serve their ambitions, the owners and managers of productive assets must do *their* job. . . .

Differently stated, officials do negotiate with particular business interests, and power struggles may well result. But their real interest lies in the level of economic performance more generally, and that is not a matter of particular businessmen coordinating their efforts, . . . deciding to invest or not, and bargaining with or attempting to coerce government, but of large numbers of businessmen responding as individuals to market incentives. . . . Officials, then, are concerned with the workings of a social process, namely, the market. Indeed, if business-state relations consisted predominantly of officials dealing with business spokesmen who were in a position to coordinate the actions of large numbers of their fellows, power considerations would play a larger role in explaining state action. For in addition to business groups trying to extract particular concessions, other businessmen would be attempting more generally to press class interests.

There is another reason that the argument presented here is not essentially about power: the division between market and state is a two-way street. Businessmen are not unschooled in the workings of the political economy. They know that if they demand too much—and if they do it in a clumsy overweening fashion—their position may become precarious. For their part, public officials see the performance of owners and managers as a central question because the latter have a *choice*. They may, for example, consume substantial portions of their capital in ways that do little for future productivity, or they may export it. But the choice is theirs, because property rights are extensively enforced; if owners and managers do not exercise discretion, they may find that the basis for their choice has been eroded. To this we may add that the division between market and state means that those who control productive assets also require various state authorizations; this, too, is understood. To be sure, the disposition of businessmen to restrain their desires is probably less powerful than that of public officials to see that economic performance is substantial: the consequences for public officials are more proximate and tangible. But as public officials pursue their concerns about economic performance, they are likely to find businessmen exercising some restraint. In summary, it is the mix of popular control and the possibility of choice in the form of property rights that provides the underlying dynamic for business-state relations.

If the story were to end here, the relationship between public officials and controllers of assets would be close and intimate, or distant but amicable. Public officials would need only to maintain business confidence and, where appropriate, directly to facilitate performance. There would be little to prevent them from taking their cues from businessmen. Businessmen could happily be left to sort out among themselves what was necessary for their performance and to convey through various means the results of their deliberations. In some contemporary liberal democratic regimes this indeed may approximate present arrangements, and historically it may well have been true at one time of most. These cases must be explained, however, because it is not obvious why popular control of authority should only find expression in an essentially passive form—simply providing the motive for public officials' concern with economic performance—and should be confined to judging the overall results. Even if citizens agree that a substantial portion of the social product should be directed toward ensuring high levels of economic performance, the question of how much may be consumed and paid out in the form of wages and public benefits is likely to be a continuing source of dispute. And even if the mass of citizens have little sense of the connection between the present division of the social product and future performance, they will certainly have an opinion on what constitutes a fair division and how those who lose out should be treated.

This potential for conflict is built into the very arrangements of liberal democratic regimes. The very existence of public forums for consideration of the public's business invites the transformation into a public matter of what might initially be thought of as a private grievance. Furthermore, because the means of achieving satisfactory economic performance—namely, the market—will force citizens to change jobs, move, or otherwise greatly alter the basic features of their life circumstances—something that we may reasonably assume they do not wish to do—they will probably turn to the available instruments of popular control to prevent it. They will, for example, seek to constrain business choice, provide compensation to those who lose out, and resist aids to business performance that contribute to major alterations in basic features of their lives. . . . Perhaps it is the notion of a "free market" that blinds us to what is otherwise obvious. Having a choice between alternatives is freedom, the freedom of the marketplace. But the ability to keep one's life circumstances as they presently are is also freedom. . . . This the market does not offer. Citizens know this and act on the knowledge when possible.

In other words, citizens will inevitably be drawn toward employing institutions of popular control in ways that will make it more difficult for public officials and businessmen to arrive at any agreement, even a tacit one, about how economic performance is to be assured. The reasons for citizens so acting may be other than specified here; that is of no consequence. It matters only that they will inevitably be drawn to act in a fashion that will make it difficult to promote economic performance. That citizens also wish for economic growth is, of course, true. Indeed, as I have said, the concern of public officials for business performance partly rests on this wish. Popular control is, however, just that: citizen concern with the full range of public matters.

The extent to which citizens make known their views and press them with vigor will vary, but the potential is always present, requiring that measures be taken to ensure that popular control does not greatly interfere with the assessment of how to promote economic performance. Unless popular control is constrained, the liberal democratic regime will collapse or be transformed. Either private control of productive assets will be markedly reduced, or businessmen will cease to perform, or both. The means by which popular control is constrained and the degree of constraint that is achieved are the principal features that distinguish liberal democratic states from one another. A number of means are, however, common to all; they simply follow from basic features of liberal democracy and operate quite apart from conscious efforts to reduce the impact that citizens have on the relations between public officials and controllers of assets.

Consider, first, that the strength of popular control is in the electoral arena. The threat of electoral penalty strongly motivates officials; and indeed, without elections, other forms of popular control would be considerably less effective. But the potency of popular control diminishes the further we move from the electoral arena, and by the time we get to decisions made by executive agencies, it is clearly weak and indirect. Yet, the administrative arena can and does serve as a forum for negotiating at least some of businessmen's concerns and some of what they may wish for by way of inducement. Liberal democracy allows for the broad facilitation of economic performance simply because the reach of popular control is limited.

Additionally, even if the methods of maintaining business confidence and facilitating performance appear on the public agenda, owners and managers have fundamental advantages in the discussion. As is already apparent, they need not press for access to public officials; the most visible of them may even be solicited. Moreover, the very fact of owning productive assets provides controllers of these assets with the solution to a problem that other interests must struggle with and indeed may not master. Opinion without benefit of organization and other resources is weak. Business enterprises, especially larger ones, are, however, already organizations with a complement of human and financial resources that may be employed to pursue other than business ends.

Finally, it is not only public officials who realize that social well-being depends heavily on business performances; so, inevitably, do many citizens, to whom businessmen appear to be more than a sectoral interest. This, plus a natural tendency to approve of those who flourish under the existing social rules, provides a substantial reservoir of positive opinion upon which public officials and businessmen may rely.

One implication of these built-in advantages must be emphasized: they operate with a kind of historical carry-over. As a group of citizens at a given moment attempt to offer an assessment of the distribution of the social product, they are, for example, attempting to do so in the context of a set of institutional arrangements. These arrangements are themselves at least partly the results of historical disputes in which the built-in advantages have operated. In short, the built-in advantages cumulate. This has the simple but profound consequence that the ordinary flow of public action works to screen out challenges. Those citizens, for example, who think that the operation of banking laws is unnecessarily weighted in favor of promoting business performance not only must object to particular actions but must also undo the institutional arrangements that created the agencies to take the actions.

Even as there are, however, certain features of liberal democratic states that work to limit the expression of popular control, citizens will still offer assessments of how to deal with the question of economic perfomance. Expressions of citizens' opinions are constrained, rather than squashed, not least because there will always be available some public officials who derive advantage from mobilizing citizens to challenge the present form of concern for business performance. However, there will be limits to the number of public officials so inclined and to the distance that they will be willing to travel. This is, after all, a dangerous road, since a citizenry that is in full cry may come to look askance at the present institutional arrangements that the existing, as well as the aspiring, officials wish to help manage. Additionally, even combative disaffected politicians are likely to be leery of inducing deep dismay in businessmen, since eventually these politicians either will have to operate a political economy in which businessmen are central or will have to deal with the consequences of poor performance that attend any major transformation. In their turn, however, businessmen are likely to recognize that officials must be seen to be responsive to strong expressions of citizen opinion, quite apart from any preference they have in the matter.

It will help to summarize the argument to this point. The facts of private control of productive assets and popular control of authority mean that public officials are inevitably drawn to promote economic performance. Because promoting satisfactory performance requires at least the tacit cooperation of controllers of productive assets (they will not do what is necessary on their own), their definition of what is required to gain the desired result will weigh heavily in the choices that officials make. Even though controllers of assets may not always agree among themselves or with public officials on what will serve economic performance, such agreement is not necessary for us to say that inevitably the state broadly serves business interests.

When we say, then, that the state promotes business interests, we are making two closely related but distinct points. First, officials are concerned about economic performance, and in their efforts to facilitate it, they attempt to see that business enterprise will flourish. Of course, particular enterprises will suffer at any given moment, but the aim is to see that in a general way, controllers of assets will reap enough rewards to induce them to continue performing at a satisfactory level. Second, in their efforts to facilitate performance, the actual definition of what is necessary is heavily shaped by what businessmen say is required. For both of these reasons, the interests of owners and controllers of assets are well served.

Public officials, however, are not unconstrained in their concern for economic performance, because citizens may and do offer their own assessments on such matters as the distribution of the social product. But basic features of regime and state operate to prevent any regular complication of the complex mutual accommodation between controllers of assets and public officials. Breaches of these limits do sometimes occur, but in no way do they alter either the dispositions of public officials to facilitate economic performance or the prominent role of businessmen in defining what this requires.

The practices of public officials give actual content to the formal institutions that are crucial to operating the state. By their efforts to pay attention both to businessmen's definitions of how to promote economic performance and to assertions of popular control, public officials make possible the coexistence of contradictory claims. They in fact lead an elaborate minuet. If there are limits on popular control, but a danger that such limits may be breached, how is business performance to be maintained? If businessmen demand too much to perform, including a substantial reduction in the exercise of popular control, what will prevent a shift from citizen acquiescence to mass mobilization?

Neither overweening businessmen nor a citizenry that is in full democratic cry can be accommodated for very long in a liberal democratic state. Ambitious politicians who are bent on exciting the citizenry need to be reminded by their peers of the consequences of excessive incitement for the state as a whole: businessmen will reduce their performance. Businessmen who are attempting to have most or all of their dealings with the state handled administratively, out of citizen view, or who are resisting democratic prerogatives to control market behavior need to be reminded that failure to concede some regulation raises the possibility of even greater efforts at popular control. They also need to be reminded that national security may demand that their prerogatives be curbed. Citizens need to be reminded that even as efforts are being made to protect and promote their ability to participate in politics, so that they may be a credible deterrent to the more greedy and overbearing among owners and managers, the health of society depends on business investment.

There is no guarantee, however, that officials will prove capable of managing the state in the manner just indicated or of maintaining these practices over time. The incentives to do so—which presumably include some mix of approval of the regime's features, of the state that has been built on them, and of a desire to pursue a career within such a state—are diffuse and long-term. Short-term gains are tempting because of their promise of immediate tangible rewards. Encouraging businessmen who think they need more inducements to invest, or exciting already mobilized citizens to demand even more, is probably easier than reminding either of them about what is required to run a liberal democratic state. In any case, even if most public officials were to take the longer view, they might be incompetent or overwhelmed by the uncertainty of social affairs. Perhaps more importantly, a vital liberal democratic state rests on more than having public officials manage state institutions. At the least, the desire for popular control must be continually renewed outside of state institutions, as must the desire individually to accumulate capital, which lies at the heart of the enterprise-based market. For any or all of the above reasons, the balance between popular control and the promotion of business performance may shift enough to transform the liberal democratic state and the regime on which it rests. . . .

Out sketch of a theory of the liberal democratic state is not yet complete. . . . The discussion has centered on the state's facilitating economic performance, and the significance of popular control has been largely interpreted in this light. Such a focus, while it is essential to any state theory, leaves too much unsaid. We cannot yet differentiate, for example, between policy making concerning tax incentives to stimulate investment and the protection of civil liberties, nor are we yet clear as to whether all state actions that might in some way facilitate economic performance are to be treated equally. Unless we can elaborate the theory further, we will inevitably be drawn into increasingly implausible assertions about the actions of public officials and the controllers of assets, since virtually all policy choices in one way or another potentially impinge on economic performance. If we mean to argue that the state inevitably facilitates economic performance, we must show that this does not mean that all aspects of public action are equally relevant to this concern. At issue is the extent to which the interests of business dominate across the spectrum of policy domains and, concomitantly, the extent to which popular control, and thus a variety of other than business concerns, shapes policy discussion. . . .

Given the argument outlined so far, the connection made by public officials and businessmen between economic performance and any particular policy question is a good first step toward explaining this variation across policy domains. . . . A well-understood connection will more readily focus the thinking and action of public officials and will make them more receptive to the approaches of business spokesmen. By the same token, owners and managers will take some trouble to indicate their preferences in the matter. Moreover, if the process of mutual accommodation between public officials and businessmen spills out into the public arena, officials are more likely to resist proposals that are offered by citizen spokesmen as they (officials) attempt to arrive at a course of action aimed at actually facilitating economic performance.

If no close connection is perceived, public officials are more likely to be guided by the variety of interest group and broader citizen concerns. But state action is still not completely free of the interests of business, as may also be inferred from the propositions already advanced. When policy choice involves complex implementation of programs and when business organizations that are capable of carrying them out are already in existence, public officials will be drawn to options that make use of such organizations. The officials' desire to be successful, whether in terms of career or larger purposes, impels them in this direction. The very fact of private ownership creates this incentive. . . . A revealing example here is the American preference for health-insurance schemes that rely on private insurers. In addition, of course, the relevant business enterprises themselves are likely to promote private alternatives, and businessmen in general argue that economic performance is itself at stake. Still, when the connection between the policy at issue and economic performance is seen to be weak, the pulling and hauling characteristic of a developed interest-group politics is most likely to occur. It is then that business groups are one among many. The other typical form of politics under these conditions is the coziness of "iron triangles."

Perhaps the best way to see the connection between these two types of policy domains (where economic performance is and is not seen to be at issue) is to note the rapidity with which iron triangles, or vital contests between equally matched interest groups, can turn into a discussion dominated by a concern with the interests of business. On their own, businessmen probably cannot bring about such a rapid shift and, indeed, may lose out to other interests; but once public officials believe that economic performance is at stake, the transformation of one sort of policy domain into another can be quick indeed.

It is important to emphasize that the proposition "The state promotes business interests" is not first and foremost an assertion about the outcome of a series of decisions but about the disposition of public officials to facilitate economic performance and why they are likely to be guided by businessmen in this regard. Empirically, the concern for business interests is likely to dominate a wide range of outcomes, but businessmen can and do lose. It is perhaps most revealing of the nature of the argument being presented that, in comparison to pluralist or ruling-class views, it is not essentially an argument about the exercise of power. It is most assuredly an argument about advantage (but not only that, as we shall see). However, the promise of the theoretical argument is precisely that we can now see the state as being active and independent, neither neutral in its actions nor up for grabs in a scramble for power among interests. *And* we can say all of this without having to rely on implausible arguments about concentrated power and its exercise; the arguments follow from the very character of the regime. Pluralist views of liberal democratic politics go astray in that they do not take the regime seriously as it shapes the actions of the state. The ruling-class thesis goes astray in thinking that the impact of the regime can be reduced to a study of the power of a business elite; that is, in a different manner, the thesis does not take the regime seriously.

The shift away from explanations that rely on the power of actors is part of a larger and common theme in social science: the search for systemic explanations. Aside from the shortcomings already noted, the *form* of actor-power explanations is inadequate. Both pluralist and ruling-class notions are essentially simple causal explanations, dealing in efficient causes. They locate an agent or agents who are supposed, by their actions, to produce an outcome. The regime argument directs our attention to the character of the whole and says, in effect, "Don't look for particular actors and efficient causes." A state of affairs is not explained by an agent and its actions but by the set of relations in which the agent is embedded. The explanation of why the state serves business interests is not only *not* business power, *neither* is it, at bottom, the disposition of public officials. Businessmen have an attentive audience, and officials are disposed in particular ways because of the very form of the regime. . . .

SELECTION 23
FROM
*Power and the Powerless**
MICHAEL PARENTI

[T]HE RESOURCES OF POWER are not randomly scattered among the population to be used in autonomous ways but are distributed within a social system, and the way the system is organized has a decisive effect on what resources are available to whom. Any listing of the resources of power would include property, wealth, organization, social prestige, social legitimacy, number of adherents, various kinds of knowledgeability and leadership skills, technological skills, control of jobs, control of information, ability to manipulate the symbolic environment, and ability to apply force and violence. This list is not exhaustive and its categories are crude and overlapping, but there probably would be fairly wide agreement among students of various persuasions that its items represent most of the essential power resources. . . .

Lacking accessibility to power resources, certain classes of people will chronically gain a deficient share of the social desiderata. In modern Western societies the social desiderata are usually thought to include such things as material comfort; financial security; adequate and safe diet; clean natural environment; good health and good medical care; sanitary living conditions; opportunities for recreation, learning, self-development, and self-esteem; autonomy of choice in personal affairs; opportunities for participation in social affairs; gratifying relationships; meaningful and useful work; freedom from exploitative and degrading labor; and other such tangible and intangible life values. . . .

What are and are not to be considered desiderata, however, is far from a settled question. Competition for the privilege of defining and ranking the desiderata is itself a point of political contention. Differences as to the significance and desirability of particular social outputs vary with class, subcultural context, and ideological commitment. The position people occupy in the social structure shapes much of their social experience, including how they define what are and are not the "good" and "bad" things in life. Consider, for instance, the distinction usually made between the "material and nonmaterial" desiderata.

*(New York: St. Martin's Press, 1978): Ch. 6, pp. 63–68, 71–72, 75–78.

For well-to-do persons who do not have to face the oppressive realities of substandard living conditions, "bad housing" is likely to be categorized as a "material" condition and one of no great urgency in their lives. But for slum dwellers, bad housing is not only a material factor but a way of life. Conditions of overcrowding, infestation, poor sanitation, and lack of proper heat and ventilation represent social and psychological realities as well as material ones, affecting one's morale, self-expectations, self-esteem, personal relations, life performances, and life chances in ways that are difficult for more comfortably situated persons to imagine.

Some Powerless Groups

Groups having the least power also have fewer of the good things in life. The dilemma of the dispossessed is that their material and nonmaterial deprivations leave them at the low end of any index of power and their relative powerlessness ensures their continued deprivation. Those with the greatest needs are thus least capable of satisfying those needs. The pluralist image of an array of groups competing for outputs across the entire breadth of society overlooks the fact that certain groups are so disadvantaged by class oppression, custom, or natural endowment as to be chronically consigned to a low measure of power and a high measure of need. Let us consider some specific categories of people.

As just noted, those who chronically suffer the lowest degree of power are persons who occupy the lowest rungs of the economic ladder. Throughout history, whether they be called the blessed or the damned, whether slave, serf, sharecropper, indentured servant, or "free laborer," they have endured a scarcity of power and an abundance of need. Possessed of little material wealth when wealth has been the greatest determinant of life chances, the lower classes have experienced the harshest exploitation as both workers and consumers; the most disease and the earliest deaths; the least opportunity for comfort, learning, autonomy, self-governance, and self-respect; and the sternest mistreatment at the hands of the law. . . . Ralph Miliband (1969) describes their condition:

> Like other classes, the working class of advanced capitalist societies has always been, and remains, highly diversified; and there are also important differences in the internal composition of the working class of one country as compared to another. Yet, and notwithstanding these differences inside countries and between them, the working class remains everywhere a distinct and specified social formation by virtue of a combination of characteristics which affect its members in comparison with the members of other classes. The most obvious of these characteristics is that here are the people who, generally, "get least of what there is to get," and who have to work the hardest for it. And it is also from their ranks that are, so to speak, recruited the unemployed, the aged poor, the chronically destitute and the sub-proletariat of capitalist society. For

> all the insistence of growing or achieved "classlessness" . . . the proletarian condition remains a hard and basic fact in these societies, in the work process, in levels of income, in opportunities or lack of them, in the whole social definition of existence. . . .

Many tens of millions in the United States, numbering neither among the very poor nor the rich, compose an amorphous category dubbed "middle Americans," which includes everyone from well-paid, middle-level managers to lowly paid clerical workers. The accepted notion is that these people are increasing in numbers as the "service sector" of the economy grows and that they enjoy affluent, comfortable lives. A closer examination of the evidence indicates that while some are well-off, a goodly number of persons in the white-collar and service sectors, like most blue-collar workers, live under the chronic threat of economic insecurity, forced early retirement, unemployment, inflation, high taxes, and heavy debts, and are employed at some of the most underpaid, menial, and mindless jobs any modern civilization could produce. . . . Occupational disability, job insecurity, job dissatisfaction, constant financial anxieties, mental stress and depression, alcoholism, and conflictful domestic relations are common woes among the mass of middle Americans who compose the aching "backbone" of America. Even if not suffering from acute want, few if any exercise much control over the conditions of their lives. If not as severely buffeted and exploited as the very poor, they still number among the powerless in regard to most of the crucial decisions affecting their livelihoods, their communities, and their nation.

The plight of the middle Americans, however, as measured by the consequences of their powerlessness, is nowhere as severe as that of the very poor, who compose about 20 percent of the United States population. Their vague feelings of alienation and estrangement are more bearable than the continued presence of uncertainty and imminent disruption, "the constant threat of having life completely overturned by forces that can be neither predicted nor controlled," which is the condition of very poor people. . . .

The disadvantages suffered by other categories of people, such as the very young, the very old, women, ethnic minorities, and those who are "institutionalized" for physical and presumably mental disabilities are greatly compounded by class position and are partly a function of class. . . .

. . . [I]f all children risk the injustices of the adult world, the offspring of the lower classes are the most victimized of all, a disproportionately high number of battered and abused youngsters coming from homes plagued by poverty, unemployment, and overcrowding. To be conceived in poverty is to suffer risks while still inside the womb. Insufficient prenatal care, poor diet, and difficult working conditions for lower-class women leave them more likely to produce miscarriages, premature births, mentally and physically damaged infants. Once born, the lower-class child faces conditions of malnutrition, infection, and inadequate health care that may lead to maldevelopment of the central nervous system and mental retardation. Indeed, the poor of *all* age brackets suffer proportionally far more than do those of higher income from tuberculosis, rheumatic fever, food poisoning, epilepsy, polio, diphtheria, brucellosis, silicosis, and venereal disease. . . .

The "institutionalized" offer further evidence of how disabilities are created by, or at least compounded by, class and race. The poorest blacks, Puerto Ricans, Native Americans, and Chicanos are heavily overrepresented in the prison population in America. The number of people involuntarily confined in American mental hospitals is twice the number of all municipal, state, and federal prisoners and consists of a population "notably devoid of white, middle-class Americans." . . . Legal protections for mental patients are even weaker than those afforded ordinary criminals. In many instances commitment comes without the benefit of investigation, trial, or other procedural safeguards, and is based on considerations and "scientific" criteria which betray a marked class and racial bias. In the words of one worker in a New York State mental institution: "The hospitals are used merely as junk heaps for poor people who are often abandoned for years to rot, without adequate psychiatric care. . . " . . . A leading critic of the tyrannies of the psychiatric profession writes:

> There is a cynical saying: a person who steals five dollars is a thief, but one who steals five million is a financier. . . . The same is true for the human events we call mental illness. The problem that sends the rich woman to Reno is likely to send the poor woman to the state hospital. When the butcher, baker, or candlestick maker thinks that the Communists are after him, he is dispatched to the mental hospital; when a Secretary of Defense thinks so, who will constrain him? . . . How can the weak constrain the strong?
>
> . . . We still tolerate appalling inequities between our treatment of the rich and the poor. . . . We regard the rich and influential psychiatric patient as a self-governing, responsible client—free to decide whether or not to be a patient. But we look upon the poor and the aged patient as a ward of the state—too ignorant or too "mentally sick" to know what is best for him. The paternalistic psychiatrist, as an agent of the family or the state, assumes "responsibility" for him, defines him as a "patient" against his will, and subjects him to "treatment" deemed best for him, with or without his consent. . . .

As stated earlier, the unequal distribution of social desiderata under modern capitalism is due largely to the unequal distribution of power resources in a society where power rather than need is the determinant of who gets what. The conditions of powerlessness and want tend to reinforce each other and those most in need are most likely to have their claims neglected or suppressed.

Inequities tend to be compounded for the haves as well as the have-nots. The possession of one power resource often creates opportunities to gain access to other resources, as when celebrity and money bring opportunities for political leadership. Thus we have instances of the rich using their wealth to gain access to public office, and of politicians using public office to gain access to wealth; generals and college presidents become corporate executives, and corporate executives become administrative leaders in state and federal governments; movie actors of fame and fortune become governors and senators, and senators have been known to become millionaires. . . .

Because there are varied resources and varied avenues for accumulating power some observers mistakenly conclude that resources are more or less widely distributed. If "inequities in political resources remain, they tend to be noncumulative," Robert Dahl writes; thus no one group either monopolizes or is totally deprived of the attributes of power. . . . Almost any group, Dahl concludes, has access to *some* resources which it can exploit to gain influence. But the enormous inequities existing among various groups and classes would suggest just the opposite: if indeed resources can be compounded, then they tend to be *cumulative* rather than noncumulative. Power resources are accumulated over time and are not up for grabs with each new issue. As already noted, those who enjoy access to resources are best able to parlay such advantages into greater advantages, using the resources they already possess to accumulate still more. While those who are most needful of reallocations of goods and services are, by that very fact, farthest removed from the resources necessary to command reallocations and least able to make effective use of whatever limited resources they do possess.

That there are great inequities in American society should come as no surprise to anyone who has moved beyond the conventional wisdom of the 1950s. Far from being distributed randomly, the allocation of resources is heavily skewed in favor of the materially better-off individuals, social groups, institutions, and classes. All other things being equal, a group with good organization, or social legitimacy, or special knowledgeability, or skill in using legal channels, or skill in manipulating symbols will be more effective than a group lacking such attributes. But all other things are rarely equal and more often than not the very ability to utilize such resources depends on the availability of still other resources which are most closely associated with class and wealth. Those groups endowed with large amounts of money, as opposed to those with limited money, are best able to command the time, energy, skills, technology, and visibility needed for durable and effective organization. Even a pluralist like Dahl seems to recognize this when he notes that there are important "objective" differences among people which limit their potential power:

> Being poor or rich, well-educated or uneducated, a professional man or an unskilled laborer, living in a slum area or a middle-class neighborhood—

these are differences in objective situations of a most persistent and general sort that are likely to show up in a variety of different ways over a long period of time.

. . . These are differences of a *class* sort which have lasting effects on the accumulation and use of power resources.

One need not conclude that the resources of power are exclusively the derivatives of wealth, nor that only the rich have access to them, but corporate wealth enjoys a superior initiative in making favorable things happen, an initiative which inheres in the ability to procure the talent, technology, loyalty, legitimacy, cultural prestige, and organized efforts of public and private institutions. . . . Pluralists to the contrary, I am arguing here that the resources of power tend to be cumulative and therefore the conditions of power and powerlessness also tend to be cumulative.

By drawing a direct link between the use of power and access to power resources, and by speaking of power conditions as "objective situations of a most persistent and general sort," I am introducing the idea that power can be delineated by means other than observing actors engaged in specific policy conflicts. The structured distribution of power resources prefigures the agenda of social decisions. Thus we can speak of someone as *having* power as well as using it. The mere possession of resources has an empowering effect by limiting the possibilities of action for others and evoking a series of anticipatory reactions from them.

Objections to this position have been raised by those who argue that access to resources is no guarantee the resources will be used properly or used at all. . . . One cannot always anticipate the specific situations in which resources will be utilized; one cannot claim that there is a predictable one-to-one relation between, say, the possession of money and the uses to which it is put. Thus, it is argued, "the distribution of [power] resources in a system tells us very little about who will *attempt influence*," or how influence is actually perceived and used. . . .

By that view, power resources are likened to commodities sitting in a warehouse, of no influence whatever unless put to use. But we might remind ourselves that the resources of power are not of that simple nature and *the existing distribution of resources frequently exercises an influence even without being actually mobilized.* Arguing that the possession of resources does not necessarily lead to the exercise of influence, Gamson cites the case of the individual who "may feel that his resources will be inadequate to meet those that are countervailing. Existing competition may raise the costs above the amount he is prepared to pay." . . . But this example more readily illustrates how the distribution of resources *does* exercise an influence of its own. The individual was deterred because he discerned the superior resources of another, the *possession* (rather than the use) of which was sufficiently persuasive to stop him.

Plainly, what makes the possession of resources so formidable is one's anticipation that they might be used. Anticipatory reaction is the mainstay of power. All ruling groups rely on it to govern. Nations rely on it for their security. It is the means whereby the possessor of power resources can enjoy the effects of such resources without having to expend them. To win a struggle is one thing, but to have your way by impressing others that struggle would be futile, that is power at its most economical and most secure. It follows that the greater one's resources, the more one is able to make efficient use of them, that is, the less one actually has to use them. The fewer one's resources, the less able is one to make efficient use of what little one has. Power is positional as well as decisional.

SELECTION 24
FROM
*Engendering Democracy**

ANNE PHILLIPS

LIBERALISM AS A WORLD OF WALLS

ON MATTERS OF POLITICAL representation, the emphasis on groups that are different as opposed to individuals who are in principle the same is an important corrective to the traditionally liberal approach, and carries with it specific implications about guaranteeing proportional representation to groups. Those who turn a blind eye to the sex of their candidates are not being as fair as they might think, for as long as societies are organized through sexual difference and each sex is assigned its own tasks, identities, responsibilities, and roles, there should be mechanisms to ensure parity in the distribution of power. Since the other side to my argument is that any discrepancy between the proportion of women in the electorate and the proportion of women elected is proof enough that the society *is* sexually ordered, there will never be a moment at which this imperative loses it force. Either society treats men and women as genuine equals, in which case they will turn up in equal numbers in any forum for making decisions, or it treats them unfairly, in which case we need special arrangements to guarantee an equal presence.

This challenges and transforms some of the founding principles of liberalism, but falls short of a complete reversal. Most notably, I have not argued for group representation in the more substantial sense of people being represented only and always as groups; and I continue to think of politics as a means of discussing and representing what are varied, and individual, beliefs. I follow a similar path of moderation in my conclusions on the public/private divide. Here, too, I see liberalism facing serious attack, but not yet abandoned for an opposite extreme. Liberalism *is* peculiarly impervious to gender, and the distinctions it makes between public and private spheres are particularly well suited to maintaining women's political subordination. Arguments that play down the political relevance of the private sphere are doing their bit to keep things just as they are, for

* (London: Polity Press, 1991): Ch. 6, pp. 156–68.

they encourage us to consider all is well despite what ought to be thought gross contradictions. Domestic tyranny, for example, is and should be seen to be thoroughly at odds with equal citizenship for, behind the facade of each having equal rights to participate and vote, it is carrying on as for centuries before these rights were conceived and won. Even in the more commonplace examples where women are "allowed" to decide for themselves whether to attend a meeting and how to cast their vote, the fact that they are being allowed should alert us to the inconsistency in the way equal citizenship is being proposed. In the most seemingly equal of conditions, the continuing inequalities of the division of labor still condemn women to a lesser political role. Frequently excluded through lack of time or lack of confidence, they do not have an equal weight with men. Graduates of Oxford and Cambridge universities used to be entitled to two votes in general elections, and it was not till 1948 that this extraordinary qualification to the principle of one person, one vote was brought to an end. The liberal obsession with the public/private divide conceals and legitimates a still more damaging inequality of weight. Pretending as it does that equal rights to vote are all that matters, it refuses to engage with the constraints placed on women through their position in the domestic sphere.

On this issue, the politics of gender confirms the case made many times over in relation to class: that formal equality can combine easily with systematic privilege and is not on its own enough. The novelty in feminism is extending this to the household and family sphere. The domestic division of labor has direct consequences for the nature and degree of political involvement and because of this should be regarded as a *political* and not just social concern. Anyone concerned with sexual equality will argue for a major redistribution of household tasks and responsibilities so as to equalize the work of women and men; what has become clear is that this is an imperative of democracy as well. The formal equalities conceded through universal suffrage do not do what they claim they have done, for without the more substantial material changes, each woman counts as less than one. Counting as half is better than not counting at all, and no one is deprecating the importance of women's right to vote. But the point of universal suffrage is that it treats each person as of equal weight to the next: if so, that point is far from being reached.

A gendered approach to democracy therefore stresses domestic equalities as part of what balances out each person's political weight and includes this in its measure of what a democracy has achieved. Not that this would then become the only measure. I can conceive, for example, of a society that had substantially eroded the sexual division of labor but in which no one had a right to a vote, and it would be eccentric to present this as more democratic than a society where elections were the norm. But as long as the division of labor between women and men has political consequences, it has to be part of the political debate. In the lengthy exchanges between liberals and socialists, the significance of formal versus substantive equality has been contested as if it referred to property arrangements alone. One of the most basic contributions feminism makes to our thinking on democracy is to raise the curtain on that more private sphere.

There is, I have argued, a more assertive version of this, where feminists stress not just the "political" consequences of "private" arrangements but the relevance of democracy to every aspect of our social life. Anthony Arblaster [1987] has commented that "in classical political thinking, 'democracy' was the name not merely of a form of government but of a whole society, and it was habitually associated, by its enemies and critics as well as its friends, with the principle of social equality." We have seen that this was far from true and that the most fervent advocates of social equality were only able to conceive of equality as a matter between men. But with the necessary adjustments to gender, this description captures many feminist concerns. In contemporary feminist politics, democracy is usually presented as something that should enter the fabric of *all* social relations, and certainly not be restricted to the way governments come about. Wherever there are decisions, there is an issue of democracy, and though some contexts will lend themselves to more formal procedures than others, all should be shaped by the same principles of equal respect. Those who joined the women's movement out of a prior experience in radical politics, or a partnership with a "radical" man, have spoken repeatedly of the gap they found between theory and practice, and the way that the most seemingly progressive of democrats distinguished between public and private affairs. Where the intentions were supposedly so good, the contrasts were that much more startling. But elsewhere, too, women have continually found themselves in an implausible mixture of public equality and private subordination. An "engendered" democracy has to query and subvert this divide.

Feminism multiplies the places within which democracy appears relevant, and then it alters the dimensions as well. "Details" matter. This is one of the most powerful and abiding messages of the contemporary women's movement, extending beyond specifically sexual equality toward more general considerations on how people relate. Liberal democracy often seems to regard the equal right to vote as the apex of a democratic society. The broader conception that develops from an analysis of women treats it more as a cornerstone on which democracy can be built. A standard objection to liberal democracy is that it is so very minimal in its ideals: that the "moment" of consent is too infrequent to count for much; that participation has been reduced to an almost gestural level; and that while the gesture matters (it still helps settle what the government will be) it cannot be seriously presented as decision making or control. The emphasis on detail comes in at a different angle, stressing not so much the degree of control people have been able to establish over decisions, but whether they relate as political equals. The means, in other words, matter as much as the ends. If the supposed equality of the vote is continually undermined by patterns of patronage and subservience and condescension, then the society is not democratic.

None of these arguments fits well with the liberal tradition, and all of them take issue with the relationship between public and private spheres. Michael Walzer describes liberalism as "a world of walls," each one of which creates a new liberty and he reworks this into his argument that justice is a matter of maintaining the boundaries between the spheres. Success in commerce, for example, should not carry with it any particular power in politics; excellence in intellectual endeavors should not give the right to have more than one vote. Walzer's *Spheres of Justice* (1983) captures much of what people object to in tyranny or nepotism or corruption, but the argument is also troubling, for it makes it harder to challenge the principles that might operate within each separate sphere. So maybe sex *should* dictate the division of labor in households, just so long as it does not dictate the arrangements that apply in schools? So maybe physical strength *is* an appropriate consideration, just so long as it stays limited to its own legitimate realm?

Walzer talks of the oppression of women in terms of the "structures of kinship" (it is not clear what is included in this) being illegitimately reiterated through other distributive spheres. They affect, therefore, women's access to jobs, education and, in an earlier period, the vote. There is nothing, in other words, particularly wrong with what goes on inside the family. The problems begin when sex or "kinship standing" stray outside their rightful domain. "The real domination of women has less to do with their familial place than with their exclusion from all other places." This is similar to the argument Jean Bethke Elshtain makes in *Public Man, Private Woman*: a woman's sex should not dictate what she does in the worlds of education or employment, but neither, however, should the principles of narrow self-interest become dominant in the familial sphere. But Elshtain does at least support some fusion or swapping of principles across the public/private divide. Walzer by contrast seems to be upholding the numerous distinctions between a plurality of separate spheres. From the perspectives of gender, the problem with this is that the walls people erect between one area and another can block the kind of parallels they might otherwise draw. Much of women's liberation has depended on taking the principles that were considered appropriate in one realm and saying they applied just as much to another. Progress has occurred precisely through breaching the wall.

Feminism has to query the separation of spheres, and on this score it has little confidence in the distinctions liberal democracy tries to make. And yet here, too, there is some accommodation that can be reached. Aside from rhetorical flourishes, few feminists have wanted to abandon all distinction, and on the issue of a woman's right to choose, many have incorporated liberal notions of what is an irreducibly private concern into their arguments for free and legal abortion. The further reservation I have noted derives from the republican rather than liberal tradition. Though feminism is often hijacked by those who dissolve differences of scale and kind into a disturbingly amorphous mess, there are crucial distinctions between being a citizen and being a nice caring person. A fully democratic society would be one in which people held one another in mutual respect and where all relationships, no matter how small or intimate the context, would be permeated by the principle that each person had equal weight. There would still be a difference of kind between the household, the workplace, and the state.

All relationships can become "political," but part of what that means is that all can become contexts in which we have to stand a bit back from ourselves. We have to be able to put our own wishes and needs in perspective, to create some momentary distance from our enthusiasms and preconceptions so as to recognize the significance of what others have to say. There is a difference between the approach we should adopt as citizens, and the more particular concerns that quite rightly preoccupy us in our everyday life. "The democratization of everyday life" is thus fair enough as a slogan that captures the importance of democratic equality in every sphere of human existence. It is misleading if it denies all distinction between politics and everyday life. Democracy is not a matter of building blocks in which each brick is equally significant and all that matters is how many we can add. So while decision making should be opened up and equalized in the household, the schools, the workplace, the housing estate, we should not regard this democratization of civil society as an alternative to a revitalized public life. The two must go hand in hand.

The Curse of the Meeting

This leads toward the perennial issue: how much popular participation can any democracy handle, and just how much active citizenship does a "revitalized" democracy require? I have argued that the sexual ordering of our societies is such that women need a politics of transformation and change, and that because their subordination enters so invidiously into the way that women perceive themselves and their needs, this sets a particularly high premium on discussion and talk. Liberal democracies work on the basis of limited and occasional participation, and voters are normally asked to choose between two or more vaguely defined parties, wrapped round in blandly expressed views. It is no coincidence that this finds its most dedicated supporters among those who resist radical change. Isolated voting dampens down the political imagination; in meetings, by contrast, we might begin to conceive of a wider range of options and test out our potential power. People change their views in the course of meeting and discussion, and not just because they get carried away by the enthusiasm of others and agree to things they do not truly believe. The change can be and frequently is "real." Vague dissatisfactions find a clearer expression, while things previously thought inevitable begin to look open to reform.

The politics of gender adds its weight to those who see isolated voting as offering too little scope for influencing the agenda and introducing new kinds of concerns. For any group that has been defined out of the mainstream of politics, this is an especially pertinent complaint. Women cannot (as women) get much purchase on a system that asks them only to register support or disapproval for existing parties or programs. It may be that none of the alternatives has any proposals for women's specific concerns; and women may not be able even to formulate their interests without a forum in which they can talk.

When this is linked to the additional problems of women's relative domestic seclusion, feminism points toward a more actively participatory democracy than has been offered in the liberal norm. Yet the more participatory a democracy sets out to be, the more it discriminates between women and men. The more emphasis it places on activity and involvement, the more it tends to exaggerate the influence of those who have greater resources of education, charm, or time. It is part of the sexually divided nature of contemporary society that women work longer than men, but with less variety of experience or length of time in formal education. Short of radical changes in the organization of paid and unpaid work, they will remain the ones least able to go out to meetings and least likely to make themselves heard. Liberal democracy has this one very strong point in its favor: by reducing the demands of participation to show a low level, it makes them more genuinely available to all.

In its own experiences of participatory democracy, the women's movement has uncovered additional strains. The circumstances of face-to-face democracy do not always promote open discussion, and when the ideals of democratic equality are set at too high a level, the resulting turmoil of guilt and accusation and resentment can drive people away from politics altogether. These are serious difficulties, and yet in the overall pattern of the "problems of democracy," they do not occupy so very large a space. Many groups must go through a similar curve of experience, in which the initial enthusiasm for democratic equality and involvement leads through a phase of impatience and bitterness, into a more sober commitment to make things as democratic as is possible under the conditions of the day. I am reminded of Eduard Bernstein's comment on socialism, that the movement is everything and the final aim nothing. In the sense that a "full" democracy can never be realized, but that we make as many approximations toward it as we can, the same thing can be said of democracy. Once this is accepted, and democracy conceived as a process instead of an impossibly elevated set of ideals, then the tensions associated with egalitarian decision making (in a movement, party, trade union, committee, in a workplace or whatever kind of group) become more manageable. In all these, of course, we are dealing with people who are there. The real problems arise when people have not yet turned up.

The higher the demands, the less widespread the involvement. The more participatory the politics, the less accountable to those who are passive or inert. There seems to be a substantive choice that democrats continually face between the precise equalities of minimal democracy and the potential risks of more intense participation. The latter *is* in many ways utopian and unwieldy, but the greatest worry is that it can become liable to bias and produce unrepresentative results. When interests conflict, and even more commonly when a minority has captured an undue concentration of power, there is only one fair way to resolve the disputes: to weight each individual equally, and give each citizen a vote. It is not that liberal democracy has such a brilliant record on accountability for, as frequently noted in the course of this book, it operates at a shallow level of consent that may be no more than deciding which of the contenders should rule. The main claim to fame is that at least it distributes this favor equally between all.

Rethinking democracy through the perspectives of gender does not substantially alter the terms of the choice between minimal equality and increased participation, and feminism has no astonishing new insight that can change this dilemma. Feminism strengthens the case for active democracy, but also highlights the importance of giving each person her vote. On this central question of democracy, the alternatives remain very much as before. On the one hand there is "the democracy of a cynical society" [Mansbridge, 1980], which expects little in the way of involvement and regards self-protection as the highest of goals: a democracy that lacks ambition, that does not inspire, that gives us no moral satisfaction. Despite its worldly acumen, it never entirely displaces the alternatives, whose ideals reappear in every age. These counter-ideals, however, bring their own discontents in their train.

My resolution follows the kind of "mixed economy" that has become the fashion of our day. Democracy means people taking decisions and will remain a formality except where this actually takes place. The only substantial ways in which people can be said to decide are when they participate in deciding the agendas and influence the choices that are made. Choosing between two parties who appear as if out of nowhere, and do not even say what they really plan to do, does not count as taking a decision. People need continuous access to all those contexts, inside political parties and outside them, at national and regional and local levels, where they can shape the decisions that are made. The curse of the meeting then remains. But democracy also means people being regarded as equals and not more important when they go out to more meetings. Arguing for greater decentralization of decisions, John Keane [1988] says we need a variety of spheres "in which different groups of citizens *could* participate, if and when they so wished," but that people will want to make themselves heard to different degrees and on different topics. Some, presumably, will never make themselves heard at all. If participation were painless, we might well dismiss these people as having indicated by their absence that they were happy for others to decide. Since participation is in fact notoriously costly—in energy, often dignity, and time—we cannot follow this path.

Though he does not discuss the problem in these terms, John Keane suggests one possible resolution when he lists a number of initiatives on which the central government could guarantee resources, but then leave it up to local constituencies to determine exactly how these resources should be deployed. Thus the government might decide to set aside a certain amount of money for child care, but those who chose to get involved in the local organization would be the ones to decide what form the child care should take. This is an immediately appealing example, but the very attraction rests on a half-submerged notion of what is a basic and what a subsidiary concern. The more decentralized a service becomes, the more it will vary from one area to another—because people differ in their preferences and ideas, but also because they differ in the degrees to which they become active and involved. In each case people would have to make choices between quality and quantity (should they improve the service, or concentrate on making more places available?), and choices over the kind and range of care (should it be nurseries or child-minders? should the emphasis be on learning or playing? how structured should the environment be?). Children living in different areas would then be offered different kinds of facilities, and some of these would be better than the rest.

If we accept this divergence as part of what a democracy is about, it is partly because the weight we attach to participation and choice is enough to balance the potential inequalities. It is also, I believe, because the precise form and quality and organization of child care are not yet considered determining influences on people's lives. We more readily accept variation and experimentation here because, rightly or wrongly, most people regard preschool child care as a subsidiary and not a central concern. (Parents and politicians alike have proved more reluctant to delegate full responsibility to local activists when it is the organization of schools that is at stake.) When it comes to issues on which there is a stronger commitment, then the fact that a decision is being taken at an open meeting which all could *in principle* attend is not regarded as enough of a protection. People have low expectations about the degree to which they might become involved. So while they might be prepared to support direct democracy in a range of subsidiary concerns, they will prefer the control that is exercised through the vote when the decisions are ones that are "basic." There are always risks associated with decentralized, meeting-based decisions, and the main risk is that the activists will be unrepresentative.

If democratic equality is to mean anything, it means that a society must submit its "ultimate" decisions to a forum in which all can take part. Realistically this means the vote, through national and local elections and, on some issues, national referendums. There may be a future scenario, when the pressures of time have been equalized between women and men and societies can afford to move up the scale and set their standards of participation a bit higher. But since gender is not the only determinant of levels of participation, this would require a great many more changes as well. For the foreseeable future, democracy has to rely on liberal minimalism for those decisions that are regarded as the more fundamental, and can only be extended by meeting-based participation for those issues thought more intermediate. That we should press for this extension in as many contexts as possible should, I hope, be clear from the arguments developed in this book. Much less clear is what principle could settle which decisions are basic and which are not, but this is because it is a question that only politics can decide.

Women's Voices: Women's Issues

The final point I want to return to hinges on the tension between feminist and republican concerns. Women have frequently commented on the spectacle of a predominantly male legislature deciding whether abortion should be decriminalized, and have noted with some bitterness that it is women who get pregnant and a woman who has to care for the child. Of all the political issues to which gender is pertinent, this is the most striking—and the relative exclusion of women from the arenas within which such decisions are made is an outrageous example of how undemocratic our democracies remain. The point is not that men oppose and women favor abortion: much of the evidence in Britain, for example, indicates that women are if anything more troubled than men by the question of late abortions, more concerned to weigh up protection of the mother against protection of the fetus, less happy-go-lucky about what abortion entails. The experiences of pregnancy and motherhood generate a complex and nuanced set of attitudes—confirmation, if any was needed, that this experience should be given more weight.

The corollary, however, is not that men should have no opinion on the issue. One of the more ambivalent side-effects of the last twenty-five years of feminist activity is the self-abasement often practised by "sympathetic" men. Just as white liberals sometimes choose to silence themselves on issues of race and ethnicity, so progressive men sometimes abdicate their responsibilities in what they now conceive as a "women's" concern. Accepting the incongruity in male legislation on such matters as abortion, child care, or affirmative action, they may apologize for their previous presumption, and ask women what they ought to do. One problem with this, as already argued, is that it too readily accepts that there is *a* women's position; another more pressing deficiency is that the stage may then be abandoned to those less reticent about their right to decide.

The further difficulty is the implication that only those with the experience have anything legitimate to say. Let me give one recent example from United States politics. When challenged to justify his political support for abortion despite his personal moral objections, Governor Mario Cuomo has noted that "there is an element of the absurd or incongruous in men making laws about something they can never experience—pregnancy." As Garry Wills argues, this conflicts with

> the citizen values of republicanism, where everyone in the community is invited to ponder together all moral issues. We do not say, in a republic, that only the military can decide on the role of the military in public life—that only the academy can frame educational issues, that only believers can frame religious issues, and so forth. Cuomo seems to be taking an enlightened stand when he apologizes, as a man, for speaking on abortion; but it is a nonrepublican position. ["Mario Cuomo's Trouble with Abortion," *New York Review of Books* 28 (June 1990)—ED.]

Given the criticisms feminists have leveled at "citizen values," this observation may not carry much weight, but I have argued throughout this book that it should certainly make us pause for thought. All members of a political community are formed and limited by their experiences, which is part of the argument that all these experiences should gain their voice. But any politics that looks toward change and transformation cannot leave things at that.

The classical liberal deals with such problems by establishing a region of private existence in which each of us makes her own moral or religious choices, and no one else is entitled to complain. The twentieth-century pluralist tackles it by the (usually dishonest) argument that all groups are free to contest with each other, and thereby contribute to the final result. From a perspective that seeks to reform or revolutionize the conditions of our existence, neither of these options is adequate, for each accepts the limits of experience as something we cannot overcome.

The most extreme alternative to liberal democracy is that associated with the Marxist tradition, some versions of which have anticipated a future beyond all significant conflict, where people act homogeneously as one. The arguments against this are too overwhelming to require further rehearsal, but it is one thing to deny conflict a voice and another to accept all conflicts as final. The recent feminist emphasis on difference and heterogeneity should be taken as a necessary corrective to those political theories and practices that have excluded sex (among other things) from the political stage. This should be viewed, however, as a starting point from which inequalities can be tackled and reduced. The crucial requirement is for women's political presence; which is not to say that only women can speak on "women's" issues, that women must speak only as a sex.

As we approach the end of the twentieth century, two major developments set the scene. The first, and most dramatic, is the extension of liberal democratic practices of universal suffrage and free elections and multiparty competition—

not only through the Soviet Union and Eastern Europe, but through the beleaguered countries of the once colonized world. One person one vote now looks imminent even in the most antidemocratic South Africa, while the heavy hand of military regimes and one-party states in other parts of Africa is being challenged again. Among those who have found liberal democracy weak and inadequate, there is considerable anxiety that these gains will sweep criticisms away and that, rejoicing in freedoms previously denied them, people will forget for another generation the substance of earlier appraisal. The problems feminists have raised, which build on and significantly extend the critical analysis of liberalism, should help to counter this risk.

The other major development is that the myths of homogeneity are being shattered, most positively through the increased awareness of gender and ethnic differentiation, more ambivalently through the rise of religious fundamentalism and the "new" nationalisms of the Soviet Union and Eastern Europe. The preoccupations of contemporary feminism are very much to the point in this development, and they put before us some of the key questions with which future democrats will have to grapple. Feminist political theorists have raised powerful criticisms of the abstract individual, and of the false universalities of much Enlightenment thought, and feminists are now leading the way toward a new politics based upon diversity and difference. Some of the routes opening up are ones I would prefer not to follow, but all of the debate is crucial to the future of democratic thought. We have to find a political language that can recognize heterogeneity and difference, but does not thereby capitulate to an essentialism that defines each of us by one aspect alone. The arguments now raging inside feminist circles provide an exhilarating guide through this terrain.

PART VII

Radical Democracy Revisited

SELECTION 25
FROM
*The Russian Revolution**

ROSA LUXEMBURG

[F]ROM THE SPECIAL INADEQUACY of the Constituent Assembly which came together in October, Trotsky draws a general conclusion concerning the inadequacy of any popular representation whatsoever which might come from universal popular elections during the revolution.

"Thanks to the open and direct struggle for governmental power," he writes,

> the laboring masses acquire in the shortest time an accumulation of political experience, and they climb rapidly from step to step in their political development. The bigger the country and the more rudimentary its technical apparatus, the less is the cumbersome mechanism of democratic institutions able to keep pace with this development.

Here we find the "mechanism of democratic institutions" as such called in question. To this we must at once object that in such an estimate of representative institutions there lies a somewhat rigid and schematic conception which is expressly contradicted by the historical experience of every revolutionary epoch. According to Trotsky's theory, every elected assembly reflects once and for all only the mental composition, political maturity and mood of its electorate just at the moment when the latter goes to the polling place. According to that, a democratic body is the reflection of the masses at the end of the electoral period, much as the heavens of Herschel always show us the heavenly bodies not as they are when we are looking at them but as they were at the moment they sent out their light-messages to the earth from the measureless distances of space. Any living mental connection between the representatives, once they have been elected, and the electorate, any permanent interaction between one and the other, is hereby denied.

Yet how all historical experience contradicts this! Experience demonstrates quite the contrary: namely, that the living fluid of the popular mood continuously flows around the representative bodies, penetrates them, guides them. How

---

* "*The Russian Revolution*" *and* "*Leninism or Marxism?*" (Ann Arbor: University of Michigan Press, 1961), pp. 59–62, 68–72.

else would it be possible to witness, as we do at times in every bourgeois parliament, the amusing capers of the "people's representatives," who are suddenly inspired by a new "spirit" and give forth quite unexpected sounds; or to find the most dried-out mummies at times comporting themselves like youngsters and the most diverse little *Scheidemaennchen* . . . suddenly finding revolutionary tones in their breasts—whenever there is rumbling in factories and workshops and on the streets?

And is this ever-living influence of the mood and degree of political ripeness of the masses upon the elected bodies to be renounced in favor of a rigid scheme of party emblems and tickets in the very midst of revolution? Quite the contrary! It is precisely the revolution which creates by its glowing heat that delicate, vibrant, sensitive political atmosphere in which the waves of popular feeling, the pulse of popular life, work for the moment on the representative bodies in most wonderful fashion. It is on this very fact, to be sure, that the well-known moving scenes depend which invariably present themselves in the first stages of every revolution, scenes in which old reactionaries or extreme moderates, who have issued out of a parliamentary election by limited suffrage under the old regime, suddenly become the heroic and stormy spokesmen of the uprising. The classic example is provided by the famous "Long Parliament" in England, which was elected and assembled in 1642 and remained at its post for seven whole years and reflected in its internal life all alterations and displacements of popular feeling, of political ripeness, of class differentiation, of the progress of the revolution to its highest point, from the initial devout skirmishes with the Crown under a Speaker who remained on his knees, to the abolition of the House of Lords, the execution of Charles, and the proclamation of the republic.

And was not the same wonderful transformation repeated in the French Estates General, in the censorship-subjected parliament of Louis Philippe, and even—and this last, most striking example was very close to Trotsky—even in the Fourth Russian Duma which, elected in the Year of Grace 1909 under the most rigid rule of the counterrevolution, suddenly felt the glowing heat of the impending overturn and became the point of departure for the revolution? . . .

All this shows that "the cumbersome mechanism of democratic institutions" possesses a powerful corrective—namely, the living movement of the masses, their unending pressure. And the more democratic the institutions, the livelier and stronger the pulse-beat of the political life of the masses, the more direct and complete is their influence—despite rigid party banners, outgrown tickets (electoral lists), etc. To be sure, every democratic institution has its limits and shortcomings, things which it doubtless shares with all other human institutions. But the remedy which Trotsky and Lenin have found, the elimination of democracy as such, is worse than the disease it is supposed to cure; for it stops up the very living source from which alone can come the correction of all the innate shortcomings of social institutions. That source is the active, untrammeled, energetic political life of the broadest masses of the people.

Lenin says: the bourgeois state is an instrument of oppression of the working class; the socialist state, of the bourgeoisie. To a certain extent, he says, it is only the capitalist state stood on its head. This simplified view misses the most essential thing: bourgeois class rule has no need of the political training and education of the entire mass of the people, at least not beyond certain narrow limits. But for the proletarian dictatorship that is the life element, the very air without which it is not able to exist.

"Thanks to the open and direct struggle for governmental power," writes Trotsky, "the laboring masses accumulate in the shortest time a considerable amount of political experience and advance quickly from one stage to another of their development."

Here Trotsky refutes himself and his own friends. Just because this is so, they have blocked up the fountain of political experience and the source of this rising development by their suppression of public life! Or else we would have to assume that experience and development were necessary up to the seizure of power by the Bolsheviks, and then, having reached their highest peak, became superfluous thereafter. (Lenin's speech: Russia is won for socialism!!!)

In reality, the opposite is true! It is the very giant tasks which the Bolsheviks have undertaken with courage and determination that demand the most intensive political training of the masses and the accumulation of experience.

Freedom only for the supporters of the government, only for the members of one party—however numerous they may be—is no freedom at all. Freedom is always and exclusively freedom for the one who thinks differently. Not because of any fanatical concept of "justice" but because all that is instructive, wholesome, and purifying in political freedom depends on this essential characteristic, and its effectiveness vanishes when "freedom" becomes a special privilege.

The Bolsheviks themselves will not want, with hand on heart, to deny that, step by step, they have to feel out the ground, try out, experiment, test now one way now another, and that a good many of their measures do not represent priceless pearls of wisdom. Thus it must and will be with all of us when we get to the same point—even if the same difficult circumstances may not prevail everywhere.

The tacit assumption underlying the Lenin-Trotsky theory of the dictatorship is this: that the socialist transformation is something for which a ready-made formula lies completed in the pocket of the revolutionary party, which needs only to be carried out energetically in practise. This is, unfortunately—or perhaps fortunately—not the case. Far from being a sum of ready-made prescriptions which have only to be applied, the practical realization of socialism as an economic, social and juridical system is something which lies completely hidden in the mists of the future. What we possess in our program is nothing but a few main signposts which indicate the general direction in which to look for the necessary measures, and the indications are mainly negative in character at that. Thus we know more or less what we must eliminate at the outset in order to free the road for a socialist economy. But when it comes to the nature of the thousand concrete, practical measures, large and small, necessary to introduce socialist principles into economy, law, and all social relationships, there is no key in any socialist party program or textbook. That is not a shortcoming but rather the very thing that makes scientific socialism superior to the utopian varieties. The socialist system of society should only be, and can only be, a historical product, born out of the school of its own experiences, born in the course of its realization, as a result of the developments of living history, which—just like organic nature of which, in the last analysis, it forms a part—has the fine habit of always producing along with any real social need the means to its satisfaction, along with the task simultaneously the solution. However, if such is the case, then it is clear that socialism by its very nature cannot be decreed or introduced by *ukase*. It has as its prerequisite a number of measures of force—against property, etc. The negative, the tearing down, can be decreed; the building up, the positive, cannot. New territory. A thousand problems. Only experience is capable of correcting and opening new ways. Only unobstructed, effervescing life falls into a thousand new forms and improvisations, brings to light creative force, itself corrects all mistaken attempts. The public life of countries with limited freedom is so poverty-stricken, so miserable, so rigid, so unfruitful, precisely because, through the exclusion of democracy, it cuts off the living sources of all spiritual riches and progress. (Proof: the year 1905 and the months from February to October 1917.) There it was political in character; the same thing applies to economic and social life also. The whole mass of the people must take part in it. Otherwise, socialism will be decreed from behind a few official desks by a dozen intellectuals.

Public control is indispensably necessary. Otherwise the exchange of experiences remains only with the closed circle of the officials of the new regime. Corruption becomes inevitable. (Lenin's words, Bulletin No. 29.) Socialism in life demands a complete spiritual transformation in the masses degraded by centuries of bourgeois class rule. Social instincts in place of egotistical ones, mass initiative in place of inertia, idealism which conquers all suffering, etc., etc. No one knows this better, describes it more penetratingly, repeats it more stubbornly than Lenin. But he is completely mistaken in the means he employs. Decree, dictatorial force of the factory overseer, draconic penalties, rule by terror—all these things are but palliatives. The only way to a rebirth is the school of public life itself, the most unlimited, the broadest democracy and public opinion. It is rule by terror which demoralizes.

When all this is eliminated, what really remains? In place of the representative bodies created by general, popular elections, Lenin and Trotsky have laid down the soviets as the only true representation of the laboring masses. But with the repression of political life in the land as a whole, life in the soviets must also become more and more crippled. Without general elections, without unrestricted freedom of press and assembly, without a free struggle of opinion, life dies out in every public institution, becomes a mere semblance of life, in which only the bureaucracy remains as the active element. Public life gradually falls asleep, a few dozen party leaders of inexhaustible energy and boundless experience direct and rule. Among them, in reality only a dozen outstanding heads do the leading and an elite of the working class is invited from time to time to meetings where they are to applaud the speeches of the leaders, and to approve proposed resolutions unanimously—at bottom, then, a clique affair—a dictatorship, to be sure, not the dictatorship of the proletariat, however, but only the dictatorship of a handful of politicians, that is, a dictatorship in the bourgeois sense, in the sense of the rule of the Jacobins (the postponement of the Soviet Congress from three-month periods to six-month periods!). Yes, we can go even further: such conditions must inevitably cause a brutalization of public life: attempted assassinations, shooting of hostages, etc. (Lenin's speech on discipline and corruption.)

SELECTION 26
FROM
*On Revolution**

HANNAH ARENDT

JEFFERSON... KNEW, HOWEVER DIMLY, that the Revolution, while it had given freedom to the people, had failed to provide a space where this freedom could be exercised. Only the representatives of the people, not the people themselves, had an opportunity to engage in those activities of "expressing, discussing and deciding" which in a positive sense are the activities of freedom. And since the state and federal governments, the proudest results of revolution, through sheer weight of their proper business were bound to overshadow in political importance the townships and their meeting halls—until what Emerson still considered to be "the unit of the Republic" and "the school of the people" in political matters had withered away . . .—one might even come to the conclusion that there was less opportunity for the exercise of public freedom and the enjoyment of public happiness in the republic of the United States than there had existed in the colonies of British America. Lewis Mumford recently pointed out how the political importance of the township was never grasped by the founders, and that the failure to incorporate it into either the federal or the state constitution was "one of the tragic oversights of postrevolutionary political development." Only Jefferson among the founders had a clear premonition of this tragedy, for his greatest fear was indeed lest "the abstract political system of democracy lacked concrete organs." . . .

The failure of the founders to incorporate the township and the town-hall meeting into the Constitution, or rather their failure to find ways and means to transform them under radically changed circumstances, was understandable enough. Their chief attention was directed toward the most troublesome of all their immediate problems, the question of representation, and this to such an extent that they came to define republics, as distinguished from democracies, in terms of representative government. Obviously direct democracy would not do, if only because "the room will not hold all" (as John Selden, more than a hundred years earlier, had described the chief cause for the birth of Parliament).

* (New York: Viking, 1963): Ch. 6, pp. 238–42, 252–68, 272–83.

These were indeed the terms in which the principle of representation was still discussed at Philadelphia; representation was meant to be a mere substitute for direct political action through the people themselves, and the representatives they elected were supposed to act according to instructions received by their electors, and not to transact business in accordance with their own opinions as they might be formed in the process. . . . However, the founders, as distinguished from the elected representatives in colonial times, must have been the first to know how far removed this theory was from reality. "With regard to the sentiments of the people," James Wilson, at the time of the convention, "conceived it difficult to know precisely what they are," and Madison knew very well that "no member of the convention could say what the opinions of his constituents were at this time; much less could he say what they would think if possessed of the information and lights possessed by the members here." . . . Hence, they could hear with approval, though perhaps not entirely without misgivings, when Benjamin Rush proposed the new and dangerous doctrine that although "all power is derived from the people, they possess it only on the days of their elections. After this it is the property of their rulers." . . .

These few quotations may show in a nutshell that the whole question of representation, one of the crucial and most troublesome issues of modern politics ever since the revolutions, actually implies no less than a decision on the very dignity of the political realm itself. The traditional alternative between representation as a mere substitute for direct action of the people and representation as a popularly controlled rule of the people's representatives over the people constitutes one of those dilemmas which permit of no solution. If the elected representatives are so bound by instructions that they gather together only to discharge the will of their masters, they may still have a choice of regarding themselves as either glorified messenger boys or hired experts who, like lawyers, are specialists in representing the interests of their clients. But in both instances the assumption is, of course, that the electorate's business is more urgent and more important than theirs; they are the paid agents of people who, for whatever reasons, are not able, or do not wish, to attend to public business. If, on the contrary, the representatives are understood to become for a limited time the appointed rulers of those who elected them—without rotation in office, there is of course no representative government strictly speaking—representation means that the voters surrender their own power, albeit voluntarily, and that the old adage, "All power resides in the people," is true only for the day of election. In the first instance, government has degenerated into mere administration, the public realm has vanished; there is no space either for seeing and being seen in action, John Adams' *spectemur agendo*, or for discussion and decision, Jefferson's pride of being "a participator in government"; political matters are those that are dictated by necessity to be decided by experts, but not open to opinions and genuine choice; hence, there is no need for Madison's "medium of a chosen body of citizens" through which opinions must pass and be purified into public views. In the second instance, somewhat closer to realities, the age-old distinction between ruler and ruled which the Revolution had set out to abolish through the establishment of a republic has asserted itself again; once more, the people are not admitted to the public realm, once more the business of government has become the privilege of the few, who alone may "exercise [their] virtuous dispositions" (as Jefferson called men's political talents). The result is that the people must either sink into "lethargy, the forerunner of death to the public liberty" or "preserve the spirit of resistance" to whatever government they have elected, since the only power they retain is "the reserve power of revolution." . . .

For these evils there was no remedy, since rotation in office, so highly valued by the founders and so carefully elaborated by them, could hardly do more than prevent the governing few from constituting themselves as a separate group with vested interests of their own. Rotation could never provide everybody, or even a sizable portion of the population, with the chance to become temporarily "a participator in government." Had this evil been restricted to the people at large, it would have been bad enough in view of the fact that the whole issue of republican versus kingly or aristocratic government turned about rights of equal admission to the public, political realm; and yet, one suspects, the founders should have found it easy enough to console themselves with the thought that the Revolution had opened the political realm at least to those whose inclination for "virtuous disposition" was strong, whose passion for distinction was ardent enough to embark upon the extraordinary hazards of a political career. Jefferson, however, refused to be consoled. He feared an "elective despotism" as bad as, or worse than, the tyranny they had risen against: "If once [our people] become inattentive to the public affairs, you and I, and Congress and Assemblies, Judges and Governors, shall all become wolves." . . . And while it is true that historical developments in the United States have hardly borne out this fear, it is also true that this is almost exclusively due to the founders' "political science" in establishing a government in which the divisions of powers have constituted through checks and balances their own control. What eventually saved the United States from the dangers which Jefferson feared was the machinery of government; but this machinery could not save the people from lethargy and inattention to public business, since the Constitution itself provided a public space only for the representatives of the people, and not for the people themselves.

It may seem strange that only Jefferson among the men of the American Revolution ever asked himself the obvious question of how to preserve the revolutionary spirit once the Revolution had come to an end, but the explanation for this lack of awareness does not lie in that they themselves were no revolutionaries. On the contrary, the trouble was that they took this spirit for granted, because it was a spirit which had been formed and nourished throughout the colonial period. Since, moreover, the people remained in undisturbed possession of those institutions which had been the breeding grounds of the revolution, they could hardly become aware of the fateful failure of the Constitution to incorporate and duly constitute, found anew, the original sources of their power and public happiness. It was precisely because of the enormous weight of the Constitution and of the experiences in founding a new body politic, that the failure to incorporate the townships and the town-hall meetings, the original springs of all political activity in the country, amounted to a death sentence for them. Paradoxical as it may sound, it was in fact under the impact of the Revolution that the revolutionary spirit in this country began to wither away, and it was the Constitution itself, this greatest achievement of the American people, which eventually cheated them of their proudest possession. . . .

"As Cato concluded every speech with the words, *Carthago delenda est*, so do I every opinion, with the injunction, 'divide the counties into wards.'" . . . Thus Jefferson once summed up an exposition of his most cherished political idea, which, alas, turned out to be as incomprehensible to posterity as it had been to his contemporaries. The reference to Cato was no idle slip of a tongue used to Latin quotations; it was meant to emphasize that Jefferson thought the absence of such a subdivision of the country constituted a vital threat to the very existence of the republic. Just as Rome, according to Cato, could not be safe so long as Carthage existed, so the republic, according to Jefferson, would not be secure in its very foundations without the ward system. "Could I once see this I should consider it as the dawn of the salvation of the republic, and say with old Simeon, 'Nunc dimittis Domine.'" . . .

Had Jefferson's plan of "elementary republics" been carried out, it would have exceeded by far the feeble germs of a new form of government which we are able to detect in the sections of the Parisian Commune and the popular societies during the French Revolution. However, if Jefferson's political imagination surpassed them in insight and in scope, his thoughts were still traveling in the same direction. Both Jefferson's plan and the French *sociétés révolutionnaires* anticipated with an almost weird precision those councils, soviets and *Räte*, which were to make their appearance in every genuine revolution throughout the nineteenth and twentieth centuries. Each time they appeared, they sprang up as the spontaneous organs of the people, not only outside of all revolutionary parties but entirely unexpected by them and their leaders. Like Jefferson's proposals, they were utterly neglected by statesmen, historians, political theorists, and, most importantly, by the revolutionary tradition itself. Even those historians whose sympathies were clearly on the side of revolution and who could not help writing the emergence of popular councils into the record of their story regarded them as nothing more than essentially temporary organs in the revolutionary struggle for liberation; that is to say, they failed to understand to what an extent the council system confronted them with an entirely new form of government, with a new public space for freedom which was constituted and organized during the course of the Revolution itself.

This statement must be qualified. There are two relevant exceptions to it, namely a few remarks by Marx at the occasion of the revival of the Parisian Commune during the short-lived revolution of 1871, and some reflections by Lenin based not on the text by Marx, but on the actual course of the Revolution of 1905 in Russia. But before we turn our attention to these matters, we had better try to understand what Jefferson had in mind when he said with utmost self-assurance, "The wit of man cannot devise a more solid basis for a free, durable, and well-administered republic." . . .

It is perhaps noteworthy that we find no mention of the ward system in any of Jefferson's formal works, and it may be even more important that the few letters in which he wrote of it with such emphatic insistence all date from the last period of his life. It is true, at one time he hoped that Virginia, because it was "the first of the nations of the earth which assembled its wise men peaceably together to form a fundamental constitution," would also be the first "to adopt the subdivision of our counties into wards," . . . but the point of the matter is that the whole idea seems to have occurred to him only at a time when he himself was retired from public life and when he had withdrawn from the affairs of state. He who had been so explicit in his criticism of the Constitution because it had not incorporated a Bill of Rights, never touched on its failure to incorporate the townships which so obviously were the original models of his "elementary republics" where "the voice of the whole people would be fairly, fully, and peaceably expressed, discussed, and decided by the common reason" of all citizens. . . . In terms of his own role in the affairs of his country and the outcome of the Revolution, the idea of the ward system clearly was an afterthought; and, in terms of his own biographical development, the repeated insistence on the "peaceable" character of these wards demonstrates that this system was to him the only possible nonviolent alternative to his earlier notions about the desirability of recurring revolutions. At any event, we find the only detailed descriptions of what he had in mind in letters written in the year 1816, and these letters repeat rather than supplement one another.

Jefferson himself knew well enough that what he proposed as the "salvation of the republic" actually was the salvation of the revolutionary spirit through the republic. His expositions of the ward system always began with a reminder of how "the vigor given to our revolution in its commencement" was due to the "little republics," how they had "thrown the whole nation into energetic action," and how, at a later occasion, he had felt "the foundations of the government shaken under [his] feet by the New England townships," "the energy of this organization" being so great that "there was not an individual in their States whose body was not thrown with all its momentum into action." Hence, he expected the wards to permit the citizens to continue to do what they had been able to do during the years of revolution, namely, to act on their own and thus to participate in public business as it was being transacted from day to day. By virtue of the Constitution, the public business of the nation as a whole had been transferred to Washington and was being transacted by the federal government, of which Jefferson still thought as "the foreign branch" of the republic, whose domestic affairs were taken care of by the state governments. . . . But state government and even the administrative machinery of the county were by far too large and unwieldy to permit immediate participation; in all these institutions, it was the delegates of the people rather than the people themselves who constituted the public realm, whereas those who delegated them and who, theoretically, were the source and the seat of power remained forever outside its doors. This order of things should have sufficed if Jefferson had actually believed (as he sometimes professed) that the happiness of the people lay exclusively in their private welfare; for because of the way the government of the union was constituted—with its division and separation of powers, with controls, checks and balances, built into its very center—it was highly unlikely, though of course not impossible, that a tyranny could arise out of it. What could happen, and what indeed has happened over and over again since, was that "the representative organs should become corrupt and perverted," . . . but such corruption was not likely to be due (and hardly ever has been due) to a conspiracy of the representative organs against the people whom they represented. Corruption in this kind of government is much more likely to spring from the midst of society, that is, from the people themselves.

Corruption and perversion are more pernicious, and at the same time more likely to occur, in an egalitarian republic than in any other form of government. Schematically speaking, they come to pass when private interests invade the public domain, that is, they spring from below and not from above. It is precisely because the republic excluded on principle the old dichotomy of ruler and ruled that corruption of the body politic did not leave the people untouched, as in other forms of government, where only the rulers or the ruling classes needed to be affected, and where therefore an "innocent" people might indeed first suffer and then, one day, effect a dreadful but necessary insurrection. Corruption of the people themselves—as distinguished from corruption of their representatives or a ruling class—is possible only under a government that has granted them a share in public power and has taught them how to manipulate it. Where the rift between ruler and ruled has been closed, it is always possible that the dividing line between public and private may become blurred and, eventually, obliterated. Prior to the modern age and the rise of society, this danger, inherent in republican government, used to raise from the public realm, from the tendency of public power to expand and to trespass upon private interests. The age-old remedy against this danger was respect for private property, that is, the framing of a system of laws through which the rights of privacy were publicly guaranteed and the dividing line between public and private legally protected. The Bill of Rights in the American Constitution forms the last, and the most exhaustive, legal bulwark for the private realm against public power, and Jefferson's preoccupation with the dangers of public power and this remedy against them is sufficiently well known. However, under conditions, not of prosperity as such, but of a rapid and constant economic growth, that is, of a constantly increasing expansion of the private realm—and these were of course the conditions of the modern age—the dangers of corruption and perversion were much more likely to arise from private interests than from public power. And it speaks for the high caliber of Jefferson's statesmanship that he was able to perceive this danger despite his preoccupation with the older and better-known threats of corruption in bodies politic.

The only remedies against the misuse of public power by private individuals lie in the public realm itself, in the light which exhibits each deed enacted within its boundaries, in the very visibility to which it exposes all those who enter it. Jefferson, though the secret vote was still unknown at the time, had at least a foreboding of how dangerous it might be to allow the people a share in public power without providing them at the same time with more public space than the ballot box and with more opportunity to make their voices heard in public than election day. What he perceived to be the mortal danger to the republic was that the Constitution had given all power to the citizens, without giving them the opportunity of *being* republicans and of *acting* as citizens. In other words, the danger was that all power had been given to the people in their private capacity, and that there was no space established for them in their capacity of being citizens. When, at the end of his life, he summed up what to him clearly was the gist of private and public morality, "Love your neighbor as yourself, and your country more than yourself." . . . [H]e knew that this maxim remained an empty exhortation unless the "country" could be made as present to the "love" of its citizens as the "neighbor" was to the love of his fellow men. For just as there could not be much substance to neighborly love if one's neighbor should make a brief apparition once every two years, so there could not be much substance to the admonition to love one's country more than oneself unless the country was a living presence in the midst of its citizens.

Hence, according to Jefferson, it was the very principle of republican government to demand "the subdivision of the counties into wards," namely, the creation of "small republics" through which "every man in the State" could become "an acting member of the Common government, transacting in person a great portion of its rights and duties, subordinate indeed, yet important, and entirely within his competence." . . . It was "these little republics [that] would be the main strength of the great one"; . . . for inasmuch as the republican government of the Union was based on the assumption that the seat of power was in the people, the very condition for its proper functioning lay in a scheme "to divide [government] among the many, distributing to every one exactly the functions he [was] competent to." Without this, the very principle of republican government could never be actualized, and the government of the United States would be republican in name only.

Thinking in terms of the safety of the republic, the question was how to prevent "the degeneracy of our government," and Jefferson called every government degenerate in which all powers were concentrated "in the hands of the one, the few, the well-born or the many." Hence, the ward system was not meant to strengthen the power of the many but the power of "every one" within the limits of his competence; and only by breaking up "the many" into assemblies where every one could count and be counted upon "shall we be as republican as a large society can be." In terms of the safety of the citizens of the republic, the question was how to make everybody feel

> that he is a participator in the government of affairs, not merely at an election one day in the year, but every day; when there shall not be a man in the State who will not be a member of some one of its councils, great or small, he will let the heart be torn out of his body sooner than his power wrested from him by a Caesar or a Bonaparte.

Finally, as to the question of how to integrate these smallest organs, designed for everyone, into the governmental structure of the Union, designed for all, his answer was:

> The elementary republics of the wards, the county republics, the State republics, and the republic of the Union would form a gradation of authorities, standing each on the basis of law, holding every one its delegated share of powers, and constituting truly a system of fundamental balances and checks for the government.

On one point, however, Jefferson remained curiously silent, and that is the question of what the specific functions of the elementary republics should be. He mentioned occasionally as "one of the advantages of the ward divisions I have proposed" that they would offer a better way to collect the voice of the people than the mechanics of representative government; but in the main, he was convinced that if one would "begin them only for a single purpose" they would "soon show for what others they [were] the best instruments." . . .

This vagueness of purpose, far from being due to a lack of clarity, indicates perhaps more tellingly than any other single aspect of Jefferson's proposal that the afterthought in which he clarified and gave substance to his most cherished recollections from the Revolution in fact concerned a new form of government rather than a mere reform of it or a mere supplement to the existing institutions.

If the ultimate end of revolution was freedom and the constitution of a public space where freedom could appear, the *constitutio libertatis*, then the elementary republics of the wards, the only tangible place where everyone could be free, actually were the end of the great republic whose chief purpose in domestic affairs should have been to provide the people with such places of freedom and to protect them. The basic assumption of the ward system, whether Jefferson knew it or not, was that no one could be called happy without his share in public happiness, that no one could be called free without his experience in public freedom, and that no one could be called either happy or free without participating, and having a share, in public power.

. . . [N]o historian will ever be able to tell the tale of our century without stringing it "on the thread of revolutions"; but this tale, since its end still lies hidden in the mists of the future, is not yet fit to be told.

The same, to an extent, is true for the particular aspect of revolution with which we now must concern ourselves. This aspect is the regular emergence, during the course of revolution, of a new form of government that resembled in an amazing fashion Jefferson's ward system and seemed to repeat, under no matter what circumstances, the revolutionary societies and municipal councils which had spread all over France after 1789. Among the reasons that recommend this aspect to our attention must first be mentioned that we deal here with the phenomenon that impressed most the two greatest revolutionists of the whole period, Marx and Lenin, when they were witnessing its spontaneous rise, the former during the Parisian Commune of 1871 and the latter in 1905, during the first Russian revolution. What struck them was not only the fact that they themselves were entirely unprepared for these events, but also that they knew they were confronted with a repetition unaccounted for by any conscious imitation or even mere remembrance of the past. To be sure, they had hardly any knowledge of Jefferson's ward system, but they knew well enough the revolutionary role the sections of the first Parisian Commune had played in the French Revolution, except that they had never thought of them as possible germs for a new form of government but had regarded them as mere instruments to be dispensed with once the revolution came to an end. Now, however, they were confronted with popular organs—the communes, the councils, the *Räte*, the soviets—which clearly intended to survive the revolution. This contradicted all their theories and even more importantly, was in flagrant conflict with those assumptions about the nature of power and violence which they shared, albeit unconsciously, with the rulers of the doomed or defunct regimes. Firmly anchored in the tradition of the nation-state, they conceived of revolution as a means to seize power, and they identified power with the monopoly of the means of violence. What actually happened, however, was a swift disintegration of the old power, the sudden loss of control over the means of violence, and, at the same time, the amazing formation of a new power structure which owed its existence to nothing but the organizational impulses of the people themselves. In other words, when the moment of revolution had come, it turned out that there was no power left to seize, so that the revolutionists found themselves before the rather uncomfortable alternative of either putting their own prerevolutionary "power," that is, the organization of the party apparatus, into the vacated power center of the defunct government, or simply joining the new revolutionary power centers which had sprung up without their help.

For a brief moment, while he was the mere witness of something he never had expected, Marx understood that the *Kommunalverfassung* of the Parisian Commune in 1871, because it was supposed to become "the political form of even the smallest village," might well be "the political form, finally discovered, for the economic liberation of labor." But he soon became aware to what extent this political form contradicted all notions of a "dictatorship of the proletariat" by means of a socialist or communist party whose monopoly of power and violence was modeled upon the highly centralized governments of nation-states, and he concluded that the communal councils were, after all, only temporary organs of the revolution. . . . It is almost the same sequence of attitudes which, one generation later, we find in Lenin, who twice in his life, in 1905 and in 1917, came under the direct impact of the events themselves, that is to say, was temporarily liberated from the pernicious influence of a revolutionary ideology. Thus he could extol with great sincerity in 1905 "the revolutionary creativity of the people," who spontaneously had begun to establish an entirely new power structure in the midst of revolution, . . . just as, twelve years later, he could let loose and win the October Revolution with the slogan: "All power to the *soviets*." But during the years that separated the two revolutions he had done nothing to reorient his thought and to incorporate the new organs into any of the many party programs, with the result that the same spontaneous development in 1917 found him and his party no less unprepared than they had been in 1905. When, finally, during the Kronstadt rebellion, the soviets revolted against the party dictatorship and the incompatibility of the new councils with the party system became manifest, he decided almost at once to crush the councils, since they threatened the power monopoly of the Bolshevik party. The name "Soviet Union" for postrevolutionary Russia has been a lie ever since, but this lie has also contained, ever since, the grudging admission of the overwhelming popularity, not of the Bolshevik party, but of the soviet system which the party reduced to impotence. . . . Put before the alternative of either adjusting their thoughts and deeds to the new and the unexpected or going to the extreme of tyranny and suppression, they hardly hesitated in their decision for the latter; with the exceptions of a few moments without consequence, their behavior from beginning to end was dictated by considerations of party strife, which played no role in the councils but which indeed had been of paramount importance in the prerevolutionary parliaments. When the Communists decided, in 1919, "to espouse only the cause of a *soviet* republic in which the *soviets* possess a Communist majority," . . . they actually behaved like ordinary party politicians. So great is the fear of men, even of the most radical and least conventional among them, of things never seen, of thoughts never thought, of institutions never tried before.

The failure of the revolutionary tradition to give any serious thought to the only new form of government born out of revolution can partly be explained by Marx's obsession with the social question and his unwillingness to pay serious attention to questions of state and government. But this explanation is weak and, to an extent, even question-begging, because it takes for granted the overtowering influence of Marx on the revolutionary movement and tradition, an influence which itself still stands in need of explanation. It was, after all, not only the Marxists among the revolutionists who proved to be utterly unprepared for the actualities of revolutionary events. And this unpreparedness is all the more noteworthy as it surely cannot be blamed upon lack of thought or interest in revolution. It is well known that the French Revolution had given rise to an entirely new figure on the political scene, the professional revolutionist, and his life was spent not in revolutionary agitation, for which there existed but few opportunities, but in study and thought, in theory and debate, whose sole object was revolution. In fact, no history of the European leisure classes would be complete without a history of the professional revolutionists of the nineteenth and twentieth centuries, who, together with the modern artists and writers, have become the true heirs of the *hommes de lettres* in the seventeenth and eighteenth centuries. The artists and writers joined the revolutionists because "the very word bourgeois came to have a hated significance no less aesthetic than political"; . . . together they established Bohemia, that island of blessed leisure in the midst of the busy and overbusy century of the Industrial Revolution. Even among the members of this new leisure class, the professional revolutionist enjoyed special privileges since his way of life demanded no specific work whatsoever. If there was a thing he had no reason to complain of, it was lack of time to think, whereby it makes little difference if such an essentially theoretical way of life was spent in the famous libraries of London and Paris, or in the coffee houses in Vienna and Zurich, or in the relatively comfortable and undisturbed jails of the various anciens régimes.

The role the professional revolutionists played in all modern revolutions is great and significant enough, but it did not consist in the preparation of revolutions. They watched and analyzed the progressing disintegration in state and society; they hardly did, or were in a position to do, much to advance and direct it. Even the wave of strikes that spread over Russia in 1905 and led into the first revolution was entirely spontaneous, unsupported by any political or trade-union organizations, which, on the contrary, sprang up only in the course of the revolution. . . . The outbreak of most revolutions has surprised the revolutionist groups and parties no less than all others, and there exists hardly a revolution whose outbreak could be blamed upon their activities. It usually was the other way round: revolution broke out and liberated, as it were, the professional revolutionists from wherever they happened to be—from jail, or from the coffee house, or from the library. Not even Lenin's party of professional revolutionists would ever have been able to "make" a revolution; the best they could do was to be around, or to hurry home, at the right moment, that is, at the moment of collapse. De Tocqueville's observation in 1848, that the monarchy fell "before rather than beneath the blows of the victors, who were as astonished at their triumph as were the vanquished at their defeat," has been verified over and over again.

The part of the professional revolutionists usually consists not in making a revolution but in rising to power after it has broken out, and their great advantage in this power struggle lies less in their theories and mental or organizational preparation than in the simple fact that their names are the only ones which are publicly known. . . . It certainly is not conspiracy that causes revolution, and secret societies—though they may succeed in committing a few spectacular crimes, usually with the help of the secret police . . . —are as a rule much too secret to be able to make their voices heard in public. The loss of authority in the powers-that-be which indeed precedes all revolutions, is actually a secret to no one, since its manifestations are open and tangible, though not necessarily spectacular; but its symptoms—general dissatisfaction, widespread malaise, and contempt for those in power—are difficult to pin down since their meaning is never unequivocal. . . . Nevertheless, contempt, hardly among the motives of the typical professional revolutionist, is certainly one of the most potent springs of revolution; there has hardly been a revolution for which Lamartine's remark about 1848, "the revolution of contempt," would be altogether inappropriate.

However, while the part played by the professional revolutionist in the outbreak of revolution has usually been insignificant to the point of nonexistence, his influence upon the actual course a revolution will take has proved to be very great. And since he spent his apprenticeship in the school of past revolutions, he will invariably exert this influence not in favor of the new and the unexpected, but in favor of some action which remains in accordance with the past. Since it is his very task to assure the continuity of revolution, he will be inclined to argue in terms of historical precedents, and the conscious and pernicious imitation of past events, which we mentioned earlier, lies, partially at least, in the very nature of his profession. Long before the professional revolutionists had found in Marxism their official guide to the interpretation and annotation of all history, past, present and future, de Tocqueville, in 1848, could already note: "the imitation [i.e., of 1789 by the revolutionary Assembly] was so manifest that it concealed the terrible originality of the facts; I continually had the impression they were engaged in play-acting the French Revolution far more than continuing it." . . . And again, during the Parisian Commune of 1871, on which Marx and Marxists had no influence whatsoever, at least one of the new magazines, *Le Père Duchêne*, adopted the old revolutionary calendar's names for the months of the year. It is strange indeed that in this atmosphere, where every incident of past revolutions was mulled over as though it were part of sacred history, the only entirely new and entirely spontaneous institution in revolutionary history should have been neglected to the point of oblivion.

Armed with the wisdom of hindsight, one is tempted to qualify this statement. There are certain paragraphs in the writings of the Utopian Socialists, especially in Proudhon and Bakunin, into which it has been relatively easy to read an awareness of the council system. Yet the truth is that these essentially anarchist political thinkers were singularly unequipped to deal with a phenomenon which demonstrated so clearly how a revolution did not end with the abolition of state and government but, on the contrary, aimed at the foundation of a new state and the establishment of a new form of government. More recently, historians have pointed to the rather obvious similarities between the councils and the medieval townships, the Swiss cantons, the English seventeenth-century "agitators"—or rather "adjustators," as they were originally called—and the General Council of Cromwell's army, but the point of the matter is that none of them, with the possible exception of the medieval town, . . . had ever the slightest influence on the minds of the people who in the course of a revolution spontaneously organized themselves in councils.

Hence, no tradition, either revolutionary or prerevolutionary, can be called to account for the regular emergence and reemergence of the council system ever since the French Revolution. If we leave aside the February Revolution of 1848 in Paris, where a *commission pour les travailleurs*, set up by the government itself, was almost exclusively concerned with questions of social legislation, the main dates of appearance of these organs of action and germs of a new state are the following: the year 1870, when the French capital under siege by the Prussian army "spontaneously reorganized itself into a miniature federal body," which then formed the nucleus for the Parisian Commune government in the spring of 1871; . . . the year 1905, when the wave of spontaneous strikes in Russia suddenly developed a political leadership of its own, outside all revolutionary parties and groups, and the workers in the factories organized themselves into councils, soviets, for the purpose of representative self-government; the February Revolution of 1917 in Russia, when "despite different political tendencies among the Russian workers, the organization itself, that is the soviet, was not even subject to discussion"; . . . the years 1918 and 1919 in Germany, when, after the defeat of the army, soldiers and workers in open rebellion constituted themselves into *Arbeiter- und Soldatenräte*, demanding, in Berlin, that this *Rätesystem* become the foundation stone of the new German constitution, and establishing, together with the Bohemians of the coffee houses, in Munich in the spring of 1919, the short-lived Bavarian *Räterepublik*; . . . the last date, finally, is the autumn of 1956, when the Hungarian Revolution from its very beginning produced the council system anew in Budapest, from which it spread all over the country "with incredible rapidity." . . .

The mere enumeration of these dates suggests a continuity that in fact never existed. It is precisely the absence of continuity, tradition, and organized influence that makes the sameness of the phenomenon so very striking. Outstanding among the councils' common characteristics is, of course, the spontaneity of their coming into being, because it clearly and flagrantly contradicts the theoretical "twentieth-century model of revolution—planned, prepared, and executed almost to cold scientific exactness by the professional revolutionaries." . . . It is true that wherever the revolution was not defeated and not followed by some sort of restoration, the one-party dictatorship, that is, the model of the professional revolutionary, eventually prevailed, but it prevailed only after a violent struggle with the organs and institutions of the revolution itself. The councils, moreover, were always organs of order as much as organs of action, and it was indeed their aspiration to lay down the new order that brought them into conflict with the groups of professional revolutionaries, who wished to degrade them to mere executive organs of revolutionary activity. It is true enough that the members of the councils were not content to discuss and "enlighten themselves" about measures that were taken by parties or assemblies; they consciously and explicitly desired the direct participation of every citizen in the public affairs of the country, . . . and as long as they lasted, there is no doubt that "every individual found his own sphere of action and could behold, as it were, with his own eyes his own contribution to the events of the day." . . . Witnesses of their functioning were often agreed on the extent to which the revolution had given birth to a "direct regeneration of democracy," whereby the implication was that all such regenerations, alas, were foredoomed since, obviously, a direct handling of public business through the people was impossible under modern conditions. They looked upon the councils as though they were a romantic dream, some sort of fantastic utopia come true for a fleeting moment to show, as it were, the hopelessly romantic yearnings of the people, who apparently did not yet know the true facts of life. These realists took their own bearings from the party system, assuming as a matter of course that there existed no other alternative for representative government and forgetting conveniently that the downfall of the old regime had been due, among other things, precisely to this system.

For the remarkable thing about the councils was of course not only that they crossed all party lines, that members of the various parties sat in them together, but that such party membership played no role whatsoever. They were in fact the only political organs for people who belonged to no party. Hence, they invariably came into conflict with all assemblies, with the old parliaments as well as with the new "constituent assemblies," for the simple reason that the latter, even in their most extreme wings, were still the children of the party system. At this stage of events, that is, in the midst of revolution, it was the party programs more than anything else that separated the councils from the parties; for these programs, no matter how revolutionary, were all "ready-made formulas" which demanded not action but execution—"to be carried out energetically in practice," as Rosa Luxemburg pointed out with such amazing clearsightedness about the issues at stake. . . . Today we know how quickly the theoretical formula disappeared in practical execution, but if the formula had survived its execution, and even if it had proved to be the panacea for all evils, social and political, the councils were bound to rebel against any such policy since the very cleavage between the party experts who "knew" and the mass of the people who were supposed to apply this knowledge left out of account the average citizen's capacity to act and to form his own opinion. The councils, in other words, were bound to become superfluous if the spirit of the revolutionary party prevailed. Wherever knowing and doing have parted company, the space of freedom is lost. . . .

However, while it may be true that, as a device of government, only the two-party system has proved its viability and, at the same time, its capacity to guarantee constitutional liberties, it is no less true that the best it has achieved is a certain control of the rulers by those who are ruled, but that it has by no means enabled the citizen to become a "participator" in public affairs. The most the citizen can hope for is to be "represented," whereby it is obvious that the only thing which can be represented and delegated is interest, or the welfare of the constituents, but neither their actions nor their opinions. In this system the opinions of the people are indeed unascertainable for the simple reason that they are nonexistent. Opinions are formed in a process of open discussion and public debate, and where no opportunity for the forming of opinions exists, there may be moods—moods of the masses and moods of individuals, the latter no less fickle and unreliable than the former—but no opinion. Hence, the best the representative can do is to act as his constituents would act if they themselves had any opportunity to do so. The same is not true for questions of interest and welfare, which can be ascertained objectively, and where the need for action and decision arises out of the various conflicts among interest groups. Through pressure groups, lobbies, and other devices, the voters can indeed influence the actions of their representatives with respect to interest, that is, they can force their representatives to execute their wishes at the expense of the wishes and interests of other groups of voters. In all these instances the voter acts out of concern with his private life and well-being, and the residue of power he still holds in his hands resembles rather the reckless coercion with which a blackmailer forces his victim into obedience than the power that arises out of joint action and joint deliberation. Be that as it may, neither the people in general nor the political scientists in particular have left much doubt that the parties, because of their monopoly of nomination, cannot be regarded as popular organs, but that they are, on the contrary, the very efficient instruments through which the power of the people is curtailed and controlled. That representative government has in fact become oligarchic government is true enough, though not in the classical sense of rule by the few in the interest of the few; what we today call democracy is a form of government where the few rule, at least supposedly, in the interest of the many. This government is democratic in that popular welfare and private happiness are its chief goals; but it can be called oligarchic in the sense that public happiness and public freedom have again become the privilege of the few.

The defenders of this system, which actually is the system of the welfare state, if they are liberal and of democratic convictions, must deny the very existence of public happiness and public freedom; they must insist that politics is a burden and that its end is itself not political. . . . If, on the other hand, taught by the profound turmoil of this century, they have lost their liberal illusion about some innate goodness of the people, they are likely to conclude that "no people has ever been known to govern itself," that "the will of the people is profoundly anarchic: it wants to do as it pleases," that its attitude toward all government is "hostility" because "government and constraint are inseparable," and constraint by definition "is external to the constrained." . . .

Such statements, difficult to prove, are even more difficult to refute, but the assumptions upon which they rest are not difficult to point out. Theoretically, the most relevant and the most pernicious among them is the equation of "people" and masses, which sounds only too plausible to everyone who lives in a mass society and is constantly exposed to its numerous irritations. . . . Terminologically speaking, one could say that the more glaring the failures of the party system are, the easier it will be for a movement not only to appeal to and to organize the people, but to transform them into masses. Practically, the current "realism," despair of the people's political capacities . . . is based solidly upon the conscious or unconscious determination to ignore the reality of the councils and to take for granted that there is not, and never has been, any alternative to the present system.

The historical truth of the matter is that the party and council systems are almost coeval; both were unknown prior to the revolutions and both are the consequences of the modern and revolutionary tenet that all inhabitants of a given territory are entitled to be admitted to the public, political realm. The councils, as distinguished from parties, have always emerged during the revolution itself; they sprang from the people as spontaneous organs of action and of order. The last point is worth emphasizing; nothing indeed contradicts more sharply the old adage of the anarchistic and lawless "natural" inclinations of a people left without the constraint of its government than the emergence of the councils that, wherever they appeared, and most pronouncedly during the Hungarian Revolution, were concerned with the reorganization of the political and economic life of the country and the establishment of a new order. . . . Parties—as distinguished from factions typical of all parliaments and assemblies, be these hereditary or representative—have thus far never emerged during a revolution; they either preceded it, as in the twentieth century, or they developed with the extension of popular suffrage. Hence the party, whether an extension of parliamentary faction or a creation outside parliament, has been an institution to provide parliamentary government with the required support of the people, whereby it was always understood that the people, through voting, did the supporting, while action remained the prerogative of government. If parties become militant and step actively into the domain of political action, they violate their own principle as well as their function in parliamentary government, that is, they become subversive, and this regardless of their doctrines and ideologies. The disintegration of parliamentary government—in Italy and Germany after World War I, for instance, or in France after World War II—has demonstrated repeatedly how even parties supporting the status quo actually helped to undermine the regime the moment they overstepped their institutional limitations. Action and participation in public affairs, a natural aspiration of the councils, obviously are not signs of health and vitality but of decay and perversion in an institution whose primary function has always been representation.

For it is indeed true that the essential characteristic of the otherwise widely differing party systems is "that they 'nominate' candidates for elective offices of representative government," and it may even be correct to say that "the act of nominating itself is enough to bring a political party into being." . . . Hence, from the very beginning, the party as an institution presupposed either that the citizen's participation in public affairs was guaranteed by other public organs, or that such participation was not necessary and that the newly admitted strata of the population should be content with representation, or, finally, that all political questions in the welfare state are ultimately problems of administration, to be handled and decided by experts, in which case even the representatives of the people hardly possess an authentic area of action but are administrative officers, whose business, though in the public interest, is not essentially different from the business of private management. If the last of these presuppositions should turn out to be correct—and who could deny the extent to which in our mass societies the political realm has withered away and is being replaced by that "administration of things" which Engels predicted for a classless society?—then, to be sure, the councils would have to be considered as atavistic institutions without any relevance in the realm of human affairs. But the same, or something very similar, would then soon enough turn out to be true for the party system; for administration and management, because their business is dictated by the necessities which underlie all economic processes, are essentially not only nonpolitical but even nonpartisan. In a society under the sway of abundance, conflicting group interests need no longer be settled at one another's expense, and the principle of opposition is valid only as long as there exist authentic choices which transcend the objective and demonstrably valid opinions of experts. When government has really become administration, the party system can only result in incompetence and wastefulness. The only nonobsolete function the party system might conceivably perform in such a regime would be to guard it against corruption of public servants, and even this function would be much better and more reliably performed by the police. . . .

The conflict between the two systems, the parties and the councils, came to the fore in all twentieth-century revolutions. The issue at stake was representation versus action and participation. The councils were organs of action, the revolutionary parties were organs of representation, and although the revolutionary parties halfheartedly recognized the councils as instruments of "revolutionary struggle," they tried even in the midst of revolution to rule them from within; they knew well enough that no party, no matter how revolutionary it was, would be able to survive the transformation of the government into a true Soviet Republic. For the parties, the need for action itself was transitory, and they had no doubt that after the victory of the revolution further action would simply prove unnecessary or subversive. Bad faith and the drive for power were not the decisive factors that made the professional revolutionists turn against the revolutionary organs of the people; it was rather the elementary convictions which the revolutionary parties shared with all other parties. They agreed that the end of government was the welfare of the people, and that the substance of politics was not action but administration. In this respect, it is only fair to say that all parties from right to left have much more in common with one another than the revolutionary groups ever had in common with the councils. Moreover, what eventually decided the issue in favor of the party and the one-party dictatorship was by no means only superior power or determination to crush the councils through ruthless use of the means of violence.

If it is true that the revolutionary parties never understood to what an extent the council system was identical with the emergence of a new form of government, it is no less true that the councils were incapable of understanding to what an enormous extent the government machinery in modern societies must indeed perform the functions of administration. The fatal mistake of the councils has always been that they themselves did not distinguish clearly between participation in public affairs and administration or management of things in the public interest. In the form of workers' councils, they have again and again tried to take over the management of the factories, and all these attempts have ended in dismal failure. "The wish of the working class," we are told, "has been fulfilled.

The factories will be managed by the councils of the workers." . . . This so-called wish of the working class sounds much rather like an attempt of the revolutionary party to counteract the councils' political aspirations, to drive their members away from the political realm and back into the factories. And this suspicion is borne out by two facts: the councils have always been primarily political, with social and economic claims playing a very minor role, and it was precisely this lack of interest in social and economic questions which, in the view of the revolutionary party, was a sure sign of their "lower-middle-class, abstract, liberalistic" mentality. . . . In fact, it was a sign of their political maturity, whereas the workers' wish to run the factories themselves was a sign of the understandable, but politically irrelevant desire of individuals to rise into positions which up to then had been open only to the middle classes.

No doubt, managerial talent should not be lacking in people of working-class origins; the trouble was merely that the workers' councils certainly were the worst possible organs for its detection. For the men whom they trusted and chose from their own midst were selected according to political criteria, for their trustworthiness, their personal integrity, their capacity of judgment, often for their physical courage. The same men, entirely capable of acting in a political capacity, were bound to fail if entrusted with the management of a factory or other administrative duties. For the qualities of the statesman or the political man, and the qualities of the manager or administrator are not only not the same, they very seldom are to be found in the same individual; the one is supposed to know how to deal with men in a field of human relations, whose principle is freedom, and the other must know how to manage things and people in a sphere of life whose principle is necessity. The councils in the factories brought an element of action into the management of things, and this indeed could not but create chaos. It was precisely these foredoomed attempts that have earned the council system its bad name. But while it is true that they were incapable of organizing, or rather of rebuilding, the economic system of the country, it is also true that the chief reason for their failure was not any lawlessness of the people, but their political qualities. Whereas, on the other hand, the reason why the party apparatuses, despite many shortcomings—corruption, incompetence, and incredible wastefulness—eventually succeeded where the councils had failed lay precisely in their original oligarchic and even autocratic structure, which made them so utterly unreliable for all political purposes.

Freedom, wherever it existed as a tangible reality, has always been spatially limited. This is especially clear for the greatest and most elementary of all negative liberties, the freedom of movement; the borders of national territory or the walls of the city-state comprehended and protected a space in which men could move freely. Treaties and international guarantees provide an extension of this territorially bound freedom for citizens outside their own country, but even under these modern conditions the elementary coincidence of freedom and a limited space remains manifest. What is true for freedom of movement is, to a large extent, valid for freedom in general. Freedom in a positive sense is possible only among equals, and equality itself is by no means a universally valid principle but, again, applicable only with limitations and even within spatial limits. If we equate these spaces of freedom—which, following the gist, though not the terminology, of John Adams, we could also call spaces of appearances—with the political realm itself, we shall be inclined to think of them as islands in a sea or as oases in a desert. This image, I believe, is suggested to us not merely by the consistency of a metaphor but by the record of history as well.

The phenomenon I am concerned with here is usually called the "elite," and my quarrel with this term is not that I doubt that the political way of life has never been and will never be the way of life of the many, even though political business, by definition, concerns more than the many, namely strictly speaking, the sum total of all citizens. Political passions—courage, the pursuit of public happiness, the taste of public freedom, an ambition that strives for excellence regardless not only of social status and administrative office but even of achievement and congratulation—are perhaps not as rare as we are inclined to think, living in a society which has perverted all virtues into social values; but they certainly are out of the ordinary under all circumstances. My quarrel with the "elite" is that the term implies an oligarchic form of government, the domination of the many by the rule of a few. From this, one can only conclude—as indeed our whole tradition of political thought has concluded—that the essence of politics is rulership and that the dominant political passion is the passion to rule or to govern. This, I propose, is profoundly untrue. The fact that political "elites" have always determined the political destinies of the many and have, in most instances, exerted a domination over them, indicates, on the one hand, the bitter need of the few to protect themselves against the many, or rather to protect the island of freedom they have come to inhabit against the surrounding sea of necessity; and it indicates, on the other hand, the responsibility that falls automatically upon those who care for the fate of those who do not. But neither this need nor this responsibility touches upon the essence, the very substance of their lives, which is freedom; both are incidental and secondary with respect to what actually goes on within the limited space of the island itself. Put into terms of present-day institutions, it would be in Parliament and in Congress, where he moves among his peers, that the political life of a member of representative government is actualized, no matter how much of his time may be spent in campaigning, in trying to get the vote and in listening to the voter. The point of the matter is not merely the obvious phoniness of this dialogue in modern party government, where the voter can only consent or refuse to ratify a choice which (with the exception of the American primaries) is made without him, and it does not even concern conspicuous abuses such as the introduction into politics of Madison Avenue methods, through which the relationship between representative and elector is transformed into that of seller and buyer. Even if there is communication between representative and voter, between the nation and Parliament—and the existence of such communication marks the outstanding difference between the governments of the British and the Americans, on one side, and those of Western Europe, on the other—this communication is never between equals but between those who aspire to govern and those who consent to be governed. It is indeed in the very nature of the party system to replace "the formula 'government of the people by the people' by this formula: 'government of the people *by an élite sprung from the people*.'" . . .

It has been said that "the deepest significance of political parties" must be seen in their providing "the necessary framework enabling the masses to recruit from among themselves their own élites," . . . and it is true enough that it was primarily the parties which opened political careers to members of the lower classes. No doubt the party as the outstanding institution of democratic government corresponds to one of the major trends of the modern age, the constantly and universally increasing equalization of society; but this by no means implies that it corresponds to the deepest significance of revolution in the modern age as well. The "elite sprung from the people" has replaced the premodern elites of birth and wealth; it has nowhere enabled the people qua people to make their entrance into political life and to become participators in public affairs. The relationship between a ruling elite and the people, between the few, who among themselves constitute a public space, and the many, who spend their lives outside it and in obscurity, has remained unchanged. From the viewpoint of revolution and the survival of the revolutionary spirit, the trouble does not lie in the factual rise of a new elite; it is not the revolutionary spirit but the democratic mentality of an egalitarian society that tends to deny the obvious inability and conspicuous lack of interest of large parts of the population in political matters as such. The trouble lies in the lack of public spaces to which the people at large would have entrance and from which an elite could be selected, or rather, where it could select itself. The trouble, in other words, is that politics has become a profession and a career, and that the "elite" therefore is being chosen according to standards and criteria which are themselves profoundly unpolitical. It is in the nature of all party systems that the authentically political talents can assert themselves only in rare cases, and it is even rarer that the specifically political qualifications survive the petty maneuvers of party politics with its demands for plain salesmanship. Of course the men who sat in the councils were also an elite, they were even the only political elite, of the people and sprung from the people, the modern world has ever seen, but they were not nominated from above and not supported from below. With respect to the elementary councils that sprung up wherever people lived or worked together, one is tempted to say that they had selected themselves; those who organized themselves were those who cared and those who took the initiative; they were the political elite of the people brought into the open by the revolution. From these "elementary republics," the councilmen then chose their deputies for the next higher council, and these deputies, again, were selected by their peers, they were not subject to any pressure either from above or from below. Their title rested on nothing but the confidence of their equals, and this equality was not natural but political, it was nothing they had been born with; it was the equality of those who had committed themselves to, and now were engaged in, a joint enterprise. Once elected and sent into the next higher council, the deputy found himself again among his peers, for the deputies on any given level in this system were those who had received a special trust. No doubt this form of government, if fully developed, would have assumed again the shape of a pyramid, which, of course, is the shape of an essentially authoritarian government. But while, in all authoritarian government we know of, authority is filtered down from above, in this case authority would have been generated neither at the top nor at the bottom, but on each of the pyramid's layers; and this obviously could constitute the solution to one of the most serious problems of all modern politics, which is not how to reconcile freedom and equality but how to reconcile equality and authority.

SELECTION 27
FROM
*Direct Action and Liberal Democracy**

APRIL CARTER

POPULAR DIRECT ACTION

ONE OF THE MAIN targets of spontaneous and local direct action in Britain has been dangerous traffic on the roads. On 8 August 1970 there was a protest which halted the traffic in the Norfolk town of Thetford. According to the *Eastern Daily Press*:

> Waving banners and chanting "We want a crossing" the mothers, their children, and a growing number of men, walked round in a large circle in the middle of the road, their chants mingling with the car horns of angry drivers held up in a mile-long queue in each direction. (Quoted in *Peace News*, 14 August 1970, I)

The protest was sparked off by the death of a fifteen-year-old girl, and was typical of a number of attempts to get local councils to take action to increase road safety. Harold Priestly in his *Voice of Protest* quotes as an example 500 villagers of Redbourn in Hertfordshire, who on 30 October 1967, walked to and fro over the zebra crossing in the High Street while traffic piled up on both sides, because they wanted a controlled crossing that could be worked from the curb. In November 1971, 500 people in Cambridge organized a "bike-in" to protest against traffic. In May 1972 a woman was taken to court for going out in the middle of the night and painting a zebra crossing where the council had failed to provide one.

Environmentalist groups have staged a number of direct action propaganda activities to advertise their cause. For example, the Earth Day plans in New York in April 1970 included free chest X-rays in Manhattan and the dumping of thousands of bottles and tins outside soft drink and beer factories; Friends of the Earth in Britain also dumped 1,500 Schweppes bottles on the doorstep of the

*(New York: Harper & Row, 1973): pp. 15–20, 24–27, 144–47, 156–59.

company in November 1971. But more relevant is the type of sustained campaign against pollution by local residents which took place in the Port Tennant area of Swansea in 1971. This action was directed against the United Carbon Black factory which emitted clouds of black smuts and dirt that fell on the surrounding houses and streets. Years of representation to the local council brought no relief—and a promise by the factory the previous year to install a new burner did not reduce the dirt. At the end of January a local meeting decided to block the road until the factory stopped spreading smuts. At the beginning of February fifty housewives went into the road in front of the factory and started turning away traffic to the firm. Shifts to fifty at a time were maintained for three weeks. In the evenings the men returning from work took over. A tent was pitched in the road and fires built. Local traders showed sympathy and brought food. After three weeks several departments of the factory had closed down, and the management negotiated a compromise agreement with the demonstrators, promising to spend £200,000 on pollution control and to stop production when easterly winds were blowing (*Solidarity*, vol. 6, no. 10).

An interesting example of spontaneous local direct action was the campaign by the wives of Hull trawlermen in 1968 after a trawling disaster in which a ship was lost, and it was revealed that the ship had no radio operator on board. Mrs. Lilian Bilocca said at the launching of a protest petition: "If ever I hear about a trawler going to sea without a full complement of crew or without a radio operator, I shall go aboard and wild horses will not drag me off until the ship is properly manned." Two days later three women tried to leap aboard a trawler about to sail without an operator, and struggled with police. The crews themselves also began to agitate. On 2 and 3 February crews refused to sail because they said that, among other faults, the life jackets were unsafe. Three days later another trawler returned to port after a dispute about the alarm in the crew's quarters. On 14 February it was announced that four inquiries were to be held into the Hull trawler disasters, including one to look into safety measures, pay, and hours of work. Tony Topham in a pamphlet on the subject commented:

> At the mass meetings of wives and mothers which have been held in Hull, the debate about *how* to achieve results has reproduced, in microcosm, all the historic strategies of the Labour movement, from Fabianism to Syndicalism. Frustration over delays and red tape, anger and grief, have brought forth determined advocates of direct action. Mrs. Bilocca, leader of much of the agitation, has proved her point that direct action can be made to pay. (*Anarchy*, no. 86, 105)

The issue which has in Britain roused widespread effective direct action campaigns is that of homelessness. The most important campaign took place immediately after World War II, in the Squatters movement of 1946. The first phase occurred in the summer of 1945, when a group composed largely of ex-servicemen moved homeless families into empty property during the night in southern seaside resorts, where many large houses were empty except when let out to holiday makers. As a result the government invested local authorities with wider powers to requisition houses. The main thrust of the Squatters movement the following year was to occupy empty army and airforce barracks and camps. The first family spontaneously took the initiative at Scunthorpe in Lincolnshire in May. By October according to the government's own figures, 39,535 people were squatting in 1,038 camps. The Ministry of Works offered Aneurin Bevan 850 former service camps "to help him in his emergency housing drive."

A member of the Squatters movement records that:

> As the camps began to fill, the squatters turned to other empty buildings: houses, shops, mansions, disused school buildings, race tracks and a stadium, were among the places occupied, and on August 26 two Aberdeen hotels and a hostel were taken . . . the final and most spectacular phase of the campaign began in London on Sunday the 8th September, when the 148 luxury flats of Duchess of Bedford House, Kensington, another block in Weymouth Street, Marylebone, and houses in Holland Park and Campden Hill, were invaded. (*Anarchy*, no. 23, 10–11)

Squatting was revived again, though on a much smaller scale, in the late 1960s. The first stage of the campaign revolved round a hostel for homeless families owned by the Kent County Council at West Malling, Kent. Some of the families themselves rebelled against a system which separated husbands from their wives, and only allowed them to visit during certain hours. After a campaign which included deliberate defiance by the husbands of the hostel regulations and of the court injunctions designed to make them obey the rules, and sustained picketing of the chief welfare officer, Kent County Council gave way.

The London Squatting Campaign was formed in November 1968. Jim Radford wrote in an article early in 1969:

> On December 1st we invaded the Hollies, a luxury block in East London, where many of the flats have remained empty since the building was completed four years ago. This was a token demonstration for the purpose of drawing public attention to a major social evil. On December 21st we went a step further. Together with a number of homeless families we took over the Old Vicarage in Capworth Street, E 11, a substantial twenty-four roomed house that has been empty ever since the vicar moved . . . three years ago. (*Anarchy*, no. 97, 80)

Families in Notting Hill and in Ilford took over houses in January and February and more squatters groups were formed. Some councils tried evictions and court injunctions to stop squatting; but in many cases squatters and councils came to an agreement, and squatters were allowed to remain. For example, the *Guardian* reported on 18 March 1970 that: "Squatting, Lewisham style, has become 'respectable' . . . the squatters now have 30 families installed in houses that would otherwise be empty awaiting redevelopment." The Squatting Association took responsibility for moving families out when redevelopment started, and for collecting low rents for the occupied houses.

Direct action centered on housing problems has not, however, been confined to the occupation of empty houses. In 1971 the Southwark Family Squatters Association barricaded themselves in at the town hall. A vigorous campaign was also undertaken to get tenants living in flats intolerably close to a new motorway rehoused. A *Guardian* article on 7 August 1970 reflected that:

> If you want to win the battle of homes versus motorways there appears to be no substitute for proletarian militancy. That seems to be the sad lesson brought home to the inhabitants of Gilda Court, a genteel decaying block of owner-occupied flats . . . there seems little hope that they will be rehoused with the alacrity shown by the Greater London Council towards some of its tenants affected by the Westway motorway.
>
> In the latter case the Walmer Road Action Committee's militancy is by no means abated. They complain that the GLC has committed itself only to rehouse the tenants of eight houses whereas 30 houses had been made uninhabitable. . . . If no satisfactory decision was forthcoming from the GLC by today there would be a "massive" campaign to disrupt traffic. (P. 5)

The tendency to resort to direct action to protect one's rights has extended to the factory floor. Faced with the threat of redundancy, in a wider context of high levels of unemployment, workers in a number of firms began in 1971 and 1972 to adopt methods more militant, and more appropriate, than the normal strike. The first and most significant action was that taken by shop stewards and workers in the yards of the Upper Clyde Shipbuilders, who, faced with the prospect of the yards being closed down, organized a "work-in," and took over control from the management. The work-in, prolonged over several months, was successful in getting the government to reverse its declared policy of not giving further financial aid to maintain the yards, though the workers had to accept compromises. The militancy of the Upper Clyde workers lay, however, more in their methods than in their long-term goals. Workers' control was used as a tactic, but not promoted as an aim.

The example of the UCS workers was followed at a number of other factories. A sit-in at the Plessey Electronics factory in Dunbartonshire began on 3 September 1971, when all the workers there had received redundancy notices. The workers took over control of the gates and refused to let machinery be moved in or out. Workers in Plessey's four factories in Ilford promised to "black" all machinery and materials from the Dunbartonshire factory. On 4 January 1972, 150 workers at an engineering factory at Mold, North Wales, took it over to prevent its closure. The gate was manned by shifts of about thirty men. Two days later a sit-in took place at the Fisher-Bendix electrical factory in Liverpool to stop the owners closing down the factory. Shop stewards reported that the management agreed to leave the factory immediately after the meeting which decided on the occupation of the factory. A more unusual example of militancy was provided by twelve women who staged a sit-in at a factory at Norfolk at the end of March 1971, and started to canvass orders for leather shoulder bags and skirts to keep the factory open. A *New Statesman* article on 28 April 1972, on a series of sit-ins in Manchester, commented:

> There are at present approximately 30 sit-ins in progress throughout the country and more are likely. And for the first time they are nearly all factory sit-ins. . . . Now in Manchester a wave of lock-outs has been countered by a wave of factory occupations.

While these tactics may be seen in part as an indication of a new militancy among industrial workers in Britain, they also reflect the prevalence of direct action as a method used both by movements committed to an ideological goal—for example, the campaign by Welsh Nationalists for use of the Welsh language—and by groups seeking redress for more immediate grievances. The *Guardian* reported, for example, on 26 May 1972, that "More than 300 prisoners staged what the Home Office described as 'a quiet, good-humoured sit-down demonstration' at Walton Prison, Liverpool, yesterday. Similar sit-downs have been staged in other prisons this week." Other prisoners at the Walton jail were said to be on hunger strike against prison conditions.

The relative respectability, as well as the prevalence, of the sit-in tactic is indicated by the fact that in September 1971, French police unions were threatening to occupy the Ministry of Finance and M. Chaban-Delmas's official residence if the prime minister would not listen to their grievances on pay and bad working conditions.

In trying to justify the direct action tactics used to stop the all-white South African cricket team touring Britain in 1970, Peter Hain [1971] appeals to the comparative legitimacy of much popular direct action:

> By attempting to stop the matches, we were accused of "infringing on people's lawful rights to watch cricket and rugby." This may have been true and, taken out of the context of the issue at stake, sounds plausible. The fact that people's "lawful rights" are just as often "infringed" by militant farmers driving tractors through towns, by industrial strikes and by disruptions of traffic by mothers demanding a zebra crossing, is conveniently forgotten. (P. 200)

The central methods of direct action comprise, in accordance with the line of analysis adopted here, the tactics evolved within the labor movement (strikes, go-slows, and boycotts) and the more recent forms of physical obstruction and intervention (sit-ins and trespassing). A third category is that of civil disobedience: deliberately breaking laws considered unjust, or the laws of a state pursuing unjust or inhuman policies. Another historical form of direct action is noncooperation with the state, for example, through tax refusal, or in the more radical form of draft resistance and disobedience inside the army. There are many other possible kinds of financial sanction, for example, the idea of a run on the banks, and many ingenious forms of protest on the margin of direct action, like taking out shares in order to disrupt shareholders' meetings. But this summary catalogue of methods indicates the general scope and nature of direct action as defined in this discussion.

While it is necessary to distinguish direct action from guerrilla warfare and street fighting, it is also necessary to mark it off, at the other end of the scale, from political activity relying on speeches, leaflets, and general propaganda which are the stock in trade of constitutional pressure groups, and a necessary element in any type of movement. They may well be a prelude to direct action, or an ancillary aspect of a direct action campaign, but they are not in themselves a form of direct action, unless undertaken as a challenge to specific laws or the authorities.

There is a rather indeterminate area, which is on the borderline of direct action, which may be termed symbolic action. This category of protest action includes parades, marches, and outdoor rallies designed to demonstrate mass opposition. It also covers vigils, fasts, and other modes of expressing individual commitment. Symbolic action may simply be an extension of other forms of propaganda, and a way of exerting public pressure on the government. In a liberal state it will normally be a legal and accepted form of protest. But symbolic demonstrations may signify a tendency to take action beyond the constitutional limits of protest, and they are usually an essential element in the creation of a movement of mass resistance. Rallies, marches, and individual acts of symbolic protest may easily be treated as illegal, especially when the authorities are nervous and regard them as acts subversive of public order. They then become a form of direct action.

A number of other criteria are relevant in identifying a model of direct action—for example, it implies organization and a conscious will to resist or to affect policy. Thus the purely religious conscientious objector escapes the category, but a campaign of conscientious objection of the kind organized in Britain in the First World War falls within it. Similarly, the individual deserter who opts out may be doing so for purely personal reasons—but in a context of political agitation inside or outside the army, desertion becomes a form of direct action. Good Soldier Schweik tactics of over-cooperation and playing dumb may also be an individual escape route, or fall into a pattern of indirect obstruction on a mass scale.

Because direct action implies organization it also implies group, if not mass, action. So where individual protest is undertaken it is with the aim of sparking off a wider movement on these lines, or as part of a planned campaign. Except in the rare case where a one-man campaign could succeed, purely individual "witness" in the Quaker or pacifist tradition does not accord with the aims and ethos of direct action. But at the other extreme, where really mass resistance or rebellion occurs, direct action may give way to insurrection or revolution. Mutiny, like the general strike, is a borderline example. If limited to particular ends, or particular sections of the armed forces, mutiny may be an extreme form of direct action. But if the aims become more ambitious, or numbers increase, it may well be the prologue to revolution.

The distinction between direct action and revolution is not ultimately one of methods—a revolution will probably involve resort to arms, but it is theoretically possible that the government could be overthrown by means of a mutiny and general strike. The crucial distinction concerns the aims and context in which the methods are used. Any movement which results in the overthrow or seizure of governmental power—whether through spontaneous insurrection, organized revolution, or a plotted coup d'état—has moved into a new dimension of political action distinct from a campaign for limited (if radical) ends within the framework of the existing state. Direct action may, however, create the conditions for overthrowing the government.

Direct action is primarily a method of protest or resistance. But it often has constructive elements. Homeless families squatting in empty houses, or workers taking over the factories where they work, are not only engaging in physical intervention but are demonstrating in embryo new forms of organization and new social solutions to their grievances. An interesting example is the idea of the "reverse strike." In Sicily Danilo Dolci led sixty-five unemployed men to repair a road just outside Partinico. Their aim was to obey Article IV of the Italian Constitution which declares all citizens have a right and a duty to work. The police ordered the demonstrators to stop work and go home. This first protest took place on 15 December 1955. Six weeks later, after a day of fasting to protest against fishing abuses, 200 men set out to repair the road. Police had banned the action in advance. Dolci and six others were arrested. Direct action demonstrations may also lead to attempts to create new institutions—for instance, the idea of a "free university" arising out of sit-ins on university campuses.

At its most ambitious level a direct action campaign may entail creating a parallel set of institutions to replace the existing authorities. This stage of a movement may merge into a conscious attempt to overthrow the existing authorities altogether. Syndicalism, which relied on the trade unions to act as the organs of a new society, combined from the start direct action methods of resistance with strengthening of alternative organizational structure. Moreover, for the syndicalist movement strikes had the same effect as direct action demonstrations have sometimes had among students today—not only did they sharpen the struggle against the powers that be, but also the very fact of taking part in action promoted a feeling of solidarity and community.

Many students advocating direct action in the late 1960s saw it as part of a wider movement aiming at direct democracy. There is a natural psychological connection between direct action protests and attempts to create direct democracy, because of the sense of community and spontaneity protests may evoke. Dave Dellinger [1971] wrote about the 1968 confrontation in Chicago:

> The triumph of Chicago was the triumph of street protesters who displayed courage, imagination, flexibility, and fraternal solidarity as they refused to knuckle under to the police. The role of centralized, formal leadership was minimal in these events. A crude but creative kind of participatory democracy was at work. The organic needs of the occasion, the interacting but spontaneous reactions of the participants, set the tone. (P. 399)

A second example arises from the 1946 Squatters movement referred to earlier. According to the account in *Anarchy*:

> A notable feature of the whole campaign was the way in which, quite spontaneously and without disputes, the accommodation was divided among the would-be squatters in accordance with their needs, the size of the families, and so on. . . . Communal cooking, laundering and nursery facilities sprang up. Fathers took turns to stoke the boilers, mothers took turns to do the settlement's shopping, and the children collected up the rubbish left by the army and made bonfires of it. . . . One of the remarkable features of the squatters' communities was that they were formed from people who had very little in common except their homelessness—tinkers and university dons were amongst them. (No. 23, 12–13)

Community organizing may encompass both direct action and institutions designed to promote direct democracy. The Notting Hill project in London, which started in 1966, has combined constructive efforts to ameliorate local problems, like housing and lack of play space, with pressure on the local authorities and direct action demonstrations. In order to give residents of the Goldborne ward direct representation, an elected neighborhood council has been integrated into the local government framework.

There is also a theoretically logical connection between direct democracy and direct action, which is a means of bypassing formal institutions and exerting direct individual pressure on policy. It can therefore be seen as one way of practicing direct democracy within a parliamentary framework. The degree to which direct action is intended to be a democratic mode of exerting power through individual and mass popular action is directly relevant to its role in a liberal democracy.

The Role of Compromise

In British and American political discourse "compromise" has acquired almost entirely positive connotations. It suggests adapting to the realities of the political situation, meeting opponents halfway, and promoting the public good by sacrificing some personal demands or preferences. It is also associated with the liberal values of reason and tolerance. As Raymond Aron [1968] has pointed out, in other languages the word for compromise has more offensive overtones— in German, for example, the equivalent is *kuhhandeln*, which is like the American "horse trading" (p. 48).

American political vocabulary includes a number of terms indicating political deals involving the crude pursuit of interest. But the link between "horse trading" among interest groups and the more exalted idea of compromise, which suggests a sublimation of interests through the mediation of reason, has not harmed the reputation of compromise. The adjudication of competing interests after the American pattern has been widely accepted as a necessary element in a liberal democratic system and a guarantee of both freedom and democratic rights. Daniel Bell [1960] notes that: "The saving grace, so to speak, of American politics, was that all sorts of groups were tolerated, and the system of the 'deal' became the pragmatic counterpart of the philosophical principle of toleration" (p. 112).

Compromise in the abstract is largely meaningless. In some senses compromise is necessary to all forms of political activity, just as cooperation is necessary, since all politics requires people to work together, and no form of politics can be explained solely in terms of domination. But the precise implications of compromise depend on the institutional context and the issues involved.

Compromise between competing interests is only advantageous if the interests are legitimate. Moreover, a fair bargain between two competing groups may still be made at the expense of a wider community. The idea of an equilibrium of pressure groups creating a situation of maximum satisfaction is as unreal as the idea of the automatic regulation by market forces, and rests on the same unrealistic assumption that perfect competition prevails between equal units. It also makes the same mistake of assuming that competition can ensure an overall social good when in practice there are no pure "interest" groups which are committed to the good of the whole. Groups promoting public "causes" are excluded from the pressure group theory based on an analogy with the market, and in practice (with certain exceptions) are excluded from political influence.

Compromise in the Anglo-American model is also often associated with the (effectively) two-party system, in which the parties are themselves coalitions of interests, and in which policies are put together by a process of adjustment. The stability and moderation resulting is seen as another virtue of compromise politics—since one of the implications of compromise is that it avoids "extremism."

The idea of compromise is therefore closely associated with the idealization of liberal democracy as a middle ground between fascism and communism, which by eschewing their ideological commitments and their methods preserves freedom and parliamentary institutions.

The built-in flaw in this model is that political processes which promote compromise and gradual reforms necessarily favor those who have most power and privilege in society. The impatience with parliamentary socialist parties arises from the conviction that parties which become parliamentary over time cease to be socialist, and that even a party in power is, so long as it accepts the rules of the game, hampered at every turn by the business and financial institutions, and by the conduct of its own civil service, or the attitudes of the armed forces. Similarly, any group suffering from discrimination which accepts the ethos of gradualism and compromise is accepting a gradualism in escaping from discrimination.

Direct action can be seen as a partial method of altering the conservatism inherent in the parliamentary approach, because it can challenge the economic and social forces which influence the political process. The evolution of trade unions, and of the strike as the central method of industrial action, represents one attempt to create some form of counterpower in an arena of conflict outside parliamentary politics. Direct action may also be seen as a means of pressurizing a government into exerting its legislative and executive capacities in order to promote the interests of a particular group. Third, direct action can be used as a form of mass resistance to particular governmental policies—as British trade unions briefly demonstrated in 1972 when dockers were sent to jail by the Industrial Relations Court for illegal picketing. At times the potential of resistance can be used not against the government, but in support of it in response to a military or economic threat—like the general strike used in Germany in 1919 to defeat the attempted Kapp Putsch.

Direct action can therefore be incorporated into an acceptance of parliamentarianism, if it is seen as a means of setting limits to compromise, and of altering the context in which decisions are taken. It may do both by altering the configurations of power, and by changing certain beliefs, attitudes, and interpretations of the situation. In contrast with the resort to guerrilla warfare, a direct action campaign is usually open at all stages to a negotiated settlement, which involves a degree of compromise; though where a head-on confrontation like the general strike occurs, one side has to accept defeat.

Apart from its potential for effecting social change direct action is also a means of asserting the importance of certain values in politics. Idealization of compromise in general obscures the fact that while adjudication of two legitimate sets of interests may be necessary and desirable, there can also be an undesirable compromise of basic values or principles. How far political activity can or should be guided by moral principle is itself a complicated and controversial question—especially in the realm of interstate relations, since politics is the art of the possible bounded by necessity. But the concept of politics requires belief in an area of free and conscious choice. It also embodies belief in certain values intrinsic to an ideal of free political activity; while commitment to parliamentary democracy means, if the implied values are taken seriously, a rejection of domination and pure violence and of extreme forms of fraudulence, trickery, and corruption. Direct action which is intended to assert an uncompromising stand on principle is an attempt to give substance to moral considerations liable to be lost in the day-to-day "realities" of government, or to be obscured by propaganda.

Whether or not the assertion of moral considerations is politically desirable depends, like the virtues of compromise, on the context. It also depends on what sort of moral principles are being asserted. Where ethical or religious commitments are a source of intercommunal conflict, or a guise for the domination of one section of the population over the rest, practical considerations of interest may conduce more to the public good than excess spiritual zeal. Even if the principles being asserted are political—for example, equality of right—there may be a genuine conflict between the remedying of injustice and the stability of the state. Lincoln is often praised, for example, because before the American Civil War he insisted that maintaining the Union was even more important than abolishing slavery. But where moral issues are being totally subordinated to realpolitik, or where the appeal to "freedom" and "democracy" is held to justify totally ruthless military and political operations, then protest centered on the morality of both ends and means is important in redressing the balance.

Once the question of democracy in other countries is considered there is a very substantial amount of evidence to suggest that governments who stress democratic precepts at home tend to subordinate them to economic or military interests in their international policies. Because it is now the major Western imperial power, in recent years the United States has most obviously pursued a policy based on military and economic aid to pro-American dictatorships, and on CIA subversion of regimes threatening American business or military interests. One of the most interesting parts of the International Telephone and Telegraph Corporation scandal, unearthed by Jack Anderson early in 1972, was not the bribing of the Nixon administration, but the revelation of ITT letters to the CIA suggesting forms of economic pressure to bring down President Allende's popularly elected Marxist government, and canvassing the possibility of an uprising by selected members of the armed forces. A minority of Americans came to the conclusion in the late 1960s that the American brand of imperialism made a mockery of its claim to respect democratic principles—and that their dissent was a form of representation of the people whose lives might be shaped, and destroyed, by American power, and whose voices clearly were not heard by the men in the inner governmental councils.

Furthermore, once the commitment to democratic principle is lost in one sphere it tends to be lost in others, and the methods employed overseas may be brought home. The corroding effects of the Indo-China War and then the Algerian War on French politics are well known; French troops became specialists in torture; parliamentary democracy was discredited and was replaced by Gaullism; and a coup d'état by the "ultras" in the French army was narrowly averted. American's Indo-China War has similar dangers; the enormous scope and power of the armed forces and security services was briefly indicated in the last chapter [of *Direct Action and Liberal Democracy*—ED.], and their power is maintained and enhanced by the defense and foreign policies pursued by successive presidents.

In the realm of foreign and defense policy there are also grounds for doubting that the elected representatives, whether the president or Congress, have full knowledge or control of the decisions being made. Even the vice-president, for example, is not informed about the activities of the CIA. The Pentagon made clear to the Senate in June 1972 that its price for accepting the Strategic Arms Limitation agreement to limit the numbers of offensive missiles, and of missile defenses, was the investment of billions of dollars in new technological development in offensive weapons.

Where direct action is a response to the usurpation of power from the elected representatives it may be seen primarily as an attempt to re-create a form of representative democracy, rather than as an attempt to alter the workings of the representative system, or to replace it altogether. But even an attempt at restoration, of what is, in any case, a partially mythical past, is in the present necessarily radical. Moreover, awareness of domination by military or business forces tends to encourage commitment to decentralized community, direct democratic control, and to antimilitarist and anticapitalist goals. The logic of using direct action does therefore lead to seeking the demise of parliamentary democracy within a free enterprise economy, and of parliamentary liberalism as it has so far been known and understood; though by no means all those who embark on direct action will follow this logic to its conclusion.

. . .[D]irect action can be justified by constitutional, liberal, and democratic principles if the existing institutions cease to embody these principles. If the radical implications of constitutionalism, liberalism, and democracy are extended direct action can be seen as an intrinsically valuable mode of expressing independence, practicing resistance, and exercising popular sovereignty.

However, direct action itself is a method of opposition, even when it takes constructive forms like the work-in or the reverse-strike, or when it serves as a focus for community feeling. Organizational forms of direct democracy may spring from a direct action campaign, but they have to be maintained and elaborated beyond a period of protest. Direct action may also have a radicalizing effect on those who take part in it (though this depends on the nature of the movement as well as the action), and it may stimulate new ideas. But it does not in itself provide any form of political theory.

Direct action is primarily a way of expressing rebellion. It creates a potential for social change by releasing new energy and determination and encouraging social imagination. But the direction it takes depends on the nature of the movement it is associated with—on the values, the ideas, and the organization which promote action and which result from it. This direction can be destructive, or lead to self-indulgence and irrelevance. Or direct action may be institutionalized, as the trade union movement has institutionalized the strike, and so lose its characteristics of rebellion. Or the impact of direct action may achieve results—but the results be limited reforms. Even if direct action does develop into full rebellion, the ideas and organization may be lacking to ensure lasting and fundamental change.

The role played by direct action is therefore necessarily limited to opposition. But this role is one of central importance wherever oppression or injustice exists. In many regimes resistance is the only means of asserting freedom or practicing democracy. The parliamentary and pressure group methods available in the "liberal democracies" of the West have not rendered direct action unnecessary. Though these constitutional channels increase the range of activity open to the individual citizen or underprivileged communities, effective protest and opposition often requires the use of direct action. And without effective opposition changes toward a better society are impossible.

The present range of dissent—from individuals sailing into a nuclear testing area to prisoners sitting-in to assert their right to human dignity—and the prevalence of direct action methods in dissent, contain both risk and promise: the risk and promise of greater democracy.

SELECTION 28
FROM
*Dissent**

MICHAEL WALZER

COMMUNISM HAS GIVEN SOCIALISM a bad name. Years of tyranny and brutality, now brought to an end almost everywhere by popular rebellions, have colored, perhaps permanently, our view of state-run economies and enforced egalitarianism.

What has been called by some Western leftists "actually existing socialism" will now disappear from the political map.

Ironically, it is likely to be succeeded by one or another version of social democracy, which is the only socialism that has ever actually existed.

This is the socialism that I mean to describe here. Anticommunist and democratic, it has played a vital role in shaping the governments and societies of the West, though it has never been more than partially realized. Like any other creed subject to the vagaries of a free electorate, its programs have become matters of negotiation and compromise. Social democracy is *socialism revised* in the course of democratic political struggle.

The socialist creed can be summed up in three principles. First, that political society should be open and accessible to all. No one should be excluded from political participation, from democratic power-sharing, because of class, race, religion, or gender.

Second, that the economy should also be open and accessible to all its members. Economic power should be shared by the same people who share political power. This second principle by no means rules out market relations; it only rules out what might be called market imperialism—the conversion of private wealth into political influence and social privilege.

Third, that the members of political society and economy are collectively responsible for each other's welfare. Citizens and workers have claims, always partial, on the resources of the whole society.

The precise forms of political participation and of economic citizenship, the precise extent of welfare provision—these are matters still subject to democratic

---

*From "A Credo for This Moment," in *Dissent* 37 (Spring 1990): no. 2, p. 160.

debate. Socialism doesn't imply a necessary commitment to any set of political or economic arrangements. In its social democratic version, it implies instead a commitment to experimentation, trial and error, institutional revision, and ideological openness.

But socialist principles do have a driving purpose, probably best understood in negative terms, which is not some simple and unqualified equality but rather the overcoming of all the gross and degrading forms of inequality.

I have described this as abolitionist politics: "No more bowing and scraping, fawning and toadying, no more fearful trembling, no more high-and-mightiness, no more masters, no more slaves."

There is also, of course, a positive program: the creation of a society of lively, energetic, active, competent people shaping their common life. But most socialists—intellectuals, militants, and politicians alike—have believed that the negative end, once realized, would bring the positive end in tow.

If people aren't active, energetic and so on, it is not because they are dull, or lazy, or incompetent, it is because they are oppressed. That may be wrong or, at any rate, too easy. Who knows? The whole of human history is a tale of hierarchy and subordination. Socialism, in the light of the ages, is a radically new idea. All its genealogies are inventions; there are no precedents—except, perhaps, within the movements and parties of the left.

The labor movement, the civil rights struggle, feminist politics, some socialist parties, some national liberation movements, the civic and democratic forums of Eastern Europe today—all have produced wonderful moments, rarely sustained, of nonhierarchical cooperation. Social democracy is the stubborn belief that these moments can be drawn out, given an ongoing institutional structure and some (imperfect) permanence.

The reason stubbornness is so necessary is well known. Oscar Wilde stated it with elegant simplicity when he said that "socialism would take too many evenings." At the height of the struggle, people will go to all the necessary meetings, join in the exciting demonstrations. But even partial victory brings rapid demobilization and then the bureaucrats and the professionals take over.

So it has happened, again and again, in the all-too-brief history of democratic politics. Efforts to sustain the excitement are contrived, inauthentic, and, finally totalitarian.

But perhaps what socialism requires is only intermittent excitement: institutional arrangements that are always open to popular insurgency, rather than always engulfed by it. That also means it requires men and women who are sometime activists, always at the ready. The political and economic arrangements would have to be really democratic and the men and women would have to be self-respecting and roughly equal citizens. Hard enough, but not impossible.

REPRINTED FROM THE LONDON *SUNDAY CORRESPONDENT*

SELECTION 29
FROM
*Praxis International**

CAROL C. GOULD

IN ITS ORIGINAL CONNOTATION, democracy meant self-rule by the people through a process of codetermination. Furthermore, at least in modern political theory, the concept of democracy was closely tied to that of individual freedom, in that political democracy was seen as the mode in which the equal individual liberty of the citizens could be preserved. Similarly, in its original connotation, socialism meant the control by the people over their own activities in economic, social, and political life, through a process of social cooperation and codetermination. Here, too, the concept of socialism is closely connected to that of freedom, in the sense of freedom from domination and exploitation and in the sense that socialism is supposed to provide an equality of condition which would permit all individuals to develop themselves freely. Hence, both democracy and socialism in their root meanings involve the ideas of self-rule and codetermination as conditions for freedom. This connection between the concepts of democracy and socialism needs to be reclaimed. However, such a synthesis cannot remain at the abstract level of the original meanings of the terms. Rather, what is required is a new theoretical framework which would provide a philosophical foundation for the intimate relation between individuality and community or social cooperation, as well as the proposal of some concrete ways in which such a synthesis might occur. . . .

PHILOSOPHICAL FOUNDATION FOR A RECONSTRUCTED DEMOCRATIC THEORY

If political theory is to satisfy the requirements which are set forth above, namely, to give an adequate account of individual freedom and social cooperation and of the relation between them, then the fundamental philosophical concepts and the normative grounds should be clarified at the outset. I would

*From "Socialism and Democracy," in *Praxis International* 1 (April 1981): no. 1, pp. 50–58.

propose that the fundamental value which a system of social relations ought to serve is that of freedom, taken in the sense of the freedom of individuals to realize themselves. This value is posited in the nature of human activity itself. Such activity is purposive, not only as involving the realization of particular purposes or intentions, but as a striving toward the fuller development of the individual and of his or her capacities. This sense of freedom may be characterized as positive freedom or freedom *to* realize or develop oneself. Yet the realization of the purposes of an individual requires social interaction as its condition. That is, particular forms of social relations are necessary for the expression and development of human purposes and capacities. In addition, various material conditions also serve as necessary conditions for individual self-realization. Together, such social and material conditions may be characterized as the objective conditions for such self-development or human freedom. Thus, freedom requires access to these objective conditions. Such availability of conditions is part of what is connoted by the term "positive" in the idea of positive freedom. Thus on this view, freedom connotes more than free choice as a capacity; it involves the freedom to realize oneself through acting with others and by transforming the material means to suit one's purposes or ends. Yet this sense of freedom presupposes free choice as a universal feature of human activity. Such free choice is implicit in the structure of human activity as a process of fulfilling purposes. This feature of human activity constitutes the capacity for freedom as self-development. However, self-development or self-realization does not follow from this capacity alone, since it requires the availability of conditions in terms of which one's purposes can be fulfilled.

Since every human being equally possesses such a capacity for freedom inasmuch as they are human, no individual has more of a right to the exercise of this capacity than any other. That is to say, they have an equal right to self-development. But, as I have said, self-development requires access to objective conditions, both social and material. Therefore, the equal right to self-realization implies an equal right of access to such conditions. . . . Such an equal right to self-realization constitutes the value of equal positive freedom which is a cornerstone of the new democratic theory.

However, inasmuch as positive freedom presupposes that one exercise free choice, such positive freedom presupposes an absence of constraint on the free choice of agents. This means absence of constraint by other agents or by the state. Such absence of constraint, or "freedom from," has been characterized in classical liberal theory as negative freedom. Thus equal positive freedom has as its presupposition equal negative freedom. Such negative freedom includes the basic liberties, namely individual civil liberties and political rights. Thus on this theory too, each individual has a right to the full realization of these basic liberties compatible with a like right on the part of each of the others. Thus the liberal rights such as freedom of speech, press, association, etc., as well as the political rights of citizenship are seen to be crucial elements in the theory of positive freedom. It may be seen that such liberties and rights are among the social conditions for freedom as self-development. Beyond this, the theory of positive freedom implies that each individual has a right to the fullest self-realization compatible with a like right on the part of the others. It therefore follows that no individual has a right to dominate or exploit any other. Each individual has the right to freedom from domination and exploitation. On this theory, therefore, the idea of negative freedom extends beyond the sphere of civil liberties and political rights and includes the right to absence of constraint in the domains of social and economic life.

Before proceeding to draw further normative conclusions from the concept of equal positive freedom, it may be useful to elaborate further the conception of social relations which pertains to this view. Social relations may be considered under two heads. The first consists of social relations among agents engaged in a common project. In such social activity, the individuals have a common purpose and share an understanding both of this end and of the means to its achievement. Their cooperation thus becomes a condition for achieving this common end. Such social activity may also serve as a way in which an individual achieves self-development, for example by the exercise or improvement of a skill, by the production of something of use to the individual, or by the satisfaction gained in the social interaction itself. The second type of social relations are those in which two or more agents act with respect to each other in order to satisfy ends which are different for each agent. Such social relations range from those in which each individual uses the other reciprocally as an instrument for the achievement of his or her own ends to those forms of the relation in which each acts so as to enhance the freedom and development of the other. This entire class of social relations may be called that of reciprocity. In general, a reciprocal social relation is one in which each agent acts with respect to the other on the basis of a shared understanding and a free agreement, to the effect that the actions of one with respect to the other are equivalent to the actions of the other with respect to the first. Thus, reciprocal social relations range from those which are merely instrumental to those which one may characterize as fully mutual. In this relation of mutuality, each individual in the relation consciously recognizes the other as free and as capable of self-realization, each acts to enhance the other's self-realization on the basis of a consideration of the other's needs and the individuals take such mutual enhancement as a conscious aim. Reciprocity in this full sense is a social condition for positive freedom, in that for each individual to develop him or herself most fully, he or she requires the fullest self-development on the part of the others.

Thus it can be seen that positive freedom as self-realization has two aspects: the activity of the agent and the conditions for this activity. Since individuals require social relations for their self-development, both in the form of social activity directed toward a common purpose and reciprocal interpersonal relations, the freedom of their activity requires their control not only over their own individual action, but also their control over their common or social action. However, since the concept of equal positive freedom entails that each individual has an equal right to such self-control, it follows from this concept that each individual has an equal right to participate in the codetermination of the social activities in which they are engaged. This may be called the *principle of democracy*, and it serves as a norm for the achievement of equal positive freedom. With respect to those social relations which are interpersonal and not institutional, the principle implies a mutual determination on the part of the individuals involved, so that none dominates or controls the activity of the others. In institutional social relations, e.g., in politics, the principle implies an equal right to democratically decide with others how such institutions are to be organized and how they are to function.

An important consequence of this view is that democratic decision making must be extended beyond the political sphere to which classical political theory had assigned it. From the principle presented here, it follows that individuals have a right to codetermine all social decisions that affect them, whether these are in the domain of politics, economics, culture, or social or community life more generally.

A second principle follows from the concept of equal positive freedom. It concerns the objective conditions of action, both material and social. It will be recalled that positive freedom requires the availability of conditions for the actions of an individual or a group of individuals, in order that their purposes may be achieved. We have also seen that equal positive freedom implies an equal right to the social and material conditions of action and further that freedom defined as self-development involves control over the conditions required for realizing one's purposes in activity. But I would argue that control over the conditions or means of activity is the meaning of property and this includes both social and material conditions. Therefore, there is an equal right to such property. This gives rise to what we may call the *principle of property right*. Namely, individuals have an equal right to means of subsistence and personal means for their own self-realization, which belong to them as their personal or private property; and they have an equal right to control the material and social conditions or means of their common activity, which take the form of social property. The first aspect of this property right, namely the right to personal property, connotes that each has a right to means of subsistence and to the conditions of their own self-expression compatible with a like right on the part of the others. The second aspect, namely the right to social property, connotes that all those who engage in a common productive activity or joint project have an equal right to control the conditions, that is, to codetermine their use and function. It therefore excludes the possibility that only some of those engaged in the activity would control it to the exclusion of others or that any external agents not engaged in the activity would be in control of it. Thus this second aspect of the principle of property rules out domination and exploitation in productive life and in social activity, just as the first aspect rules out domination in personal relations. Thus the principle excludes private ownership of social means of production, and it also excludes control by others over the means or conditions which individuals need for their individual or social activity.

It may be seen that this principle of property right entails conclusions about decision making concerning the means of social production which are similar to the consequences of the first principle concerning the right of democratic participation in social decisions. Thus the principle of social property entails the right to control with others the means of a common productive activity and thus to participate equally in decision making concerning such social production. Thus democratic decision making is required both in economic production and in social and political activity.

From the analysis of the philosophical foundations thus far, it is clear that the concepts of democracy and socialism, on a certain interpretation, entail each other. For the principle of democracy states that each individual has an equal right to participate in the codetermination of all social activities in which he or she is engaged. As we have seen, this includes not only the sphere of political decision making, but also decisions in economic, social and cultural life as well. But such codetermination or common control over social activity in these spheres, if it is to be meaningful, requires also codetermination or common control over the conditions for this activity. For if control over the conditions of such activity belongs to others, then the democracy involved in control over the conditions by those engaged in the activity is precisely what I designated as social property, which is one of the fundamental aspects of socialism. Conversely, the principle of social property was seen to involve common control over the social and material conditions of social production by means of democratic participation in decision making concerning the use of such means. But this is a mode of democratic decision making concerning the means which is closely related to the principle of democracy.

The equal right to participate in social decisions concerning both the activity and the means, as I have discussed it earlier, also has implications for the form and nature of the democratic process. Specifically, it implies that where feasible, the form of democratic decision making should be participatory. For where such participation is feasible and an individual is excluded from such participation, then others are making decisions for that individual and violating the equal right which he or she has to codetermine these decisions. Furthermore, a participatory rather than a representative process is the most direct and surest way of taking into account each individual's choices. In addition, participation serves to develop the range of choices which an individual has, as well as the individual's capacities to deal with diverse situations. In this sense, also, it is a means for the fuller development of an individual's freedom. The realization of equal rights in social decision making thus requires the extension and development of participatory processes. However, such processes of direct participation clearly cannot be instituted in all contexts, as for example in large-scale and centralized policy-making in government, industry, and cultural affairs. Here, what is required is an adequate system of representation founded on participation at the lower levels. Such participation and representation would not only characterize the political sphere but would also apply to decisions in economic, social, and cultural life as well. In these various spheres, each would have an equal right to be represented and to serve as a representative. Furthermore, the representatives or delegates would be held accountable to those whom they represent by regular elections and regular consultations with those whom they represent, as well as by being subject to recall.

Among the social conditions necessary for the realization of positive freedom is not only equality but also what I have called reciprocity and mutuality. Reciprocity as I discussed it earlier characterizes a social relation in which agents or groups of agents freely take each other's actions to be equivalent. It may be seen that the democratic process in social decision making embodies this relation of reciprocity. In the process of codetermination, each individual takes the others as having equal rights to participate in the decision. In this sense, each takes the relation to the other to be equivalent. But beyond this, a democratic process may come to encourage the development of mutual social relations among individuals, in which each recognizes the other's rights to self-realization and each acts to enhance the other's agency. In the process of participatory decision making which aims at a common agreement, people would most likely learn to take each other's needs and purposes into account and would learn to respect differences among themselves. Furthermore, in the course of such interactions, they would create a richer mutual environment of ideas, options, and practices which would in turn enhance the possibilities of self-realization for each of them.

The philosophical foundations for the theory of democracy which I have sketched here may be seen to imply a distinctive conception of the basic entities and relations which constitute social reality. Such a conception of the nature of social reality may be characterized as a social ontology. In the social ontology which underlies this theory, the basic entities are individuals-in-relations, or social individuals. Such individuals in relations constitute social institutions and society as a whole through their various interactions. The social relations among these individuals may be regarded as internal in the sense that these individuals are essentially changed through their interactions with each other. Yet, since these individuals are agents, they fundamentally constitute or change these social relations by their choices. Thus this view contrasts with the ontology presupposed by the classical liberal theories of democracy which takes as its basic entities isolated individuals who relate to other individuals only in external relations and on the basis of self-interest. Yet the view here shares with the liberal conception an emphasis on individuals as free agents who act to realize their purposes. Furthermore, the ontology implied by the view I have proposed contrasts with socialist views as they have developed inasmuch as most of these views regard individuals as being who they are by virtue of their place within the totality or social whole and do not see social relations and the social whole as constituted by agents who are fundamentally free. Yet the ontology presented here shares with the socialist view an emphasis on the internality of social relations.

THE NEW DEMOCRACY—SOME CONCRETE PROPOSALS

The theoretical model of democracy and the value of equal positive freedom on which it is based need to be interpreted in terms of concrete social and institutional forms which would serve to realize them. The general political, economic, and social forms which I will propose here seem to me to be required by the principles which I have discussed, although particular details of these forms may vary. In the formulation of these concrete proposals, I am concerned not only with the realization of these principles and values, but also with the feasibility of the institutional forms. In particular, it is important that they be suitable for large, complex societies and not serve simply as suggestions for small social experiments.

There are several general remarks which may be made before turning to the specific proposals. First, it follows from the theory that all the institutions of society—social, economic, political, and cultural—should be democratized. Furthermore, the legitimation of the functioning of such institutions on the grounds of equal positive freedom requires the fullest degree of participatory decision making feasible. Also, the institutions should be designed so that the political, economic, and sociocultural spheres each function separately, although they bear on each other. Such a separation contributes to the preservation of balance among these spheres, and to the prevention of any monolithic control of the society as a whole. It also contributes to diversity in the options for democratic participation and individual self-development. Finally, democracy in these institutional contexts has to be founded on reciprocity and mutuality in interpersonal relations. It is not sufficient to propose changes in objective institutional structures without at the same time recognizing the importance of changes in relations among people.

The first set of concrete proposals concerns the economic sphere. The four points I will deal with here are workers' self-management, the market, planning and regulatory functions, and the distribution of income. One of the most decisive features of the proposed social structure is the democratic management of economic activity by the workers themselves. This would be in the form of ownership, control, and management of each firm by those who work there. . . . Such worker self-management means that the workers in a given firm jointly determine the planning and production for the firm, and the work process (including allocation of work, rates of production, hours of work, and work discipline). They also decide on the distribution of the firm's income, including reinvestment in production, depreciation costs, and the division of wages to be paid among themselves. In addition, the workers control the sale of their firm's products. The capital of the firm is the workers' joint or social property, which is to say that they have the legal rights to possess, use, manage, or alienate this property.

Such workers' self-management does not entail that all the workers decide on every feature of the production and sale of their products. They may well decide to appoint directors or managers of various aspects of the firm's activities. However, such delegation of powers and functions rests entirely upon the democratic decision of the workers. This democratic decision making should involve the direct and immediate participation by the workers up through as many levels of the firm's activities as is feasible.

It may be seen that these forms of democratic and participatory control by the workers of their own economic activity are required by the principle of equal positive freedom. For, as will be recalled, such equal positive freedom implies each individual's right to control the conditions of his or her activity, and thus it implies the right to codetermine those common activities in which an individual is engaged, as well as the conditions for such activity. Therefore, the workers' activity as well as the objective conditions of this activity, namely the means of production, must be under their own control. This requirement is realized in workers' self-management, as I have described it.

The second major feature of the proposed economic structure is the market. Firms are free to buy and sell to other firms, institutions, or to individual consumers. The market therefore determines prices and serves as an instrument for adjusting supply and demand. Thus, the market functions as the locus for the exchange of commodities. However, unlike the capitalist market, what is excluded here is the market between capital and labor. Rather, the workers' incomes are determined by their own division of the net revenue or profits of the firm among themselves.

In terms of the values and principles discussed earlier, the virtues of such a market scheme are three: First, it preserves the freedom of workers to determine what to produce and the freedom of consumers to determine what, and from whom, to buy. In the market, the firms relate to each other and to individual consumers as free and equal exchangers. Second, the market is an efficient means of reflecting the needs and wants of consumers and of adjusting supply to meet the effective demand. Third, the market fosters variety in what is produced because it expresses the multiplicity of wants and it leaves producers free to satisfy them. In all these respects, the market is superior to a centralized planning scheme in which decisions are made from the top down, as they are in many contemporary socialist countries. Such centralized planning removes the autonomy of the workers in determining production, is often inefficient, and fails to provide variety because the planning bureaucracies tend to be insensitive to differentiated demands and cumbersome in adjusting supply to demand. . . . However, in claiming that the market is well-suited to realize the principles, I do not mean to imply that it is the only system that could satisfy these principles. But the market form is already available and well-developed and requires no third party to intervene between producers and consumers, or to validate their choices.

The third feature of the proposed economic structure is that there should be planning and market-regulatory commissions. The planning commissions would affect the direction of production in the economy indirectly, by making funds available for new investment to existing or prospective worker-managed firms. The commissions would derive these funds from taxation of the social capital of firms. They would operate regionally where possible, though some national planning would be necessary.

All of these commissions would be political bodies in the sense that they would be made up of elected representatives of the people. They would not be chosen as representatives of the workers in the firms, but rather by the workers in general, in their capacity as citizens, who would presumably be in a better position to make decisions in the interests of society as a whole. The unit to be represented on the planning commissions will, therefore, be a political unit at the most local levels possible, rather than an economic unit (e.g., a firm or an industry).

The market-regulatory commissions will function to see to it that the market is free of abuses, such as price-fixing, monopolistic practices, violations of contract, or deceptive advertising or merchandising practices. Thus, these commissions are not intended to control the market, but to permit it to operate fairly and effectively. Like the planning commissions, the market-regulatory commissions will also be democratically elected entities representing the public.

Both the planning commissions and the market-regulatory commissions are necessary to correct malfunctions of the economy and to help it to meet social needs. Thus, although worker self-managed firms together with the market are seen as the principal moving force and adjustment mechanism, respectively, of the economy, nonetheless, these cannot be expected to meet all needs optimally, or may sometimes meet them in a haphazard or distorted way. The commissions, in representing the general social interest, are thus balancing and corrective mechanisms, and can also foster innovation to meet important social and economic needs.

The fourth feature of the proposed scheme concerns the principles and mode of distribution of income. It combines elements of the two well-known principles of distribution according to work and distribution according to needs. The scheme excludes deriving income from investment or from exploitation of the work of others.

Most generally, income will be distributed by the workers in each firm, by a process of participatory democratic decision in which they determine the allocation of the net revenue of that firm among themselves. Since this is an autonomous democratic procedure, the principle that they use for distributing income is up to them. However, since the amount of net revenue to be distributed among the workers in a firm depends in part on their work, the principle of distribution of income is to this degree a principle of distribution according to work.

In terms of the principle of equal positive freedom, the justification of such democratic allocation of income follows from the requirement for common control over the activity of production. I take such activity to include not only the conception and process of production, but also its product. Therefore, each worker has an equal right to control the common product of his or her work, and therefore also an equal right to codetermine the distribution of the income from that work.

This principle is complemented by the principle of distribution according to need in important areas of social and economic life. Thus, every individual is assured of free access to education and health care according to his or her needs. In the case of education, this should be taken to include the provision of higher education to all those who want it. A principle of need should also be in effect with regard to subsistence needs which should be available to all regardless of their work. With respect to those unable to work because of age or illness, or those who are unemployed, this would mean that they should be provided with incomes approximating the average of those who work. With respect to those (hopefully few) who refuse to work, this principle would mean the provision of minimal subsistence needs. The principle of distribution according to need may also require that the state guarantee a minimum income for those who work, which would provide not merely means of subsistence but also means of self-development.

It may be seen that this combination of principles of distribution according to work and need is required by the value of equal positive freedom as discussed above, at least under the conditions of scarcity. This value was seen to imply not only the equal right to control over the work activity, but also the right of each individual to the means of subsistence and the conditions for self-realization, compatible with a like right on the part of each of the others. This latter aspect of the principle excludes exploitation of some by others, or some profiting from the work of others, in two senses: it excludes the accumulation and control of capital by those who have not produced it; and it also excludes parasitism, in the sense of those unwilling to work benefiting from the labor of others. Yet, because of the supreme value of human life, the principle of equal positive freedom implies that everyone has a right to the means of subsistence. These interpretations of the second part of the principle of equal positive freedom, combined with the first part which asserts the equal rights of everyone to control their activity, seem to me to yield the principles of distribution sketched above.

SELECTION 30
FROM *Retrieving Democracy**

PHILIP GREEN

AT ANY LEVEL OF political life, it is *representation* that we must think about. We certainly want to extend institutions of collective, participatory decision making as far as we possibly can, but they cannot be the whole of a democratic decision-making process. Town meeting democracy—direct democracy—is not a form through which great numbers of people can govern themselves, or even cooperate together consensually when that is what they actually want to do. And in fact, the most interesting aspect of direct democracy is that far from its being the antinomy of representative government, the two are profoundly linked. . . .

For what happens at a town meeting, after all? A decision is reached, after discussion, by the assembled citizens, and some official—the town engineer, the town manager, the town counsel, etc.—is then authorized to carry out that decision. Town meeting democracy, in other words, results in the empowering of authorized representatives by citizens. This makes town meeting democracy decisively different from our own pseudorepresentative system; for the meeting authorizes its agents to do *something*, whereas we authorize our representatives to do *anything*. And the citizens of the town have participated in something close to the full sense of the term during the authorization process; whereas in the pseudorepresentative system we cast only abstract, alienated votes. However, town-meeting democracy without a representative system of some kind to receive its democratically made decisions would be radically incomplete.

The same is true of the various modes of mass democracy such as the referendum. Unless it provides carefully crafted and seriously supported forums for public discussion in small groups, mass democracy can only ape the worst features of pseudodemocracy without even having the one real virtue of even the most spuriously representative government: the virtue of providing a forum for informed and educative public debate. . . . But neither mass democracy nor

*(Totowa, NJ: Rowman and Allanheld, 1985): Ch. 9, pp. 176–99.

town meeting democracy eliminates our need for a democratic theory and practice of representation, of "adversary democracy."

The best way to begin to think about democratic representation is to take as a point of departure the pseudorepresentative system we inhabit. The most striking aspect of this system is that political elites and their deputies lead lives grossly different from those of ordinary persons. Transportation policies are made by people who fly in (subsidized) private planes, are driven by chauffeurs, and generally travel first class in every possible way. Safety legislation is voted on by people most of whom have never worked in a factory or a mine.

The administrators of national health services never wait in a doctor's waiting room. Housing codes for public housing are drafted by people who will never live in public housing. Education policy is set by people who send their children to private schools. Cities are governed and administered by people who live in suburbs, or in special enclaves away from the high-crime, high-poverty districts. Agricultural policy is made by people who have never tried to keep a family farm going. Obviously there are exceptions in all nations to these generalizations, and also differences among nations: the small proprietor is probably better represented in the French Parliament than in the American Congress, for example. But the generalizations hold as such.

Especially, since legislators and high-level public servants in all democratic nations are paid considerably more than the national average wage, the rounds of periodic belt-tightening they engage in, to combat inflation by increasing unemployment and lowering living standards, create a pinch which most of them along with other members of their class will never feel themselves. One could multiply such examples endlessly; perhaps we should conclude this catalogue with the note that ex-President Eisenhower, who continually threw the weight of his office against proposals for a national health insurance program in the United States on the grounds that it's bad for people's character not to pay for their own medical care, never paid a cent of his own medical bills from the age of eighteen to his death. The tears of the political elite in the pseudodemocracies are almost always crocodile tears.

In addition, not only are political elites of a different effective social class from the bulk of their constituents, they are also professionals at governing and managing. Both in legislatures and bureaucracies a large proportion of the governing class stay in the realms of power all their adult lives, barring wholesale political upsets. Even as governments change, the number of persons who return to ordinary community life, away from the new world of influence created by their political and business contacts, is small, and usually consists of young persons who were close winners in marginal constituencies in elections to a lower house. Otherwise the professional member of the governing class, even the middle-rung administrator, usually moves in a heady and permanent world of favors and contacts.

Governing elites in the pseudorepresentative system themselves lack the essential quality of citizenship. They know how to rule, but they don't know how to be ruled. Whatever the extent of party competition here or there, politicians and administrators form, in effect, a separate governing class, removed from contact with most citizens, and, whether in legislatures or public bureaucracies, fundamentally out of their control.

What is nondemocratic about all forms of pseudorepresentative government—whether unitary or federalist, whether based on centralized or fragmented political parties, and no matter what social and material circumstances it encounters—is that it turns political access and influence into an episodic and occasional or even nonexistent event in the lives of most people. It makes experts at political action of people who have had something visibly important to gain or to protect from that action, and apathetic incompetents of the rest. . . .

A representative is someone chosen by a group of people to represent them on some matters which they consider ought to be the agenda for action at a forthcoming legislative meeting or administrative hearing, or on any other matters which they have reason to believe will be placed on that agenda by the representatives of other groups. That is the basic act of representation. Every self-defined group, whether their community is defined by the geography of their residences or their places of work or their minds, must be represented in this way for self-government to be a reality.

The most important thing to note about this prescription is that it offers a model of representation for a society of equals. Thus, it ought not to be subject to the complaint, correctly leveled against group theory in a pseudodemocratic setting, or vanguardism in Leninist theory, that all members of an interest group or a class do not necessarily have the same interest; and that active leaders may misrepresent apathetic or alienated followers. The point about a society of social equals is that the occurrence of apathy should be randomized, a mere function of that mysterious entity we think of as personality, rather than correlating with class or caste membership.

There is, in fact, nothing new about this version of representation; it goes on all around us all the time. Only its contemporary theorization is new (or reconstructed). There is nothing utopian about it either, for here and there it is practiced all the time. Some people get together and draw up a manifesto, a commentary on some existing proposals, an agenda for some kind of action, etc. They circulate it to friends and neighbors, coworkers, etc., with whom they hope to join in a group, for their consideration, comments, amendments, and ultimately signatures. The final group of signatories then meets to approve the "agreement of the people" and to choose one or more spokespersons. Out of a given group of say a hundred signatories there might be one candidate for that position, or fifty, but that is a matter of absolute indifference. There is no question of the losers in the election going unrepresented, as in existing winner-take-all elections everywhere. There is no question of some candidates being more or less remote from, unknown to, and unrepresentative of their constituents on actual issues. There is no question of candidates selling themselves like soap to constituents who by purchasing them give them the effective power to make their own agenda for action with little or no reference to their electors, as in most existing electoral systems. Whoever is chosen is an equal member of a solidary group, no more so or less so than anyone else in the group. That is the group's true representative.

These are the basic building blocks of democratic self-government. As to what their size should be, that (to follow Rousseau) must obviously vary from one political community to another, depending on the intensity with which a given people adhere to common moral guidelines in their thinking and to neighborliness in their daily lives. The maximum feasible size would doubtless, for example, be greater in a Parisian arrondissement than in a neighborhood of equal population in New York City; would be greater in a factory, among people performing a common task, than among the residents of any diverse, geographically defined neighborhood. My own thinking circles around numbers in the hundreds, but that is really beside the point. The sole purpose of radical democratic theory today is to inspire people to struggle for a vision of self-government; if it succeeds in any way, it will be the real historical nature of the struggle that will determine the way people relate to each other politically, not off-the-cuff observations by political theorists. What is important is only that we recognize the need for limits on the size of constituencies, or else we will wind up recreating the impersonal oligarchic polity founded in coalitions of notables, of pseudorepresentatives. In that respect the traditional concentration of democratic theorists on size has always been correct.

It is not just to ensure real personal contact, and preclude impersonal salesmanship from above as the source of political action, however, that we have to emphasize formal limitation on the size of constituencies. The strongest criticism of pseudorepresentation is that it destroys the foundations of real citizenship. Any substitute that does not instead maintain those foundations is no substitute at all. If for the most part we cannot have universal citizen participation in actual governance in complex modern societies, we can at least have it in the choice of those who will do the governing. In a sense Joseph Schumpeter and Walter Lippmann were right when, in criticism of Rousseau, they said that the only thing "the people" could really do was to choose their leaders; but they were fatally wrong to consider pulling a lever for a fantasized leader figure as an expression of either choice or participation. . . . (For this reason political science courses in "participation" that focus on voting behavior should be seen as no more than exercises in public relations for the pseudorepresentative system, even though that may in no way be the intention of those who teach them.)

If being involved in the choice of leaders is to be a major component of effective citizenship, the involvement must be intense, educational—in a word, *participatory*. What is intended by the aforementioned phrase beginning "Some people get together" is that groups of citizens feel empowered to choose representatives for each and every separate arena of public business that they wish to attend to, or feel threatened by. If a society where the business of controlling, authorizing, and implementing actions taken in the name of a national, regional, or local public interest were defined as broadly as I have suggested it should be, it could well be that everyone from some group of like-minded people might wind up being a representative to some function or another, elective, supervisory, administrative, productive, or whatever. Participation and representation are not antithetical; on the contrary, they demand and strengthen each other. Even among those who, for whatever reasons, never serve but are only served, being represented properly will almost certainly demand, and potentially receive, a self-enhancing amount of civic commitment and energy. Simply to negotiate unanimous agreement on some group need or demand or action will involve every member of the group in active political life: in participatory democracy.

A democratic as opposed to pseudodemocratic polity will be one in which legitimate public policy at whatever level will be made by representatives who have the kinds of ties to their constituents that are described above; and who, if they must form governing coalitions in order to govern, will be authorized to form them, accountable to those who have given the authorization, and subject to recall if they violate the terms of their authorization, through those same kinds of ties. A mass democratic party (such as the Swedish Social Democratic party) will not generate policies that eventuate in political equality unless it is mobilized by constituencies to which its leaders are directly accountable. And political equality will not subsist for long unless these acts of what we might call "reverse mobilization," continue to be the fundamentally defining acts of citizen sovereignty. It is indicative, indeed, that I feel compelled here to refer to the process of mobilization from below as reverse mobilization. That is not because I agree that this is the opposite of the more real kind of mobilization, namely mobilization from above; but rather because social scientists have so overwhelmingly agreed that mobilization is something leaders do to (or for) followers. Democracy can only take place when that consensus is overthrown. . . .

Negatively, on the other hand, in addition to our finding a proper balance between centralization and decentralization, in a democracy there ought also to be constitutional mechanisms designed to prevent the growth of Caesarism, or of any political relationships that are essentially exploitative or manipulative. The representative system in some trade unions or labor movements accomplishes this directly in the Madisonian manner: workers elect shop stewards, who in turn elect delegates, etc. This is the ideal model for how layers of authorized representation can be built from the bottom up. However, not all kinds of social life, as I've remarked, have the communality of the workplace; and in any event, no society of any reasonable size—that is, where the political process is intended to sum the desires of millions of people—will be able to dispense with the mass electoral process for at least some levels of representation and leadership. . . . Moreover, no matter how savagely we criticize the shadow world of political life, we must understand that civic liberty is likely to flourish only in the space between the world of impersonal, abstract representation and the world of immediate, neighborly political life. It is true that without layers of truly direct democracy at the base, we will be subject to familiar forms of elective autocracy; but it is equally true that absent the checks and balances of impersonal, supracommunal politics, local democracy is sure to turn into a stifling parochialism. It is no accident that society-wide universal suffrage is what the working class, the women's movement, and popular forces generally have fought for. Egalitarians can hope to add more fully democratic institutions to that historical incarnation of democracy; but should neither hope nor want simply to replace it. . . .

However, that centralized policy making is necessary does not mean that its scope must be as unlimited as it is among us. In a democracy, as opposed to a pseudodemocracy, central executives ought to be limited to implementing those mandates, as well as conducting negotiations between regions or localities that can't find any other legitimate authority, superior to both in jurisdiction, that they are willing to listen to. No democratic constitution ought to provide an executive with explicit emergency powers. (It is sobering to reflect on how few emergencies have actually existed in the recent history of even so imperial a power as the United States, if we discount those of its own making—i.e., flights of geese erroneously identified as incoming missile attacks, etc.) When emergencies do arise, they will be met anyhow. To prepare for them beforehand in the structure of government is to insure that wielders of a routinized emergency power will aggrandize every power potentially within their grasp, great or small, as an allegedly necessary component of that power. In general, an egalitarian community will have to be dedicated to being pacific except in clear self-defense, for powers of self-government can never outlast the insatiable demands of national security, once the latter's military aspect is accepted as being uppermost. Renunciation of international power is the very requirement of democracy.

On the other hand, it's utopian to assume that the role of armed force can be renounced by a people merely because they are equals among themselves. Thus, no discussion of executive power is complete without discussion of the relationship between democracy and the military, as well as their domestic arm, the police.

Absent civilian control of the military, democracy is not just unlikely but impossible; history attests to that very authoritatively. And civilian control will never be achieved if military leaders are permitted to become a socially hermetic and self-selecting caste. As for the police, their two most important domestic functions in contemporary industrial societies are to prevent members of the underclass from disturbing whatever version of social peace is built around their subordination, and to enforce existing legal class relations between workers and employers. The former function ought to disappear when the reserve army of labor (along with all the excrescences of racism and other forms of discrimination that are everywhere attached to it) is abolished. The latter function ought to disappear, at least in large part, when the managers of productive operations, on whose behalf the police maintain order, are the workers, or the workers and their neighbors, themselves. Whatever remaining kind of police force might be necessary in a democracy, its leaders ought to be civilians; and a good many of its remaining functions ought probably to be performed by civilians as well. And a national secret police, we should add, is incompatible with democratic equality. A state with a secret police is a police state, however attenuated. . . .

The simplest and probably most effective way to ensure that representatives function as responsible and responsive agents is to enforce very strictly the traditional principle of rotation in office. Whether by election, lot, or appointment—and the most appropriate method depends on the office to be filled—rotation is as important for preventing the development of a separate political class with a separate way of life as it is for preventing the development of a separate social class of experts within the division of labor.

Again, it is less important that everyone hold office than that no one who holds office think of it as a permanent career, with its own lines of advancement and group consciousness. The idea of rotation must therefore be taken seriously and literally. Parties and other elite political groups develop their own reward and punishment systems. They make their own attempts to secure a monopoly on definitions of the public good, a private version of their institutional well-being, and a well-kept distance from all those of their constituents or would-be constituents who are not inner-group activists.

In a different way, the same thing is true of those more professional administrative offices that are not disposed of by party or electoral fiat. Those too become spoils, though the victor who claims them does so not by winning elections but by winning credentials. The difference is often trivial. And although Europeans more than Americans have always thought that administration demands more measurable expert skills than does politics, it is hard to find evidence for that belief. The senior French civil service, for example, is the envy of technocrats everywhere: almost all of its members are graduates of the technocratic Ecole Nationale d'Administration. But nothing on the record demonstrates that the French government in its administrative functions has been either more or less effective an instrument of public good than any other—no matter what standard of good one uses. Generally speaking the most favorable testimony to the merit of permanent civil servants who have passed through special training programs is offered by themselves; and although democrats can sympathize with the recognizable human impulse that prompts it, there's no reason for us to take it seriously. . . .

At the same time, though, we must recognize that the principle of rotation in office is a defensive, negative principle. By implementing it we protect ourselves against the monopolization or corruption of office; but why should a society of civic equals assume the normality of monopolization and corruption in the first place? In the first instance, that is, it is much more important for us to discuss the ways in which officeholding itself can be reconceptualized so as to be appropriate to the philosophy of political equality.

Beyond rotation in office, then, civic equals would surely require that any candidate for a high-level elective office must have already performed some agreed-upon amount of service as one kind or another of constituency representative. In this way, and probably in this way only, could we implement the requirement that when national legislatures reach an agreement on general rules, they do so with an inspiration that has come to them from the basic democratic constituencies. (Here and elsewhere in this chapter I use the word "national" to mean any jurisdiction that is too large to be governed solely by the consensus of representatives from local communities, and yet is recognized by the inhabitants of those communities as somehow politically legitimate.) We could hope that those whose experience of representation has been solely the experience of an instructed delegate from solidary communities, will not easily throw over the cast of mind that such an experience ought to induce.

In our own pseudodemocracy that requirement might not seem to imply anything especially positive about the outcome of representation. But in the egalitarian political and social milieux of democracy the experience of service ought to have a different meaning and a different effect.

The idea of politics as an independent career dedicated to the search for power and glory is probably inescapable. Some people simply have more talent at being aggressively self-seeking than others do. In any event the motivations for public service are emotionally and intellectually inseparable from desires for personal success. People possessed of a burning drive to fulfill a personal moral vision by entering public life, might well find more support than they do now, if they lived in a social order infused with a deeper appreciation of communal ties than is common among us (even though they would find less support for naked personal ambition). Moreover, representation at the most generalized levels of policy making will always entail some freedom from constituency discipline; even the direct constituency delegate in the style of the Levellers, armed with remonstrances from the people, will often have to negotiate in a constituency's interest without being able to engage in constant referral for further instructions. Representation is an institution that to some extent always inescapably transcends the purely mechanical amalgamation of crudely individual interests. The kind of representation I am describing here should accomplish that transcendence as often as is necessary to generate collectively ethical behavior; but not so often as to subordinate individual and group needs to the actions of an uncontrolled elite. Even our ideal of the legislator as romantic hero or heroine, on the model of James Stewart in *Mr. Smith Goes to Washington*, is not necessarily repudiated by the democratic demand that representatives be truly representative. We have only to think of that Leveller spokesman, a regimental agitator at the Putney Debates, who when asked not to "make a public disturbance upon a private prejudice," replied, "Concerning my making rents and divisions in this way. As a particular, if I were but so, I could lie down and be trodden there; [but] truly I am sent by a regiment, [and] if I should not speak, guilt shall lie upon me, and I [should] think I were a covenant-breaker." There is as much heroism and glory, potentially in fulfilling obligations as in escaping from them. . . .

In addition, even the discipline of experience as a democratic representative will only take hold if it is preceded and accompanied by the more fundamental experience of living in a community that manifests democratic relationships in its core commitments. Assuming that the expert-amateur distinction must continue to be real, that at any historical juncture some people will be expert at very important types of production or reasoning, and others will not, then experts must be of and by rather than merely for communities. Specifically, all our notions of the training of experts ought to be turned around. An understanding of the ideals of service and representation ought to replace the acquisition of technique as the first skill demanded of the trained professional; and the first of these ideals would be, as I have already indicated, that the highest accomplishment of the trained person is to render his or her own skills obsolete by finding ways to convert them to general usage. Beyond that simple statement, if such an ideal is to become a social reality, it will only be because we have come to conceive of the opportunity for training itself as something both desired by individuals and given to them, as a token of their citizenship in a democracy, by communities. It should not be, as now among us, the product of almost nothing but the drive to advance a privatized version of self-interest, paid for either by individual resources or by public financing so remote from any intimate connection with its beneficiaries that it carries no weight of moral dedication to public service with it. . . .

. . . The idea of choosing public servants by taking a random sample of the total population is obviously absurd. But it is only slightly more absurd, if more obviously so, than the alternative method of using educational attainments, examination results, and interviews to give an implicit rank ordering of that same total population for every single skilled task. The point that democrats must insist on, in confrontation with meritocratic arguments, is that the defenders of the merit principle, and everything it has come to imply in the way of nonresponsive expert bureaucracies, fail to understand what capability and talent really are in the realm of public services. . . .

What after all do we mean by the merit of a person? Nothing more, surely, than that person's ability to do an assigned task in the most appropriate manner. In the case of the kinds of tasks about which we are talking here, the most appropriate manner is that which best fulfills the needs of those on whose behalf the task is being done. How are we best to know those needs then becomes the crucial question in any discussion of merit, democracy, and public service. The proponents of recruitment and promotion by competitive examination and civil service standards, indeed, have never added anything to the Platonic conception that a pilot must be an expert navigator, a doctor an expert surgeon, a chef an expert cook, and so on; nor have they got beyond the simplistic exposition by Thrasymachus of the medical analogy: a physician is a physician only if he treats his patients correctly, and a ruler is a ruler only if he rules correctly. . . .

A democratic society, then, is not one in which the leaders, policymakers, administrators, and their subordinates are the best men, but rather one in which they are representative of well-trained men and women. Nor do we turn our backs, with that epigraph, on Aristotle's parenthetical comment that positions requiring "some practical experience or professional skill" should be exempted from the operation of appointment by lot. Where such positions are exempted from that method of recruitment, representation is still achieved so long as it remains to the constituencies to decide what they want to mean by those wholly equivocal phrases. The crucial thing for the achievement of democracy in action is that citizens come to appreciate that they are almost always equally as capable of making judgments about relevant qualifications as anyone else; and often, when their needs are directly at stake, most capable of all.

The merit of a public employee is twofold. He or she knows how a particular service or good can be produced or distributed, and what kinds of services or goods their prospective users prefer. If a society consists of a multiplicity of interests, therefore, its employees must generally be from a multiplicity of backgrounds (to which they feel some kinship). Where a particular producer of a good or service has one or two particular collections of interests as his or her primary prospective clients, then policies concerning that product must be made, at least in major part, by people sharing the same interests or backgrounds, or else by those who have their seal of approval.

That needs are best appreciated when they are shared, in other words, is one of the things we must understand when we talk about capability and talent in a democratic society. Among the chief merits of a city planner is that he or she lives with an ordinary income in a representative area of the city to be planned; of a policymaker in an energy agency, that he or she know what it means to face debt or frost as permanent alternatives; of the public member of an oil industry advisory board, that he or she has no friends in the industry and no faith in the veracity of its spokespersons when they report on their proven reserves, their profits, or their international relations. The role of public servants in a democracy is to be representative, and the role of a representative is to represent; to do otherwise is to be ultra vires, to be incompetent. . . .

. . . [F]or example, men might go on desiring to command the dominant position in fields of medical practice that serve mostly women, but not many constituency groups would be found to waste their precious energies and powers on trying to get male doctors to be the administrators of such services. On the other hand, in the absence of a spontaneous movement in the direction of greater administrative power for females in those areas, numerous constituencies of women would spring up with precisely that end in view. Given democratic recruitment, that is, positions of service and authority would come to be filled by the solicitations of one kind of affected group or another, rather than being most open, as now, to ambitious individuals representing primarily their own desires. This change from the job as an individual good to the job as a locus for the fulfillment of specific community needs would be accomplished without any "quotas" whatsoever.

As for merit, whether its requirements are real or fancied, it should always be judged (to combine Aristotle with Bentham) by those who know their own interests best—the diners at the feast, the patients of the surgeon, the dwellers in the house. If the people persisted in nominating incompetents and dolts for technically exigent positions then no one would suffer the consequences more than themselves in the end, as they would come to realize: learning by doing. The technocratic ideology, contrarily, is based on assiduous cultivation among the public, by experts, of the belief that every day in every way society is in such a state of crisis that learning by doing is impossible. Unless the experts are given free rein, without interference, machines will run amok, explosives will explode, the economy will grind to a halt, and nuclear war will instantly break out. Thus a kind of surplus value is extracted from citizen-clients, who surrender a part of their personal capabilities to enhance the creative opportunities and powers of those who monopolize the term, "professional." The message that this form of exploitation is necessary is thrust on a worldwide public by the spokespersons for estimable professions, without exception.

Those professions, however, to revert to my earlier catalogue of those who rule but are not ruled, also contain thousands of architects who design buildings with windows that won't open, doctors who prescribe unnecessary drugs in the interest of pharmaceutical companies, teachers who dislike children, economists who can neither predict nor understand inflation or depression, scientific administrators whose public statements about the problems of nuclear power are without exception false, and political elites who manage consistently to arrange costly wars in the wrong place at the wrong time. Theirs is a message designed to prevent democracy from happening; the only way to test its validity is to open up positions of responsibility to those communities (through their representatives) on whose behalf that responsibility is supposed to be exercised. . . .

SELECTION 31
FROM
*Strong Democracy**

BENJAMIN BARBER

LIBERAL CRITICS OF PARTICIPATION, imbued with the priorities of privatism, will continue to believe that the neighborhood-assembly idea will falter for lack of popular response. "Voters," writes Gerald Pomper, "have too many pressing tasks, from making money to making love, to follow the arcane procedures of government." . . . If the successful and industrious will not participate because they are too busy, and the poor and victimized will not participate because they are too apathetic, who will people the assemblies and who will give to talk a new democratic life? But of course people refuse to participate only where politics does not count—or counts less than rival forms of private activity. They are apathetic because they are powerless, not powerless because they are apathetic. There is no evidence to suggest that once empowered, a people will refuse to participate. The historical evidence of New England towns, community school boards, neighborhood associations, and other local bodies is that participation fosters more participation.

The greater danger for the neighborhood-assembly idea would come from the success, not the failure, of participation: from the tendency of communes and local assemblies to fall prey to peer pressure, eloquence, social conformity, and various forms of sub-rosa manipulation and persuasion not known in larger adversary systems. Thus, in his provocatively one-sided account of prerevolutionary New England (Puritan) towns, Michael Zuckerman contended that "sociability and its attendant constraints have always governed the American character more than the individualism we vaunt." . . . And Jane J. Mansbridge found considerable evidence that justice was skewed and fairness corrupted by social coercion in the modern Vermont town meeting she studied. . . . Historical studies of communal self-government in Switzerland have uncovered evidence of the same abuses, which are peculiar to parochialized, hothouse communities governed autonomously from within. . . . But urban neighborhoods and rural regions are no longer seared by Puritan zest, and local assemblies

*(Berkeley: University of California Press, 1984): pp. 272–86.

in modern America are more likely to be troubled by mirror-image sectarianism and special-interest conflict than by uniformitarian coerciveness. In his recent study of neighborhood democracy, Douglas Yates reports that "there was almost no evidence of monopolistic control by either minorities or majorities. In fact," he concludes, "just the opposite pattern obtained. Widespread internal conflict was the dominant characteristic of neighborhood governance." . . . As one element in the American pluralist pressure system, the neighborhood assembly would be unlikely to reproduce the consensualist pressure of the villages and towns of an earlier era.

. . . It is time to rescue the neighborhood from nostalgia and restore it to its position as the cellular core of the democratic body politic.

Neighborhood assemblies offer vital forums for ongoing political talk, but they reach only local constituencies and can divide and parochialize both regions and the nation as a whole. Forums for regional and national talk are needed as well. Representative assemblies on the model of the representative town meetings can solve the problem of scale, particularly if their members are selected by lot (see below). But representation is always a second-order solution that (I have argued) exacts costs in civic activity and competence that its virtues fail to pay for.

What strong democracy requires is a form of town meeting in which participation is direct yet communication is regional or even national. Because scale is in part a function of communication, the electronic enhancement of communication offers possible solutions to the dilemmas of scale. Although it brings new kinds of risks, modern telecommunications technology can be developed as an instrument for democratic discourse at the regional and national level. . . . The wiring of homes for cable television . . . the availability of low-frequency and satellite transmissions in areas beyond regular transmission or cable, and the interactive possibilities of video, computers, and information retrieval systems open up a new mode of human communications that can be used either in civic and constructive or in manipulative and destructive ways. The capabilities of the new technology can be used to strengthen civic education, guarantee equal access to information, and tie individuals and institutions into networks that will make real participatory discussion and debate possible across great distances. Thus for the first time we have an opportunity to create artificial town meetings among populations that could not otherwise communicate. There is little doubt that the electronic town meeting sacrifices intimacy, diminishes the sense of face-to-face confrontation, and increases the dangers of elite manipulation. Yet it would be foolish to allow these dangers to stop us from exploring television as a civic medium. . . .

The development of the medium to service civic participation in a strong democratic program would call for a linkage among neighborhood assemblies that permitted common discussion of shared concerns as well as national discussions among selected individuals on national initiatives and referenda. The New

York–New Jersey–Connecticut Tristate League of the League of Women Voters has run a series of television town meetings, using telephone/television interactive hookups. . . . Advocates of "teledemocracy" in California and Hawaii have developed more ambitious schemes for civic interaction via television; the University of Hawaii group designed a "televote" for New Zealand's Commission for the Future that appears to have had a considerable success. . . . A Honolulu electronic town meeting succeeded in producing a remarkably sophisticated political debate in 1982, and a similar proposal is now under consideration in Los Angeles. . . .

In other words, there is already a body of evidence that testifies to the civic utility of electronic town meetings and that answers the fears of those concerned with simplistic abuses of interactive systems. . . .

. . . Strong democracy can also be served by representative town meetings, office-holding by lot, and decriminalization and lay justice.

The representative town meeting compromises the principle that all citizens should engage fully in local deliberative processes, but it thereby rescues the town meeting from the eroding impact of scale. Thus Massachusetts has thirty-two representative town meetings in communities where full and direct participation is no longer feasible. When the representatives to the town meeting are chosen by lot and membership is rotated, over time all will be able to participate. It turns out to be easier in large-scale societies for everyone to have some participation for some of the time.

The same principle can be applied to local office-holding. The great majority of local offices in towns and municipalities can be filled by citizens chosen by lot on a rotating basis. The expertise required is not so great and the responsibility involved not so onerous that members of local boards of selectmen, of planning boards, of road, water, and conservation commissions, of zoning, housing, and education boards, and of other bodies such as library committees, the registry of voters, and cemetery commissions could not be selected by lot. The lot principle . . . is a natural extension of the democratic principle to large-scale societies.

The democratization of local offices also has a place in the criminal and civil justice system. Students of the judiciary have recently argued that a variety of small offenses should be decriminalized and have proposed alternative forums of justice for trying such cases. . . . The Europeans have successfully experimented with empowering lay juries and judges or other surrogate civic bodies to mediate, arbitrate, and settle disputes. . . . Although intended primarily to alleviate the courts' case load, the experiment in decriminalization has in fact engaged the larger civic community in the judicial process in a fashion that supports strong democracy. A cooperative, mediatory, participatory approach to petty misdemeanors, family quarrels, moving traffic violations, and small-sum civil disputes educates and involves the community in the justice system at the same time that it makes the judiciary more efficient. If civic participation were made a conscious goal rather than merely a side benefit of experiments in decriminalization, strong democracy would be very well served at no additional cost. . . .

. . . A national initiative and referendum act would permit Americans to petition for a legislative referendum either on popular initiatives or on laws passed by Congress. Petitioners would be allowed from twelve to eighteen months to collect signatures from registered voters in at least ten states. The number of signatures would have to equal two or three percent of the number of ballots cast in the previous presidential election. Such initiatives would then be submitted to a popular vote; if they passed, there would ensue a waiting period of six months followed by a second vote. A third vote might be required if Congress vetoed the second popular vote (or in the case of congressional laws that had been brought to the referendum by petition). The waiting period, and the resulting debate, would give the public ample opportunity to review its positions, to take into account the advice of political leaders, and to discuss the decision in the neighborhood assemblies. Since the intent of the process is to increase participation rather than to produce immediate legislative innovations, the deliberate (even ponderous) pace of a two- or three-stage procedure would be more than justified. Certainly it would help to calm any fears felt by advocates of the Madisonian representative screen.

. . . Because civic education is an important feature of the referendum process, a national referendum and initiative act would mandate local and national discussion in the assemblies and in the print and broadcast media of the issues on the ballot. Regulations integral to the referendum bill would fund informational documents offering pro and con arguments on each issue . . . would limit the spending by interest groups on campaigns for or against bills; would organize television discussions . . . and would sponsor town meetings on the air. The general aim of these regulations would be to maximize public debate and to guarantee open and fair discussion. With them, the dangers of plebiscitary abuse of the referendum would be diminished and the utility of the multichoice format confirmed.

PART VIII

Democratic Rights

INTRODUCTION TO PART VIII

AS THE INTRODUCTION TO Parts I–VII suggests, there is still a fundamental question not settled, or even really addressed, by all of our discussions of participation and representation; of genuine majority rule and the obstacles to achieving it. This unsettled question has to do with the treatment of minorities, or dissident or deviant individuals, in a democracy based on majority rule. Is democratic majority rule, however we accomplish it, really likely to be more tolerant than, say, benevolent despotism, or a more aristocratic form of elitism? Plato and Aristotle both considered "democracy" to be among the inferior forms of government (although Aristotle thought it the best of the bad), not so much because classical democracy was direct, or overly egalitarian, but because of what they thought of as its tendency to turn majority rule into mob rule. Plato, moreover, was certainly helped in reaching this conclusion by the fate of his teacher, Socrates, at the hands of Athenian democracy.

This is not quite the same point that agitated Madison in the tenth *Federalist* (Selection 5). A "rage for paper money," like any policy with economic implications, will help some people and injure others, but it does not necessarily leave anyone without human or civil rights; even socialization of large-scale means of production leaves everyone with equal property rights, although it may have deleterious consequences otherwise. (See Christian Bay's discussion of fundamental rights in Selection 34.) The problem of rights in a democracy only truly arises when there are, or threaten to be, structurally *permanent* majorities and minorities formed into dominant and subordinate blocs: white/black, Christian/Jewish, Jewish/Arab, Catholic/Protestant, sexually conventional/sexually deviant, etc. (Conditions of civil war, or minority domination resulting from conquest, as in Northern Ireland or South Africa, do not, or at least do not yet, raise the problem of *democratic* rights.) In addition, as discussed earlier, the one obvious case in which the problem of rights is not one of majorities and minorities is the case of gender inequality in all contemporary societies; a system of authority such as male domination/female subordination may be so deeply embedded in social, legal, and economic institutions as to be ineradicable by the practices of normal democratic politics.

The most well-known statement on individual rights is that of John Stuart Mill (Selection 33). However, Mill's utilitarian defense of individual rights (that, in effect, free speech leads to progress) is not always compelling, especially to people (and there are many) who doubt the utility of "progress" itself. Furthermore, Mill couches his argument in such a way that it does not always seem part of an argument for democracy, and may even at times, as in his assaults on the conformism of the majority, seem antidemocratic. From the standpoint of democratic theory, the case for individual rights is probably stronger if put differently. It is located in the distinction between institutions that are *constitutive* of a political system, and those that, however laudable, are incidental to it. Freedom of speech for dissenting individuals, to take Mill's concern, is such a constitutive institution; along with related institutions such as the right to vote, freedom of association, accountable government, equality before the law, and equal opportunity, it is constitutive of the political system we call "democratic." Unless these institutions are protected, the voluntary formation of groups of persons with like-minded views about what the public good or public interest requires—the essence of any version of democracy—cannot move forward.

As for the status of *groups* in a democratic society built around the institution of majority rule, it poses a more complex problem. Rousseau earlier set out the logic of maintaining group equality (Selection 32). Unfortunately, the two positions, on individual rights and on group equality, often seem to many people to be in conflict with each other (as when someone complains that he "made it on his own"; why do those other people need affirmative action programs?). Especially, we think of the vote, the most fundamental right of all, as belonging to *individuals*, who participate equally in (at the very least) choosing representatives. In any of its meanings, therefore, "democracy" would seem to require that every individual have an equal chance to have voted, win or lose, for the representative of his or her choice (see Selection 7). But if we equalize the representation of groups of unequal size, individuals will, in effect, have different voting power: the individual member of a smaller but equally represented group will have more say than a member of a larger group, other things (such as the internal relationships of the groups) being equal.

If group size could be truly equal in Rousseau's sense, or if a complex society could truly be founded on a single general will, then no problem would seem to arise. But the latter solution simply wishes the difficulties of pluralism away by fiat. To say there are no conflicts in the general will is to say that there is really only *one* sociocultural identity among a group of people large enough to constitute a social order: a prescription unlikely to be realized even by the most stringent tyranny, as the fate of the Soviet Union attests. As for equal group size, as a historical matter it seems to occur infrequently if at all. The Netherlands, of which the population is divided into roughly equal thirds of Catholics, Protestants, and "others" (secularists or religious/racial minorities), is, with the self-destruction of Lebanon, the only true example we have. The experience of the Netherlands, where affirmative action for minorities is endorsed by all groups and practiced as a matter of course, does indeed seem to bear out the supposition that a demographically balanced society is likely to be more tolerant of all sorts of differences than so-called pluralist societies, such as the United States, in which a single religious group was historically dominant and an unequal racial division is the essence of the nation's history. At the same time, the Dutch experience illustrates the potential incompatibility of group-oriented and individualist political cultures. Any group of Netherlanders is free to construct itself as a religion or a nationality or a sexual orientation or a political ideology, and on that basis to receive a prorated share of access to television channels, government funding for schools, its own newspaper, etc. But no one can define himself or herself as more than one kind of person: a Muslim or a Turk or a gay man or woman or a socialist. The rule is necessary to prevent inhabitants from making multiple claims on funding or institutions, but it seems to deny the reality that personality itself is diverse and senses of identity likely to be plural and overlapping. In any event, extending the Dutch system to representation itself (e.g., legislating that half of elected representatives must be women, etc.) is even more problematic from an individualist perspective, and even more constricting of possibilities for self-definition; it is also, to return to Rousseau's conception of the general will, impossible or indefensible if the issues that divide groups in the polity are defined by deep and uncompromisable moral differences (see Selection 35). On the other hand, as Young points out (Selection 36), to ignore "difference," especially the difference between "normal" politics and oppression, in constituting legitimate access to public spaces and political institutions, is to ratify histories of discrimination and exclusion. The question of how to reconcile group and individual rights thus remains perhaps the thorniest of all questions for democratic theory, and democratic practice.

SELECTION 32
FROM
*The Social Contract**

JEAN-JACQUES ROUSSEAU

BOOK I, CHAPTERS VII AND IX

[T]HE BODY POLITIC OR the Sovereign, drawing its being wholly from the sanctity of the contract, can never bind itself, even to an outsider, to do anything derogatory to the original act, for instance, to alienate any part of itself, or to submit to another Sovereign. Violation of the act by which it exists would be self-annihilation; and that which is itself nothing can create nothing.

As soon as this multitude is so united in one body, it is impossible to offend against one of the members without attacking the body, and still more to offend against the body without the members resenting it. Duty and interest therefore equally oblige the two contracting parties to give each other help; and the same men should seek to combine, in their double capacity, all the advantages dependent upon that capacity.

Again, the Sovereign, being formed wholly of the individuals who compose it, neither has nor can have any interest contrary to theirs; and consequently the sovereign power need give no guarantee to its subjects, because it is impossible for the body to wish to hurt all its members. We shall also see later on that it cannot hurt any in particular. The Sovereign, merely by virtue of what it is, is always what it should be.

This, however, is not the case with the relation of the subjects to the Sovereign, which, despite the common interest, would have no security that they would fulfill their undertakings, unless it found means to assure itself of their fidelity.

In fact, each individual, as a man, may have a particular will contrary or dissimilar to the general will which he has as a citizen. His particular interest may speak to him quite differently from the common interest: his absolute and naturally independent existence may make him look upon what he owes to the common cause as a gratuitous contribution, the loss of which will do less harm to

**The Social Contract* and *Discourses*, G. D. H. Cole (Trans.) (New York: E. P. Dutton [Everyman's Library], 1950). From *The Social Contract*, Book I, Chs. 7 and 9; Book II, Chs. 3, 4, 6, and 11.

others than the payment of it is burdensome to himself; and, regarding the moral person which constitutes the State as a *persona ficta*, because not a man, he may wish to enjoy the rights of citizenship without being ready to fulfill the duties of a subject. The continuance of such an injustice could not but prove the undoing of the body politic.

In order then that the social compact may not be an empty formula, it tacitly includes the undertaking, which alone can give force to the rest, that whoever refuses to obey the general will shall be compelled to do so by the whole body. This means nothing less than that he will be forced to be free; for this is the condition which, by giving each citizen to his country, secures him against all personal dependence. In this lies the key to the working of the political machine; this alone legitimizes civil undertakings, which, without it, would be absurd, tyrannical, and liable to the most frightful abuses.

. . . I shall end this chapter and this book [Book I] by remarking on a fact on which the whole social system should rest: i.e., that, instead of destroying natural inequality, the fundamental compact substitutes, for such physical inequality as nature may have set up between men, an equality that is moral and legitimate, and that men, who may be unequal in strength or intelligence, become every one equal by convention and legal right.*

BOOK II, CHAPTER III

. . . If when the people, being furnished with adequate information, held its deliberations, the citizens had no communication one with another, the grand total of the small differences would always give the general will, and the decision would always be good. But when factions arise, and partial associations are formed at the expense of the great association, the will of each of these associations becomes general in relation to its members, while it remains particular in relation to the State: it may then be said that there are no longer as many votes as there are men, but only as many as there are associations. The differences become less numerous and give a less general result. Lastly, when one of these associations is so great as to prevail over all the rest, the result is no longer a sum of small differences, but a single difference; in this case there is no longer a general will, and the opinion which prevails is purely particular.

It is therefore essential, if the general will is to be able to express itself, that there should be no partial society within the State, and that each citizen should think only his own thoughts: . . . But if there are partial societies, it is best to have as many as possible and to prevent them from being unequal, . . . These

*Under bad governments, this equality is only apparent and illusory; it serves only to keep the pauper in his poverty and the rich man in the position he has usurped. In fact, laws are always of use to those who possess and harmful to those who have nothing: from which it follows that the social state is advantageous to men only when all have something and none too much.

precautions are the only ones that can guarantee that the general will shall be always enlightened, and that the people shall in no way deceive itself.

CHAPTER IV

. . . The undertakings which bind us to the social body are obligatory only because they are mutual; and their nature is such that in fulfilling them we cannot work for others without working for ourselves. Why is it that the general will is always in the right, and that all continually will the happiness of each one, unless it is because there is not a man who does not think of "each" as meaning him, and consider himself in voting for all? This proves that equality of rights and the idea of justice which such equality creates originate in the preference each man gives to himself, and accordingly in the very nature of man. It proves that the general will, to be really such, must be general in its object as well as its essence; that it must both come from all and apply to all; and that it loses its natural rectitude when it is directed to some particular and determinate object, because in such a case we are judging of something foreign to us, and have no true principle of equity to guide us.

Indeed, as soon as a question of particular fact or right arises on a point not previously regulated by a general convention, the matter becomes contentious. It is a case in which the individuals concerned are one party, and the public the other, but in which I can see neither the law that ought to be followed nor the judge who ought to give the decision. In such a case, it would be absurd to propose to refer the question to an express decision of the general will, which can be only the conclusion reached by one of the parties and in consequence will be, for the other party, merely an external and particular will, inclined on this occasion to injustice and subject to error. Thus, just as a particular will cannot stand for the general will, the general will, in turn, changes its nature, when its object is particular, and, as general, cannot pronounce on a man or a fact. When, for instance, the people of Athens nominated or displaced its rulers, decreed honors to one, and imposed penalties on another, and, by a multitude of particular decrees, exercised all the functions of government indiscriminately, it had in such cases no longer a general will in the strict sense; it was acting no longer as Sovereign, but as magistrate. This will seem contrary to current views; but I must be given time to expound my own.

It should be seen from the foregoing that what makes the will general is less the number of voters than the common interest uniting them; for, under this system, each necessarily submits to the conditions he imposes on others: and this admirable agreement between interest and justice gives to the common deliberations an equitable character which at once vanishes when any particular question is discussed, in the absence of a common interest to unite and identify the ruling of the judge with that of the party.

From whatever side we approach our principle, we reach the same conclusion, that the social compact sets up among the citizens an equality of such a kind, that they all bind themselves to observe the same conditions and should therefore all enjoy the same rights. Thus, from the very nature of the compact, every act of Sovereignty, i.e., every authentic act of the general will binds or favors all the citizens equally; so that the Sovereign recognizes only the body of the nation, and draws no distinctions between those of whom it is made up. What, then, strictly speaking, is an act of Sovereignty? It is not a convention between a superior and an inferior, but a convention between the body and each of its members. It is legitimate, because based on the social contract, and equitable, because common to all; useful, because it can have no other object than the general good, and stable, because guaranteed by the public force and the supreme power. So long as the subjects have to submit only to conventions of this sort, they obey no one but their own will; and to ask how far the respective rights of the Sovereign and the citizens extend, is to ask up to what point the latter can enter into undertakings with themselves, each with all, and all with each.

We can see from this that the sovereign power, absolute, sacred, and inviolable as it is, does not and cannot exceed the limits of general conventions, and that every man may dispose at will of such goods and liberty as these conventions leave him; so that the Sovereign never has a right to lay more charges on one subject than on another, because, in that case, the question becomes particular, and ceases to be within its competency.

When these distinctions have once been admitted, it is seen to be so untrue that there is, in the social contract, any real renunciation on the part of the individuals, that the position in which they find themselves as a result of the contract is really preferable to that in which they were before. Instead of a renunciation, they have made an advantageous exchange: instead of an uncertain and precarious way of living they have got one that is better and more secure; instead of natural independence they have got liberty, instead of the power to harm others' security for themselves, and instead of their strength, which others might overcome, a right which social union makes invincible. . . .

Chapter VI

. . . I have already said that there can be no general will directed to a particular object. Such an object must be either within or outside the State. If outside, a will which is alien to it, cannot be, in relation to it, general; if within, it is part of the State, and in that case there arises a relation between whole and part which makes them two separate beings, of which the part is one, and the whole minus the part the other. But the whole minus a part cannot be the whole; and while this relation persists, there can be no whole, but only two unequal parts;

and it follows that the will of one is no longer in any respect general in relation to the other.

But when the whole people decrees for the whole people, it is considering only itself; and if a relation is then formed, it is between two aspects of the entire object, without there being any division of the whole. In that case the matter about which the decree is made is, like the decreeing will, general. This act is what I call a law.

When I say that the object of laws is always general, I mean that law considers subjects en masse and actions in the abstract, and never a particular person or action. Thus the law may indeed decree that there shall be privileges, but cannot confer them on anybody by name. It may set up several classes of citizens, and even lay down the qualifications for membership of these classes, but it cannot nominate such and such persons as belonging to them; it may establish a monarchical government and hereditary succession, but it cannot choose a king, or nominate a royal family. In a word, no function which has a particular object belongs to the legislative power.

On this view, we at once see that it can no longer be asked whose business it is to make laws, since they are acts of the general will; nor whether the prince is above the law, since he is a member of the State; nor whether the law can be unjust, since no one is unjust to himself; nor how we can be both free and subject to the laws, since they are but registers of our wills.

CHAPTER XI

. . . If we ask in what precisely consists the greatest good of all, which should be the end of every system of legislation, we shall find it reduces itself to two main objects, liberty and equality—liberty, because all particular dependence means so much force taken from the body of the State, and equality, because liberty cannot exist without it.

I have already defined civil liberty by equality; we should understand, not that the degrees of power and riches are to be absolutely identical for everybody, but that power shall never be great enough for violence, and shall always be exercised by virtue of rank and law; and that in respect of riches, no citizen shall ever be wealthy enough to buy another, and none poor enough to be forced to sell himself: . . . which implies, on the part of the great, moderation in goods and position, and, on the side of the common sort, moderation in avarice and covetousness.

Such equality, we are told, is an unpractical ideal that cannot actually exist. But if its abuse is inevitable, does it follow that we should not at least make regulations concerning it? It is precisely because the force of circumstances tends continually to destroy equality that the force of legislation should always tend to its maintenance.

SELECTION 33
FROM
*On Liberty**
JOHN STUART MILL

[I]N POLITICAL AND PHILOSOPHICAL theories, as well as in persons, success discloses faults and infirmities which failure might have concealed from observation. The notion, that the people have no need to limit their power over themselves, might seem axiomatic, when popular government was a thing only dreamed about, or read of as having existed at some distant period of the past. Neither was that notion necessarily disturbed by such temporary aberrations as those of the French Revolution, the worst of which were the work of a usurping few, and which, in any case, belonged, not to the permanent working of popular institutions, but to a sudden and convulsive outbreak against monarchical and aristocratic despotism. In time, however, a democratic republic came to occupy a large portion of the earth's surface, . . . and made itself felt as one of the most powerful members of the community of nations; and elective and responsible government became subject to the observations and criticisms which wait upon a great existing fact. It was now perceived that such phrases as "self-government," and "the power of the people over themselves," do not express the true state of the case. The "people" who exercise the power are not always the same people as those over whom it is exercised: and the "self-government" spoken of is not the government of each by himself, but of each by all the rest. The will of the people, moreover, practically means the will of the most numerous or the most active *part* of the people; the majority, or those who succeed in making themselves accepted as the majority; the people, consequently, *may* desire to oppress a part of their number; and precautions are as much needed against this as against any other abuse of power. The limitation, therefore, of the power of government over individuals loses none of its importance when the holders of power are regularly accountable to the community, that is, to the strongest party therein. This view of things, recommending itself equally to the intelligence of thinkers and to the inclina-

*David Spitz (Ed.) (New York: W. W. Norton [A Norton Critical Edition], 1975): pp. 5–9, 15–18, 22–24, 31–32, 46–50, 63–65, 69–78.

tion of those important classes in European society to whose real or supposed interests democracy is adverse, has had no difficulty in establishing itself; and in political speculations "the tyranny of the majority" is now generally included among the evils against which society requires to be on its guard.

Like other tyrannies, the tyranny of the majority was at first, and is still vulgarly, held in dread, chiefly as operating through the acts of the public authorities. . . . But reflecting persons . . . perceived that when society is itself the tyrant—society collectively over the separate individuals who compose it—its means of tyrannizing are not restricted to the acts which it may do by the hands of its political functionaries. Society can and does execute its own mandates; and if it issues wrong mandates instead of right, or any mandates at all in things with which it ought not to meddle, it practices a social tyranny more formidable than many kinds of political oppression, since, though not usually upheld by such extreme penalties, it leaves fewer means of escape, penetrating much more deeply into the details of life, and enslaving the soul itself. Protection, therefore, against the tyranny of the magistrate is not enough: there needs protection also against the tyranny of the prevailing opinion and feeling; against the tendency of society to impose, by other means than civil penalties, its own ideas and practices as rules of conduct on those who dissent from them; to fetter the development, and, if possible, prevent the formation, of any individuality not in harmony with its ways, and compels all characters to fashion themselves upon the model of its own. There is a limit to the legitimate interference of collective opinion with individual independence: and to find that limit, and maintain it against encroachment, is as indispensable to a good condition of human affairs, as protection against political despotism. . . .

The likings and dislikings of society, or of some powerful portion of it, are thus the main thing which has practically determined the rules laid down for general observance, under the penalties of law or opinion. And in general, those who have been in advance of society in thought and feeling, have left this condition of things unassailed in principle, however they may have come into conflict with it in some of its details. They have occupied themselves rather in inquiring what things society ought to like or dislike, than in questioning whether its likings or dislikings should be a law to individuals. They preferred endeavoring to alter the feelings of mankind on the particular points on which they were themselves heretical, rather than make common cause in defense of freedom, with heretics generally. The only case in which the higher ground has been taken on principle and maintained with consistency, by any but an individual here and there, is that of religious belief: a case instructive in many ways, and not least so as forming a most striking instance of the fallibility of what is called the moral sense: for the *odium theologicum*, . . . in a sincere bigot, is one of the most unequivocal cases of moral feeling. Those who first broke the yoke of what called itself the Universal Church, . . . were in general as little willing to permit differences of religious opinion as that church itself. But when the heat of the conflict was over, without giving a complete victory to any party, and each church or sect was reduced to limit its hopes to retaining possession of the ground it already occupied, minorities, seeing that they had no chance of becoming majorities, were under the necessity of pleading to those whom they could not convert, for permission to differ. It is accordingly on this battlefield, almost solely, that the rights of the individual against society have been asserted on broad grounds of principle, and the claim of society to exercise authority over dissentients openly controverted. The great writers to whom the world owes what religious liberty it possesses, . . . have mostly asserted freedom of conscience as an indefeasible right, and denied absolutely that a human being is accountable to others for his religious belief. Yet so natural to mankind is intolerance in whatever they really care about, that religious freedom has hardly anywhere been practically realized, except where religious indifference, which dislikes to have its peace disturbed by theological quarrels, has added its weight to the scale. In the minds of almost all religious persons, even in the most tolerant countries, the duty of toleration is admitted with tacit reserves. One person will bear with dissent in matters of church government, but not of dogma; another can tolerate anybody, short of a Papist . . . or a Unitarian, . . . another every one who believes in revealed religion; a few extend their charity a little further, but stop at the belief in a God and in a future state. Wherever the sentiment of the majority is still genuine and intense, it is found to have abated little of its claim to be obeyed.

Apart from the peculiar tenets of individual thinkers, there is also in the world at large an increasing inclination to stretch unduly the powers of society over the individual, both by the force of opinion and even by that of legislation; and as the tendency of all the changes taking place in the world is to strengthen society, and diminish the power of the individual, this encroachment is not one of the evils which tend spontaneously to disappear, but, on the contrary, to grow more and more formidable. The disposition of mankind, whether as rulers or as fellow citizens, to impose their own opinions and inclinations as a rule of conduct on others, is so energetically supported by some of the best and by some of the worst feelings incident to human nature, that it is hardly ever kept under restraint by anything but want of power; and as the power is not declining, but growing, . . . unless a strong barrier of moral conviction can be raised against the mischief, we must expect, in the present circumstances of the world, to see it increase.

. . . No argument, we may suppose, can now be needed, against permitting a legislature or an executive, not identified in interest with the people, to prescribe opinions to them, and determine what doctrines or what arguments they shall be allowed to hear. This aspect of the question, besides, has been so often and so triumphantly enforced by preceding writers, that it need not be specially insisted on in this place. Though the law of England, on the subject of the press, is as servile to this day as it was in the time of the Tudors, . . . there is little danger of its being actually put in force against political discussion, except during some temporary panic, when fear of insurrection drives ministers and judges from their propriety; . . . and, speaking generally, it is not, in constitutional countries, to be apprehended, that the government, whether completely responsible to the people or not, will often attempt to control the expression of opinion, except when in doing so it makes itself the organ of the general intolerance of the public. Let us suppose, therefore, that the government is entirely at one with the people, and never thinks of exerting any power of coercion unless in agreement with what it conceives to be their voice. But I deny the right of the people to exercise such coercion, either by themselves or by their government. The power itself is illegitimate. The best government has no more title to it than the worst. It is as noxious, or more noxious, when exerted in accordance with public opinion, than when in opposition to it. If all mankind minus one were of one opinion, and only one person were of the contrary opinion, mankind would be no more justified in silencing that one person, than he, if he had the power, would be justified in silencing mankind. . . . Were an opinion a personal possession of no value except to the owner; if to be obstructed in the enjoyment of it were simply a private injury, it would make some difference whether the injury was inflicted only on a few persons or on many. But the peculiar evil of silencing the expression of an opinion is that it is robbing the human race, posterity as well as the existing generation, those who dissent from the opinion, still more than those who hold it. If the opinion is right, they are deprived of the opportunity of exchanging error for truth; if wrong, they lose what is almost as great a benefit, the clearer perception and livelier impression of truth, produced by its collision with error.

In the present age—which has been described as "destitute of faith, but terrified at scepticism" . . . —in which people feel sure, not so much that their opinions are true, as that they should not know what to do without them—the claims of an opinion to be protected from public attack are rested not so much on its truth, as on its importance to society. There are, it is alleged, certain beliefs so useful, not to say indispensable, to well-being that it is as much the duty of governments to uphold those beliefs, as to protect any other of the interests of society. In a case of such necessity, and so directly in the line of their duty, something less than infallibility may, it is maintained, warrant, and even bind, governments to act on their own opinion, confirmed by the general opinion of mankind. It is also often argued, and still oftener thought, that none but bad men would desire to weaken these salutary beliefs; and there can be nothing wrong, it is thought, in restraining bad men, and prohibiting what only such men would wish to practice. This mode of thinking makes the justification of restraints on discussion not a question of the truth of doctrines, but of their usefulness; and flatters itself by that means to escape the responsibility of claiming to be an infallible judge of opinions. But those who thus satisfy themselves, do not perceive that the assumption of infallibility is merely shifted from one point to another. The usefulness of an opinion is itself matter of opinion: as disputable, as open to discussion, and requiring discussion as much as the opinion itself. There is the same need of an infallible judge of opinions to decide an opinion to be noxious, as to decide it to be false, unless the opinion condemned has full opportunity of defending itself. And it will not do to say that the heretic may be allowed to maintain the utility or harmlessness of his opinion, though forbidden to maintain its truth. The truth of an opinion is part of its utility. If we would know whether or not it is desirable that a proposition should be believed, is it possible to exclude the consideration of whether or not it is true? In the opinion, not of bad men, but of the best men, no belief which is contrary to truth can be really useful: and can you prevent such men from urging that plea, when they are charged with culpability for denying some doctrine which they are told is useful, but which they believe to be false? Those who are on the side of received opinions never fail to take all possible advantage of this plea: you do not find *them* handling the question of utility as if it could be completely abstracted from that of truth; on the contrary, it is, above all, because their doctrine is "the truth," that the knowledge or the belief of it is held to be so indispensable. There can be no fair discussion of the question of usefulness when an argument so vital may be employed on one side, but not on the other. And in point of fact, when law or public feeling do not permit the truth of an opinion to be disputed, they are just as little tolerant of a denial of its usefulness. The utmost they allow is an extenuation of its absolute necessity, or of the positive guilt of rejecting it.

In order more fully to illustrate the mischief of denying a hearing to opinions because we, in our own judgment, have condemned them, it will be desirable to fix down the discussion to a concrete case; and I choose, by preference, the cases which are least favorable to me—in which the argument against freedom of opinion, both on the score of truth and on that of utility, is considered the strongest. Let the opinions impugned be the belief in a God and in a future state, or any of the commonly received doctrines of morality. To fight the battle on such ground gives a great advantage to an unfair antagonist; since he will be sure to say (and many who have no desire to be unfair will say it internally): Are these the doctrines which you do not deem sufficiently certain to be taken under the protection of law? Is the belief in a God one of the opinions to feel sure of which you hold to be assuming infallibility? But I must be permitted to observe, that it is not the feeling sure of a doctrine (be it what it may) which I call an assumption of infallibility. It is the undertaking to decide that question *for others*, without allowing them to hear what can be said on the contrary side. And I denounce and reprobate this pretension not the less, if put forth on the side of my most solemn convictions. However positive any one's persuasion may be, not only of the falsity but of the pernicious consequences—not only of the pernicious consequences, but (to adopt expressions which I altogether condemn) the immorality and impiety of an opinion; yet if, in pursuance of that private judgment, though backed by the public judgment of his country or his contemporaries, he prevents the opinion from being heard in its defense, he assumes infallibility. And so far from the assumption being less objectionable or less dangerous because the opinion is called immoral or impious, this is the case of all others in which it is most fatal. These are exactly the occasions on which the men of one generation commit those dreadful mistakes which excite the astonishment and horror of posterity. It is among such that we find the instances memorable in history, when the arm of the law has been employed to root out the best men and the noblest doctrines; with deplorable success as to the men, though some of the doctrines have survived to be (as if in mockery) invoked in defense of similar conduct toward those who dissent from *them*, or from their received interpretation.

. . . What is boasted of at the present time as the revival of religion, is always, in narrow and uncultivated minds, at least as much the revival of bigotry; and where there is the strong permanent leaven of intolerance in the feelings of a people, which at all times abides in the middle classes of this country, it needs but little to provoke them into actively persecuting those whom they have never ceased to think proper objects of persecution. . . . For it is this—it is the opinions men entertain, and the feelings they cherish, respecting those who disown the beliefs they deem important, which makes this country not a place of mental freedom. . . .

In politics, again, it is almost a commonplace, that a party of order or stability, and a party of progress or reform, are both necessary elements of a healthy state of political life; until the one or the other shall have so enlarged its mental grasp as to be a party equally of order and of progress, knowing and distinguishing what is fit to be preserved from what ought to be swept away. Each of these modes of thinking derives its utility from the deficiencies of the other; but it is in a great measure the opposition of the other that keeps each within the limits of reason and sanity. Unless opinions favorable to democracy and to aristocracy, to property and to equality, to cooperation and to competition, to luxury and to abstinence, to sociality and individuality, to liberty and discipline, and all the other standing antagonisms of practical life, are expressed with equal freedom, and enforced and defended with equal talent and energy, there is no chance of both elements obtaining their due; one scale is sure to go up, and the other down. Truth, in the great practical concerns of life, is so much a question of the reconciling and combining of opposites, that very few have minds sufficiently capacious and impartial to make the adjustment with an approach to correctness, and it has to be made by the rough process of a struggle between combatants fighting under hostile banners. On any of the great open questions just enumerated, if either of the two opinions has a better claim than the other, not merely to be tolerated, but to be encouraged and countenanced, it is the one which happens at the particular time and place to be in a minority. That is the opinion which, for the time being, represents the neglected interests, the side of human well-being which is in danger of obtaining less than its share. I am aware that there is not, in this country, any tolerance of differences of opinion on most of these topics. They are adduced to show, by admitted and multiplied examples, the universality of the fact that only through diversity of opinion is there, in the existing state of human intellect, a chance of fair play to all sides of the truth. When there are persons to be found who form an exception to the apparent unanimity of the world on any subject, even if the world is in the right, it is always probable that dissentients have something worth hearing to say for themselves, and that truth would lose something by their silence.

I do not pretend that the most unlimited use of the freedom of enunciating all possible opinions would put an end to the evils of religious or philosophical sectarianism. Every truth which men of narrow capacity are in earnest about, is sure to be asserted, inculcated, and in many ways even acted on, as if no other truth existed in the world, or at all events none that could limit or qualify the first. I acknowledge that the tendency of all opinions to become sectarian is not cured by the freest discussion, but is often heightened and exacerbated thereby; the truth which ought to have been, but was not seen, being rejected all the more violently because proclaimed by persons regarded as opponents. But it is not on the impassioned partisan, it is on the calmer and more disinterested bystander, that this collision of opinions works its salutary effect. Not the violent conflict between parts of the truth, but the quiet suppression of half of it, is the formidable evil; there is always hope when people are forced to listen to both sides; it is when they attend only to one that errors harden into prejudices, and truth itself ceases to have the effect of truth, by being exaggerated into falsehood. And since there are few mental attributes more rare than that judicial faculty which can sit in intelligent judgment between two sides of a question, of which only one is represented by an advocate before it, truth has no chance but in proportion as every side of it, every opinion which embodies any fraction of the truth, not only finds advocates, but is so advocated as to be listened to.

I have said that it is important to give the freest scope possible to uncustomary things, in order that it may in time appear which of these are fit to be converted into customs. But independence of action, and disregard of custom, are not solely deserving of encouragement for the chance they afford that better modes of action, and customs more worthy of general adoption, may be struck out; nor is it only persons of decided mental superiority who have a just claim to carry on their lives in their own way. There is no reason that all human existence should be constructed on some one or some small number of patterns. If a person possesses any tolerable amount of common sense and experience, his own mode of laying out his existence is the best, not because it is the best in itself, but because it is his own mode. Human beings are not like sheep; and even sheep are not undistinguishably alike. A man cannot get a coat or a pair of boots to fit him unless they are either made to his measure, or he has a whole warehouseful to choose from: and is it easier to fit him with a life than with a coat, or are human beings more like one another in their whole physical and spiritual conformation than in the shape of their feet? If it were only that people have diversities of taste, that is reason enough for not attempting to shape them all after one model. But different persons also require different conditions for their spiritual development; and can no more exist healthily in the same moral, than all the variety of plants can in the same physical, atmosphere and climate. The same things which are helps to one person toward the cultivation of higher nature are hindrances to another. The same mode of life is a healthy excitement to one, keeping all his faculties of action and enjoyment in their best order, while to another it is a distracting burthen, which suspends or crushes all internal life. Such are the differences among human beings in their sources of pleasure, their susceptibilities of pain, and the operation on them of different physical and moral agencies, that unless there is a corresponding diversity in their modes of life, they neither obtain their fair share of happiness, nor grow up to the mental, moral, and aesthetic stature of which their nature is capable. Why then should tolerance, as far as the public sentiment is concerned, extend only to tastes and modes of life which extort acquiescence by the multitude of their adherents? Nowhere (except in some monastic institutions) is diversity of taste entirely unrecognized; a person may, without blame, either like or dislike rowing, or smoking, or music, or athletic exercises, or chess, or cards, or study, because both those who like each of these things, and those who dislike them, are too numerous to be put down. But the man, and still more the woman, who can be accused either of doing "what nobody does," or of not doing "what everybody does," is the subject of as much depreciatory remark as if he or she had committed some grave moral delinquency. . . .

There is one characteristic of the present direction of public opinion peculiarly calculated to make it intolerant of any marked demonstration of individuality. The general average of mankind are not only moderate in intellect, but also moderate in inclinations: they have no tastes or wishes strong enough to incline them to do anything unusual, and they consequently do not understand those who have, and class all such with the wild and intemperate whom they are accustomed to look down upon. Now, in addition to this fact which is general, we have only to suppose that a strong movement has set in toward the improvement of morals, and it is evident what we have to expect. In these days such a movement has set in; much has actually been effected in the way of increased regularity of conduct and discouragement of excesses; and there is a philanthropic spirit abroad, for the exercise of which there is no more inviting field than the moral and prudential improvement of our fellow creatures. These tendencies of the times cause the public to be more disposed than at most former periods to prescribe general rules of conduct, and endeavor to make every one conform to the approved standard. And that standard, express or tacit, is to desire nothing strongly. Its ideal of character is to be without any marked character; to maim by compression, like a Chinese lady's foot, every part of human nature which stands out prominently, and tends to make the person markedly dissimilar in outline to commonplace humanity.

The combination of all these causes forms so great a mass of influences hostile to individuality, that it is not easy to see how it can stand its ground. It will do so with increasing difficulty, unless the intelligent part of the public can be made to feel its value—to see that it is good there should be differences, even though not for the better, even though, as it may appear to them, some should be for the worse. If the claims of individuality are ever to be asserted, the time is now, while much is still wanting to complete the enforced assimilation. It is only in the earlier stages that any stand can be successfully made against the encroachment. The demand that all other people shall resemble ourselves grows by what it feeds on. If resistance waits till life is reduced *nearly* to one uniform type, all deviations from that type will come to be considered impious, immoral, even monstrous and contrary to nature. Mankind speedily become unable to conceive diversity, when they have been for some time unaccustomed to see it.

Though society is not founded on a contract, and though no good purpose is answered by inventing a contract in order to deduce social obligations from it, . . . every one who receives the protection of society owes a return for the benefit, and the fact of living in society renders it indispensable that each should be bound to observe a certain line of conduct toward the rest. This conduct consists, first, in not injuring the interests of one another; or rather certain interests, which, either by express legal provision, or by tacit understanding, ought to be considered as rights; and secondly, in each person's bearing his share (to be fixed on some equitable principle) of the labors and sacrifices incurred for defending the society or its members from injury and molestation. These conditions society is justified in enforcing, at all costs to those who endeavor to withhold fulfillment. Nor is this all that society may do. The acts of an individual may be hurtful to others, or wanting in due consideration for their welfare, without going to the length of violating any of their constituted rights. The offender may then be justly punished by opinion, though not by law. As soon as any part of a person's conduct affects prejudicially the interests of others, society has jurisdiction over it, and the question whether the general welfare will or will not be promoted by interfering with it, becomes open to discussion. But there is no room for entertaining any such question when a person's conduct affects the interests of no persons besides himself, or need not affect them unless they like (all the persons concerned being of full age, and the ordinary amount of understanding). In all such cases, there should be perfect freedom, legal and social, to do the action and stand the consequences.

But the strongest of all the arguments against the interference of the public with purely personal conduct is that, when it does interfere, the odds are that it interferes wrongly, and in the wrong place. On questions of social morality, of duty to others, the opinion of the public, that is, of an overruling majority, though often wrong, is likely to be still oftener right; because on such questions they are only required to judge of their own interests; of the manner in which some mode of conduct, if allowed to be practiced, would affect themselves. But the opinion of a similar majority, imposed as a law on the minority, on questions of self-regarding conduct, is quite as likely to be wrong as right; for in these cases public opinion means, at the best, some people's opinion of what is good or bad for other people; while very often it does not even mean that; the public, with the most perfect indifference, passing over the pleasure or convenience of those whose conduct they censure, and considering only their own preference. There are many who consider as an injury to themselves any conduct which they have a distaste for, and resent it as an outrage to their feelings; as a religious bigot, when charged with disregarding the religious feelings of others, has been known to retort that they disregard his feelings, by persisting in their abominable worship or creed. But there is no parity between the feeling of a person for his own opinion, and the feeling of another who is offended at his holding it; no more than between the desire of a thief to take a purse, and the desire of the right owner to keep it. And a person's taste is as much his own peculiar concern as his opinion or his purse. It is easy for any one to imagine an ideal public which leaves the freedom and choice of individuals in all uncertain matters undisturbed, and only requires them to abstain from modes of conduct which universal experience has condemned. But where has there been seen a public which set any such limit to its censorship? or when does the public trouble itself about universal experience? In its interferences with personal conduct it is seldom thinking of anything but the enormity of acting or feeling differently from itself; and this standard of judgment, thinly disguised, is held up to mankind as the dictate of religion and philosophy, by nine-tenths of all moralists and speculative writers. . . .

SELECTION 34
FROM
*The Structure of Freedom**

CHRISTIAN BAY

IT IS CONVENIENT TO think of freedom demands as "human rights" and in this way relate the issue before us to a perennial issue in writings on democracy: What is the proper balance between majority rule and minority rights? Perhaps the present concept of "human right" can contribute toward an acceptable answer to this problem. As I have just implied, I use this term to refer to a demand for a specified sphere of freedom around every individual. A human right has been "realized" to the extent that this demand is in fact generally honored. . . . Human rights in this sense are not God-given or inalienable. In a democratic society there is usually a law or constitutional clause enforcing every human right, or there is a demand for such a law or constitutional clause. For this reason the term "civil right" is often used in the same sense. . . .

The problem of freedom maximization, to the extent that it can be conceived as a problem of maximal realization of freedom demands, is best approached by making a distinction between human rights and social privileges. . . . A human right is a freedom demand that can, in principle, be vindicated for all human beings. The right of free speech is such a human right. . . . Other examples are the right to work, the right to health services, the right to leisure. A social privilege, on the other hand, is a right that by its very nature must be limited to some. A privilege is not necessarily something bad. Social privileges—for example, the private ownership of factories—tend to extend the freedom of the few at the expense of the freedom of the many. However, if this kind of an economic system is believed to be particularly effective in delivering goods that men need, it may conceivably contribute in other respects to extend the freedom of everybody. Such a possibility should not be rejected offhand. But since there are always two sides to questions of social privilege, it is reasonable to hold that they should be regulated by majority rule.

When it comes to human rights, however, majority rule should not apply. If

*(New York: Atheneum, 1965): pp. 6–7, 371–74. Originally published in 1958 by Stanford University Press.

an exercise of a particular freedom by an individual does not interfere with someone else's freedom, he should not be denied his right no matter how small the minority of which he is a member. This position, to which I shall later refer as the *human rights approach*, is a value orientation that differs sharply from that of Bentham and the orthodox utilitarians. It is my faith, as it was theirs, that society exists for the benefit of all. But Bentham's method for assigning priorities between freedom demands was a simple addition of pleasures and subtraction of pains to achieve the highest sum of happiness. My method is instead to assign top priority to the removal of the heaviest constraints on freedom first, throughout society, before one should worry about the less serious constraints. A society is as free as its underdogs are.

In other words, in my value position the extension of the more basic human rights to the last few individuals takes precedence over the extension of less basic rights to much larger numbers of individuals. Although Bentham, too, believed in the equality of all individuals, his notion of equality was essentially a computation device. For me, a society is free only to the extent that its least privileged and its least tolerated members are free. . . .

. . . This philosophy of human rights can be considered analogous in certain respects to the philosophy of natural law. I assume that there are certain principles of justice that are potentially acceptable to all mankind. They correspond to objective requirements pertaining to certain universal human needs and can therefore be claimed as valid, potentially at least, in all cultures that permit and encourage an expanding individual freedom.

I am assuming only the most general categories of needs. In fact, it suffices for my argument to assume only one universal need—for self-expression. But I would wish to add also the need for growth: the need for expression of the potential self, or of what the individual is capable of becoming.

On this double assumption, the universal desirability of a maximal freedom for all individuals is a clear conclusion. Psychological freedom makes the individual capable of knowing and expressing what is in him; it realizes to this extent the two objectives of "know thyself" and "be thyself." Social freedom, especially freedom from coercion, gives the individual the opportunity to express himself in accordance with his inclinations, insofar as they are compatible with the essential needs of others. Potential freedom, especially resistance against special interest manipulation, rescues the individual from becoming the willingly exploited tool of the interests of others, and it permits him to be concerned both with the development of his own needs according to their own dynamics and with acquiring the knowledge that facilitates their optimal satisfaction.

Let me further assume that a maximal freedom is considered equally desirable for all men and women; that each human life is equally deserving of maximal opportunities for developing all its potentialities, insofar as these are not self-defeating or defeating the potentialities of others.

Here is precisely where the most difficult empirical problem arises: how do we determine the criteria for compatibilities between various freedom values for the same individual and between various freedom demands of different individuals? And in cases of conflict, how is it possible to lay down priority criteria that are potentially acceptable to all?

I cannot solve this problem, but I suggest that the most promising avenue toward a never fully attainable solution is opened up by the political and legal instrumentality of human rights. Even the most basic human rights are not natural rights in any traditional sense, for they presuppose either a government able and willing to enforce them or a demand of enforcement directed at some political authority. . . . But it is possible that they can *become* natural rights in a different sense, to the extent that the behavioral sciences can demonstrate that each right corresponds to a universal human need—a need actually or potentially rooted in all human beings everywhere.

Yet, even if and when this happens, it still is less misleading to speak of human rights rather than natural rights. A huge sum of long-term achievements in civilization and culture has developed human nature to the point at which human beings can sense a need for—to cite one example—freedom of speech. In the extreme state of nature, there are few needs beyond biological essentials common to all men. At an extremely high level of cultural development, on the other hand, one may assume that all or most men, regardless of their particular strain of culture, will experience an actual need for free speech, if not also more specialized needs such as artistic experience. . . . Throughout this argument, I presuppose the probable validity of some such theory as Maslow's, on the hierarchy of human motives. New and "higher" motives are born only as more basic and essential motives receive satisfaction, and the individual comes to take their satisfaction for granted. . . .

There is at least one more respect in which my conception of human right departs from the traditional notions of natural right. Needs that in fact can be realized for all individuals *within a given society* should provide the basis for establishing the corresponding array of human rights within that society. Human rights are freedoms that are demanded by some and are of such a nature that they can be extended to all individuals within a given society without curtailing comparable or more basic freedoms in the same or in any other society. Some cultures may stress some needs or enforce some human rights at the expense of other possibilities, while other cultures may reverse these priorities between conflicting freedom demands.

The problem of determining priorities between human rights is perhaps the thorniest of all the problems raised by my approach toward a theory of the free society. What should the majority's role be in this decision-making process? We remember Solomon's advice to the father who wanted to divide his lands justly between his two sons: let the older son divide the lands in two halves, and let the younger one choose his half. Let the majority of citizens, I suggest, choose which freedoms or rights are of the more basic importance for human well-being and establish a set of general priorities—guided by the information of social scientists, but yet autonomously according to the prevailing and enduring attitudes. But let the minority of responsible rulers see to it that the more basic rights are granted under the law to all citizens without exception before conflicting and less basic rights or privileges are granted to anyone.

This is in a broad sense a statement affirming the desirability of constitutional governments for the establishment and expansion of human rights everywhere. Constitutions are, according to my position, primarily instruments for the growth of human freedom by the gradual expansion of human rights. To the extent that a constitution serves this function, it should be imbued with sanctity. To the extent that it obstructs it, or fails to protect past accomplishments in human rights, it should be disobeyed. Democratic constitutions have on the whole been favorable to the growth of effective human rights. Perhaps the reverse is also true, that the growth of freedom has been favorable to the preservation of democratic constitutions. . . .

There are several basic advantages to a constitution, particularly a constitution that enjoys the protection of an *enlightened* judicial review, in the struggle for protecting and expanding human rights. First, there is the power of a constitution, backed up by an alert court, to prevent popular majorities from abolishing the human rights of unpopular minorities.

Second, there is the establishment of a permanent presumption favoring established rights if there are conflicts with new freedom demands. The drawback to this presumption is that it also tends to favor established privileges against human rights demands. But among rights, the loss in freedom by curtailing established ones generally outweighs the gains won by instituting new ones, unless the new rights are consensually considered more essential. In such cases the heavy machinery of constitutional amendments is available, and heavy it ought to be for these purposes.

Third, constitutions are important symbols, capable of vesting the rights of the humblest minority with great national significance. Constitutions alone are capable of making minority human rights—rights desired only by minorities, though open to all who wish to claim them—permanently strong enough to prevail against majority preferences.

Fourth, constitutions provide procedural stability for the political struggle. They furnish the rules of the game for the democratic or pluralist political process. They offer a set of enduring criteria for the making of decisions when powerful groups are in conflict. The various sources of economic, professional, and cultural influence operate as an extraconstitutional system of checks and balances, but the constitution provides the procedures for checking and balancing.

Needless to say, the constitution proper is surrounded with a mass of social institutions and psychological incentives, which might in theory prevail even if the constitution one day were abolished. But in the last resort it is the constitution itself, insofar as people with power are loyal to it, that enjoys the protection of legal sanctions. Indirectly, however, these sanctions support also political practices that are not themselves matters of law.

SELECTION 35 FROM *Political Science Quarterly**

GEORGE KATEB

A READING OF JOHN Calhoun's speeches, state paper, and formal writings leaves a clear impression of masterly intellect. . . . From his earliest days as congressman from South Carolina to his last years as genius of the slave states, Calhoun spoke and wrote with a rare force and elegance. One might almost say that his words were in excess of the occasions: he philosophized, he generalized, he expressed himself as if his audience were made up of political scholastics. For this quality of irrepressible intellectual excess the idle student of political ideas should be grateful. More to the point, however, is the capacity of his thought to demoralize all those who subscribe to the principles of democratic government. For it is not easy to repel Calhoun's arguments, to repel his theory of concurrent majority. . . .

. . . Not to try would be to leave democratic theory exposed to serious incursions.

I

For the sake of rough analysis, let us take a simple model of democratic government which is highly faithful to the majority principle. . . . The model would have six elements:

1. Universal suffrage.

2. The votes of electors weigh equally. Among other things, this means that constituencies have roughly equal populations.

3. Representatives are elected by the majority (or plurality) in the constituencies. This excludes all forms of indirect election.

4. Representatives vote according to the sense of the majority that elected them.

*"The Majority Principle: Calhoun and His Antecedents," in *Political Science Quarterly* 84 (December 1969): pp. 595–617.

5. There is majority rule among the representatives. This excludes such practices as filibuster.

6. There are no extralegislative restrictions on the will of the majority of the representatives.

Such a model assumes that a system in which everything is directly decided by the people in frequent referenda would be too crude, even though yet more faithful to the majority principle. The division of the country into constituencies reflects the diversity of the country. Each constituency putatively has a "character"; it is in some respects different from all the rest. A gathering of representatives is thus a gathering of men who bring to bear on any problem a multitude of viewpoints and concerns. Furthermore, the political process requires continuous discussion, negotiation, and inquiry; it therefore requires a class of politicians. Then, too, the class of politicians is needed to superintend the work of execution and administration, putatively in the hands of agencies separate from the legislature. For all these reasons, a representative system with the above six elements is to be preferred to a system of unmediated consultation with the people.

This model leaves much out, including the frequency of elections, the nature and place of parties, the complexities involved in ascertaining the sense of the majority, the difficulties raised by the fact that different issues call into being differently composed majorities, the question of electoral apathy and ignorance, the unequal political influence among the electorate, and a host of other considerations. Nevertheless it does provide a syndrome of elements that can be used to guide the critic in his judgment of the workings of democratic systems in the real world. It is apparent that the *moral* reason for subscribing to these elements—to leave aside practical or utilitarian reasons—is that they are indispensable to the realization of formal political equality. An attack on them, an attack on majoritarianism is, at the same time, an attack on formal political equality. And when the American system is judged by such a model, it soon becomes apparent that plain majoritarianism has suffered a rather hard fate in this country. . . .

The very idea of living politically by a written constitution offends item 6 (no extralegislative restrictions on the will of the majority of the representatives). The legislature is meant to play according to certain rules, and within a larger framework; the rules and the framework are meant to be binding on the generations of men. The powers and relations of the legislature are defined. Though the definition is general, it is not so vague as to permit unlimited interpretive freedom. To be sure, everything in the Constitution (except the equal representation of the states in the Senate) is subject to amendment. But the states, unequal in population, count equally; each has one vote. And three-fourths of the states must agree to any proposed amendment, indeed the one-fourth plus one opposed may contain a proportion of the population significantly less than one-fourth of the whole. A minority can turn back a majority. We see that the amending process systematically offends item 2 (the votes of electors weigh equally), if we suppose that there is a fairly strict correspondence between the wishes of the people in a state and the votes of the state legislature or the state convention, and that there is in each state a decisive majority behind the state position on the proposed amendment. Or figuring each state as a single representative, we see that item 5 (majority rule among representatives) is offended by the amending process. In actuality, item 4 (representatives or delegates vote according to the sense of the majority in their constituencies) may also be offended.

Beyond the offense given to item 6 by the very idea of a written constitution, there is the offense to several items especially given by some of the content of the American Constitution and its amendments. The Constitution contains not only prescriptions for the structures and relations of federal public agencies, but also specific prohibitions on the will of the majority of the representatives in Congress and in the states (item 6).

Item 2 (the votes of electors weigh equally) is offended by the equal representation of states in the Senate. Item 3 (representatives are elected by the majority in the constituencies) is offended by the provision for the indirect election of senators; and in an extended sense of "constituency," by the provision for the indirect election of the president and vice-president.

What, then, can be said to defend these encroachments on the requirements of our model, on the requirements of a system of democratic government which is highly faithful to the majority principle? A different defense suits each of the different considerations we have mentioned.

We must take into account the political necessities inherent in creating a political unit out of smaller political units already in existence, in the very idea of a written constitution. It was not a question of inheriting a customary set of arrangements, but of making a break with the past. The need for explicitness was absolute. Obviously, however, the historical conditions give only a partial explanation. Those who framed the Constitution must have thought that their work embodied something more than expedience in the face of historical circumstances. They must have thought that their work embodied principles which men of succeeding generations, as well as their contemporaries, would have to acknowledge as *the* principles of political rationality. Through changes of fashion or mood, through periods of calm or turmoil, men would see the great superiority of free, republican, representative government. The benefits enumerated in the Preamble will accrue not only to "ourselves" but also to "our Posterity."

The federal nature of the American union dictated the requirement that the states, rather than the people directly, pass on proposed amendments. The requirement, however, that three-fourths of the states, rather than a bare majority, must approve a proposed amendment reflects the view that changes in the fundamental law must command widespread assent. In *The Social Contract* Rousseau stated this view succinctly: ". . . the more grave and important the questions discussed, the nearer should the opinion that is to prevail approach unanimity.". . . Rousseau is not referring explicitly to fundamental law; but his point has a wide range of implication. It is important to notice that what is involved here is not merely a lack of trust in, or a suspiciousness of, the bare majority. Rather, some version or other—it is hard to be precise—of the doctrine of consent could supply much of the basis for the sentiment voiced by Rousseau and procedurally defined in Article 5 of the American Constitution.

There can be no doubt that the specific prohibitions of the American Constitution were conceived in suspiciousness of majority will, whether the will of the majority of the people translated into the will of their representatives, or the will of the majority of representatives acting selfishly or misguidedly as a political class and able to manipulate the people into accepting an erosion of their rights, claims, and liberties. Today one may go so far as to assert that these rights, claims, and liberties would ideally be placed altogether out of the reach of the amending process, out of the reach of even overwhelming majorities. They have the status of absolutes because without them free government could not function; they are indispensably instrumental for the practice of citizenship in a democratic society. Beyond that they compose the legal and political preconditions for the creation of a society of free individuals. Thus they are among the means needed to achieve free government which, in turn, is among the means needed to achieve a society of free individuals; they are also among the means directly needed to achieve a society of free individuals. The creation of such a society is the ultimate standard by which everything political is to be judged. The hope must be that the enumeration of prohibitions on majority will (it is simultaneously an enumeration of guarantees for all) would work as a standing reminder to all men in society of what they must honor if their society is to honor the ultimate political standard, rather than as a continuously irritating obstacle to be weakened in one way or another. But should the temptation be present to chip away at the obstacle, the legitimacy of resistance to such efforts is increased by the explicit prohibitions of the fundamental law.

The offense given by the equal representation of states in the Senate to item 2 (the votes of electors weigh equally) is explained by the exigencies faced by the men who framed the Constitution. The explanation, in this instance, constitutes the defense.

Narrow suspiciousness of the people lay behind the provisions establishing indirect election of the president, vice-president, and senators. In the course of time direct election became the norm.

II

The antimajoritarian impulse found in *The Federalist* papers, and to which Calhoun alludes at several places in the *Disquisition*, is so notorious as to need very little attention from us. . . .

In the name of what political value did Madison attack majoritarianism? In Numbers 10 and 51 he speaks of justice. "Justice is the end of government. It is the end of civil society.". . . Of course Madison was interested in other values, including especially liberty. It would be foolish to reduce his passion to a single-minded anxiousness over justice. But the burden of the argument in *The Federalist* deals with the perils to justice raised by majority rule. By "justice" is meant the preservation of every man in what is his own, the preservation of property. In reality the many are pitted against the few; the many seek to use political power to make transgressive incursions against the property rights of the few. Unless the social structure is complicated enough, and unless the governmental structure provides checks on the legislative will of the popular branch of public authority (the House of Representatives), the existent relations of property are put in jeopardy. Madison refers in Number 10 to "a rage for paper money, for an abolition of debts, for an equal division of property . . ." and hints at other "improper or wicked" projects. *The Federalist* papers are full of dark thoughts about human nature, but it is the human nature of the less well-advantaged many that dominates the discussion. There will be free government—what alternative is there?—but a free government neutralized, rendered incapable of any action that looks to disturb the status quo. . . .

We have seen so far that prior to Calhoun's writings American thought and practice had mounted a quite severe assault on majoritarian democracy. Calhoun was not breaking new ground when he assayed a theoretical critique of it. At work before he began the exposition of his views were certain principles that informed the political life of the United States. Though not usually explicit, a doctrine of consent could be relied on to make amendment of the fundamental law a legitimate process only when there was near unanimity. Though originally derived from the philosophy of natural rights certain personal rights, claims, and liberties of a legal and political sort could be held to be indefeasible and championed as inherent in the nature of that political society which otherwise strove to see immediate majoritarianism. Though also derived from the philosophy of natural rights, the protection of property in the name of justice could be advocated, without metaphysical reference, as the central end of government; and, as such, it would be morally entitled to force curtailments on majoritarianism. Whatever the mode chosen to articulate and support these political values—and one cannot impose a monolithic coherence or insist on a premature full self-consciousness—American statesmen had managed, with varying degrees of success, to make plausible the idea that there were political values as high as, or higher than majoritarianism. Which is to say that there were values as high as, or higher than *political equality*.

The qualifications of majoritarianism would themselves suffer qualification as time went on. The rights of property especially would undergo marginal encroachment, in the name of other values. The putatively indefeasible personal rights would trace a remarkably complex career, a career still in flux, and one that will remain in flux. But the most ardent majoritarian would have to concede that the debate between political equality and the other political values was more a family quarrel than a competition of alien and mutually unassimilable principles. Humane idealism, in the most expanded sense, was not the monopoly of the majoritarian side. Was Calhoun's contribution yet another voice in the family quarrel, or something else?

III

The presiding value in Calhoun's political theory is justice. Though the word is avoided in *A Disquisition on Government*, and liberty and power are declared the ends of government, it is clear that justice serves him as the ultimate standard by which political life is to be judged. . . .

Two matters—one issue and one condition—elicited from Calhoun the strenuous exertion of systematic thought. The issue was protective tariffs in the period (roughly) of 1828 to 1833. The condition was the division of the Union into free states and slave states, a condition increasingly vexatious from 1835 on. The two matters are linked; the debate over tariffs turned out to be a proving ground for many of the conceptions and intellectual strategies involved in the defense of slavery. . . .

The most eloquent passages in Calhoun's longest and last work, *A Discourse on the Constitution and Government of the United States*, deal with the threat posed to slave institutions by the growing strength of abolitionist feeling and of the nonslave states in general. In a Senate speech delivered on 23 February 1837, he asserted that on the subject of tariffs, the Southern states composed a "permanent minority.". . . In the *Discourse* he extends the application of that phrase to all the questions associated with slavery, especially the question of allowing slavery in the territories. . . . Where Madison's oppressed minority was a class, Calhoun's was a section. Calhoun was certain that the abolitionist movement (and presumably the sentiment for "containing" slavery) could not be appeased, and would, what is more, be courted by the class of politicians in the North and West who, in their quest for a majority coalition able to win the presidency, would take any support they could find. The Constitution, however, was made and accepted by men who countenanced the institution of slavery; in the most general way, the Constitution enjoined on public authority the protection of slavery, not its containment, and certainly not its abolition. And what the

Constitution protected deserved protection. Calhoun, in his Senate speech of 6 February 1837, pronounced slavery to be ". . . instead of an evil, a good—a positive good." He touched on arguments in defense of slavery that were to become Southern commonplaces: slavery was the suitable state for the black race; slavery meant the absence of the conflict of labor and capital, and hence was the best foundation for free institutions; ". . . there never has yet existed a wealthy and civilized society in which one portion of the community did not, in point of fact, live on the labor of another." . . . In any case, the "peculiar institution," however hated or however praised, had to be preserved; the status quo had to be maintained.

IV

How, then, was a permanent minority—in the electoral college and in both houses of Congress—if not now a permanent minority, then inevitably one day soon—to protect itself against selfishness and fanaticism? How was it to secure its preservation, to secure justice for itself? Calhoun's answer, in a renowned phrase, was concurrent majority. He first used the phrase in a letter in 1832; . . . that is, after he had written the "Exposition." It recurs frequently thereafter, variously illustrated with examples foreign and domestic. It was Calhoun's mature view that the American Constitution, in its inception and by design, in its spirit and its specific prescriptions, reflected the theory of the concurrent majority.

The theory is stated abstractly in the *Disquisition*; it is stated in the language of American constitutionalism in the *Discourse*.

In the *Disquisition* Calhoun says that the only way in which to prevent an interest or combination of interests from aggrandizing at the expense of other interests is

> . . . by taking the sense of each interest or portion of the community which may be unequally and injuriously affected by the action of the government separately, through its own majority or in some other way by which its voice may be fairly expressed, and to require the consent of each interest either to put or to keep the government in action . . . give to each division or interest, through its appropriate organ, either a concurrent voice in making and executing the laws or a veto on their execution. . . .

Calhoun is thus making unanimity the required condition for all measures that affect interests importantly, that carry with them the possibility of injustice. Since no community of any size or diversity can be counted on to achieve justice, all interests must be armed with the right to say no. Concurrent majority is the unanimous agreement of (the majorities within) all interests. One cannot tell from the *Disquisition* the meaning which "interests" had for Calhoun in the

American context. However, in the same letter in which Calhoun first mentioned concurrent (or concurring) majority, he said that he viewed ". . . a confederated community as composed of as many distinct political interests as there are States. . . ." . . .

In the *Discourse*, as well as in speeches, Calhoun spells out the various features of the American constitutional system, some unfortunately altered in practice, some still intact, that incorporate the theory of concurrent majority. The key point is that ". . . the States, regarded in their corporate character, and the population of the States, estimated in federal numbers, are the two elements of which the government is exclusively composed; and that they enter, in different proportions, into the formation of all its departments." . . . American government does not move by majority will of its people alone; the fact that it is a federal republic establishes it as a system loyal to concurrent majority. He says:

> It thus appears, on a view of the whole, that it was the object of the framers of the constitution, in organizing the government, to give to the two elements, of which it is composed, separate, but concurrent action; and, consequently, a veto on each other, whenever the organization of the department, or the nature of the power would admit: and when this could not be done, so to blend the two, as to make as near an approach to it, in effect, as possible. . . .

Apart from the construction and workings of the federal government, the retention by the states of their reserved powers reinforces the restrictions on the majority will of the people, as reflected in the House of Representatives.

There is no need to follow Calhoun through all the intricacies of the American system as he explains it. His work is indubitably impressive. The heart of the matter is that, as originally made, the American political system, in its division of powers, its separation of powers, its checks and balances, and the rigors of its amending process, would have made it almost impossible for injustice to be regularly forthcoming; American politics was to be largely the politics of the status quo. If change were to come about, it would have to have overwhelming support. The real meaning of concurrent majority in America was to be that two elements of our above majoritarian model would be offended: item 2 (the votes of electors weigh equally), and item 6 (no extralegislative restrictions on the will of the majority of the representatives). To put it another way, the most important consequence of extralegislative restrictions would be to render the votes of electors unequal in weight. The interests, one for each state, would be safe. . . .

. . . What could restore the capacity of a minority—a permanent minority—to impede the course of injustice? As early as the "Exposition" of 1828 Calhoun saw in the amending process the possibility of salvation. The procedure would be for an aggrieved state to nullify the objectionable law made by Congress and to thrust on it the duty to propose an amendment affirming the power it had already claimed. It is clear that Calhoun thought that though the South was a minority, it would never be such a small minority as to compose a fraction insufficient to defeat proposed amendments it did not like. Concurrent majority thus meant the unanimity of sections. . . . For this procedure to function, a state's right of nullification or interposition had, of course, to be granted. And if the state failed to gain enough support to block passage of the amendment, secession was morally justified.

Calhoun also wanted certain past measures repealed, measures which in his view violated the constitutional division of powers. Calhoun suggests yet another possibility toward the end of the *Discourse*. Something more than restoring the government to its federal character was now needed, something to supplement the procedure of interposition and amendment. Calhoun says that "perhaps" the United States should have two presidents, one elected by the North, one by the South, and each with the power to veto acts of Congress. . . . In short, the guarantees against majoritarian abuse had to become far more formal and institutionalized than the framers of the Constitution had made them.

V

Our concern is not with the correctness of Calhoun's understanding of the nature of the federal Union. Rather it is with his assault on majoritarianism. Has he successfully defended his curtailments of the majority principle? I would say that he had, if the following conditions existed in the period in which he spoke and wrote.

1. The interests of a nation are on a plane of moral equality. No plausible case could be made for the contention that one interest was parasitic on others, or exploited others. All the interests are equally entitled to continued existence because none violates more than any other the moral standards all accept.

2. The concept of interest has sufficient precision. The interests are clearly identifiable.

3. Each interest is more or less homogeneous. The numbers of people included within each one are like-minded in their view of what serves their interest; they are all equally served by the same policies.

4. The political arrangement through which each interest expresses and defends itself contains no other competing interest whose wishes could be ignored in favor of the dominant interest.

5. Whenever the interest works through its political agency to impose a veto on a policy approved by the majority in the higher legislature, it does so only in situations that clearly threaten its continued existence, that clearly threaten it with grave and irreparable injustice. . . . It does not exercise its veto capriciously, or for the pleasure of exercising it. . . . The membership of the interest

assumes that there is a prima facie case against exercising the veto, which case can be rebutted only after anguished examination.

6. There is a lack of consensus in the community. In the absence of obstacles, serious injustice can be expected.

Unless condition (1) holds, room is left for other moral and political values than the preservation of an interest to be introduced into the controversy. Justice itself could be cited against the claim made in the name of justice for continued and unimpaired existence.

Unless condition (2) holds, the theory of concurrent majority disintegrates. It could not be said with enough certainty who stands to benefit, who stands to suffer, from any policy.

Unless condition (3) holds, the interest can be seen as a cluster of interests. Any in the cluster may be harmed by what is done in the name of the interest as a whole; any in the cluster may have more in common with other interests or parts of interests than it does with those who are nominally included with it in the same interest. It may suffer injustice, whereas the structure of concurrent majority supposedly obstructs injustice.

Unless condition (4) holds, the same possibility of injustice mentioned in the preceding paragraph exists.

Unless condition (5) holds, the structure of concurrent majority, ostensibly reared to avoid the tyranny of the majority, turns into an instrument for control by the minority over the majority, if not for the tyranny of the minority.

Unless condition (6) holds, what moral or political value or values germane to *this* decision would qualify as ample enough to restrict the workings of the majority principle, to force concessions from the value, political equality?

The terrible irony is that by the time Calhoun set to write his *Disquisition* and *Discourse* (1845–50) the theory of concurrent majority as a solution to the problem of conflicts of interest was no longer appropriate. The problem of these years was the institution of slavery; the earlier problems of tariff and fiscal management had lost their salience.

A reasonable case could be made for the view that as far as tariffs were concerned, all the above conditions held, even when allowance is made for Calhoun's characteristic ferocity and immoderation. If one is willing to leave aside the manner in which slavery could affect the analysis of the struggle over tariffs—and the protectionists left it aside—then Calhoun's pleading is undoubtedly compelling. In a nation dedicated to the preservation of property, it is no eccentricity or exaggeration to say that the agricultural interests deserved justice. One of the great ends of government was being programmatically subverted. The most that one can say against Calhoun is that he probably underestimated the potentialities which the American political system contained for changing harmful policies, for allowing new sentiments to emerge and to be translated into new laws that rectified old wrongs. In actuality, the tariff was altered in a direction favorable to the South. Other appeals could have been made to Calhoun. The welfare of the majority could have been cloaked in phrases like "the common good" or "the public interest." . . . An effort could have been made to show that in the long run the South would have benefited from the prosperity of the other sections of the country. Other than economic benefits could have been offered as substitutions for the loss of economic ones. But these arguments would sound somewhat hollow, especially at a time and place notoriously materialistic.

The only trouble is that the great question of slavery could not legitimately be discussed within the conceptual framework of the *Disquisition*. Sentiment for abolition, for containing slavery, or for refusing to comply with laws relating to fugitive slaves did not represent an interests or cluster of interests ranged against some other interest, the slave interest. Abolition, containment, and noncompliance were not interests at all. They were moral feelings seeking political power to achieve moral ends. It will not do to impute the sadism of virtue, or hypocrisy, or blindness to deplorable injustice at home, or whatever, to those who had antislavery sentiments. The evil of slavery was so gross as to forgive any imperfection that went into the making of the feeling that it was absolutely wrong, as wrong as anything in man's organized social life could be, and to forgive any imperfection that went into the effort to limit or destroy it. It is no accident that the language of interests does not figure in the *Discourse*, and that in this work Calhoun relies purely on technical constitutional arguments, of a historical and legal sort, to make his case for the right of a minority to veto majority will. Furthermore, given the nature of the evil, it is hardly surprising that the minority represented by Calhoun should have experienced attacks on what it thought of as its rights. Slavery had to breed fanatical hatred. The question of slavery cannot be taken as paradigmatic of the eternal clash between majority rule and minority rights. The question of which slavery was paradigmatic was the eternal clash between right and wrong—a clash, in this instance, as free of moral (as opposed to practical) ambiguities as clashes ever get. Calhoun himself knew that sin, not a battle of moral equals, not a battle of men standing for equally good or equally bad causes, was the kernel of the controversy.

VI

. . . [H]is theory forces on the attention of those who cherish the model of majoritarian democracy the problem of consensus—but not quite in the way his admirers think.

Calhoun's vision of society—it is also Madison's—is one of factions straining to despoil each other, and barely kept from doing so by artful political devices. The view of human nature is Hobbesian disjoined from the political system advocated by Hobbes. It is hard to see, however, how any society made up of more than a few people could hold together if this view were adequate to the facts. Not all the artful arrangements in the world would suffice without a preponderance of civil feelings. A continuous and extensive fear of injustice is incompatible with the life of a society that means to remain one society. Fear of injustice cannot therefore be imagined as the basis for the requirement of unanimity, of concurrent majority. Even if it could, there is no guarantee that other motives would not govern a minority's use of its veto. That would lead to minority rule, a result that is morally unacceptable for any point of view. There is only one basis for the requirement of unanimity that is morally acceptable and that could conceivably be grounded realistically in the facts of democratic social life: self-determination. On the rare occasions when the fundamental law is being revised, an approximation to unanimity is morally desirable; at the same time, there would be a widespread understanding that such an approximation is, in fact, morally desirable. There would be consensus on the proposition that, on these rare occasions, consensus is again called for. By and large, revisions in the fundamental law would not pertain to the clash of interests, would not involve the contest of economic groups, but would rather deal with purely political arrangements.

Nevertheless, there may be situations in which a minority group in society stands in constant peril from the majority. There may be situations in which a society is fundamentally divided into a permanent majority and a permanent minority, and in which the majority does not extend civil feelings toward the minority. A normal society could not exist in the absence of widespread civil feelings, no matter how much diversity it contains, no matter how many factions and conflicts of interest it contains. But a certain group within it may, for one reason or another, arouse the murderous animosity of the rest. Ethnic, religious, racial, and linguistic minorities come to mind from our own present experience. The rights of these groups could perhaps be designated as "interests," if the meaning of that word were extended. Calhoun's analysis would apply. It would then be an open question whether the majority would choose to be just and respect minority rights by complying with the arrangements meant to protect them. In any case, whether they did so or not, right is on the side of the minority.

SELECTION 36
FROM
*Justice and the Politics of Difference**

IRIS MARION YOUNG

I HAVE ARGUED THAT participatory democracy is an element and condition of social justice. Contemporary participatory democratic theory . . . inherits from republicanism a commitment to a unified public that in practice tends to exclude or silence some groups. Where some groups are materially privileged and exercise cultural imperialism, formally democratic processes often elevate the particular experiences and perspectives of the privileged groups, silencing or denigrating those of oppressed groups.

In her study of the functioning of a New England town meeting government, for example, Jane Mansbridge demonstrates that women, blacks, working-class people, and poor people tend to participate less and have their interests represented less than whites, middle-class professionals, and men. White middle-class men assume authority more than others, and they are more practiced at speaking persuasively; mothers and old people find it more difficult than others to get to meetings. . . . I cited Amy Gutmann's example of how increasing democracy in some school systems led to increased segregation because the more numerous, materially privileged, and articulate whites were able to promote their perceived interests against blacks' just demand for equal treatment in an integrated system. . . .

In these and similar cases, the group differences of privilege and oppression that exist in society have an effect on the public, even though the public claims to be blind to difference. Traditionally political theory and practice have responded to evidence of such bias by attempting yet once again to institute a genuinely universal public. Such a pure perspective that transcends the particularity of social position and consequent partial vision . . . is impossible. If the unified public does not transcend group differences and often allows the perspective and interests of privileged groups to dominate, then a democratic public can

---

* (Princeton, NJ: Princeton University Press, 1990): pp. 183–91.

counteract this bias only by acknowledging and giving voice to the group differences within it.

I assert, then, the following principle: a democratic public should provide mechanisms for the effective recognition and representation of the distinct voices and perspectives of those of its constituent groups that are oppressed or disadvantaged. Such group representation implies institutional mechanisms and public resources supporting (1) self-organization of group members so that they achieve collective empowerment and a reflective understanding of their collective experience and interests in the context of the society; (2) group analysis and group generation of policy proposals in institutionalized contexts where decisionmakers are obliged to show that their deliberations have taken group perspectives into consideration; and (3) group veto power regarding specific policies that affect a group directly, such as reproductive rights policy for women, or land use policy for Indian reservations.

Specific representation for oppressed groups in the decision-making procedures of a democratic public promotes justice better than a homogeneous public in several ways, both procedural and substantial. . . . First, it better assures procedural fairness in setting the public agenda and hearing opinions about its items. Social and economic privilege means, among other things, that the groups which have it behave as though they have a right to speak and be heard, that others treat them as though they have that right, and that they have the material, personal, and organizational resources that enable them to speak and be heard. As a result, policy issues are often defined by the assumptions and priorities of the privileged. Specific representation for oppressed groups interrupts this process, because it gives voice to the assumptions and priorities of other groups.

Second, because it assures a voice for the oppressed as well as the privileged, group representation better assures that all needs and interests in the public will be recognized in democratic deliberations. The privileged usually are not inclined to protect or advance the interests of the oppressed, partly because their social position prevents them from understanding those interests, and partly because to some degree their privilege depends on the continued oppression of others. While different groups may share many needs, moreover, their difference usually entails some special needs which the individual groups themselves can best express. If we consider just democratic decision making as a politics of need interpretation, as I have already suggested, then democratic institutions should facilitate the public expression of the needs of those who tend to be socially marginalized or silenced by cultural imperialism. Group representation in the public facilitates such expression.

In the previous section I argued for the assertion of a positive sense of difference by oppressed groups, and for a principle of special rights for those groups. I discussed there the legitimate fears of many in emancipatory social movements that abandoning group-blind policies and adopting group-specific ones will restigmatize the groups and justify new exclusions. Group representation can help protect against such a consequence. If oppressed and disadvantaged groups can self-organize in the public and have a specific voice to present their interpretation of the meaning of and reasons for group-differentiated policies, then such policies are more likely to work for than against them.

Group representation, third, encourages the expression of individual and group needs and interests in terms that appeal to justice, that transform an "I want" into an "I am entitled to," in Hannah Pitkin's words . . . publicity itself encourages this transformation because a condition of the public is that people call one another to account. Group representation adds to such accountability because it serves as an antidote to self-deceiving self-interest masked as an impartial or general interest. Unless confronted with different perspectives on social relations and events, different values and language, most people tend to assert their perspective as universal. When social privilege allows some group perspectives to dominate a public while others are silent, such universalizing of the particular will be reaffirmed by many others. Thus the test of whether a claim upon the public is just or merely an expression of self-interest is best made when those making it must confront the opinion of others who have explicitly different, though not necessarily conflicting experiences, priorities, and needs. . . . As a person of social privilege, I am more likely to go outside myself and have regard for social justice when I must listen to the voice of those my privilege otherwise tends to silence.

Finally, group representation promotes just outcomes because it maximizes the social knowledge expressed in discussion, and thus furthers practical wisdom. Group differences are manifest not only in different needs, interests, and goals, but also in different social locations and experiences. People in different groups often know about somewhat different institutions, events, practices, and social relations, and often have differing perceptions of the same institutions, relations, or events. For this reason members of some groups are sometimes in a better position than members of others to understand and anticipate the probable consequences of implementing particular social policies. A public that makes use of all such social knowledge in its differentiated plurality is most likely to make just and wise decisions.

I should allay several possible misunderstandings of what this principle of group representation means and implies. First, the principle calls for specific representation of social groups, not interest groups or ideological groups. By an interest group I mean any aggregate or association of persons who seek a particular goal, or desire the same policy, or are similarly situated with respect to some social effect—for example, they are all recipients of acid rain caused by Ohio smokestacks. Social groups usually share some interests, but shared interests are not sufficient to constitute a social group. A social group is a collective of people who have affinity with one another because of a set of practices or way of life; they differentiate themselves from or are differentiated by at least one other group according to these cultural forms.

By an ideological group I mean a collective of persons with shared political beliefs. Nazis, socialists, feminists, Christian Democrats, and anti-abortionists are ideological groups. The situation of social groups may foster the formation of ideological groups, and under some circumstances an ideological group may become a social group. Shared political or moral beliefs, even when they are deeply and passionately held, however, do not themselves constitute a social group.

A democratic polity should permit the expression of all interests and opinions, but this does not imply specific representation for any of them. A democratic public may wish to provide representation for certain kinds of interests or political orientations; most parliamentary systems, for example, give proportional representation to political parties according to the number of votes they poll. The principle of group representation that I am arguing for here, however, refers only to social groups.

Second, it is important to remember that the principle calls for specific representation only of oppressed or disadvantaged groups. Privileged groups are already represented, in the sense that their voice, experience, values, and priorities are already heard and acted upon. . . . Once we are clear that the principle of group representation refers only to oppressed social groups, then the fear of an unworkable proliferation of group representation should dissipate.

Third, while I certainly intend this principle to apply to representative bodies in government institutions, its application is by no means restricted to that sphere. In earlier chapters I have argued that social justice requires a far wider institutionalization of democracy than currently obtains in American society. Persons should have the right to participate in making the rules and policies of any institution with authority over their actions. The principle of group representation applies to all such democratized publics. It should apply, for example, to decision-making bodies formed by oppressed groups that aim to develop policy proposals for a heterogeneous public. Oppressed groups within these groups should have specific representation in such autonomous forums. The black caucus should give specific representation to women, for example, and the women's caucus to blacks.

. . . A principle of group representation has been implicitly and sometimes explicitly asserted in several contemporary social movements struggling against oppression and domination. In response to the anger and criticism that women, blacks, gays and lesbians, American Indians, and others have leveled against traditionally unitary radical groups and labor unions, many of them have implemented some form of group representation in their decision-making bodies. Some political organizations, unions, and feminist groups have formal caucuses for blacks, Latinos, women, gay men and lesbians, disabled people, and old people, whose perspectives might be silenced without explicit representation. Frequently these organizations have procedures for giving the caucuses a voice in organization-wide discussion and caucus representation in decision making. Some organizations also require representation of members of disadvantaged groups in leadership bodies.

At the height of efforts to occupy nuclear power construction sites, for example, many antinuclear power actions and organizations responded to criticisms by feminists or people of color that the movement was dominated by straight white men. Social group affinity groups formed and were generally encouraged, providing solidarity and representation to formerly invisible groups. The National Women's Studies Association, to take another example, has a complex and effective system of representation for group caucuses in its decision-making bodies.

The idea of a Rainbow Coalition expressed a heterogeneous public with forms of group representation. The traditional coalition corresponded to the idea of a unified public that transcends particular differences of experience and concerns. In traditional coalitions diverse groups work together for specific ends which they agree interest or affect them all in a similar way, and they generally agree that the differences of perspective, interests, or opinion among them will not surface in the public statements and actions of the coalition. This form ideally suits welfare state interest-group politics. In a Rainbow Coalition, by contrast, each of the constituent groups affirms the presence of the others as well as the specificity of their experience and perspective on social issues. . . . In the Rainbow public blacks do not simply tolerate the participation of gays, labor activists do not grudgingly work alongside peace movement veterans, and none of these paternalistically concede to feminist participation. Ideally, a Rainbow Coalition affirms the presence and supports the claims of each of the oppressed groups or political movements constituting it, and arrives at a political program not by voicing some "principles of unity" that hide difference, but rather by allowing each constituency to analyze economic and social issues from the perspective of its experience. This implies that each group maintains significant autonomy, and requires provision for group representation. . . .

A principle of representation for oppressed or disadvantaged groups has been implemented most frequently in organizations and movements that challenge politics as usual in welfare capitalist society. Some more mainstream organizations, however, also have implemented this principle in some form. The national Democratic party has had rules requiring representation of women and people of color as delegates, and many state Democratic parties have had similar rules. Many nonprofit agencies call for representation of specific groups, such as women, blacks, Latinos, and disabled people, on their boards of directors. In a program that some of them call "valuing difference," some corporations have instituted limited representation of oppressed social groups in corporate discussions. One can imagine such a principle of group representation extended to other political contexts. Social justice would be enhanced in many American cities, for example, if a citywide school committee formally and explicitly represented blacks, Hispanics, women, gay men and lesbians, poor and working-class people, disabled people, and students.

Some might object that implementing a principle of group representation in governing bodies would exacerbate conflict and divisiveness in public life, rendering decisions even more difficult to reach. Especially if groups have veto power over policies that fundamentally and uniquely affect members of their group, it seems likely, it might be claimed, that decision making would be stalled. This objection presupposes that group differences imply essential conflicts of interest. But this is not so; groups may have differing perspectives on issues, but these are often compatible and enrich everyone's understanding when they are expressed. To the extent that group differences produce or reflect conflict, moreover, group representation would not necessarily increase such conflict and might decrease it. If their differences bring groups into conflict, a just society should bring such differences into the open for discussion. Insofar as structured relations of privilege and oppression are the source of the conflict, moreover, group representation can change those relations by equalizing the ability of groups to speak and be heard. Thus group representation should mitigate, though not eliminate, certain kinds of conflict. If, finally, the alternative to stalled decision making is a unified public that makes decisions ostensibly embodying the general interest which systematically ignore, suppress, or conflict with the interests of particular groups, then stalled decision making may sometimes be just.

A second objection might be that the implementation of this principle can never get started. For to implement it a public must be constituted to decide which groups, if any, deserve specific representation in decision-making procedures. What principles will guide the composition of such a "constitutional convention"? Who shall decide what groups should receive representation, and by what procedures shall this decision be made? If oppressed groups are not represented at this founding convention, then how will their representation be ensured at all? And if they are represented, then why is implementation of the principle necessary?

These questions pose a paradox of political origins which is not specific to this proposal, and which no philosophical argument can resolve. No program or set of principles can found a politics, because politics does not have a beginning, an original position. It is always a process in which we are already engaged. Normative principles such as those I have proposed in this chapter can serve as proposals in this ongoing political discussion and means of envisioning alternative institutional forms, but they cannot found a polity. In actual political situations application of any normative principle will be rough and ready, and always subject to challenge and revision. If democratic publics in American society accept this principle of group representation, as I have suggested a few have, they also are likely to name candidates for groups within them that deserve specific representation. Such an opening might sensitize the public to the need for other groups to be represented. But if it does not, these groups will have to petition with arguments that may or may not be persuasive. I see no practical way out of this problem of origin, but that does not stand as a reason to reject this or any other normative principle.

One might ask how the idea of a heterogeneous public which encourages self-organization of groups and group representation in decision making differs from . . . interest-group pluralism. . . . Interest-group pluralism, I suggest, operates precisely to forestall the emergence of public discussion and decision making. Each interest group promotes its own specific interest as thoroughly and forcefully as it can, and need not consider the other interests competing in the political marketplace except strategically, as potential allies or adversaries in its own pursuit. The rules of interest-group pluralism do not require justifying one's interest as right, or compatible with social justice. A heterogeneous public, however, is a *public*, where participants discuss together the issues before them and come to a decision according to principles of justice. Group representation, I have argued, nurtures such publicity by calling for claimants to justify their demands before others who explicitly stand in different social locations.

Implementing principles of group representation in national and local politics in the United States, or in restructured democratic publics within particular institutions such as factories, offices, universities, churches, and social service agencies, would obviously require creative thinking and flexibility. There are no models to follow. European models of consociational democratic institutions, for example, cannot be removed from the contexts in which they have evolved, and even within them it is not clear that they constitute models of participatory democracy. Reports of experiments with institutionalized self-organization among women, indigenous peoples, workers, peasants, and students in contemporary Nicaragua offer an example closer to the conception I am advocating. . . .

Social justice entails democracy. Persons should be involved in collective discussion and decision making in all the settings that depend on their commitment, action, and obedience to rules—workplaces, schools, neighborhoods, and so on. When such institutions privilege some groups over others, actual democracy requires group representation for the disadvantaged. Not only do just procedures require group representation in order to ensure that oppressed or disadvantaged groups have a voice, but such representation is also the best means to promote just outcomes of the deliberative process.

I have argued that the ideal of the just society as eliminating group differences is both unrealistic and undesirable. Instead justice in a group-differentiated society demands social equality of groups, and mutual recognition and affirmation of group differences. Attending to group-specific needs and providing for group representation both promotes that social equality and provides the recognition that undermines cultural imperialism.

BIBLIOGRAPHY

Arblaster, Anthony. 1987. *Democracy*. London: Open University Press.

Aristotle. 1962. *The Politics of Aristotle*. Ernest Barker, ed. and trans. New York: Oxford University Press.

Aron, Raymond. 1968. *Democracy and Totalitarianism*. London: Weidenfeld & Nicolson.

Bachrach, Peter, and Morton S. Baratz. 1962. Two Faces of Power. *American Political Science Review* 56: 947–55.

Bell, Daniel. 1960. *The End of Ideology*. Glencoe, IL: The Free Press.

Bledsoe, Timothy, and Mary Herring. 1990. Victims of Circumstances: Women in Pursuit of Political Office. *American Political Science Review* 84: 213–24.

Block, Fred. 1977. The Ruling Class Does Not Rule. *Socialist Review* 7 (May): 6–28.

Cockburn, Cynthia. 1977. *The Local State*. London: Pluto Press.

Curry, Richard O., ed. 1988. *Freedom at Risk: Secrecy, Censorship, and Repression in the 1980s*. Philadelphia, PA: Temple University Press.

Dahl, Robert A. 1956. *A Preface to Democratic Theory*. Chicago, IL: University of Chicago Press.

Dellinger, Dave. 1971. *Revolutionary Nonviolence*. New York: Doubleday Anchor Books.

Eisenstein, Zillah. 1988. *The Female Body and the Law*. Berkeley, CA: University of California Press.

Elshtain, Jean. 1981. *Public Man, Private Woman: Women in Social and Political Thought*. Princeton, NJ: Princeton University Press.

Hain, Peter. 1971. *Don't Play with Apartheid*. London: Allen & Unwin.

Horwitz, Robert. 1989. *The Irony of Regulatory Reform: The Deregulation of American Telecommunications*. New York: Oxford University Press.

Keane, John. 1988. *Democracy and Civil Society*. London: Verso.

Lindblom, Charles E. 1977. *Politics and Markets*. New York: Basic Books.

Lippmann, Walter. 1925. *The Phantom Public*. New York: Harcourt Brace.

Lipset, Seymour Martin. 1960. *Political Man*. Garden City, NY: Doubleday.

Mackenzie, Midge. 1975. *Shoulder to Shoulder: A Documentary*. New York: Alfred Knopf.

MacKinnon, Catherine. 1989. *Toward a Feminist Theory of the State*. New York: Cambridge University Press.

Mansbridge, Jane. 1980. *Beyond Adversary Democracy*. New York: Basic Books.

Miliband, Ralph. 1969. *The State in Capitalist Society*. New York: Basic Books.

Mill, John Stuart. 1957. *Autobiography*. New York: Liberal Arts Press.

Morgenthau, Hans. 1960. *The Purpose of American Politics*. New York: Alfred Knopf.

Newfield, Jack. 1988. *City for Sale*. New York: Harper & Row.

Nozick, Robert. 1974. *Anarchy, State, and Utopia*. New York: Basic Books.

Okin, Susan Moller. 1979. *Women in Western Political Thought*. Princeton, NJ: Princeton University Press.

———. 1989. *Justice, Gender, and the Family*. New York: Basic Books.

Pateman, Carol. 1983. Feminist Critiques of the Public/Private Dichotomy. In *Public and Private in Social Life*, eds. Stanley I. Benn and G. Gaus. London: Croom Helm.

———. 1988. *The Sexual Contract*. Stanford, CA: Stanford University Press.

Schattschneider, E. E. 1960. *The Semi-Sovereign People*. New York: Holt, Rinehart and Winston.

Schiller, Herbert. 1989. *Culture Incorporated: The Corporate Takeover of Expression*. New York: Oxford University Press.

Walzer, Michael. 1983. *Spheres of Justice: A Defense of Pluralism and Equality*. New York: Basic Books.

INDEX

Abortion, 200–201
Adams, John, 101, 210, 228
Affirmative action, 2, 275; in the Netherlands, 275–76
African Americans, 8, 100, 143, 188, 309, 312–14
Agenda-setting, 6, 61–63
Allende, Salvador, 241
American Civil War, 100, 112, 241
American Revolution, 41, 209, 211, 213, 216
American Voter, The (Campbell et al.), 112
Antimajoritarianism, 301
Apathy: and democracy, 95–97, 100, 259, 269
Aquinas, Thomas, 20
Arblaster, Anthony, 194
Arendt, Hannah, 15, 17, 172
Aristotle, 2, 6, 19, 266–67, 274
Aron, Raymond, 239
Athenian democracy, 2, 3, 14, 36, 41, 274, 279
Authority: and democracy, 101–3
Autobiography (Mill), 4, 8

Bachrach, Peter, 5, 6, 8
Bakuninism, 79, 221
Baratz, Morton, 6
Bay, Christian, 274
Bell, Daniel, 239
Bentham, Jeremy, 17, 20, 86, 173, 267, 293
Bernstein, Eduard, 197
Bevan, Aneurin, 233
Bill of Rights, 136, 167, 213, 215
Block, Fred, 176
Bonaparte, Louis Napoleon, 8
Bridges, Harry, 17
British Constitution, 50
British Parliament, 54
Bryce, Lord James, 96
Bureaucracy, 74–82; and democracy, 76–82, 259
Burke, Edmund, 21, 92, 173

Caesarism, 262
Calhoun, John, 297, 301–8. *See also* Concurrent majority
Capitalism: and bureaucracy, 75; and democracy, 10, 146–57, 168–84, 188–91
Censorship, 158, 165
Chaban-Delmas, Jacques, 235
Civil disobedience, 235–36
Civil liberties, 206, 275, 281
Civil rights, 292–93
Civil Rights Act (1964), 15
Civil rights movement, 16, 245
Civil War. *See* American Civil War
Civilian control of the military, 262–63
Class conflict, 33
Classical democratic theory, 14, 84, 87–88, 97–98, 129
Cockburn, Cynthia, 18
Communism, 33, 244
Compromise, 239–43
Concurrent majority, 297–308
Conscientious objection, 236
Consensus, 99, 110, 117–18
Considerations on Representative Government (Mill), 3, 4, 7
Constitution of the United States, 48, 100, 146, 209–15, 298–300, 304–5
Corruption, 214
Council system, 221–30. *See also* Workers' councils
Crisis, 8
Cromwell, Oliver, 221
Crusoe, Robinson, 148
Culture of democracy, 169, 171
Cuomo, Mario, 201

Dahl, Robert, 3, 4, 5–9, 11, 14, 17, 189
Davidson, Emily Wilding, 15
Dellinger, Dave, 238
Democracy: as favorable term, 7; as unfavorable term, 4, 19–20; definitions of, 4, 19–22
Democracy and Its Critics (Dahl), 7

Democratic creed, 14, 99, 110–18
Democratic elitism. *See* Theory of democratic elitism
Democratic process, 6–9, 14–16, 57–63, 126–27
Democratic spirit, 102
Dewey, John, 9, 11
Dictatorship of the proletariat, 206, 218
"Difference," 309–16
Direct action, 14–18, 210, 226, 231–43
Direct democracy, 3, 30–31, 47, 209, 238
Disadvantaged: representation of, 312–13. *See also* Oppression; Worst-off, the
Discourse on the Constitution and Government of the United States, A (Calhoun), 302, 304–6
Disquisition on Government, A (Calhoun), 301–3, 306–7
Distribution of income, 255–56
Division of labor, 169–70
Dolci, Danilo, 237
Domestic life. *See* Private sphere
Donald, David, 100

East European revolutions of 1989, 2, 13, 15, 202, 245
Ecole Nationale d'Administration, 264
Economic democracy, 9, 17, 128, 252–56
Economic performance: and democracy, 175–76
Economic theory, 168
Education: and democracy, 168, 206, 309
Eisenhower, Dwight D., 134, 258
Eisenstein, Zillah, 13
Elections, 17, 58–60, 137, 140
Elites: and democracy, 6, 113–44, 166, 228–30, 258–59, 263
Elshtain, Jean Bethke, 195
Emerson, Ralph Waldo, 209
Empirical democratic theory, 4–6, 12, 14, 97–98
Engels, Friedrich, 151, 225
Equal opportunity, 16, 129, 275
Equal rights, 18, 194, 250–51, 280–81
Equality, 277–81; and democracy, 38–42, 58–60, 100, 164, 278
Ethnic minorities, 8, 187–88, 312–14

Excess of democracy, 99
Executive power, 262
Experts, 11, 81–82, 120–25, 263–68

Fable of the Bees, The (Mandeville), 173
Factions, 45–47, 278–79
Faraday, Michael, 124
February Revolution of 1848 (Paris), 220–21
Federalist, The, papers, 4, 301
Feminism, 193–94, 200–202, 245, 312–13
First Amendment, 12. *See also* Bill of Rights
Formal equality, 77
Founding fathers, 210
Free enterprise. *See* Free market: and democracy
Free market: and democracy, 10, 146–57, 167, 169–74, 178–79, 252–54
Free press, 158, 164, 208, 285
Free speech, 21, 164, 208, 275, 284–91, 292, 294
Freedom: and democracy, 89–90, 247–49, 292–95. *See also* Positive freedom
Freedom of information, 60–61
Freedom rides, 16
French Revolution, 16, 20, 212, 219–21, 282
Friedman, Milton, 10, 153–57, 171

Gamson, William, 190
Gay men, 312–14
Gender: and democracy, 13, 192–202, 274, 312–13
General strikes, 15, 21, 240
General will, 88, 277–79
Government and business, 176–84
Greek democracy, 19, 25, 29. *See also* Athenian democracy
Grotius, 31
Group representation. *See* Group rights
Group rights, 192, 275–76, 308–16
Group theory, 259
Group veto, 305–6, 310. *See also* Concurrent majority
Gutmann, Amy, 309

Hain, Peter, 235

Hamilton, Alexander, 20
Hobbes, Thomas, 307
Horwitz, Robert, 12
Human nature: and democracy, 105–8, 307–8
Human rights, 292–93. *See also* Civil rights
Hungarian Revolution, 222, 225
Huntington, Samuel, 9

Ideological groups, 311–12
Ideology, 159, 162
Imperialism, 241
Individual development, 130, 293
Individual rights, 274–75, 277, 282–91
Inequality: in democracy, 104, 109–10, 185–91
Inflation, 103
Interest groups. *See* Pressure groups
"Iron law of oligarchy," 69
Irrationality, 85, 94

Jacksonianism, 100
Jefferson, Thomas, 87, 209–12, 214–17
Johnson, Lyndon, B., 139
Judicial review, 167, 295
Justice, 302–3, 306–8. *See also* Social justice

Keane, John, 198–99
Kennedy, John F., 139
Koch, Edward, 8
Kronstadt rebellion, 218

Labor movement, 245
Leadership: competition for, 88–89; necessity of, 102
League of Women Voters, 271
Lenin, V. I., 205–8, 213, 218, 220, 259
Lesbians, 312–14
Levellers, 265
Lewis, John L., 17
Liberal democracy, 21, 175–84, 197, 231–43
Liberal democrats, 9, 10, 16
Liberalism and liberal theory, 126, 172, 192–93, 201, 247, 252, 269
Liebling, A. J., 164, 167
Lincoln, Abraham, 241
Lindblom, Charles, 176
Lippmann, Walter, 11, 260
Lipset, Seymour Martin, 6, 137
"Long Parliament," 205
Louis Philippe, Emperor (France), 205
Luxemburg, Rosa, 15, 223

McCarthy, Senator Joseph, 134, 136
McClellan, Senator John, 135
MacKinnon, Catherine, 13
Macpherson, C. B., 10
Madison, James, 3, 4, 9, 12, 210, 272, 274, 301, 307
Majority rule, 2–4, 12–13, 20, 57–59, 90–91, 122, 274, 292, 297, 300–302, 307
Majority tyranny, 47–49, 282–84, 295
Mandeville, Bernard, 173
Mansbridge, Jane, 18, 198, 269, 309
March on Rome, 16
Markets. *See* Free market: and democracy
Marx, Karl, 3, 8, 12, 213, 217–19, 221
Marxism, 201, 220, 221
Maslow, Abraham, 294
Mass democracy, 257
Mass media: and democracy, 10, 158–67, 228–29
Masses, danger from the. *See* Threats to democracy
Means of communication, 75. *See also* Mass media: and democracy
Meritocracy, 266–68
Michels, Robert, 18
Miliband, Ralph, 186
Mill, John Stuart, 3, 4, 7, 17, 274–75; as "Socialist," 4, 9
Minorities and minority rights, 2, 102–3, 122, 274, 285–96, 307–8
Mitchell, Attorney General John, 135
Morgenthau, Hans, 13
Mosca, Gaetano, 137
Mr. Smith Goes to Washington, 265
Mumford, Lewis, 209
Mussolini, Benito, 16

NAACP, 143
National Labor Relations Act (1935), 15
Nationalism, 202
Natural rights, 294–95
Needs, 293–95
Newfield, Jack, 9

Newton, Sir Isaac, 124
1984 (Orwell), 162–63
Nixon administration, 241
Northern Ireland, 274
Nozick, Robert, 12
Nullification, 305

O'Brien, Denis, 173
Okin, Susan Moller, 13
Oligarchy: and democracy, 68–73, 121–23, 224, 260. *See also* "Iron Law of Oligarchy" (Michels)
Oppression, 186, 276, 309–12. *See also* Worst-off, the
Orwell, George, 162
"Overload" of government, 102–3

Pacifism, 237
Parisian Commune, 212–13, 217–18
Parliamentarianism: and democracy, 204–8, 240
Participation: and democracy, 8, 17, 32–37, 128, 172, 196–200, 204–30, 261, 268–72, 274
Participatory democracy, 66, 250–51, 261, 309
Pateman, Carol, 13
Permanent minority, 302–4, 308
Pitkin, Hannah, 311
Plato, 19, 131–34, 136, 274
Platonism, 121, 266
Pluralism, pluralist democracy, 18, 104–18, 139–44, 166, 172, 184, 186, 190, 275, 315
Political equality, 302
Political parties, 68–73, 92, 97, 101, 142, 223–29, 239, 261–62
Political stability, 95, 99–103
Polyarchy, 3–8, 13–15, 17–18, 63–66
Pomper, Gerald, 269
Poor, the. *See* Worst-off, the
Popular sovereignty, 29–40, 70, 277–80
Positive freedom, 164, 248–49, 255–56, 293–94
Poverty, 187, 278. *See also* Worst-off, the
Power: and social class, 142–43, 185–91, 193, 258, 281
Pressure groups, 139–44
Private property, 214–15
Private sphere: and democracy, 192–96
Privilege, 292, 309–11
Propaganda, 158–60
Property: and democracy, 45–46, 49, 249–50, 278, 292, 301. *See also* Private property
Proportional representation, 90
Proudhon, Pierre, 221
Pseudodemocracy, 257–68
Public Man, Private Woman (Elshtain), 195
Public opinion: and democracy, 83–87, 289–91
Putney Debates, 265

Race, 188
Rainbow Coalition, 313
Räterepublik ("Red Republic") of Bavaria, 222
Reagan, Ronald, 8
Referendum, 257, 272
Reflections on the Revolution in France (Burke), 21
Religion, 202
Religious freedom, 284, 287
Representation, representative government, 3, 5–9, 13, 21, 27–29, 47–56, 87, 140, 209, 223, 257–68, 270, 274
Republic, The (Plato), 19, 131–33, 136
Republican principle, republicanism, 46–49, 200–201, 215–17, 309
Resources of power, 185–91
Reuther, Walter, 17
Revolution, revolutionary spirit, 204–8, 212–22, 237
Rights: in a democracy, 22, 274–76. *See also* Civil rights; Group rights; Individual rights
Robbins, Lionel, 168
Roman Republic, 21, 29, 212
Rotation in office, 211, 263–64, 271
Rousseau, Jean-Jacques, 3, 5, 9, 62, 260, 275–76, 300
Rovere, Richard, 134
Ruling-class thesis, 184
Rush, Benjamin, 210
Russian Revolution (1905), 207, 213, 217, 218–19, 221
Russian Revolution (1917), 204–8, 218–19, 221. *See also* Soviet Union

Sandinistas (Nicaragua), 160–61, 315
Santayana, George, 124
Schattschneider, E. E., 142
Schiller, Herbert, 11, 163
Schumpeter, Joseph, 5, 6, 11, 136, 260
Shah of Iran, 162
Sit-down strikes, 16–17
Slavery, 302–3, 306–7
Smith, Adam, 173
Smith, Al, 99
Social class: and democracy, 33, 38–42. *See also* Power: and social class
Social contract, 280
Social Contract, The (Rousseau), 3, 62, 300
Social democracy, 245
Social justice, 312–16. *See also* Justice
Socialism: and democracy, 21, 71, 151, 206–7, 244–56
Socialists, 166, 193
Socrates, 19, 274
Solon, 19
South Africa, 274
Southern Christian Leadership Conference, 143
Soviet Union, 202, 218, 275. *See also* Russian Revolution
Spheres of Justice (Walzer), 195
Spinoza, 20
Squatting, 238
"Strong democracy," 271
Supreme Court of the United States, 113
Switzerland, 269
Syndicalism, 237

Technology: and democracy, 13, 124
"Teledemocracy," 10, 270–71
Thatcherism, 12
Theory of democratic elitism, 5, 8, 12, 126–30
Thrasymachus, 266
Threats to democracy, 100–103, 117–18, 129, 131–33, 141
Thucydides, 19
Tilden, Samuel J., 122
Tocqueville, Alexis de, 3, 4, 122, 171, 220
Town meetings, 3, 17, 139, 257, 269–71, 309
Trade unions, 102, 139, 240, 262
Trilateral Commission, Trilateral countries, 99, 101, 102
Trotsky, Leon, 204–6, 208

Underprivileged, the. *See* Worst-off, the
Universal suffrage, 193, 201, 262
Utilitarianism, 274, 293

Vietnam War, 139, 242
Voting: and democracy, 93–98, 172, 194, 196, 261, 269

Wagner, Senator Robert, 16
Walzer, Michael, 195
Ward system, 215–17
Welfare state, 157, 224
Who Governs? (Dahl), 8, 11, 14
Wilde, Oscar, 245
William, Raymond, 2
Wills, Gary, 201
Wilson, James, 210
Women. *See* Feminism; Gender: and democracy
Women's liberation, 195
Women's Social and Political Union (WSPU), 15, 17
Women's suffrage movement, 15–17
Workers' control, workers' self-management. *See* Economic democracy
Workers' councils, 212, 217, 221–27
Working class, 8, 33, 142, 186–87, 314
Worst off, the, 12, 186–89, 293
Written constitutions, 295–96, 298

Yates, Douglas, 270
Young, Iris Marion, 13, 276

Zuckerman, Michael, 269